SEEING NATURE THROUGH GENDER

DEVELOPMENT OF WESTERN RESOURCES

The Development of Western Resources is an interdisciplinary series focusing on the use and misuse of resources in the American West. Written for a broad readership of humanists, social scientists, and resource specialists, the books in this series emphasize both historical and contemporary perspectives as they explore the interplay between resource exploitation and economic, social, and political experiences.

John G. Clark, University of Kansas, Founding Editor
Hal K. Rothman, University of Nevada, Las Vegas, Series Editor

SEEING NATURE THROUGH GENDER

Edited by Virginia J. Scharff

University Press of Kansas

Cover: *Persephone*, by Thomas Hart Benton, courtesy of The Nelson-Atkins Museum
of Art, Kansas City, Missouri. (Purchase: acquired through the Yellow Freight Foundation
Art Acquisition Fund and the generosity of Mrs. Herbert O. Peet, Richard J. Stern,
the Doris Jones Stein Foundation, the Jacob L. and Ella C. Loose Foundation,
Mr. and Mrs. Richard M. Levin, and Mr. and Mrs. Marvin Rich.) F86-57.
Photograph by Mel McLean. T.H. Benton and R.P. Benton Testamentary
Trusts/Licensed by VAGA, New York, NY.

Published by the University Press of Kansas (Lawrence, Kansas 66049), which was
organized by the Kansas Board of Regents and is operated and funded by Emporia State
University, Fort Hays State University, Kansas State University, Pittsburg State University,
the University of Kansas, and Wichita State University.

Library of Congress Cataloging-in-Publication Data

Seeing nature through gender / edited by Virginia J. Scharff.
p. cm. — (Development of western resources)
Includes bibliographical references.
ISBN 0-7006-1284-X (cloth : alk. paper) — ISBN 0-7006-1285-8 (pbk. :
alk. paper)
1. Human ecology--Philosophy. 2. Philosophy of nature. 3. Sex
role--History. 4. Sex role—Environmental aspects. 5. Body,
Human–Social aspects. I. Scharff, Virginia. II. Series.
GF21.S44 2003
304.2--dc21
2003012332

British Library Cataloguing in Publication Data is available.

Printed in the United States of America

10 9 8 7 6 5 4 3 2 1

The paper used in this publication meets the minimum requirements of the American
National Standard for Permanence of Paper for Printed Library Materials Z39.48-1984.

To Sam and Annie

CONTENTS

ILLUSTRATIONS

ACKNOWLEDGMENTS

I have long thought that a book about gender and environmental history could be of use. That notion has grown into this volume as a consequence of my great fortune in joining conversations in feminist, environmentalist, and environmental history circles over the last twenty years. My earliest colleagues and mentors, Katherine Jensen, Janice Harris, Jean Schaeffer, Judy Smith, Diane Sands, Corky Bush, Susan Armitage, Susan Tweit, Mary Rothschild, and Karen Anderson, helped me to see the first connections.

Many scholars have encouraged me to imagine how gender might matter for the history of human relationships with each other and the world around us, even as they've critiqued, with vigor, rigor, and generosity, the answers I've begun to formulate. I want especially to thank Beth Bailey, Melissa Bokovoy, Kathy Brosnan, Bill Cronon, Bill De Buys, Dan Flores, Sandra Harding, John Herron, Paul Hirt, Suellen Hoy, Scott Hughes, Jenn Huntleigh-Smith, Paul Hutton, Andy Kirk, Dorothee Kocks, Patricia Limerick, Kim Little, Les McFadden, Maria Montoya, Judy Morley, Vera Norwood, Jenny Price, Bob Righter, Hal Rothman, Andrew Sandoval-Strausz, Jane Slaughter, Michael Anne Sullivan, Sam Truett, Marsha Weisiger, Elliott West, Chris Wilson, Richard White, and David Wrobel. I also extend deep thanks to all the contributors to this book, who have been partners in its conception, gestation, and (at last!) journey to your hands.

Cindy Tyson, colleague and friend, prepared the manuscript and offered much good counsel. Scott Meredith, promising young environmental historian, also provided brains and legwork and a whole lot of good cheer. My graduate students at the University of New Mexico continue to teach me, and I am grateful to them all.

Nancy Scott Jackson midwifed and mentored this book into existence. She has been a dream editor—deeply engaged, widely read, imaginative, brilliantly tough-minded, patient, and nurturant. This projects owes its virtues to her and none of its faults. My most heartfelt thanks to Nancy for endeavor far and above the call of duty and for her remarkable friendship.

Hal Corbett, Katie Curtiss, and John Meehan have been thoughtful companions in many wild places. Peter Swift guided me along many nature trails with patience and love. He showed me what it means to be outdoors, looking carefully and breathing and thinking hard, with exhilaration, reflection, and understanding. I can't convey what that's meant.

Sam and Annie Swift, this one's for you, with all my love.

INTRODUCTION
Virginia J. Scharff

Humans know nature in varied and changing ways—by accident and deliberately, through work and contemplation, with intent to transform, and with desire to enjoy. Our ways of encountering all the things we call "nature"—butterflies and volcanoes, prickly pear cacti and penicillin molds—are as many as the encounters themselves. But every one is as mediated by our mental maps of the world as they are by the limits of our bodies and our surroundings.

Humans have in common the curious practice of knowing nature through the categories by which we know ourselves. To observe, for example, that most Americans would have little trouble referring to nature as "Mother" may elicit a "duh" from discerning scholars of environmental history, but that figure of speech should clue us in to something important. Gender, the bundle of habits and expectations and behaviors that organizes people and things according to ideas about the consequences of sexed bodies, is a crucial, deep, and far-reaching medium through which we encounter nature. Gender varies from time to time and place to place. But all humans, in all cultures, think in and act in gendered terms. In turn, gendered ideas and actions respond to all the things we see and feel and hear and smell and taste, what we do with the world around us, and how we think about it.

In short, humans know nature, at least in part, through gender.

The essays in this volume demonstrate how gendered ideas, things, and actions have shaped, and been molded in turn, by the myriad ways in which people have represented, experienced, consumed, manipulated, and produced ourselves and the world of which we are part. If, as I would like to argue, nature and gender are mutually constitutive, historically variable clusters of things and ideas, then seeing gender at work offers a new way to approach the fascinating enterprise of environmental history.

First, some definitions. We begin where pathbreaking scholars have led us, defining environmental history as Donald Worster has as the scholarly field that "deals with all the interactions people have had with nature in past times."[1] William Cronon, in *Nature's Metropolis*, employed Karl Marx's distinction between "first" and "second" nature to try to get at the difference between animals, vegetables, and minerals existing in their own right, and those same substances processed by human hearts, minds, and hands. Both things-in-themselves and things-transformed fall into the category of "nature" ordered numerically.[2] These definitions reflect a larger debate among environmental historians about the meaning of nature, a dispute that remains lively and occasionally rancorous to this day.[3] Acknowledging, always, that there is a material world that exists outside human agency and imagination, many scholars have nonetheless come to question an environmental history that rests on any firm distinction between man and nature. As my own contribution to this book will attest, it is possible to have as much trouble with the category of "man" as of "nature."[4]

Seeing Nature through Gender proceeds from the assumption that humans are fully embedded in, inextricable from, accountable to, and for the world around us: we are within nature. The ways in which humans imagine that they transcend nature are, in my view, historical artifacts to be examined rather than assumptions to be shared. In like manner, the ways in which humans have divided the world according to gender are not descriptions of some "authentic" reality but, instead, forces in environmental history. Thus, the environmental history we imagine here operates not as the action of one thing upon another but instead, following Richard White's recent model, as a recombinant hybrid, a mutable organic machine that does not work according to any grand "intelligent design," but rather according to a process that incorporates both pattern and contingency.[5]

Gender is a component of this organic machine. At a biological level, most human beings encounter the world through bodies that are pretty much alike but differ according to sexual variation in certain organs that make us male and female. But what those sexual differences *mean* to us— culturally, economically, historically—are questions we work out socially. To say that a person is male because certain of his organs are designed to play a particular role in biological reproduction tells us little about the social meaning of that set of biological attributes: masculinity. In one situation, a man might be expected to join his fellows hunting bison with spears; in another, to wear lace and velvet and excel at court intrigue; in still others, he might weave, or devote his life to prayer, or drink beer and chomp hot dogs at Busch Stadium. Femininity, likewise, varies according to time, place, class, ethnicity, occupation, sexual orientation: eighteenth-century Plains Indian women butchered bison with knives; early-twenty-first-century Hollywood starlets shop for spindly shoes. Even just within what has become the United States, the historical and cultural diversity of gender practices boggles the mind.

Each chapter in this book shows how a person or group of people in American history has understood nature (including human animals) in gendered terms and acted accordingly, with consequences for people and other organisms and systems. We demonstrate how nature and gender come together time and again, in varied times and places, with material and often unpredictable, paradoxical, ironic results for both. Gender matters for nature. Nature matters for gender.

Environmental historians have failed to see gender at work because they have told, almost exclusively, men's stories and have examined, nearly as exclusively, men's activities. This volume includes women's history alongside and in dynamic relation to that of men and tries to understand how women's actions, desires, and choices have shaped the larger world, including the things men have done. As cultural historian Natalie Davis suggested in 1975, "It seems to me that we should be interested in the history of both women and men, that we should not be working only on the subjected sex any more than a historian of class can focus entirely on peasants. Our goal is to understand the significance of the sexes, of gender groups in the historical past. Our goal is to discover the range in sex roles and in sexual symbolism in different societies and periods, to find out what meaning they had and how they functioned to maintain the social order or to promote its change."[6]

Gender is relational and permeable, not a solid object to be carried from place to place. It is more like a grammar, employed in all conversations, not always perfectly executed, and indeed often misunderstood but providing at least the potential for order in a world full of wild possibility, unacknowledged context, and inexplicable consequence. In this book, we add women to the record of environmental history. But more broadly, we will examine the ways in which gender conditions historical relations between humans and nature, looking at the intertwined histories of women and men and myriad other things. We don't argue that men's actions are always different from women's, or that men and women always act according to gender scripts, or that all interactions with nature have equal transformative potential. Instead, we seek to put women in the picture, along with men, as more or less knowledgeable agents of ecological transformation, as people who shape and are shaped by their environments. And we seek to look at the ways in which gendered thinking engraves itself upon humans and the world around them.

We also work, in this volume, to undermine the perception that men and women are essentially different creatures, with biologically different destinies. This notion is embraced by all kinds of people, including religious fundamentalists of many kinds. It is also identified with the environmental and political movement known as ecofeminism. The ecofeminist position that some scholars have mapped out—that the exploitation and degradation of women and the earth arise from the same patriarchal impulses and have followed parallel paths—remains historically important and continues to shape writing in environmental history.[7] But that is not the position of this book.

Gender both structures and escapes men's and women's physical embodiment, is larger than human bodies, stunningly historically powerful, and sometimes, for both better and worse, ridiculously easy to alter. We cannot address in a short volume the many ways in which gender operates in environmental history. Instead, we consider four major concerns of environmental history in new ways. We focus here on the representation of both humans and "nature," on the complex reciprocal relations between human bodies and changing landscapes, on questions about consumption, and on environmental politics. In at least these four areas of inquiry, we hold that gender analysis has exciting explanatory power for environmental historians.

My own provocative and frankly irreverent chapter "*Man and Nature! Sex Secrets of Environmental History*" opens the first part, "Representation." I show how scientists see nature through the lens of gender by looking at one influential example from evolutionary biology, a study of breeding behavior in finches. When the researchers focused entirely on the behavior of male birds, they came to the conclusion that reproductive behavior in finches was—surprise!—a matter of male choices, from "adultery" to "rape." But once researchers shifted their field of view, and their notions about gender, to contemplate the possibility that females of the species might make choices too, a far richer and more complex biological story emerged.

The same could be said for environmental history. Environmental historians have done a fine job of showing how men's work in and on nature—mining, fishing, and timbering, for example—has transformed human society and the larger world. What might happen if we put women's work into the picture, taking the home as seriously as fishery or factory? Every day, American consumers make small but significant choices about living in nature. The history of the Amazon rain forest, as any schoolchild knows, is bound up with the history of Happy Meals; Happy Meals may not actually make those who eat them happier, but they make sense in an era when mothers must work for pay as well as feed their families. Seeing women at work and at home can help reveal heretofore obscure dimensions of contemporary environmental history.

Feminist historians of science have for some time investigated the ways in which science institutionalizes various kinds of inequality, including male dominance and imperial conquest.[8] Their work has much to offer environmental history. In "Naturalizing Power: Land and Sexual Violence along William Byrd's Dividing Line," Paige Raibmon considers two accounts of one of the landmark scientific and political expeditions in American history, Byrd's famous 1728 survey of the border country between Virginia and North Carolina. She analyzes the ways in which Byrd segregated stories of sexual conquest and violence into a *Secret History*, detailing sexual encounters with local women, and replaced those stories with accounts of flora and fauna for public consumption in his far more staid *History of the Dividing Line.* Bringing the two stories together, Raibmon shows how colonial British "masculine" activities—claiming and cataloguing women and nature—went hand in hand. She provides an exemplary starting place for examining the relation between ecological imperialism and sexual subordination.

Peter Boag takes a humorous cue from a classic essay in environmental history to offer an intriguing, wonderfully entertaining reading of what is arguably the nation's most visible meeting ground of nature and culture, the Mount Rushmore memorial in the Black Hills of South Dakota. His "Thinking Like Mount Rushmore: Sexuality and Gender on the Republican Landscape" engages the ways in which mountains and memorials, and the landscape of an expanding nation, embody gendered logics and power arrangements. As Boag demonstrates, masculinity and heterosexuality are powerful components of the American impulse to dominate nature, enshrined and engraved at Mount Rushmore.

Mount Rushmore, of course, grafts human bodies directly onto nature's face. In Part II, "Bodies," we see how gender operates in a world that encompasses complex and changing relations between human bodies and environmental changes. We begin with a chapter that brings together the insights of gender scholarship with urban environmental history, Mark Tebeau's "Scaling New Heights: Heroic Firemen, Gender, and the Urban Environment, 1875–1900." There can be few more volatile combinations in nature than the mixing of wood, air, and heat to produce fire. And there are few more powerful testaments to the connections between humans and nature than the enduring presence of fire in cities. Tebeau shows, in lively and beautifully detailed fashion, how the ecology of fire in a changing built environment reshaped both firefighting practices and firefighters' gendered bodies and identities. As American cities built up and out, they became riskier environments in ways the designers and inhabitants had never anticipated. The increasing dangers of firefighting in tall buildings and congested spaces, and the efforts of those who fought fire to establish themselves as worthy of public support, produced a new icon in American culture: the heroic fireman. Tebeau's essay will surely strike post-9/11 readers as both illuminating and poignant.

As Bryant Simon vividly demonstrates in "'New Men in Body and Soul': The Civilian Conservation Corps and the Transformation of Male Bodies and the Body Politic," such gendered identities have been central both to the ways Americans have known nature through work and sought to create political institutions. Simon shows how reformers in the Roosevelt administration sought to promote the CCC, one of the New Deal's most celebrated programs, as a way to "beef up" male bodies and strengthen the state. Putatively turning puny American boys into men by putting them to work in nature, New Dealers hoped to alleviate fears about chaos, decadence, industrialization, and cities and, not coincidentally, to create soldiers fit to defend the nation. If even the most malnourished American male could be transformed into a muscular embodiment of American might, both natural obstacles and political enemies would be no match for Nature's Nation.

These histories of urban firefighters and CCC workers show how expectations about the control of nature relied on, but also created, expectations about the power of manly bodies. But what happened when such bodies were imperiled by the very efforts to control nature that they were supposed to enable? In a story laden with multiple ironies, Maril Hazlett's "Voices from the *Spring*: *Silent Spring* and the Ecological Turn in American Health" reveals the ways in which gendered ideas about human bodies shaped American responses to Rachel Carson's pathbreaking work. Hazlett explains that Carson's book catalyzed an "ecological turn" in many Americans' notions about humans' place in nature, revealing the connections between vulnerable human bodies, science and technology, and the natural world. But at the same time, gendered understandings of bodies, science, nature, and power constrained Americans' capacity to come to terms with the vast implications of Carson's work. Seeing the modern world through both the sympathetic, intuitive, feminized eyes of the naturalist and at the same time applying the rigorous scrutiny of "masculine" science to the problem of pesticides, Carson transcended gender and offered an embracingly human way of knowing nature. But as Hazlett's chapter helps us to understand, contemporary American gender scripts shaped both the successes and limits of environmentalism in postwar America.

The dynamic relations between nature and nurture, between gender, science, and bodies, penetrate far beyond the political; gender, if social in origin, has consequences for sex itself. Nancy Langston offers a chilling and crucial portrait of the complicated ways in which gender, human bodies, and the environment remake each other in "Gender Transformed: Endocrine Disruptors in the Environment." In unforgettable prose, she shows how our ways of constructing gender and consuming our world are reinventing humans, animals, and water systems from the cellular level out. The story is as complicated as it is alarming, linking growing populations, burgeoning consumer goods, the health of female humans, the sexual biology of other creatures. Readers may never look at a plastic bottle of "purified drinking water" the same way again.

As Langston reveals, consumption matters. In a world in which humans can only view nature from the inside, the processes of production and consumption appear not separate but deeply intermeshed. Still, we manage to keep them apart in our minds and daily activities, in great measure, by invoking gender. Douglas Sackman's "Putting Gender on the Table: Food and the Family Life of Nature" shows how American families make gender and identity when they consume nature as food; gendered identities, in turn, shape that consumption of nature. Sackman writes that "if environmental history finds its main story at the place where nature and culture intersect, then the home should not fall outside of its purview." Instead, charting a sweeping course of American history, encompassing changing ideals and habits from the farm family to the consumer family, Sackman puts families and households at the center of humans' engagement with the rest of nature. "As we cook nature," he explains, "we also cook ourselves."

Cooking nature is a process with large as well as small possibilities. In "From Snow Bunnies to Shred Betties: Gender, Consumption, and the Skiing Landscape," Annie Gilbert Coleman invites us to see how mountains, markets, and women's changing roles came together in the form of new landscapes, traversed in new ways, by thrill-seeking female sports enthusiasts. Mountains have long been a staple setting in the literature of environmental history, and mountaineers, climbers, and wilderness seekers have assuredly been revered personages in that same literature. But here, for the first time, we meet agents of environmental change who have been all but invisible to historians. The fashion-conscious Snow Bunnies of the 1950s and 1960s and the slope-ripping, baggy-pants Shred Betties of the current snowboarding generation may at first glance appear frivolous figures, but Coleman treats them with both the verve and the seriousness they deserve. Although the ski industry initially saw women as an accoutrement to men, the "real" skiers, the mountains proved as much a challenge and invitation to women as to men. Surprising the ski industry with their determination to transcend the bounds of femininity in search of physical challenge and perilous speed, women skiers' and snowboarders' consumption of mountains would in turn catalyze the industry's expanding transformation of mountain landscapes. Tearing through the door their Snow Bunny mothers opened by getting out of the lodge and onto the black diamond runs, Shred Betties, far from contenting themselves with "feminine" passivity in nature, devour mountains with all the voraciousness of their boarding brethren. Coleman's women skiers emphatically demonstrate what Dan Flores once wrote about mountain climbing: "It won't do to dismiss climbing a mountain out of hand as an arrogant and peculiarly male desire to conquer nature. There is, after all, the question of knowledge. . . . What about mountains as ladders of transcendence to the spiritual?"[9]

Coleman's essay makes a large point: to know environmental history, we must know women's history. In the fourth part, "Politics," scholars examine the ways in which both women's activities and gendered ideas and practices have shaped environmental crusades from the conservation movement of the early twentieth century to countercultural

back-to-the-land experiments in the late twentieth century to land and resource battles and environmental justice campaigns that continue into the
new millennium.

Most Americans today would not know the name of Gene Stratton-
Porter; indeed most environmental historians, who ought to know better,
don't know who she was. In her time, however, Porter was an international celebrity, a best-selling novelist, a screenwriter, a celebrated nature
photographer, and founder of the Isaak Walton League. Her passionate
pleas on behalf of wild and beautiful places reached an audience num-
bering in the tens of millions; far more people read her *Girl of the Limberlost* than ever heard of John Muir.

In response to her society's constraining expectations about how
women should know nature, Porter fashioned a "muscular womanhood"
that both played off and stretched the bounds of femininity. Not surprisingly for this woman of hybrid sensibility, she combined an ardent love for
nature with an equally avid pursuit of wealth. Like many in her generation, she saw no contradiction between conservation and consumption.

Historians of the conservation movement have often depicted their
subject in polarized terms, focusing on the activities of male leaders, or in
Amy Green's words, on "battles between mountaineer John Muir and
forester Gifford Pinchot, promoters of use and advocates of preservation," with Theodore Roosevelt playing referee. But examining Porter's
long, influential, and contradictory life and work in "'She Touched Fifty
Million Lives': Gene Stratton-Porter and Nature Conservation," Green reveals a more complicated cultural politics of "nature work," exemplified
by the remarkable career of Porter, bound up in making and breaking
rules about gender. If we follow Amy Green's lead, what other lost figures in the history of environmental politics might we recover? And how
would taking such people seriously reshape our expectations about what
environmentalism has been and might be?

By the 1960s, culture, politics, and nature work came together in an
environmental movement of breathtaking diversity. Catherine Kleiner's
"Nature's Lovers: The Erotics of Lesbian Land Communities in Oregon,
1974–1984" offers a richly detailed portrait of one small but surprisingly
influential variant of environmental politics, the lesbian back-to-the-land
movement. As Kleiner reveals, land lesbians fused radical politics, countercultural antimaterialism, and separatist feminism in utopian experiments squarely in the tradition of American communitarian endeavors
from Nashoba and Brook Farm to the Llano colony and the Hog Farm.
Land lesbians developed a "spirit politics" based on the idea that women
were not simply close to nature. Nature *was* a woman: a mother, lesbian
lover, sister, womb, who could be nurtured and nurturing under
women's stewardship. Land lesbians elevated their interactions with na-

ture to a level of consciousness both practical and erotic. They committed themselves to nonviolence, to caring for the earth, to consuming as little as possible. Their vision of a good life raises once again questions posed in Sackman's and Coleman's essays: how do our gender scripts shape our ideas about the right way to consume nature?

Kleiner's story of land lesbians and Katherine Jensen's "Saving Centennial Valley: Land, Gender, and Community in the Northern Black Hills" both testify to the ways in which gender operates in rural Americans' struggle to stay on the land. The story of the Frawley Ranch controversy shows how a group of Black Hills ranching families drew on both well-established gender patterns, in which women and men knew their places but worked as full partners on the land, and the new expertise and experience of various family members to mobilize opposition to development. The Save Centennial Valley Again Association embraced a grassroots environmental politics that put human community and land stewardship at the center of its vision. Looking at the multigenerational ranch families who organized the SCVAA, Jensen shows how the activists mobilized family solidarity, traditional divisions of labor on the ranch, and political savvy and skills garnered through participation in sixties' protest movements and work in international development to bring both local and global strengths to the land struggle. Her warm, thoughtful portrait takes us far beyond the picture of battles between developers and ranchers as simply contests between "men in suits and men in boots."

In the Black Hills, activists drew on a vision of community based in preexisiting land use patterns and human relations. But along the Santa Cruz watershed, flowing from Arizona into Sonora, environmental justice organizers, many of them poor women of color, created a political and social network that began in neighborhoods and ultimately spanned a fortified national border, took on a host of polluting industries, and ultimately created not simply a new movement but indeed a new borderland ecology. In "Steps to an Ecology of Justice: Women's Environmental Networks across the Santa Cruz River Watershed," Giovanna di Chiro shows how environmental justice networks are made, one flyer, one meeting, one tank of gas at a time, as she tags along with remarkable organizer Rose Marie Augustine. As di Chiro explains, "Like the 'natural' flow of rivers, air currents, and toxic chemicals within and across geographical landscapes, political borders, residential neighborhoods and bodily tissues, the 'extraordinary' circulation of women's environmental networks reveals the quintessential ecological threads connecting desert-dwelling peoples and desert nature. This *is* the stuff of remarkable, and even more 'fertile,' environmental history."

These chapters range from colonial borderlands to transnational boundaries, from mountain to marketplace, from irony and playfulness to earnest explanation and political argument. But they have in common the attempt to understand how gender situates humans in the world of fire, air, earth, and water, and how that world can remake the gendered patterns we've engraved on ourselves and the planet. We offer them as a contribution to an ongoing conversation about how to tell useful stories about the history of humans' place in nature.

NOTES

1. Donald Worster, ed., *The Ends of the Earth: Perspectives on Modern Environmental History* (Cambridge: Cambridge University Press, 1988), vii.
2. William Cronon, *Nature's Metropolis: Chicago and the Great West* (New York: W. W. Norton, 1991).
3. See William Cronon, "The Trouble with Wilderness, or Getting Back to the Wrong Nature," *Environmental History* 1, no. 1 (January 1996): 7–28, with comments by Samuel P. Hays, Michael P. Cohen, Thomas R. Dunlap, and Cronon's response. See also the extremely hostile reactions to Cronon's essay in *Wild Earth* (Winter 1996–1997) by Gary Snyder, Dave Foreman, Donald M. Waller, and George Sessions.
4. See Virginia J. Scharff, "Man and Nature! Sex Secrets of Environmental History," Chapter 1 in this volume.
5. Richard White, *The Organic Machine: The Remaking of the Columbia River* (New York: Hill and Wang, 1995).
6. Natalie Zemon Davis, "Women's History in Transition: The European Case," *Feminist Studies* 3 (1975–1976): 90.
7. For a critique of this literature, see Virginia J. Scharff, "Are Earth Girls Easy? Feminism, Women's History, and Environmental History," *Journal of Women's History* 7, no. 2 (Summer 1995): 163–75.
8. Ruth Hubbard, Mary Sue Henifin, and Barbara Fried, eds., *Women Look at Biology Looking at Women: A Collection of Feminist Critiques* (Cambridge, Mass.: Schenkman, 1979); Evelyn Fox Keller, *Reflections on Gender and Science* (New Haven, Conn.: Yale University Press, 1985); Ann Fausto-Sterling, *Myths of Gender: Biological Theories about Women and Men* (New York: Basic Books, 1985); Donna Haraway, *Primate Visions: Gender, Race, and Nature in the World of Modern Science* (New York: Routledge, 1989); Ludmilla Jordanova, *Sexual Visions: Images of Gender in Science and Medicine between the Eighteenth and Twentieth Centuries* (Madison, Wis.: University of Wisconsin Press, 1989); Ruth Hubbard, *The Politics of Women's Biology* (New Brunswick, N.J.: Rutgers University Press, 1990); Donna J. Haraway, *Simians, Cyborgs, and Women: The Reinvention of Nature* (New York: Routledge, 1991); Evelyn Fox Keller, *Secrets of Life, Secrets of Death: Essays on Language, Gender, and Science* (New York: Routledge, 1992); Londa Schiebinger, *Nature's Body: Gender in the Making of Modern Science* (New York: Beacon Press, 1993); Sandra Harding, *The Science Question in Feminism* (Ithaca, N.Y.: Cornell University Press, 1986); Sandra Harding, *Whose Science, Whose Knowledge? Thinking from Women's Lives* (Ithaca, N.Y.: Cornell University Press, 1991); Sandra Harding, *Is Science Multicultural? Postcolonialism, Feminism and Epistemologies (Race, Gender, Science)* (Bloomington: Indiana University Press, 1998).
9. Dan Flores, *Horizontal Yellow: Nature and History in the Near Southwest* (Albuquerque: University of New Mexico Press, 1999), 202.

PART I: REPRESENTATION

CHAPTER ONE

Man and Nature! Sex Secrets
of Environmental History

Virginia J. Scharff

> My image of History would have at least two bodies in it, at least two per-
> sons talking, arguing, always listening to the other as they gestured at their
> books; it would be a film, not a still picture, so that you could see that some-
> times they wept, sometimes they were astonished, sometimes they were
> knowing, and sometimes they laughed with delight.
> —*Natalie Zemon Davis*[1]

I tease and entice you, reader, with this title, "Man and Nature! Sex Secrets of Environmental History." But it is likely I shall disappoint you. If
you have read *Masters and Johnson* or the *Kinsey Report,* you know that
works that put *sex* in the title seduce the reader with the promise of titil-
lation but deliver the goods in a manner more consistent with school-
marms than strippers. So it is with me. In the past, I have worked to
create what I have called a "tender coupling" between environmental history, women's history, and feminist analysis, a triple conjunction that the
environmental historian Dan Flores memorably called a "ménage à
trois."[2] In this chapter, however, I come not to supplicate but to lecture.

My subject is environmental history, which I identify as a body of
writing and a set of professional techniques, institutions, and practices, or
to use the earthier term of the most distinguished and provocative environmental historian, Donald Worster, environmental history is a "field."
According to Worster, this scholarly field "deals with all the interactions
people have had with nature in past times."[3] I applaud such an enterprise,
but like many fields that exist mostly in the domains of words, thoughts,
and paper, the objects buried in *this* field are ideas. I will argue here that
environmental history, at present, does not begin to answer Worster's description because buried within it is a sex secret. It remains at present not
a story of people and other things but is instead a story of man and nature.

Environmental historians have devoted unending energy to answer-

This essay originally appeared in *Human/Nature* (1999) and is reprinted courtesy of University of New Mexico Press.

ing the question, "What do we mean by nature?"[4] They have spent a whole lot less time trying to define who or what they mean when they write about *humanity*. The relation between the terms *human* and *nature* in environmental history has, however, endless and intimate connections, as when, in seeking moral and political lessons for humans from the collection of diverse things we call nature, we write about nature as if it were singular, a term parallel and comparable to the singular term *man*.

Critics of the very sciences environmental historians incorporate in their scholarship have demonstrated that categories like "man" and "nature" are not only socially constructed but intellectually and politically salient; the words we use to capture knowledge of our world matter, in the here and now.[5] We should heed critiques of science for practical reasons. Environmental historians often use biology, for example, but biology requires interrogation rather than appropriation. Scholars including Carolyn Merchant, Stephen Jay Gould, Evelyn Fox Keller, Donna Haraway, and Londa Schiebinger have shown how the sociopolitical categories of gender, race, and class construct scientific understandings of who, and what, counts as a human as well as what counts as natural.[6]

I believe that humans are best understood as historical animals. Part of what makes us what we are today is a centuries-long struggle within our species, *Homo sapiens*, over the right to be classed as "human" and therefore to claim legitimate right to the powers and privileges of humanity. Among those powers are the right to speak publicly, the right to possess one's own home, the right to own one's own body.

But pause for a moment over this word *species*, the linguistic emblem of a scientific, biologically based view of humanity. If humans are understood biologically, as a species, it is a tautology to say that knowing humanity means understanding the differences and commonalities between males and females. One common definition of species is "a group of intimately related and physically similar organisms that actually or potentially interbreed and are less commonly capable of fertile interbreeding with members of other groups."[7] Since humans propagate sexually, our species includes at a minimum men and women and moreover is *defined* with reference to sexual division according to humans' function in biological reproduction. Sigmund Freud famously explained that anatomy was destiny; many before and since have argued that this biological difference of sex tells us nearly everything we need to know about creatures I want to call "historical animals."[8] I think, however, that continuing differences in women's and men's histories are products of contentiously shared experience, a wide realm, more than narrowly mechanistic outcomes of bodily complementarity. There is far more to the enterprise of reproducing the species than the generation and gestation of viable human fetuses, a subject I'll be getting back to by and by.

Environmental historians, who wish to situate human thought and action in a world of other flora and fauna, have good reasons to try to understand humans as animals. But the biological concept of species, as we have just seen, is a rather dull categorical tool. At the same time it is also a complex, contradictory device. Even as biologists have put fruitful sexual congress at the heart of their professional understanding of human beings, biological science has perpetuated a naming practice that creates confusion, error, and inequality. I refer, of course, to the practice of referring to the human species as "man" or "mankind." I cannot do justice to the numerous elegant feminist critiques of the use of the male generic in English, so I refer you to a useful book first published in 1976, Casey Miller and Kate Swift's *Words and Women: New Language in New Times*.

As Miller and Swift point out, citing the *Oxford English Dictionary*, in Old English the term *man* referred to individual persons of both sexes. The word *mankind* did not appear in Old English, first coming into usage around 1300. However, by the end of the first millennium after Christ, speakers of Old English had begun to use *man* in another sense, to distinguish a person of the male sex from one of the female sex. The older meaning, of course, persisted. As a consequence English would come to be a language in which no one could ever be truly sure when the words *man* and *men* meant males and when they meant humans in general.

By the eighteenth century, as Western Europeans and European Americans struggled over access to "the rights of man," defining the term had potentially immense political consequences. David Hume, who aimed for precision, referred in his 1752 *Political Discourses* to "all men, male and female." Alexander Pope, however, was a little less clear. His famous *Essay on Man*, published in 1733, admonished his friend Lord Bolingbroke to "know then thyself. . . . The proper study of mankind is man." Presumably he meant that all persons, male and female, should have self-understanding, but Pope left a puzzle behind in the essay, with a later reference to "thy dog, thy bottle, and thy wife."[9] When Thomas Jefferson wrote that "all men are created equal," he would make available a political argument for universal rights, an argument he by no means wished to extend to all humans, not even all males.[10]

Enlightenment science understood generic "man" as male, building on the classical tradition of seeing males as normative and females as deformed. The male generic has permeated not only Western science but also common English usage. As a consequence, both small children and scientists have tended not only to imagine that women's actions must be insignificant but moreover to assume "that all creatures are male unless they are known to be female." As Miller and Swift noted, English speakers often refer to animals as "he," and "only ladybugs, cows, hens, and mother animals with their young are predictably referred to as *she*."[11]

The repercussions of speaking and thinking in male generics may sometimes be trivial, but they are also substantial. And science is rife with the male generic. Environmental historians rely on science as an analytical tool; they should be sensitive to the ways in which gender ideology constructs scientific knowledge. Biologists, for example, have shaped their assumptions about animal behavior, natural selection, and even genetics in conformity with the idea that males of a species are biologically normative, active, and essential, and females are somehow auxiliary, or perhaps vehicular, even when the species cannot propagate itself without both.

This kind of thinking leads to some fairly weird and historically interesting science. My favorite recent example of such scientific work involved experiments by a team of researchers at the University of Sheffield in England, led by the globally eminent ornithologist Timothy R. Birkhead. Birkhead's group studied sperm morphology and sperm production in Australian zebra finches (*Taeniopygia guttata*).[12] Whatever the scientific merits of studying sperm morphology, the larger purpose of these experiments was, I think, to say something not simply about zebra finch sperm or even sperm of various species but to speculate about "natural" sexual behavior in zebra finches and in animals in general, including the human. In our time, when sociobiology claims even the attention of historians, biological experiments bear heavy burdens of meaning. Indeed, as E. O. Wilson explains, in the sociobiologist's "macroscopic view the humanities and social sciences shrink to specialized branches of biology."[13]

Zebra finches are among those birds that were reputed to mate and rear young with one lifetime partner, a notion Birkhead and others have attributed to Charles Darwin's "touchingly naive" Victorian sexual mores.[14] Birkhead's Sheffield team, hailing from the other side of the sexual revolution, reported instead that such birds "occasionally enjoy sexual dalliances with other birds. Indeed, individual out-of-wedlock copulations have a higher fertilization rate than single mating efforts at home." To test this hypothesis, according to a summary account in *Science News*:

> The team collected sperm by allowing male zebra finches to mate with a freeze-dried female equipped with an artificial sperm receptacle. When prevented from copulating for a week, a male would ejaculate several times into the dead female. Sperm from the second ejaculate moved at half the speed of sperm from the first go-around, a computerized sperm tracker revealed. Quantity decreased as well. . . . "The vagina is an incredibly hostile zone to sperm," so the faster they zip through, the better their chances of surviving, suggests Birkhead. . . . A male zebra finch has affairs only after he has re-

covered from copulating with his mate during her fertile period. As a result, he releases more sperm during one act of intercourse with his one-time lovers than with his regular gal, Birkhead says. "Waiting until your own female is no longer fertile before you go looking for extra-pair copulations is part of the male strategy," he asserts.[15]

Now, this experiment certainly raises some questions about thinking in male-generic terms when it comes to understanding the intimate lives of zebra finches. Do the nonfertile females have "affairs" too? (You may or may not buy the assumptions underlying this question at all. If you do, they do; see below.) Do they seek out as partners males who would rather copulate with living than dead specimens? Do the females who indulge in "one-night stands" with aging males suffer social stigma, or do they have no trouble attracting younger males with speedier sperm? An "artificial sperm receptacle" installed in a freeze-dried female zebra finch may be "an incredibly hostile environment," but is it really a "vagina"? Is it more hostile yet when such a receptacle is equipped with "a computerized sperm tracker"? And I wonder how, exactly, it is possible to see a male zebra finch's willingness to copulate (repeatedly) with a dead female as a strategy for reproductive success?

Clearly I envision a somewhat more active role for female zebra finches in the whole enterprise of sex and biological reproduction than such an experimental design can contemplate. And these days so does Professor Birkhead, who has spent endless hours watching and manipulating the matings of birds, including chickens, finches, sooty terns, rock ptarmigans, swallows, hawks, and spoonbills. Birkhead and Anders Pape Moller, his coauthor of the definitive work *Sperm Competition in Birds: Evolutionary Causes and Consequences* (1992), have devoted a lot of work quite recently to investigating "female control." As they explained in an article in *Animal Behaviour*, "At the time we were writing *Sperm Competition in Birds,* the idea of female control was still at an early stage. . . . The idea of female control has subsequently been explored more fully, both in terms of behavior . . . and physiology . . . and there is now some good evidence for it."[16]

It turns out that despite their many years of observing bird copulations, these two scientists had not until recently paid much attention to the fact that female birds had copulated with numbers of male birds in a dazzling array of settings and that after the acts, the females routinely ejected sperm from their bodies. Not until 1992, in fact, did Birkhead and Moller burst the epistemological straitjacket of the generic male and begin to wonder what those birds were doing, and why it might matter.

And why did the scientists change their minds? As Birkhead and Moller admitted, "After more careful research, and the occasional verbal batterings from female colleagues, most behavioral ecologists have come to realize that such notions [of male activity and female passivity] were founded on the blinkered observations of male chauvinists. In reality, many female birds actually seek adulterous copulations. Far from being passive victims of adultery, they are active and willing participants."[17]

I personally am not prepared to encumber zebra finches or other birds with all the cultural baggage that comes along with adultery, but I think it is much to Professor Birkhead's credit that he learned from those batterings from female colleagues and as a consequence has gone on to explore a rich, wide-open new field for inquiry in his research specialty. How much more interesting those long hours of sitting quietly in the copse must have become now that both parties observed in the act of union may be presumed to have interests, strategies, desires, and significance. Awareness of his own cultural blinders, evidently, has transformed his work.

In recent years, environmental historians have also been self-critical about the ways cultural notions inform seemingly scientific observations of nature.[18] Still, the man/nature formulation continues to pop up in the most interesting places, for example, in a book much admired by environmental historians, Michael Pollan's erudite and fetching *Second Nature: A Gardener's Education*. Pollan is a beguiling writer and evidently a gifted gardener, but as I read along in this book I was continually brought up short by his insistence on referring to humans collectively as "man" and to nature in aggregate as "she." In this formulation, "man" tends to be purposeful but misguided, perpetually intervening in processes "he" can't quite fathom and always creating consequences "he" didn't intend. "Nature," on the other hand, is energetic and alluring, but utterly witless. *"Nature herself,"* Pollan writes, *"doesn't know what's going to happen here.* Nature has no grand design . . . chance events can divert her course into an almost infinite number of different channels."[19]

Pollan is acutely aware that people who write about nature perforce use metaphors, some of which he finds misleading (nature as a watch or other machine), others "more apt" ("an organism or a stock exchange").[20] But for all his sensitivity to ecological contingency and human folly, why is he so unself-conscious about reducing complex, diverse people to "man" and everything not human to a "her"? What are the implications of this rhetorical choice? Man, in Pollan's world, is a deeply reflective Shandyan character, a less dyspeptic Henry Adams seeking education but settling for experience, a Ricky Ricardo, shaking his head and muttering, "Lucy, Lucy, Lucy." Nature—earthworms, Norway pines, tomato plants, tornadoes, what have you—is in Pollan's world little more ultimately than a flighty dame, determined to seduce man with the promise of conquest but ultimately coy, elusive, and unreflective.

But "nature" is not one thing. Why shove zebra finches, saguaro cacti, tidal waves, uranium ore, and the AIDS virus into one vessel or, as engineers might put it, one "black box"? Such a formula is nowhere near adequate for the immense mission of environmental history.

Most environmental historians would, I think, find Pollan's personification of people as "man," and nature as "her," to be at least quaint or even embarrassing in the same way we are embarrassed when we hear a small boy tell his female classmate, "You can't play Little League. Girls aren't allowed." No, we want to say, that isn't polite. But in some senses, Pollan's overtly sexist language is preferable to the sex secret created when writers use seemingly neutral language while focusing almost exclusively on men's activities. There are a number of ways of measuring the extent to which environmental historians emphasize male humans' stories. We might look at the subjects and settings of environmental history studies, asking, for example, why scholars in the field have found forest fires more fascinating than cooking fires.[21] We might ask questions about analysis of data, as I shall presently. But another way to measure the disproportionate attention given to male activities in environmental history is to study the field's taxonomy. In field guides to birds, taxonomic distinctions are revealed in book indexes. So it is with environmental history.

Schoolmarm that I am, I recently investigated the taxonomy of environmental history by creating and performing a simple, even crude exercise in arithmetic. I looked at the indexes of seven important works in environmental history, all books I admire greatly, some of them written by contributors to this anthology. I counted up the number of male proper names and female proper names indexed. Then I calculated the percentage of male versus female names indexed. The results of this tabulation are in Table 1.

It is possible to interpret these figures in a number of ways. First, note that indispensable works of environmental history have made specific reference to, almost exclusively, men. Carolyn Merchant's pathbreaking *Ecological Revolutions*, a book best known for the author's revealing use of gender as a category of analysis in environmental history, still takes note of strikingly few historical woman. All these books claim to be about human beings' relations with nature, but their indices suggest that the humans being represented here are overwhelmingly male. On the other hand, Vera Norwood's *Made from This Earth* narrows its human subjects to "American women" and comes closer, taxonomically anyhow, to telling a story with persons of both sexes in it; one-third of the people to whom Norwood refers are men. Suellen Hoy alone refers to roughly equal numbers of women and men, and my own estimate is that this taxonomic parity reflects her conscious and successful attempt to write a gender-balanced environmental history of cleanliness in the United States.

Table 1. Incidence of Male and Female Proper Names in the Indexes of Environmental History Books

Author, Title	No. of Male Names	No. of Female Names	Percentage of Male Names
De Buys, *Enchantment and Exploitation*	137	3	97.9
Worster, *Rivers of Empire*	313	13	96.0
Cronon, *Nature's Metropolis*	146	9	94.2
Rothman, *On Rims and Ridges*	272	24	91.2
Merchant, *Ecological Revolutions*[a]	173	25	87.4
Hoy, *Chasing Dirt*	113	102	52.6
Norwood, *Made from This Earth*	75	151	33.2

[a]Tabulations for this index exclude names of gods and goddesses.

Perhaps the other environmental historians, whose works lean so much more heavily upon men's stories, have reached the conclusion that men's activities end up transforming "nature" more than women's. They have thus simply focused on what's important. I do not wish to argue either that men's actions are always different from women's or that we can make a simplistic correlation between the environmental impact of a group's actions and the size of its population—Americans, for example, are a minority of the earth's people but use most of its fossil fuels. But how can we *know* women's relative significance as agents of ecological transformation if we haven't consulted, in any serious way, their words and works? Without studying women's history, we will never know, for example, how women's actions, desires, and choices have shaped the world, including the things men have done, among them those things so ably and elegantly detailed in the works for environmental historians.

The idea that men have simply been more important environmental actors than women also begs the question of how we identify what constitutes "transformation" of nature. Building a dam or clear-cutting a forest obviously impress us as epic ecological events, but bigness is no guarantee of ecological significance, as Alfred Crosby's work on the role of viruses in ecological imperialism reminds us.[22] Mistaking size for significance also confuses the goal of documenting and interpreting the ways humans (or here, significant humans, i.e., men) have left a mark on nature with Worster's far more ambitious goal of describing *interactions between people and all the other kinds of things on earth.*

Another possibility is that environmental historians' sources limit their ability to see the significance of women's actions. Women's historians have long pointed out the ways that traditional historical sources obscure women's lives. And given the sometimes terminal sanctions against speaking out, acting up, even eating "too much," women the world over have extended themselves, with dismaying success, to cover their own tracks. But this concealment hasn't stopped women's historians from finding out a lot about women's past, and it shouldn't stop environmental historians either. Rivers and forest fires, woodchucks and white pine trees do not speak, but the literature of environmental history testifies eloquently to the presence and the significance of these mute entities. Women, unlike woodchucks, have the power of speech, but environmental historians have not listened very well.

At the risk of appearing downright waspish, I have to admit that there are times when the very best environmental histories almost foreground their silencing of women's history. As I was working my way through the index of Bill Cronon's splendid *Nature's Metropolis*, for example, I found an entry for one Patrick O'Leary. Turning to the text, I read about "the blaze that began in the barn behind Patrick O'Leary's cottage." This passive construction of the origins of the Great Chicago Fire of 1871 blandly skirts a story of human, more particularly, female agency familiar to every schoolchild in the land: "One dark night, when we were all in bed / Mrs. O'Leary left the lantern in the shed / And when the cow kicked it over, she winked her eye and said / There'll be a hot time in the old town tonight." Mrs. O'Leary does not make an appearance in Cronon's magisterial book. How can this be?

The *Oxford English Dictionary*, and Miller and Swift, remind us that "man" is sometimes human and sometimes male, and the confusion between the two constructions leads not only to further confusions but also contributes to social inequalities. But this linguistic heritage has spawned a further confusion, the "sex secret" of the literature of environmental history, in which all too often "human" *also* means "male." I want to stress here the political importance of this contest over what or who counts as "human" and remind you that just as science was launching its sustained takeoff into growth, the philosopher Mary Wollstonecraft was finding it impossible to convince most of the advanced thinkers of her day that women possessed enough of the stuff that made men naturally "human" to claim title to the Rights of Man. It is thus not surprising, as feminists from Wollstonecraft to Sherry Ortner and Carolyn Merchant have pointed out, to find human women perpetually slipping into the category of "nature" or to see the pervasiveness of gender as an organizing force in environmental thinking in the tradition of regarding "nature itself" as female and feminine.[23]

Numerous scholars have called attention to the identification of women with nature and of nature with women. I want to endorse the idea that women are, in crucial ways, embedded in nature; so are men. But in keeping with my waspish and pedantic desire to cavil over categories and claim the power of lecturing, I insisted once again that women share with men the pernicious and noble attribute of being human. Thus, taking up Worster's charge to write a history that "deals with all the interactions people have had with nature in past times," I insist that environmental historians must own up to their sex secrets in order to begin to account for human activity, if nothing else.

And so I turn, as humans sometimes do, from sex to work. In 1979 feminist educator and organizer Judy Smith told a Missoula, Montana, audience that environmentalists needed to think more about the ways their attempts to advocate on nature's behalf might have consequences for women's work. In the years since Smith made this suggestion, environmental historians like Merchant, Vera Norwood, and Suellen Hoy have taken up the task of describing precisely those changes and consequences.[24] In 1995 Richard White echoed Smith's suggestion in *The Organic Machine*, writing that "one of the great shortcomings—intellectual and political—of modern environmentalism is its failure to grasp how human beings have historically known nature through work."[25] I agree wholeheartedly. Environmental history needs a broader, more nuanced, and far more gender-conscious understanding of work than the fundamentally Marxist formulation embraced by most scholars working in the field.

Here, at the risk of oversimplifying, I am forced to be brief and schematic. The environmental history I have read, from Donald Worster to cultural critic Mike Davis, conceptualizes work in relation to what Marx called "modes of production," one of which is, of course, capitalism. Most environmental historians treat the rest of capitalism as a process that rationalized, mechanized, and commodified work; alienated people from nature; transformed workers from producers into consumers; and in the process created distinct boundaries between work and leisure.

The following describes the capitalist transformation of work:

rationalization
mechanization
commodification
alienation from nature
from production to consumption
separation of work and leisure

However, feminist activists, labor historians, and feminist social scientists have demonstrated that industrialization and capitalist development led to the creation of all kinds of nonrationalized, nonmechanized, uncommodified (i.e., unpaid) productive work. As feminists have long noted, much of this work has been and remains women's work, often identified as "reproduction" or "consumption."[26] Following Anthony Giddens rather than Marx, I argue the need to abandon the distinction between production and reproduction, to instead see *all* human work as *action* entailing the *reproduction and transformation* of available rules and resources.[27] Those rules and resources may be as large and complex as the federal reserve banking system or as tiny as a lamp flame flickering in a shadowy cowshed.

Sometimes even spectacular ecological transformations may be traced back to mundane moments in women's history. Cronon's passing mention of Patrick O'Leary's shed inspired me to think about how to imagine an environmental history that includes women. Return with me to that dark night in 1871, when that horrible fire in the by then supposedly rationalized, mechanized, commodified city of Chicago was about to start. Experts disagree about what happened—most recently Chicago Title Insurance Company lawyer Richard F. Bales has used the techniques of a claims adjuster to cast doubt on Mrs. O'Leary's culpability—but contemporaries and modern schoolchildren swore that most people were in bed and that Mrs. O'Leary left a lantern in the shed, and the cow kicked it over, and the rest was history.[28]

What might Mrs. Catherine O'Leary have been doing in the shed long after everyone else was in bed? Evidently she kept five cows, earning money selling milk to families in her working-class Irish neighborhood. Cows need to be milked, or they get extremely uncomfortable.[29] If Catherine O'Leary was in the shed, she was presumably there to do that overdue milking. Women like her tended to have busy days, still doing their work long after dark. A cow in the city, a woman attending to her domestic chores late into the night. That night the men of the Chicago Board of Trade had left off dealing in mechanized rivers of grain they had never seen and had gone home to a dinner somebody else cooked, maybe read the evening paper while somebody else cleaned up, and then they stretched, yawned, and went up to bed. While they were enjoying a few hours of shut-eye, Catherine O'Leary's cows needed tending. The board of inquiry that investigated the fire exonerated both Mrs. O'Leary and her cow, a forgiving but, folklorically speaking, futile gesture.[30]

But let's not turn Catherine O'Leary into a sentimental heroine of history. Try another story. We know that she kept cows in the city, but consider a wholly undocumented conjecture: Perhaps she wasn't always a responsible dairywoman. Maybe she didn't get around to milking that night because she got drunk in the morning and spent the whole day passed out in bed. Patrick, returning filthy and exhausted from his twelve-hour day, shook her awake and said to her, "That damnable cow is mooing her head off. What's the matter with you—didn't you milk her yet?" Mrs. O'Leary, bleary, staggered out to the shed with the lantern and then remembered she'd forgotten something in the house. But she left the lantern in the shed. Consider what happens when women *don't* do their work.

Ross Miller, who has examined the Great Chicago Fire as both an event in social history and a formative cultural myth, pointed out that in 1871, "in Chicago, a thriving cosmopolitan downtown still coexisted with Mrs. O'Leary's rural homestead."[31] You would probably get arrested for keeping a cow in Chicago today. But that doesn't mean that all work has been rationalized, mechanized, socialized, and commodified. Instead the gendered division of labor, symbolized by Catherine O'Leary in the shed, has structured the relation between nature, markets, and work to this very day. Even today domestic work remains productive, relatively unmechanized, unrationalized, generally uncommodified, connected to nature, often unseparated from leisure, and performed chiefly by women.

If, as far as we know, women have not recently burned down any American cities (and that assumption may simply reflect our ignorance rather than their actions), their domestic work remains ecologically transformative in ways that tend to be small and incremental rather than cataclysmic, easier to see in the aggregate than in the particular (and perhaps this distinction, to be charitable, accounts in part for those skewed indices). Let me try to make a trivial part of that work visible by turning a personal anecdote into a story about environmental history. One fall day, I returned from the grocery store annoyed, as I often am, by the fact that getting food into our household had once again cost me an hour and a half of valuable writing time. As I began to unload the grocery bags from the car and ferry them into the house, I was reminded of that revolutionary moment, so brilliantly narrated by William Cronon, when grain dealers realized they could save endless money and labor by transporting wheat using steam-powered machines rather than human muscles and by storing grain in bins and mechanized grain elevators rather than sacks.[32]

Trudging back and forth from car to kitchen with my dozen bags, I began to wonder just how much freight I was carrying that day. And so, turning annoyance into science, I went into the bathroom, got the scale, and put it on the kitchen floor. Then I weighed those groceries sack by sack. That day's load, comprising most but by no means all of what I would purchase and carry during an average week's grocery shopping, weighed in at seventy-eight pounds.

Most weeks I end up at a grocery store four or five times because we've run out of milk or lettuce or coffee, or somebody has to take something to school for a class snack. I figure those extra trips add up, conservatively, to another twenty-five pounds of freight, but let's round off my weekly total to one hundred pounds of groceries for a family of four.

Multiply that by fifty-two weeks per year, and you've got me carrying fifty-two hundred pounds of groceries a year. That doesn't seem too bad; only a bit over two and a half tons. But in the course of each shopping trip, I heft each item five times—from the shelf into the cart, from the cart onto the conveyor belt (then somebody else, a bagger, is paid to lift things twice, from the counter into bags and then into my cart), from the cart into the car, from the car to the house, and once in the house to wherever constitutes being "put away" in my house. So it seems fair to me to multiply the total weekly weight of groceries by five in order to account for the number of times I lift and carry items to complete the job of "grocery shopping." Reckoned this way, I haul a total of twenty-six thousand pounds, or thirteen tons, of groceries a year before I've so much as opened a single can of tomatoes to make dinner.

Calculating the weight of my groceries may seem like a Taylorist exercise in whining; yes, it is that. And like much of arithmetic, this problem is pretty boring. But being tiresome doesn't rule it out as a description of a meaningful encounter with nature through work.[33] I have risked boring you in order to demystify the mingling of production and consumption, of work and leisure, of mechanization and labor power, of nature and culture: a woman shopper's encounter with gravity, a tomato's encounter with a can. This isn't very sexy stuff, but it is, I assure you, essential to reproducing human organisms. If I don't do this work, people in my house don't eat.

So, think: What percentage of that tonnage is packaging? Where does all that varied and hefty stuff comes from? Why do I choose to buy and carry and process and dispose of the particular things I do—Mexican tomatoes and South American ground beef, spaghetti from Italy and oranges from Florida, Corn Pops from Battle Creek and Budweiser from St. Louis? Pretty soon I am thinking about bulk marketing and recycling, about takeout fast food and home delivery pizza, about McDonald's hamburgers and the Amazon rain forest, about the global economy and ecology of eating in middle-class America today. Follow the trails of human encounters with nature outward, from the grocery bags in my kitchen, and I think you'll see some of the possibilities of women's environmental history.[34]

Imagine taking account of all the unpaid domestic work still done, mostly by women who also work in paid jobs, bringing home the bacon in more ways than one. How do they calculate their interests? To what extent has environmental history come to grips with the economic and ecological consequences of what they think and do? What new problems and challenges in environmental history does this kind of subject open up?

Let me make this unoriginal but still important point in the clearest possible terms. If environmental history is ever to come close to describing relations between humans and other things, it will have to look at, take seriously, and understand women's lives and attitudes and work and the environmental consequences of what women do. Environmental history will have to try to see things from women's points of view.

Take Mrs. O'Leary and me and the uncounted others whose work and thoughts couple together humans and other things. Given the choice of keeping a cow or circulating between my house and the supermarket, I emphatically prefer carting milk home from the store. For your information, a plastic gallon jug of milk weighs a bit more than seven pounds. We drink two gallons a week. I could, in the spirit of F. W. Taylor, save some work by buying powdered milk, but it just doesn't taste the same. I do seventy pounds of hauling each week, or 3,640 pounds each year, in milk alone, and I haven't even poured it on anyone's Cheerios yet. Or tried to detach four-day-old, formerly milk-soaked Cheerios from the underside of my daughter's chair or thrown away the week-old, half-full milk glass my son left sitting by the heater in his room. Try to read forward and backward from these acts to see where they come from, why I do them, where they go.

These tedious domestic details are not, I know, heroic rendezvous between man and nature, dramas of dominance and submission, tragedies or triumphs. They are little didactic lessons, seemingly devoid of sex or secrecy, significant only because they are endlessly iterated and replicated. They are the acts that keep the species going, boring, idiotic, fascinating. I suppose they have at least those attributes in common with the kinds of sex secrets I haven't revealed in this essay.

I do not insist that all works of environmental history focus on women, or even that they must each and all do a very good job of accounting for the presence and significance of women. It is perfectly possible to write a decent book about men mostly or even men only; many of the finest works of environmental history appear to be just such books. It is also quite possible to write books primarily or exclusively about women; I have read many such books and articles, and I commend them to environmental historians. I also know that women and men will often act in the *same* ways: we talk, we eat, we sleep, we are, together, historical animals. And we are, after all, far more like one another than are, say, hogs, diamonds, and rivers. Indeed, we should wonder if the only way to reduce the endless multiplicity of things to the unit "nature" is to pair that term with "man," an act of reduction arguably far loonier than leaving half of humanity out of environmental history.

But environmental history can no longer afford even the liability of concentrating so exclusively on male humans' interactions with nonhuman things. If ornithologists can learn from birds, historians can learn from ornithologists. Professor Timothy Birkhead has seen the exciting possibilities offered by believing that there might be two knowledgeable parties to the fleeting couplings in the barnyard and the bosky glen. Imagine with me, for a moment at least, an environmental history multiplied by the power of two, a history even richer, more complicated, and, yes, more fertile than we have seen so far.

NOTES

I would like to thank the participants in the New Mexico Environmental Symposium, who offered numerous comments on the paper I originally presented, along with those who have since read and carefully critiqued drafts of this chapter: Melissa Bokovoy, Nancy Langston, Les McFadden, Jane Slaughter, Kate Swift, Peter Swift, and Marsha Weisiger.

1. Natalie Zemon Davis, "History's Two Bodies," *American Historical Review* 93, no. 1 (February 1988): 30.
2. Virginia J. Scharff, "An Earth of One's Own" (paper presented at the Organization of American Historians, Washington, D.C., March 1995, with comment by Dan Flores); see also Virginia J. Scharff, "Are Earth Girls Easy? Ecofeminism, Women's History, and Environmental History," *Journal of Women's History* 7, no. 2 (Summer 1995): 164–75.
3. Donald Worster, ed., *The Ends of Earth: Perspectives on Modern Environmental History* (Cambridge: Cambridge University Press, 1988), vii.
4. See, for example, essays in *Uncommon Ground: Toward Reinventing Nature*, ed. William Cronon (New York: Norton, 1995).
5. Carolyn Merchant, *The Death of Nature: Women, Ecology, and the Scientific Revolution* (San Francisco: Harper and Row, 1980).
6. Ibid.; Stephen Jay Gould, *The Mismeasure of Man* (New York: Norton, 1981); Evelyn Fox Keller, *Reflections on Gender and Science* (New Haven, Conn.: Yale University Press, 1985), and *Secrets of Life, Secrets of Death: Essays on Language, Gender, and Science* (London: Routledge, 1992); Donna Haraway, *Primate Visions: Gender, Race and Nature in the World of Modern Science* (New York: Routledge, 1989), and *Simians, Cyborgs, and Women: The Reinvention of Nature* (New York: Routledge, 1991); and Londa Schiebinger, *Nature's Body, Nature's Mind: Gender in the Making of Modern Science* (Boston: Beacon Press, 1993).
7. *Webster's Third New International Dictionary of the English Language, Unabridged* (Springfield, Mass.: G. C. Merriman, 1971), 2187.
8. See, for example, Edward Clarke, *Sex and Education: A Fair Chance for Girls* (Boston: Osgood, 1873). For the best historical study of early-twentieth-century American scholarly attempts to combat the biases and consequences of biological determinist arguments about women's capacities, see Rosalind Rosenberg, *Beyond Separate Spheres: Intellectual Roots of Modern Feminism* (New Haven, Conn.: Yale University Press, 1982). In this volume Max Oelschlaeger traces the philosophical roots of biologicalist arguments about sex and gender, while Dan Flores offers a contemporary sociobiological version of the biologicalist argument about sex.

9. Casey Miller and Kate Swift, *Words and Women: New Language in New Times* (New York: HarperCollins, 1991), 21–42.

10. On Jefferson's Declaration of Independence, see Garry Wills, *Inventing America: Jefferson's Declaration of Independence* (New York: Vintage, 1978).

11. Miller and Swift, *Words and Women*, 34–35.

12. More generally see T. R. Birkhead and A. P. Moller, *Sperm Competition in Birds: Evolutionary Causes and Consequences* (London: Academic Press, 1992).

13. The classic work on the topic is, of course, Edward O. Wilson, *Sociobiology: The New Synthesis* (Cambridge, Mass.: Harvard University Press, 1975). Physiologist Jared Diamond, *The Third Chimpanzee: The Evolution and Future of the Human Animal* (New York: HarperPerennial, 1992), explains that some sociobiologists argue that "our peculiar societies . . . have their closest parallels in colonies of seabirds" (p. 71). Feminists have of course practiced, interrogated, inveighed against, and historicized sociobiology; for a prescient critique, see Ruth Herschberger, *Adam's Rib* (New York: Pellegrini and Cudahy, 1948), 68–84. See also Haraway, *Primate Visions* and *Simians, Cyborgs, and Women*; Ruth Hubbard, *The Politics of Women's Biology* (New Brunswick, N.J.: Rutgers University Press, 1990), 67–141; Susan Sperling, "Baboons with Briefcases vs. Langurs in Lipstick: Feminism and Functionalism in Primate Studies," in *Gender at the Crossroads of Knowledge: Feminist Anthropology in the Postmodern Era*, ed. Micaela di Leonardo (Berkeley: University of California Press, 1991), 204–34; and Keller, *Secrets of Life, Secrets of Death*, especially 113–60.

14. Tim Birkhead and Anders Moller, "Faithless Females Seek Better Genes," *New Scientist* 135, no. 1828 (July 4, 1992): 34.

15. "Secret to Birds' Mating Score: Speedy Sperm," *Science News* 148 (October 7, 1995): 231.

16. Birkhead and Moller, "Faithless Females"; T. R. Birkhead, A. P. Moller, and W. J. Sutherland, "Why Do Females Make It So Difficult for Males to Fertilize Their Eggs?" *Journal of Theoretical Biology* 161 (1993): 51–60; Fiona M. Hunter, Marion Petrie, Merja Otronen, Tim Birkhead, and Anders Pape Moller, "Why Do Females Copulate Repeatedly with One Male?" *Trends in Ecology and Evolution* 8 (1993): 21–26; T. R. Birkhead and A. P. Moller, "Extra-Pair Copulation and Extra-Pair Paternity in Birds," *Animal Behavior* 49 (1995): 846–48.

17. Birkhead and Moller, "Faithless Females," 34.

18. Richard White, "Environmental History, Ecology and Meaning," *Journal of American History* 76 (1990): 1111–16, and "Discovering Nature in North America," *Journal of American History* 79 (1992): 874–91; William Cronon, "The Trouble with Wilderness; or Getting Back to the Wrong Nature," in *Uncommon Ground.*

19. Michael Pollan, *Second Nature: A Gardener's Education* (New York: Atlantic Monthly Press, 1991), 183.

20. Ibid., 184.

21. Stephen Pyne, *Fire in America: A Cultural History of Wildland and Rural Fire* (Princeton, N.J.: Princeton University Press, 1982).

22. Alfred Crosby, *The Columbian Exchange* (Westport, Conn.: Greenwood Press, 1972), and *Ecological Imperialism: The Biological Expansion of Europe, 900–1900* (Cambridge: Cambridge University Press, 1986).

23. Sherry Ortner, "Is Female to Male as Nature Is to Culture?" in *Woman,*

Culture, and Society, ed. Michelle Zimbalist Rosaldo and Louise Lamphere (Stanford, Calif.: Stanford University Press, 1974), 66–87; Susan Griffin, *Woman and Nature: The Roaring Inside Her* (New York: Harper and Row, 1978); Merchant, *The Death of Nature*; Chaia Heller, "For the Love of Nature: Ecology and the Cult of the Romantic," in *Ecofeminism: Women, Animals, Nature,* ed. Greta Gaard (Philadelphia: Temple University Press, 1993).

24. "Deciding What's Appropriate" (conference proceedings, University of Montana, Missoula, April 27–29, 1979), 5.

25. Richard White, *The Organic Machine* (New York: Hill and Wang, 1995), 2.

26. Raphael Samuel, "Workshop of the World: Steam Power and Hand Technology in Mid-Victorian Britain," History Workshop, 6–72; Wally Seccombe, "The Housewife and Her Labour under Capitalism," *New Left Review* 83 (January–February 1974): 3–24; Pat Mainardi, "The Politics of Housework," in *Sisterhood Is Powerful: An Anthology of Writing from the Women's Liberation Movement,* ed. Robin Morgan (New York: Random, 1970), 447–54; A Redstocking Sister [Ellen Willis], "Consumerism and Women," in *Woman in Sexist Society: Studies in Power and Powerlessness,* ed. Vivian Gornick and Barbara K. Moran (New York: Signet, 1971), 658–64; Heidi Hartmann, "The Unhappy Marriage of Marxism and Feminism: Towards a More Progressive Union," in *Women and Revolution: A Discussion of the Unhappy Marriage of Marxism and Feminism,* ed. Lydia Sargent (Boston: South End Press, 1981), 1–41; Laura Balbo, "The Servicing Work of Women and the Capitalist State," *Political Power and Social Theory* 3 (1982): 251–70; Susan Strasser, *Never Done: A History of American Housework* (New York: Pantheon, 1982); Nancy Hartsock, *Money, Sex, and Power: Toward a Feminist Historical Materialism* (New York: Longman, 1983); and Ruth Schwartz Cowan, *More Work for Mother: The Ironies of Household Technology from the Open Hearth to the Microwave* (New York: Basic Books, 1983).

27. Anthony Giddens, *A Contemporary Critique of Historical Materialism* (New York: Macmillan, 1981).

28. Pam Belluck, "Barn Door Reopened on Fire after Legend Has Escaped," *New York Times,* 17 August 1997.

29. Pam Belluck and Christine Meisner Rosen, *The Limits of Power: Great Fires and the Process of City Growth in America* (Cambridge: Cambridge University Press, 1988), 92.

30. Karen Sawislak, *Smoldering City: Chicago and the Great Fire* (Chicago: University of Chicago Press, 1995), 43–46.

31. Ross Miller, *American Apocalypse: The Great Fire and the Myth of Chicago* (Chicago: University of Chicago Press, 1990), 2.

32. William Cronon, *Nature's Metropolis: Chicago and the Great West* (New York: W. W. Norton, 1991), 107–15.

33. As Richard White has pointed out regarding the Bonneville Power Agency, "The BPA is a large and boring agency, and boredom has served it well" (*The Organic Machine,* 71).

34. A growing literature investigates this topic. See, for instance, Arlie Hochschild with Anne Machung, *The Second Shift* (New York: Avon, 1989); Warren J. Belasco, 1988 (New York: Pantheon, 1989); and Marjorie L. De Vault, *Feeding the Family: The Social Organization of Caring as Gendered Work* (Chicago: University of Chicago Press, 1991).

CHAPTER TWO

Naturalizing Power: Land and Sexual Violence along William Byrd's Dividing Line

Paige Raibmon

> The border surrounds us
> without clarity.
> There is no certain way to see,
> to cross into the good revolution
> from the diseased heart of power.
> —*Karen Connelly*

Colonialism is about asserting dominance over far-flung lands; colonialism is about asserting dominance over far-flung peoples. These statements are commonplaces, though the connection between them is not. William Byrd's *History of the Dividing Line Betwixt Virginia and North Carolina* and its companion *Secret History* reveal this interrelationship at work in the colonial South. Hailed as "the most literarily and historically valuable of southern colonial memoirs" and a "double masterpiece," these chronicles of the 1728 survey are unusually rich sources for exploring the workings of links between human beings and their environments.[1] Byrd planted sex and scandal liberally throughout the *Secret History*, intended only for the eyes and ears of close friends. He weeded these lurid details out of his public *History*, replacing them with accounts of the region's flora and fauna. Through his own "creative censorship," Byrd replaced sex with nature.[2]

The relationship between these aspects of the two *Histories* is crucial to Byrd's works, yet it has long been overlooked. Although scholars have paid homage to Byrd's invaluable record of natural history, they have given his descriptions of sexual encounters literary rather than historical treatment, viewing them as superior examples of eighteenth-century satirical wit. Attempts, such as Kathleen Brown's, to treat Byrd's sex life as a historical rather than a literary event have prompted calls to return our attention to his narrative multiplicity and strategies of literary emplotment.[3] This literary perspective has diverted attention away from the disturbing issues raised when we admit the sexual encounters as historical fact, for in his *Secret History*, Byrd chronicled a series of repeated sex-

20

ual assaults on local women. The victims of these incidents varied from a "Dark Angel" who "struggled just enough to make her Admirer more eager," to a "Tallow-faced Wench . . . disabled from making any resistance by the Lameness of her Hand," to a farmer's "tal straight Daughter of a Yielding Sandy Complexion," to a kitchen maid who "wou'd certainly have been ravish't, if her timely consent had not prevented the Violence."[4]

Byrd addressed his account of these events to contemporaries of his own class. The *Secret History* was "designed for reading aloud around a colonial fireplace, where congenial gentlemen and ladies accustomed to ribaldry engaged the talk of a western adventure by people they knew."[5] These were stories colonial elites told themselves about themselves and as such belong within a broader context of colonial politics, power, and culture. The image of Byrd and his peers reading the *Secret History* at a party or as part of a fireside chat confronts us with an elite culture where such acts were part of young men's training. For the elite women among the fireside audience, hearing about such acts must have reinforced both their sense of vulnerability as women and their sense of racial and class distance from the female victims of male "ribaldry."[6]

Byrd's accounts provide a privileged glimpse into the culture and ideology of an elite colonial class, a class for whom the manipulation of sex and nature, or more broadly of people and the environment, was not so much interchangeable as intertwined. His assumptions about class, sex, gender, and the environment combined to mandate joint manipulation of land and society. In his natural history, Byrd did more than itemize flora and fauna; he naturalized the power structures of colonial domination. He framed the *Histories* within a dual enclosure of environmental and human potential, evaluating the land and its inhabitants in terms of their susceptibility to colonial improvement and increased productivity.[7] Throughout the *Histories*, Indians and settlers, as much as swamps and forests, were features of the landscape along the dividing line. Byrd described women in particular as akin to nature, not unlike soil or trees or animals, even describing them in similar terms. The assaults on women were closely associated with Byrd's other colonial goals, not aberrations from them. The social reform and social control that he craved necessitated transformations of landscape. At the same time, his vision of changes in the land necessitated human transformations. In the *Histories*, Byrd candidly displayed the ideological tools that men of his class used to create a dialectic of justification and necessity for their New World domination of land and people.

Byrd's own roots were deeply sunk in a landscape of class, race, and gender privilege. Born into the Virginia planter class in 1674, he was sent to school in England in the wake of Bacon's Rebellion. He subsequently alternated his home between England and Virginia until, in his early fifties, he settled in the colonies for good in 1726, residing there until his death in 1744. In 1728, he accepted an appointment as chief commissioner for Virginia on the survey expedition organized to settle a long-standing border dispute between his home colony and North Carolina.[8] The survey party consisted of representatives from both sides of the border and totaled between forty and fifty men, organized into a strict hierarchy. The boundary commissioners, three from Virginia including Byrd and four from North Carolina, perched at the apex of the pyramid. All were men whose pedigree, education, political involvement, and landholdings imbued them with the status and authority of gentlemen. Below the commissioners were the four surveyors. Their status rested upon their technical knowledge of surveying, their familiarity with the landscape, and, for some, their large landholdings. These formally trained surveyors commanded the "woodsmen" who performed technical roles marking and measuring the land and handling the instruments. All three tiers rested upon the "base" of the pyramid: the black and white servants who toiled at the most physical and menial work. The hierarchy of the survey team replicated southern society at large, in which status, privilege, and landholdings were closely linked. At Byrd's insistence, the assembled party was large enough to ensure that this social hierarchy survived the trials of travel over the unfamiliar territory from the north shore of Currituck Inlet through the Great Dismal Swamp to the foothills of the Appalachian mountains, two hundred and forty-one arduous miles west of the coast. In his survey team, Byrd assembled a microcosm of the social and political order he sought to extend to the unsocialized and, he was convinced, uncivilized people along the dividing line.[9]

Sometimes the links between Byrd's assessments of land and people are buried beneath the surface of his natural history entries. To find the connections, we have to dig a little. For Byrd, good land was either along a riverbank or wooded with large, deciduous trees. He wrote, for example, that the lands between Fountain Creek and the Roanoke River and between Caskade/Casquade Creek and the Dan River were especially fertile.[10] In several other instances, he used "the largeness of the Trees," particularly walnut, poplar, hickory, and white oak, as "certain Proofs of a Fruitful Soil."[11] These two standards were sometimes at odds with one another within Byrd's text as well as with what we now know about the natural and human history of the area surveyed. Although his first standard resonates with current notions of land fertility, the second does not. Byrd's preference for large deciduous stands was consonant with the contemporary English exaltation of the solid "heart of oak," national symbol of English colonial power, liberty, and identity.[12] Yet it was inconsistent with the fact that much of the most fertile land would have been kept clear of deciduous stands by Native American agricultural and hunting practices, which included frequent burnings. This tendency was especially true along the coastal plain.

The larger Indian (and later settler) population in eastern North Carolina ensured that burnings were more frequent there than elsewhere, and the sandy soils and extensive peat bogs of the coastal plain meant burnings were more extensive and harder to control.[13] Although many Native American agricultural fields and villages had been abandoned by Byrd's time because of disease and warfare, such sites would not yet have reverted to large deciduous forests. They would instead have been characterized by the fire subclimax of longleaf pines. Byrd himself recognized that "Indian Towns . . . are remarkable for a fruitful Situation," yet he still lauded the hardwood forests as superior land.[14] The inconsistencies of his categorization are apparent again in his declaration that "the Land . . . had all the Marks of Poverty, being for the most Part Sandy and full of Pines. This kind of Ground, tho' unfit for Ordinary Tillage, will, however, bring Cotton and Potatoes in Plenty."[15] Clearly, Byrd measured "good" land by more than mere fruitfulness.[16]

When Byrd assessed land, he also implicitly assessed the inhabitants and their way of life. Indians situated their towns in fertile locales, he concluded, because "being by Nature not very Industrious, they choose such a Situation as will Subsist them with the least Labour."[17] He pronounced similar judgments upon the white and black inhabitants of these sandy pine-covered regions. Byrd claimed that land suited for growing potatoes and cotton was land suited for those who were "easily contented, and like the Wild Irish, find more Pleasure in Laziness than Luxury."[18] In this assessment, Byrd ignored the labor-intensive nature of cotton farming. And in his judgment of the potato, an archetypal New World product, he referenced widespread colonial associations between potatoes and Irish savagery.

In the hands of "uncivilized" inhabitants, laziness was the lamentable by-product of natural bounty. "Surely there is no place in the World where the Inhabitants live with less Labour than in N Carolina," wrote Byrd. "It approaches nearer to the Description of Lubberland than any other, by the great felicity of the Climate, the easiness of raising Provisions, and the Slothfulness of the People."[19] According to him, laziness was literally in the air. Simply living in the environs of the Great Dismal Swamp produced in settlers "Agues . . . which Corrupt all the Juices of their Bodies, give them a cadaverous complexion, and besides a lazy, creeping Habit, which they never get rid of."[20] Swamp "Borderers" subsisted on free-range cattle and hogs, a diet that Byrd believed left them ridden with yaws and "hoggish in their Temper" to the point that many "seem to Grunt rather than Speak in their ordinary conversation."[21] Like many aspects of his natural history, these observations were gendered. He placed the blame for ill health on the men whose lazy dispositions, he believed, led them to locate their families in unhealthy locales.[22] Although certain illnesses were linked to environmental conditions of the southern lowlands, Byrd's fear of disease was less reflective of actual biological threats than of his condemnation of land-use practices that he deemed inadequately rigorous.[23] Just as Spanish colonists could believe the savagery of the South American rain forest was contagious, so English colonists feared the contagion of southern swamps and pocosins.[24]

Byrd's fear that environmentally induced laziness would infect settlers was compounded by his worry that the temperate climate and bountiful environment actually attracted indolent individuals: "To Speak the Truth, tis a thorough Aversion to Labor that makes People file off to N Carolina, where Plenty and a Warm Sun confirm them in their Disposition to Laziness for their whole Lives."[25] Thus, for Byrd, land could be poor because it had too much rather than too little fertility; environments could be problematic because of the human behavior they facilitated.

But why should Byrd have been so preoccupied with the work ethic of backcountry settlers? In fact, laziness was not the issue in and of itself. The real problem lay in the social relations of power signaled by the possibility of a "lazy" existence. Byrd worried that New World abundance might pose a serious obstacle to elite attempts to harness others' labor. Like most Virginia planters, he realized these people who had "filed off to North Carolina" were primarily former Virginia indentured servants, overworked and underrewarded, who had headed south when faced with a lack of available land and an officious gentry class at home. As in other colonial settings, the labor shortage resulted not from a scarcity of laborers, but from an abundance of those who would scarcely labor; the failure to work "appropriately" was a sociopolitical and cultural issue rather than a demographic one.[26]

Byrd had good reason to be preoccupied with labor issues. He needed people to work his own vast landholdings, which included twenty thousand acres of the most fertile borderlands surveyed by the dividing-line commissioners.[27] Dubbing this tract the "Land of Eden," Byrd boasted that it was "as fertile as the Lands were said to be about Babylon, which yielded, if Herodotus tells us right, an Increase of no less than 2 or 300 for one."[28] He later claimed in his 1737 promotional tract, "New found Eden," that Indian corn "yields the planter in good soil seven to eight hundred fold or still more."[29] But planters needed laborers in order to reap this spectacular yield. Byrd, who self-identified as Adam in this newfound Eden, feared that the bountiful New World environment might produce a new social world. Would poor white and enslaved African-American men still submit to working his Eden if they believed they could become Adams of their own gardens?[30]

Byrd's Eden required not only laborers but also laborers who produced for commercial surplus rather than personal subsistence. "Valuable" land for Byrd was land that supported trade and commerce. As he wrote, the border region contained land that "would be a Valuable Tract of Land in any Country but North Carolina, where, for want of Navigation and Commerce, the best estate affords little more than a coarse Subsistence."[31] His perspective was representative of contemporary mercantilist values that saw commercial people as the final products of "the natural advancement of human society."[32] If England and Virginia were to display this superior state of civilization, workers had to be persuaded to produce goods to fuel the engine of colonial commerce.[33] Poor immigrant settlers, whom elite colonialists such as Byrd judged to be inferior, incapable of self-discipline, and barely civilized, were in particular need of persuasion.[34]

Byrd transformed these class-specific economic values into universal moral ones by invoking the biblical flood. He explained that "there is no climate that produces every thing, since the Deluge Wrencht the Poles of the world out of their Place, nor is it fit it shou'd be so, because it is the Mutual Supply one country receives from another, which creates a mutual Traffic and Intercourse amongst men." Trade and commerce were not only natural but also necessary aspects of the postdiluvial world. "And in Truth," he continued, "were it not for the correspondence, in order to make up for each other's Wants, the Wars betwixt Bordering Nations, like those of the Indians and other barbarous People, wou'd be perpetual and irreconcilable."[35] Byrd thus naturalized the production of commercial surplus, conflating it with the Christian duty to prevent a Hobbesian war of all against all. Fertile land and independent folk whose self-sufficiency hindered the execution of this duty would have to be civilized, or coerced, into working.

Biblical precedent was a useful way for Byrd to promote his own commercial ventures, such as his plan to drain the Great Dismal Swamp.[36] Though it could only be done at great expense to the "Publick Treasure," he claimed that the drainage project would improve the health of settlers and "at the same time render so great a Tract of Swamp very Profitable, besides the advantage of making a Channel to transport by water-carriage goods from Albemarle Sound into Nanismond and Elizabeth Rivers, in Virginia."[37] Casting industriousness and trade as inherent moral goods allowed Byrd to argue that the general population would benefit from planting the colonial garden adjacent to a major transportation route under his control.

Byrd's personal concerns and interests mirrored those of the planter class at large. From the beginning, colonial settlements in Virginia and North Carolina failed to reproduce some of the most important structures of English ruling class authority. The refusal of backcountry residents to marry formally through the church was but one example.[38] Dispersed settlement patterns undermined effective centralized control, a problem the English upper class had confronted in Ireland.[39] Still more problematic, as one historian has shown, was the fact that the poor settlers who were excluded from the benefits of elite English civility "did not accept the arguments of English social and cultural superiority that were expounded by their betters."[40]

The experiences of the survey team reproduced in microcosm the difficulties that this lack of deference caused for elite colonists in general. In these, as in other, colonial borderlands, elite knowledge was hopelessly inadequate. Unable to survive in the backwoods without the assistance of knowledgeable locals, the survey party was dependent upon local people for everything from directions to sustenance.[41] Colonial elites who succeeded in establishing their authority relied on the appropriation rather than the replacement of indigenous knowledge to a far greater degree than men such as William Byrd would have been willing to admit. Much of the information he included in the History about medicinal herbs and plants, the uses of "Dogwood Bark" and "Seneca Rattle-Snake-Root," for example, probably originated with indigenous and other local sources including African slaves.[42] But many local residents were notably reluctant to share their hard-won knowledge of the terrain and environment with Byrd and his cohorts. When pressed for directions, residents sometimes fled and sometimes pleaded an unlikely degree of ignorance of local geography.[43] Both strategies could be risky, as Byrd's party threatened the uncooperative with imprisonment.[44] Local inhabitants were aware that Byrd could use the knowledge they shared against them, just as he was aware that their lack of cooperation was symptomatic of larger issues of social control.

Rejection of elite superiority and resistance to elite domination were closely linked to the style of agriculture that took root on the colonial frontier. Dispersed settlement patterns that facilitated the evasion of elite control went hand in hand with the practices of extensive agriculture and free-range grazing. To elites, landscapes marked by such practices looked more like "barbaric" Native American or even Irish patterns than the English tradition of intensive agriculture and enclosed pastures.[45]

Byrd knew how to read the human relations imprinted upon physical landscapes. Swidden agriculture and free-ranging livestock bespoke the presence of independent (and, from his perspective, uncooperative), backcountry inhabitants, settlers who produced for personal subsistence rather than commercial surplus. Byrd's New World Eden, by contrast, would require neatly planted orchards, crops in orderly monoculture fields, and enclosed livestock. Land would be brought under control through "Ordinary Tillage."[46] Forests could (and indeed should) be cleared to obtain pastures or fields or wood products because after all Eden itself had only two trees.[47] Domesticated animals—cattle, sheep, and goats—were an integral component of his pastoral vision. Just as ordered, agricultural fields represented "civilized" land, so sheep, goats, and cattle represented "civilized" animals.[48] Of course, this re-created Eden was to be planted not in virgin soil, but on top of an age-old Native American landscape, whose inhabitants presented still other obstacles to colonial domination. Eden would have to be very carefully constructed and managed.[49]

Changes in the land were integral to the process of civilizing and controlling its inhabitants. Byrd's vision required reorienting the relationship not only between people and land but also between men and women. He wanted to transform the Virginia and Carolina wilderness into a garden comparable to the one where Adam delved and Eve span. In this endeavor, women had less distance to travel than men. Byrd noted that local women "Spin, weave and knit, all with their own Hands, while their Husbands, depending on the Bounty of the Climate, are Sloathfull in every thing but getting of Children."[50] Throughout the *Histories*, he largely exempted women from the environmentally induced infection of lassitude, claiming that "the Distemper of Laziness seizes the Men oftener much than the Women."[51] The fact that women worked hard was less a sign, for Byrd, of their own virtue than it was of the savagery and laziness of the men who forced them into this unnatural role.

Judging men by how they treated women, Byrd wrote that "the Men for their Parts, just like the Indians, impose all the work upon the poor Women."[52] Male lassitude and female drudgery inverted his view of the natural order and were therefore signs of savagery. Although men were savages if they didn't work enough, women were savages if they worked too much or if they worked at "male" tasks such as agriculture. Byrd inherited the dual images of the "squaw drudge" paired with that of the "indolent brave" from his seventeenth-century Virginian predecessors.[53] Countless colonizers before him used this stereotype to attack Native American rights, and many others would continue to draw upon it as a "prime index of savagism" through the turn of the twentieth century.[54] In Byrd's Eden, landscape and humanscape would be mutually transformative; civilized inhabitants would be producers *and* products of the civilized environment.

The survey team was the vanguard of this mission to "civilize" the savage along the dividing line. In this respect too, it was a microcosm of broader colonial experience. The labor force Byrd sought to recruit through his rhetoric of human and environmental "civilization" was primarily male, and the lessons he derived from the Garden of Eden were purely patriarchal. The implications for women were chilling. Local women felt the impact of this civilizing mission through sexual violence; they experienced the dividing line as a frontier of sexual fear.

Members of the survey party assaulted women at least nine times during the expedition. Byrd took obvious pleasure both in observing and recounting the sexual assaults on white, African-American, and Native American women. His *Secret History* often made the dividing-line expedition seem like one great sexual romp, more reminiscent of soldiers pillaging a captured city by assaulting its women and girls than anything as high-minded and officially sanctioned as a survey mission.[55] On March 9, for example, members of Byrd's party occupied a man's house without permission and "endulg'd themselves so far as to ly in the House. But it seems they broke the Rules of Hospitality," he continued, "by several gross Freedoms they offer'd to take with our Landlord's Sister."[56]

Two days later Byrd and another member of the party were surprised by the "Charms" of a "Dark Angel" who "struggled just enough to make her Admirer more eager." Byrd described the encounter: "Her Complexion was a deep Copper, so that her fine Shape & regular Features made her appear like a Statue en Bronze done by a masterly hand. Shoebrush [Byrd's pseudonym for John Lovick, commissioner for North Carolina] was smitten at first Glance, and examined all her neat Proportions with a critical Exactness."[57] This woman was a member of a mulatto family, whose "Master" avoided the survey party, perhaps fearing they would doubt his free status, as indeed they did. In the *History*, Byrd expressed a measure of sympathy for the family, implying that their neighbors took economic advantage of their tenuous claim to freedom, "well knowing their Condition makes it necessary for them to Submit to any Terms."[58] But the sexual assault in the corresponding entry of the *Secret History* reveals that Byrd's party likewise took advantage of vulnerable backcountry residents. Being forced to submit to "any Terms" also meant enduring sexual violence at the hands of men like Byrd, against whom local people had no hope of recourse.[59]

The following day Byrd's party took advantage of another woman who was both injured and intoxicated.

In the Gaiety of their Hearts, they invited a Tallow-faced Wench that had sprain'd her Wrist to drink with them, and when they had raise'd her in good Humour, they examined all her hidden Charms, and play'd a great many gay Pranks. When Firebrand [Byrd's pseudonym for Richard Fitz-William, commissioner for Virginia] who had the most Curiosity, was ranging over her sweet Person, he pick't off several Scabs as big as Nipples, the Consequence of eating too much Pork. The poor Damsel was disabled from making any resistance by the Lameness of her Hand.[60]

On March 15, a farmer's daughter became the next victim. Byrd described her in the *Secret History* in terms much like those used for the natural environment. She was "tal" and "straight" rather like the pine trees that took root in the region's sandy soils, of which her "Yielding Sandy Complexion" was reminiscent.[61] Byrd's writings imply that it was more than the girl's complexion that was "yielding." He claimed it was her own curiosity that led to her encounter with Puzzlecause (William Little, commissioner for North Carolina), who took her inside one of the tents where the Parson (the Reverend Peter Fontaine) also awaited "to keep him honest, or peradventure, to partake of his diversion if he shou'd be otherwise."[62] Byrd alluded to this incident in the *History* by stating simply that at this locale, the men in his party "were furnisht with every thing the Place afforded."[63] Read in conjunction with the corresponding portion of the *Secret History*, this comment suggests Byrd's inclination to include women among a region's natural resources. He counted women and nature alike among the things "the Place afforded."

On March 25, Firebrand, dissatisfied with the supper he received, "endeavour'd to mend his Entertainment by making hot Love to honest Ruth, who wou'd by no means be charm'd either with his Perswasion, or his Person. While the Master was employ'd in making Love to one Sister, the man made his Passion known to the other, Only he was more boisterous, & employ'd force, when he cou'd not succeed by fair means."[64] Master and servant alike attempted to exercise sex privileges along the dividing line. And on April 1, Byrd seemed to interpret the smile of his "Landlord's" daughter as indication that she would welcome his kisses: "I discharg'd a long Score with my Landlord, & a Short one with his Daughter Rachel for some Smiles that were to be paid for in Kisses."[65]

Byrd described an assault on a kitchen maid in both histories. In the *History*, he recounted how brandy caused some men to be "too loving; Insomuch that a Damsel, who assisted in the Kitchen, had certainly Suffer'd what the Nuns call Martyrdom, had she not capitulated a little too soon."[66] He elaborated in the *Secret History*: "A Damsel who came to assist in the Kitchen wou'd certainly have been ravish't, if her timely consent had not prevented the Violence."[67] Feeling similarly threatened, the landlady of the house hid in her bedroom, armed with a chamberpot of "Female Ammunition."[68] Byrd claimed not to know the assailant's identity, though "Firebrand & his Servant were the most suspected, having been engag'd in those kind of Assaults once before."[69]

On still another occasion, Byrd described how Meanwell (William

Dandridge, commissioner for Virginia) and Captain Stith "pretended to go a hunting, but their Game was 2 fresh colour'd Wenches, which were not hard to hunt down."[70] This rhetoric of women as game again reflected Byrd's conflation of the natural and female resources along the dividing line.

The survey party treated Native American women similarly. Describing a visit to a village of Nottoway Indians, Byrd reported that the survey team "visited most of the Princesses at their own Appartments, but the Smoke was so great there, the Fire being made in the middle of the Cabbins, that we were not able to see their Charms."[71] Again linking women with the natural world, he explained that he "could discern by some of our Gentlemen's Linnen, discolour'd by the Soil of the Indian Ladys, that they had been convincing themselves in the point of their having no furr."[72] Byrd's words suggest that he and the survey team viewed these women as akin to animals and that they treated them accordingly. The "Volley of small Arms" fired at Byrd's party when they "march't out of the Town" suggests that Nottoway communities knew the difference between sexual assault and their own traditions of "trading girls."[73]

In several instances, Byrd claimed to have stepped in at the last moment to save the women from rape, a contention that seems incredible when set in the context of his own sexual history.[74] He was a man accustomed to having power over the lower classes. Repeatedly rejected by women of his own class, Byrd lorded sexual power over women of lesser status long before the dividing-line expedition. His London diaries include explicit descriptions of nonconsensual sexual encounters. Describing a morning visit to a friend, he recalled that he "committed uncleanness with the maid because the mistress was not at home," then "when the mistress came I rogered her."[75] According to one of Byrd's admiring editors, he "was not above picking up a stray wench in St. James's Park and consummating the affair in the weeds nearby."[76] From the days of his youth, Byrd had struggled to control his sexual urges.[77] As he aged, his sexual encounters were characterized more frequently than not by gross imbalances of class position and power, and toward the last years of his life, his sexual partners regularly included female slaves.[78]

The expedition's sexual violence sheds disturbing light on Byrd's exemption of women along the dividing line from the immoral indolence of men. The inverted sexual division of labor seems part of a twisted rationale for a different form of "civilizing" action for women than for men. Byrd's acceptance of the "squaw-drudge" stereotype provided ideological justification for assaults on "savage" women supposedly in need of European rescue from Native American men. A vocal advocate of intermarriage between white men and Native American women, he argued that "a sprightly Lover is the most prevailing Missionary that can be sent amongst these or any other Infidels."[79] Byrd may have been aware that these views echoed those previously espoused by other prominent southern colonists, including his brother-in-law, Robert Beverley II, and John Lawson; he did not know how well they anticipated the assimilation policies proposed for Alaskan Natives by Catherine the Great and for Native Americans by Thomas Jefferson.[80]

Regardless, Byrd was blunt in linking sex with colonial policy. Perhaps recalling the legendary story of John Rolfe and Pocahontas, he wrote that "the poor Indians would have had less reason to Complain that the English took away their Land, if they had received it by way of Portion with their Daughters."[81] Although not official policy, intermarriage between white traders and Indian women was commonplace on the eighteenth-century southern frontier. The specter of sexual violence in the *Secret History* complicates our picture of these relationships, problematizing the notion of consent between colonizer and colonized.[82] It suggests the need to locate intermarriage along a continuum of sexual interaction that includes sexual assaults and rape. And it suggests the need to bind our understanding of the appropriation of land to the appropriation of women.

Sexual relations served Byrd as a justification not only for land appropriation but also as further means to coerce labor from the male inhabitants along the dividing line. The threat of sexual violence demonstrated to fathers, sons, brothers, and husbands alike the value of voluntarily conforming to the prescriptive vision for land and society that men like Byrd propounded. Men feared that the cost to their families would be more than economic if they chose to forgo the surplus goods Byrd urged them to produce. The sexual threat ensured a human cost for environmental inadequacy. Here again, Byrd's frontier paralleled other colonial settings. Colonizers employed gendered coercion to obtain labor in the pelagic sea otter trade in Russian Alaska and in the rubber industry in Colombia, where traders took women and children hostage until the men returned with pelts or rubber.[83] One anthropologist has identified a "culture of terror" in Colombia, where indigenous men as well as women were subjected to horrific sexual and other physical violence in the name of procuring rubber.[84] Although the records do not suggest a "culture of terror" of the same degree in Virginia and North Carolina, the sexual violence detailed in Byrd's *Secret History* begs a reassessment of commonalities across colonial frontiers. And it again complicates our notion of consent: the consent not only of women but of men who gave their labor under conditions tainted by the perverse coercion of sexual fear.[85]

Through acts of sexual violence elite men reaffirmed their power not only over women but also over entire classes and races of people they deemed beneath them as well as over vast tracts of land they deemed unfinished country.[86] Acts of sexual violence in colonial settings are not just personal but are deeply political as well.[87] Violence and abuse against women were inseparable from Byrd's colonial project of subjugating land and people. Here again, Byrd was not unique; this constellation of power, land, class, and sex extended far beyond the dividing line. Authors of other colonial texts may well have exercised the same sort of self-censorship that Byrd did when he wrote his public *History* hoping to promote land sales and settlement.[88] Although accounts of sexual violence were accepted and understood around elite fireplaces, Byrd could not have been certain of their reception in other circles, particularly among the families he hoped to attract to domesticate his vast holdings of back-country land.

Historically, colonial ruling elites have attempted to legitimate their power with precariously balanced justifications of the imperial enterprise and its suspect alignment with their personal wealth and status. Byrd's paradoxical concern that natural overabundance would encourage human underproduction is but one example of such a justification. The object of his discourse was not to render a plentiful environment less so but rather to ensure that it would yield its plenty to an elite class of which he was, of course, a member. This undertaking involved altering the human and natural landscapes in ideological and material ways. In his natural history, Byrd erected specific environmental values as fortifications around his Eden; he established particular configurations of land and power as entrance requirements. His invocations of Eden and the flood naturalized his self-interested definitions of the proper relationships between people and nature and between men and women. Biblical metaphors cast political questions of power in moral terms. The laziness that seeped from the swamps and pocosins into the men of the colonies justified both the physical alteration of the land itself and attempts to instill among settlers the work ethic required to effect such alterations. The drudgery inflicted upon women by uncivilized men appeared as further proof of these people's savagery, even as it served to sanction the abuse of women.

Byrd buttressed the exertion of elite, colonial power by a multifaceted appeal to nature. He presented his role as Adam in a restored Eden as part of the natural order of things while at the same time condemning those "contented with Nature as they find Her."[89] Human nature was intertwined with the natural environment in a way that facilitated their mutual redirection. But ultimately there was very little that was "natural" about either the landscape or humanscape that Byrd desired. Colonial elites did not rule naturally. They achieved and maintained dominance through the manufacture of ideological coercion and physical violence.

Byrd may well have been, as scholars have argued, a representative Virginia gentlemen of his day.[90] The convergence of environmental and social policies apparent in his *Histories* was certainly characteristic of the colonial enterprise. This convergence masked, justified, and facilitated the brutality of colonialism in general and of Byrd's survey expedition in particular. The survey team was indeed a microcosm of colonial relations. We must move beyond viewing Byrd as a "sophisticated, satirical, man of letters"[91] if we are to confront the unsettling implications of this violence for race, class, and gender relations in the colonial South, relations that characterized the public and political realms as much as the private and personal ones. Byrd's *Histories* offer powerful illustrations of how attitudes toward land and attitudes toward people can be mutually sustaining. In his colonial Eden, the environment was much more than a neutral assemblage of rock, water, and woods. It was the terrain in which he and men like him rooted their cultural identities, values, and human interactions. This fact is no more a relic of the colonial past than the acts of sexual violence that he described. Natural science and social science remain as inextricable today as when Byrd first traversed the dividing line.

NOTES

I would like to thank David Cecelski, Kirsten Fischer, Nancy Hewitt, Virginia Scharff, Daniel Levinson Wilk, Gwenn Miller, Peter Wood, and Susan Yarnell for their valuable encouragement and assistance with this chapter.

1. Richard Beale Davis, *Intellectual Life in the Colonial South, 1585–1763* (Knoxville: University of Tennessee Press, 1978), 901, 1438. Byrd used his detailed personal diaries as the basis for his *History of the Dividing Line betwixt Virginia and North Carolina, Run in the Year of Our Lord, 1728,* which was first published in 1841 by the pioneering southern agronomist Edmund Ruffin. *The Secret History of the Line,* which Byrd actually composed prior to the *History,* remained unpublished until 1929. Hereafter, I refer separately to the *History* and *Secret History* where appropriate. When making statements applicable to both, I refer simply to the *Histories.* All citations come from the 1929 joint publication of the two histories. See William Byrd, *Histories of the Dividing Lines Betwixt Virginia and North Carolina,* ed. William K. Boyd (Raleigh: North Carolina Historical Commission, 1929).

2. Kenneth A. Lockridge, *The Diary and Life of William Byrd II of Virginia, 1674–1744* (Chapel Hill: University of North Carolina Press, 1987), 136.

3. Douglas Anderson, "Plotting William Byrd," *William and Mary Quarterly* 56, no. 4 (1999): 701–22.

4. Byrd, *Histories,* 57, 59, 67, 149.

5. Davis, *Intellectual Life,* 1371; Charles Reagan Wilson and William Ferris, eds., *Encyclopedia of Southern Culture* (Chapel Hill: University of North Carolina Press, 1989), 679.

6. Here is powerful evidence indeed for Kathleen M. Brown's assertion that "in [Byrd's] life and in the lives of an unknown number of planters, power and sex were mutually reinforcing, especially when played out on the bodies of female subordinates" (*Good Wives, Nasty Wenches, and Anxious Patriarchs* [Chapel Hill: University of North Carolina Press, 1996], 334). In her discussion of American literature, Dawn Landner links the frontier's promise of sexual adventure for men with assumptions about white women's unfitness for frontier life: "Contrary to its surface appearance, America promises not a land of men without women, a Paradise without Eve, but a wilderness where the white man will have the best sex of his life. The assertion that wilderness life is too difficult for women, and the subsequent insistence upon the exclusion of white women, often assumes, unspoken, the retention of a non-white female sexual object (not peer or partner) and a sexuality which is without responsibility" ("Eve among the Indians," in *The Authority of Experience: Essays in Feminist Criticism,* ed. Arlyn Diamond and Lee R. Edwards [Amherst: University of Massachusetts Press, 1977], 201).

7. Byrd was typical in his use of categories of civilization and improvement to understand and control the "New World." On the seventeenth- and early-eighteenth-century ideology and literature of improvement, see Joyce Chaplin, *An Anxious Pursuit: Agricultural Innovation and Modernity in the Lower South, 1730–1815* (Chapel Hill: University of North Carolina Press, 1993), 26ff.

8. On William Byrd's life, see Lockridge, *Diary;* Kenneth A. Lockridge, *On the Sources of Patriarchal Rage: The Commonplace Books of William Byrd and Thomas Jefferson and the Gendering of Power in the Eighteenth Century* (New York: New York University Press, 1992); and Pierre Marambaud, *William Byrd of Westover, 1674–1744* (Charlottesville: University Press of Virginia, 1971).

9. For the above characterization of the survey team I have drawn on David Smith, "William Byrd Surveys America," *Early American Literature* 11 (1977): 300–303. On Byrd's emphasis on order among the survey team, see Smith, "William Byrd," 303; and Brown, *Good Wives,* 280. On Byrd's concern with establishing a civilized order along the length of the dividing line, see A. James Wohlpart, "The Creation of the Ordered State: William Byrd's (Re)Vision in the *History of the Dividing Line,*" *Southern Literary Journal* 25, no. 1 (1992): 3–18.

10. Byrd, *Histories,* 150, 210, 211.

11. Ibid., 154, 166, 188.

12. Simon Schama, *Landscape and Memory* (New York: Alfred A. Knopf, 1996), 163–64.

13. Harry Roy Merrens, *Colonial North Carolina in the Eighteenth Century: A Study in Historical Geography* (Chapel Hill: University of North Carolina Press, 1964), 192.

14. Byrd, *Histories,* 208.

15. Ibid., 102.

16. Here as along other colonial frontiers, the evaluation of land could not occur without an external benchmark. As a scholar of colonial Peru points out, "'good' and 'bad' environments are defined as such in terms of a given productive system" (Karen Spalding, *Huarochiri: An Andean Society under Inca and Spanish Rule* [Stanford, Calif.: Stanford University Press, 1984], 298). Thus, for example, the Andes represented a "problem climate" for Spanish conquerors and colonialists be-

cause it was a landscape that presented "great difficulties to the technology developed by Europeans for the cultivation of their temperate, relatively flat agricultural lands" (p. 13). Since any productive system is tied to those who produce within it, Spalding's insight can be extended to the conclusion that judgments of land use were simultaneously judgments of land users.

17. Byrd, *Histories,* 208.

18. Ibid., 102.

19. Ibid., 92, 304.

20. Ibid., 74.

21. Ibid., 55, 152.

22. Ibid., 74.

23. Hookworm, a parasite that can cause lethargy, dullness, and physical malformation, was likely prevalent among the population of the colonial South and may account for some of Byrd's observations. The impact of this "germ of laziness" should not be overstated, however, lest it become, as it did for some early-twentieth-century public health reformers, a "scientific" validation for long-established prejudices about the South. See Albert E. Cowdrey, *This Land, This South: An Environmental History* (Lexington: University of Kentucky Press, 1996), 133–34.

24. Michael Taussig, *Shamanism, Colonialism, and the Wild Man: A Study in Terror and Healing* (Chicago: University of Chicago Press, 1987), 76.

25. Byrd, *Histories,* 92.

26. Taussig, *Shamanism,* 54.

27. Byrd's landholdings began with an inheritance of some 14,000 acres in 1705. By 1744, when he died, he was the owner of 179,440 acres of land and had been negotiating for the Great Dismal Swamp. See William Byrd, *The Prose Works of William Byrd of Westover: Narratives of a Colonial Virginian,* ed. Louis B. Wright (Cambridge, Mass.: Harvard University Press, 1966), 28. Byrd was not alone in his acquisition of especially fine specimens of surveyed land. David Smith notes that "there was hardly a commissioner who did not return from the survey in possession of the rights to title of thousands of acres of choice real estate" ("William Byrd," 303).

28. Byrd, *Histories,* 268–270.

29. William Byrd, *William Byrd's Natural History of Virginia or The Newly Discovered Eden,* ed. Richard Croom and William J. Mulloy (Richmond, Va.: Dietz Press, 1940), 20; see also Byrd, *Histories,* 92. Here, Byrd seized upon the most outstanding symbol of overabundance in the colonial imagination. In 1588, Thomas Hariot had claimed that with less than twenty-four hours' labor, twenty-five square yards of land would yield enough corn for twelve months' sustenance; see *A Brief and True Report of the New Found Land of Virginia* (New York: History Book Club, 1951), C3.

30. Kenneth Lockridge, *On the Sources,* 93, notes Byrd's self-identification with Adam in the *History.* See also, for example, Byrd, *Histories,* 178.

31. Byrd, *Histories,* 52. The contrast between the accessible Chesapeake and the barrier of the Outer Banks was well known to colonial Virginians and North Carolinians alike. In Byrd's view, the natural impediments to extensive seaborne trade in North Carolina meant that North Carolinians needed to work harder to measure up.

32. Chaplin, *Anxious Pursuit*, 33.

33. Ibid., 27.

34. Nicholas P. Canny, "The Permissive Frontier: Social Control in English Settlements in Ireland and Virginia, 1550–1650," in *The Westward Enterprise: English Activities in Ireland, the Atlantic, and America, 1480–1650*, ed. K. R. Andrews, N. P. Canny and P. E. H. Hair (Detroit: Wayne State University Press, 1979), 19.

35. Byrd, *Histories*, 270.

36. Ibid., xxvi. See William Byrd, *Description of the Dismal Swamp and a Proposal to Drain the Swamp*, ed. Earl G. Swen, Heartman's Historical Series, no. 38 (Metuchen, N.J.: C. F. Heartman, 1922). George Washington would later invest some of his wealth and his slaves in the digging of the Dismal Swamp canal.

37. Byrd, *Histories*, 84–86.

38. Anderson, "Plotting William Byrd," 717; Byrd, *History*, 74.

39. Canny, "The Permissive Frontier," 40.

40. Ibid., 34.

41. Byrd, *Histories*, 37, 50, 160, 220, 286, 312.

42. Ibid., 145, 148, 152, 154, 155, 156, 160, 162, 163, 178, 242, 287. On the dependency of southern colonial culture and lifestyle on the unacknowledged appropriation of expertise and skill from African slaves, see Peter Wood, "'It was a Negro Taught Them,' A New Look at African Labor in Early South Carolina," *Journal of Asian and African Studies* 9, nos. 3–4 (July–October 1974): 160–89.

43. Byrd, *Histories*, 37, 50.

44. Ibid., 50.

45. Susan Yarnell, "Half-Ploughed Fields: English Bias in Southern Agricultural Sources: 1580–1860" (master's thesis, Duke University, 1992), 17, 18, 23.

46. Byrd, *Histories*, 102.

47. Schama, *Landscape and Memory*, 226.

48. About a pleasing view across a valley, for example, Byrd wrote that it "had a most agreeable Effect upon the Eye, and wanted nothing but Cattle grazing in the Meadow, and Sheep and Goats feeding on the Hill, to make it a Compleat Rural Landscape" (*Histories*, 296). See also Keith Thomas, *Man and the Natural World: A History of the Modern Sensibility* (New York: Pantheon Books, 1983), 20.

49. Byrd's own plantation, of course, became a carefully constructed and well-managed English Eden, at least as he described it, though slavery certainly made it a "post-Fall" environment.

50. Byrd, *Histories*, 66.

51. Ibid., 66, 92, 116, 304.

52. Ibid., 92.

53. David D. Smits, "The 'Squaw Drudge': A Prime Index of Savagism," *Ethnohistory* 29, no. 4 (1982): 281. This trope was apparent in Australia too. See Patricia Grimshaw, "Maori Agriculturalists and Aboriginal Hunter-Gatherers: Women and Colonial Displacement in Nineteenth-Century Aotearoa/New Zealand and Southeastern Australia," in *Nation, Empire, Colony: Historicizing Gender and Race*, ed. Ruth Roach Pierson and Nupur Chaudhuri (Indianapolis: Indiana University Press, 1998), 32–38.

54. Smits, "The 'Squaw Drudge,'" 281–306.

55. "William Byrd," 305–7, Smith points out that the spring and fall portions of the survey expedition had markedly different characters. The accounts of sexual violence all occurred during the spring portion, which Smith argues had "something of the nature of a light-hearted group pilgrimage." The fall months of the survey, which traversed more westerly and less inhabited lands, had a more exclusively homosocial spirit akin to that of a great male hunting party.

56. Byrd, *Histories*, 53.

57. Ibid., 57.

58. Ibid., 56.

59. Douglas Anderson reads this passage from the *History* somewhat differently, identifying in it what he terms Byrd's "complex neutrality" ("Plotting William Byrd," 718). Byrd seems rather more complicit than neutral in my reading of the passage, however, as he himself was among those who dictated the terms to vulnerable escapees.

60. Byrd, *Histories*, 59.

61. Ibid., 67.

62. Ibid.

63. Ibid., 66.

64. Ibid., 91.

65. Ibid., 105.

66. Ibid., 146.

67. Ibid., 149.

68. Ibid.

69. Ibid.

70. Ibid., 151.

71. Ibid., 123.

72. Ibid.

73. Ibid.

74. Even if we were to accept Byrd's dubious claim that actual rape was usually averted during the survey expedition, it is clear that it was not by much. In several instances, he based his contention that rape did not occur on his assertion that the women ultimately consented. And if Byrd actually did intervene to prevent intercourse, he did so only after he had voyeuristically watched events proceed to the brink against the woman's will.

75. William Byrd, *The London Diary (1717–1721) and Other Writings*, ed. Louis B. Wright and Marion Tinling (New York: Oxford University Press, 1958), 180.

76. Byrd, *Prose Works*, 14.

77. Lockridge, *Diary*, 49.

78. Brown, *Good Wives*, 334, 355. For a graphic quantitative accounting of Byrd's sexual encounters as recorded in his diaries, see Lawrence Stone, *Family, Sex, and Marriage in England, 1500–1800* (London: Wiedenfield and Nicolson, 1977), 563–68. Byrd's sexual history must also be placed in the context of an elite culture in which marriage was a primary mechanism for acquiring and maintaining gentry status. Courtship was thus a period in which young elite women enjoyed an increased degree of social power; Brown, *Good Wives*, 249, 253–255. Byrd felt the sting of this superiority when women rejected him as a suitor, and male resentment of such power inspired misogyny in him and others. Lockridge,

On the Sources, 86, accepts Byrd's claims of sexual temperance and restraint, believing that his expressions of misogyny were limited to his commonplace book. Donald J. Siebert Jr., "William Byrd's *Histories of the Dividing Line:* The Fashioning of a Hero," *American Literature* 47 (1975): 533–51, however, is less convinced by Byrd's self-descriptions as regular, ordered, and sexually restrained. The *Secret History* and Byrd's London diary certainly establish that his backlash was not limited to literary jibes. When elite women frustrated Byrd's attempts to fashion himself as a Virginian gentleman, separate from but equal to his English counterparts, he and men of his class could and did take recourse against the nonwhite, nonelite women to whom the power of courtship did not accrue.

79. Byrd, *Histories* 2, 4, 118, 120.

80. On Robert Beverly II and John Lawson, see, for example, Davis, *Intellectual Life,* 134, 163; Brown, *Good Wives,* 243; and Gary B. Nash, "The Image of the Indian in the Southern Colonial Mind," *William and Mary Quarterly* (3d ser.) 29 (1972): 227. On intermarriage between Russian fur traders and Native women, see Gwenn A. Miller, "'Handsome but Tattooed': Native Women and Russian Fur Traders at the Intersection of Cultures in Russian America, 1784–1819," (master's thesis, Duke University, 1997), 42. For Jefferson's ideas on assimilation and intermarriage, see Bernard J. Sheehan, *Seeds of Extinction: Jeffersonian Philanthropy and the American Indian* (Chapel Hill: University of North Carolina Press, 1973), 174; and Brian W. Dippie, *The Vanishing American: White Attitudes and U.S. Indian Policy* (Lawrence: University Press of Kansas, 1982), 5, 260. Support for the idea of intermarriage between whites and Native Americans was prominent enough to almost pass into Virginia law in the late eighteenth century. In 1784, Patrick Henry, supported by John Marshall, authored a bill proposing that incentives of cash, livestock, and clothing be offered to white men and women alike who married Native Americans. The bill also provided for mixed-race children to receive an education at the government's expense. It passed two readings but failed the third. See James Hugo Johnston, *Race Relations in Virginia and Miscegenation in the South* (Amherst: University of Massachusetts Press, 1970), 269–70.

81. Byrd, *Histories,* 4. For an analysis of racial attitudes in Byrd's *Histories,* see Dana D. Nelson, *The Word in Black and White: Reading "Race" in American Literature, 1638–1867* (New York: Oxford University Press, 1992), 29–37. Nelson argues that Byrd's call for intermarriage, far from being a liberal manifestation of racial tolerance, was, in fact, profoundly conservative.

82. Kathleen Brown, *Good Wives,* 356, similarly sees sexual relationships between masters and enslaved women as a case in which the gross imbalance of power renders the notion of "consent" extremely problematic, if not completely untenable.

83. For this phenomenon in Colombia, see Taussig, *Shamanism,* 25. For the Russian Alaskan example, see Miller, "Handsome but Tattooed," 32, 37.

84. Taussig, *Shamanism,* 30, 41, 47, 48, 49, 51, 52, 100, 121.

85. The implications of domination in Byrd's narrative have not gone entirely unnoticed by scholars. Historian Kenneth Lockridge recognizes that the *History of the Dividing Line* is not only an epic of running the line but is also "the epic of William Byrd's natural mastery over those around him," and he notes that "in the Secret History, much of the mastery is the shared mastery of men over

women" (*Diary,* 132). Ultimately, however, Lockridge treats the *Secret History's* "obsession with sex" as a flaw in the text's literary merit rather than as a key to understanding gender and power in colonial society; ibid., 134. In this analysis, Lockridge is aligned with Byrd's many other editors and commentators who have treated his *Secret History* as a literary work of art, a "witty social satire" that is "rich in racy humor" (Davis, *Intellectual Life,* 1372; Wilson and Ferris, *Encyclopedia of Southern Culture,* 679). For a more recent literary take on Byrd that emphasizes his role in the production of a distinctly southern regional literature, see Susan Manning, "Industry and Idleness in Colonial Virginia: A New Approach to William Byrd II," *Journal of American Studies* 28, no. 2 (1994): 169–90. When historians have addressed the acts of sexual violence, they have most often treated them dismissively as an "eye for feminine charms" or as "amorous activities" (Byrd, *Histories,* xiv; Byrd, *Prose Works,* 15). More than twenty years ago, David Smith recognized that it was no longer enough to agree with such assured complacent judgments of Byrd. Smith, "William Byrd," 308–9, identified some of the complex questions regarding masculinity, sexuality, power, and colonialism raised by the *Histories,* though he left them unanswered.

86. For an extended look at the gendered dynamic of the discourses of discovery, conquest, and settlement in an earlier period, see Louis Montrose's analysis of Sir Walter Raleigh, "The Work of Gender and Sexuality in the Elizabethan Discourse of Sexuality," in *Discourses of Sexuality: From Aristotle to AIDS,* ed. Domna C. Stanton (Ann Arbor: University of Michigan Press, 1992), 138–84.

87. See Antonia Castañeda, "Sexual Violence in the Politics and Policies of Conquest: Amerindian Women and the Spanish Conquest of Alta California," in *Building with Our Hands: New Directions in Chicana Studies,* ed. Adela de la Torre and Beatriz M. Pesquera (Berkeley: University of California Press, 1993), 25; and Susan Brownmiller, *Against Our Will: Men, Women, and Rape* (New York: Simon and Schuster, 1975), 153.

88. On Byrd's intent in writing the *History,* see Davis, *Intellectual Life,* 59.

89. Byrd, *Histories,* 202.

90. Historian Richard Davis, *Intellectual Life,* 59, 1367, 1373, has argued, for example, that Byrd was representative of his age and that the survey expedition was emblematic of the American experience.

91. Byrd, *Prose Works,* 22–23.

CHAPTER THREE

Thinking Like Mount Rushmore: Sexuality and Gender in the Republican Landscape

Peter Boag

On April 1, 1944, Aldo Leopold wrote his cursory and since celebrated essay "Thinking Like a Mountain." In a few short words the famed naturalist made the case that mountains in wild country contain a "hidden meaning" or a "secret opinion" about nature and its processes that humans cannot fully decipher. In reality, Leopold projected his own ecological ideas onto the landscape as others had before him. In the late-eighteenth-century Western world, for example, poets counted mountains among the most sublime of landscapes—places where God might most likely reveal himself and in ways that struck terror into the soul. Thus, at this time mountains might best be avoided. In the nineteenth century, the more joyous concept of the picturesque replaced the sublime in Western landscape perception. Mountains then were sought out for the delight that they could bring. By the time Aldo Leopold contemplated mountains in the mid–twentieth century, he had witnessed the environmental and social horrors of the dust bowl and had begun lamenting his role, performed during his earlier and less thoughtful years, in extirpating wolves from the American Southwest. At this precise moment mountains became for Leopold repositories for ecological ideas that he had only recently worked out in his mind and that for the vast majority of his fellow Americans remained obtuse.[1]

Leopold's mountains, then, are not "natural" places so much as they are cultural sites. In fact, the story is pretty much the same wherever they exist: in the Himalayas or the Adirondacks, in the Alps or at Disneyland, mountains are a complex blend of both nature and culture—concepts and realities that cannot really be disentangled from each other. South Dakota's Mount Rushmore is an example of a mountain that seems, at first glance, especially cultural. There "art" did not so much imitate "nature" as it transformed it into a sculpture of four male American heroes. Less obviously cultural than the peering visages of George Washington, Thomas Jefferson, Theodore Roosevelt, and Abraham Lincoln are certain

Mount Rushmore National Memorial. (Courtesy National Park Service)

elements of this Black Hills setting that might otherwise be understood as natural. While ponderosa pine and the least chipmunk have long inhabited the area, mountain goats and bighorn sheep are both introduced species. Ancestors of the former, a gift from Canada in 1924, escaped from their pens at nearby Custer State Park. Bighorns were brought in to replace the native Audubon sheep that overhunting had helped drive to extinction early in the twentieth century. Yet after many years both "wild" species of goats and sheep scramble among Rushmore's cliffs and precipices as though they have known them forever. In lieu of reading the fine print of tourist brochures, many visitors undoubtedly accept them as natural.

   The Mount Rushmore National Memorial blends nature and culture in yet more surprising and complex ways than these. It does so in the multiple and contending meanings and opinions about nature, politics, sexuality, and gender that visitors read into and sense when viewing the colossal sculpture located there; in those that its creator intended and did not intend when he put chisel to stone in the Black Hills between 1927 and 1941; and in those represented in the real lives, historic reputations, and political ideologies of the men whose likenesses now look out from this otherwise isolated granite edifice. In this chapter I explore these meanings and opinions, asserting that in its ideal form, Rushmore symbolizes a social-political story that many, perhaps most, Americans have long accepted as natural. It is a story, furthermore, that has long promoted "heterosexuality" and its incumbent gender system as "natural," too. And it is a story, therefore, that has significantly influenced the American environment and how people act on and think about it. Yet while this story has in past and present times formed the solid bedrock of America, an investigation of the history of the memorial and of the biographies of its subjects reveals "hidden meanings" and "secret opinions" that, when brought to the surface, destabilize what otherwise seems to be the firm foundations of the nation and its dominant environmental ethos. In doing such, these hidden meanings and secret opinions have the potential to significantly alter how Americans think about this mountain and thus their own social and natural landscapes.

At the July 4, 1930, dedication of George Washington's head—the first portion of the National Memorial completed—observers of the scene coined the moniker the "Shrine of Democracy" and applied it to the monument. It has been known as such ever since. The National Park Service promotes it.[2] Many Americans accept it as an appropriate summation of the site: the political and patriotic meanings and opinions attending the phrase "Shrine of Democracy" are conjured in the viewer, as if by some natural force, while gazing at the memorial. But what is natural about such obviously cultural meaning and opinion? Although present by the time of Rushmore's birth, they were not necessarily there at its conception. The idea for a monument in the Black Hills first occurred to Doane Robinson, South Dakota state historian, in 1924. He wished to attract tourists to his otherwise out-of-the-way state that was, like other agricultural areas in the early 1920s, suffering a major economic downturn. Robinson initially felt that a sculpture of western characters such as Lewis and Clark, Buffalo Bill Cody, or Red Cloud might best suit the Black Hills site. He contacted the sculptor Gutzon Borglum who recently had gained national attention for his attempt to carve up a large mountain in Georgia. Upon arriving in western South Dakota, Borglum suggested that the national figures of Washington and Lincoln might be more appropriate for a sculpture. They were, in his estimation, "the nation's two greatest heroes." But, like the historian, the artist also originally had more earthly considerations in mind. When he suggested Washington and Lincoln, Borglum thought money! "If we pitch the note high enough," he announced, "we will arouse the nation," and support would thereby flow in.[3]

The "high note" also led to Borglum's subsequent suggestion of adding Jefferson to the memorial. After all, he had drafted the Declaration of Independence. He also was responsible for bringing the Black Hills within the bounds of the young republic when he acquired the Louisiana Territory. This latter theme of national expansion came in handy when Borglum and his champion, South Dakota's U.S. senator Peter Norbeck, later desired to include in the sculpture the more controversial choice of Theodore Roosevelt. Both Borglum and Norbeck had known Roosevelt, had worked in his 1912 campaign, and greatly admired his Progressive politics. To justify this addition, Borglum turned Jefferson's expansionist vision to Roosevelt's advantage. In the words of an early chronicler of the memorial, it was with "Roosevelt and . . . the Panama Canal . . . and the Spanish-American War, [that] the United States . . . had suddenly gained an impressive maturity as a world power."[4] Thus Roosevelt's form of expansion seemed to complement Jefferson's continental territorial acquisitions. In the final sum, and in the later words of Borglum's wife, Mary, the four likenesses carved on Rushmore expressed a "sincere patriotic effort to preserve and perpetuate the ideals of liberty and freedom on which our government was established and to record the territorial expansion of the Republic."[5]

The meaning of Rushmore was, therefore, only naturalized in stone after the memorial's conception. Regardless, the linking of politics and expansion actually long predates Rushmore. Americans early on connected democracy with territorial gain as the Manifest Destiny of their country: God ordained them with the right and duty to take their unique political institutions around the world. Gutzon Borglum himself referred to what many of his era assumed to be the "natural" aspects of this exceptional history in an essay he penned in 1930 as part of that year's George Washington dedication. "But strangely enough, by some humour of nature," Borglum confidently began,

out of confusion grew and developed a small tribe of independent, self-reliant souls, in whose veins flowed the blood of Europe, of Greece, of Rome, of England. . . . America, a nation, was conceived and born, sired by aeons of upward struggle, out of hair and leaves, out of mud and fear, out of slavery in galleys and cells, out of bigotry, out of injustice into fair play. The right each in his own way to be happy was written by them across the sky, firmly there, where a world could read it as if it had been wrought by volcanic eruption and, like the rocky back-bone of America, it has girdled the world.[6]

This "natural" history of the American people, in Borglum's mind, would ideally be commemorated in the nation's natural "rocky back-bone": the

Black Hills, or what South Dakota geologist Cleophas C. O'Harra referred to at the 1930 dedication as "the Birthplace of the Americas."[7]

Inextricably linking expansion and democracy, Americans also from the beginning attached political meaning to the land itself, particularly to the lands of the West, as Borglum and O'Harra suggested. When amalgamated, democracy, expansion, and western lands became American republicanism. Although the origins of republicanism lay in European history, it was Thomas Jefferson, more than any other national founder, who did so much to transform it into a significant political myth for the United States. Jefferson's view embraced an agricultural society composed of small family farms that would ever expand into the West through natural reproduction. It would be impossible for wealth and power to become concentrated in the hands of a few in this dispersed group of people who enjoyed limitless access to land and could support themselves. The central figure in this social system was the yeoman. He personified independence, the ingredient necessary for ensuring the survival of democracy. The yeoman also had a divine connection that, oddly enough, sprang from the soil. "Those who labour in the earth," Jefferson wrote, "are the chosen people of God, if ever he had a chosen people, whose breasts he has made his peculiar deposit for substantial and genuine virtue."[8]

Gutzon Borglum firmly believed in Jeffersonian republicanism. He was also from the West, having been born in Idaho in 1867. Like many Americans of northern European ancestry who lived when he did, Borglum also harbored nativist sentiments. He blended his regional, racial, and political convictions when he warned that the greatest threat to the America of his day emanated from the East: that region's great financial and political centers, its overabundance of non–Anglo-Saxon immigrants, and its teeming cities. Borglum looked to rural America, namely the white farmer of the northern West whom he called the "hardy pioneer," for the salvation of the country. While still clinging to these notions, he began sculpting the Black Hills.[9]

In espousing such ideas, Borglum obviously inherited much from Thomas Jefferson, including certain of his opinions about race. Jefferson had also envisioned Anglo-Saxon peoples dominating his farming republic and expressed grave concern over immigrants. He worried that "the greatest number" of the latter would come to America from the "absolute monarchies." Either they will "bring with them the principles of the governments they leave . . . or, if able to throw them off, it will be in exchange for an unbound licentiousness."[10] Jefferson also opposed the intermixing of European Americans and African Americans (although he did not feel the same way about whites and Indians). Of course, complicating these feelings was his own sexual relationship with his slave Sally Hemings. Combined, recent DNA tests, historical gossip, and oral tradition confirm that Jefferson fathered children by her. His children, then, became his slaves; he only slowly liberated them. Hemings earned her freedom only after her lover died.[11]

Jefferson's views of African Americans and slavery and their relationship to republicanism were not consistent, undoubtedly because he was a slaveholder and likely due to the complications of his personal relationships. At one time he might justify slavery because he felt that African Americans could not govern themselves, claiming that they "are inferior to the whites in the endowments both of body and mind." Thus logically they should be made dependents of whites. Jefferson also felt that emancipated African Americans could not live together with whites because of the long history of hurts that they had endured. The stigma of racism would always exist and could not be forgotten. Consequently, he also advocated colonization to rid the Republic not just of the trap of slavery but also of a race that he believed could not compatibly live alongside whites in freedom. To Jefferson, slavery, combined with the environmental conditions of the South, might undermine republicanism in other ways as well. "For in a warm climate," he asserted, "no man will labour for himself who can make another labour for him. This is so true, that of the proprietors of slaves a very small portion indeed are ever seen to labor." In depending on others' exertions, masters eschewed the lifestyle of the yeoman—the rugged individualist who relied, theoretically, only on himself. At another time Jefferson felt slavery subverted republicanism because white masters, while naturally able to control their passions for women within the all-white republican family, could not do so when they wielded power over the bodies of African-American females.[12]

Sexuality, then, was certainly something that Jefferson considered when he thought about republicanism. Regardless of its racial aspects, his republicanism in fact promoted "heterosexuality," and it also reinforced patriarchy and the separate male-female genders that have traditionally accompanied that sexuality.[13] Jefferson envisioned *family* farms and expansion especially through reproduction, and reproduction at high rates (up to a "dozen" children per woman). Although he felt that his political ideology elevated women to "their natural equality" with men, in reality it demanded that they, whom Jefferson referred to as the "weaker" sex, as well as their dozens of children be subservient to the yeoman. It was imperative, in his mind, that women be locked up on the land under the control of men. Such would allow women to achieve the greatest contentment in their "natural" roles as wives, mothers, and domestics.

Moreover, such tutelage, to paraphrase the historian Virginia Scharff, would eliminate the potential for women's instinctively seductive presence to corrupt vulnerable men, the very men who needed to maintain reason and control passion as they governed the republic.[14] The land itself, then, played a role in the preservation of the "natural" gender system that Jefferson and other eighteenth-century Americans believed in. In the final analysis, Jefferson's agricultural society would offer no sanctuary for workshops, industrial operatives, the mobs of urban areas, or those detached from the newly appearing "modern" male-female nuclear family. Thus, and within the context of just slightly later times, this pastoral utopia would likewise exclude from its embrace independent women and men (in particular those of the cities) who composed the rank and file of the first modern lesbian and gay communities.

Calling Jeffersonian republicanism a "heterosexual" ideology is somewhat problematic, of course. At the time Jefferson refined his beliefs, Western society did not have the understanding developed later that divides people into heterosexuals and homosexuals. Back in Jefferson's day, if one did participate in a same-sex sex act, then one would be considered a transgressor of community standards—probably a sinner and even a criminal—but not as someone who had a sexual identity based on his or her conduct. Thus, anyone had the possibility to transgress. It was only at the end of the nineteenth century that heterosexual and homosexual categories and identities began to emerge in the Western world. They did not become fixed, or "naturalized," until the early twentieth century. Although it is anachronistic to push back onto Jefferson's republican ideology and landscape a heterosexist interpretation, it is fair to conclude that same-sex sex acts were not acceptable and, theoretically, not even possible in or on them.

Jefferson asserted that the "corruption of morals in the mass of cultivators is a phaenomenon of which no age nor nation has furnished an example."[15] And his society did indeed consider same-sex sexual activities a "corruption of morals"—it lumped them together with bestiality and termed them "crimes against nature." They violated laws given by God that proclaimed reproductive sex—sex that resulted in population increase, sex that resulted in expansion and eventually global domination—as the only acceptable kind. The waste of sperm undercut male virility and the family and thereby undermined American political, social, and cultural institutions. Needless to say, Jeffersonian America dealt harshly with those whose morals, for whatever reason, did become corrupted. In colonial days they could be sentenced to death. Jefferson called for the more lenient punishment of castration. In the final analysis, while Jeffersonian republicanism is not a heterosexual myth in the strictest sense, it nonetheless did enshrine a certain set of values about sexuality, the primacy of the male-female couple, the family, and gender behaviors and roles and their relationship to the land.

Republicanism influenced expansion into the West through motivating and informing the Northwest Ordinance; the Louisiana Purchase; the Lewis and Clark expedition; the Homestead (1862), Dawes (1887), Carey (1894), and Newlands (1902) Acts; and even elements of the New Deal's public works projects of the 1930s. Moreover, with the male-female couple and the family as a core concern, republicanism also necessarily affected the society that it encouraged through western expansion. Take for example its influence on nineteenth-century Oregon in the form of the Donation Land Act (DLA). Congress passed the DLA in 1850. By its generous provisions a male who was white or half white/half Native American, was over the age of eighteen, and had cultivated his land for four consecutive years before 1 December 1850 received 320 acres of land. If married, he procured an additional 320 acres that was held in his wife's name (a total of one square mile per couple). The provision for mixed bloods considered the fact that a number of white American fur trappers had produced children with Native wives and had settled in Oregon and taken up farming years before. But after Congress initially considered these historical realities, it subsequently applied a revised law only to white people. A white male who was twenty-one or older and had arrived between December 1, 1850, and December 1, 1853 (later extended to 1855) received a 160-acre parcel and an additional 160 acres for his wife (a total of one-half square mile).[16]

Although partly designed to reward those who made their way to Oregon before it fell under the jurisdiction of the United States, the DLA and its generous allotments also had the purpose of encouraging more (white) migration to the far distant North Pacific Coast. Consider, for example, the story of Elizabeth Richey. Her husband died in Iowa before the two with their children could make the journey west. The overwhelming lure of free land in the wake of her husband's demise led Richey to undertake the remarkable crossing anyway. Once in Oregon in 1853, she proved to officials that her husband had intended all along to make the trip as well but death had interfered with those plans. Richey was thereby able to qualify for the 160 acres that she would have automatically received had her husband lived.

It is to be additionally noted that only because of her relationship with a man (in fact, a dead one) that Richey could acquire Oregon land. She was, therefore, also caught in the patriarchal system that the DLA recognized and reinforced. It also promoted it. For example, because of its double allowance, the DLA encouraged marriage in early Oregon. "Since single adult women were as scarce in Oregon as in other frontier societies," historian Dorothy Johansen found, "very young girls suddenly became marriageable and were soon wives." Sometime girls as young as eight or ten, Vernon Carstensen noted, stood as the wife of record.[17] An excellent example of Jeffersonian republicanism in action, the DLA encouraged national expansion in the form of (especially white) settlement but also in the form of increased fertility rates as Oregon women, at least for a time, married at a very young age. It also perpetuated patriarchy. Women gained access to land only through their relationship to men. Very young women and even girls were wed to men likely without their full understanding of what they were doing.

Extraordinarily large land grants available through the DLA privileged male-female couples in mid-nineteenth-century Oregon. They also influenced the course of economic and environmental history there.[18] With up to one square mile of land per family, farmers ended up leaving large quantities uncultivated, which limited economic growth and impeded town development in parts of Oregon's Willamette Valley. It also encouraged the increase of shrubs and trees on the valley's prairies that Native Americans had, previous to Euroamerican settlement, maintained with fire. Soon, parts of the Willamette became more forested than had been the case just a few years before. Certain plants that took hold in these now more woodsy environments (for example, deep-rooted and tenacious ferns) sent unwanted progeny into neighboring pastures and cultivated fields, causing endless headaches and backaches for nineteenth-century farmers and ranchers.

On the aesthetic level, responses to the economic and environmental conditions to which the DLA contributed varied according to the observer's perspective on "progress." Those who desired thriving towns with bustling economies, such as male resident L. B. Judson, decried the legacy of the DLA, lamenting in 1874 what he termed the Willamette Valley's "state of wilderness." But just two years earlier Frances Fuller Victor opined that the DLA claimant's "uncultivated prairie lands . . . make a large extent of country still in its primeval condition." Victor also described the valley's numerous "'Arcadian' groves" that bestowed in her a feeling of "romantic freedom." She even defended them from the defilement that they endured at the hands of agriculturalists. Victor declared it a "profanation" that a valley farmer she observed "allowed one of these grand forest cathedrals to be used as a shelter for his stock."

Regardless of what they thought "wilderness" or a "primeval condition" to be, Judson and Fuller reacted to an environment that a patriarchal and "heterosexist" political ideology helped to create. Their reactions also serve as examples of how the two different genders of this same system might stereotypically respond to nature in the mid–nineteenth century. The masculine that inhabited the public realm sought to transform nature or wilderness into fruitful farms and productive towns. Although the feminine also had in mind converting nature and the wild, it did so only to the point that these might provide a refuge for domesticity. To westering women of the nineteenth century, this amalgamated setting would, in turn, produce the moral anodyne to the acquisitiveness of the male sphere and, therefore, strengthen republicanism.[19] In many ways (along the lines of race, gender, sexuality, and environment conditions), the mid-nineteenth-century western Oregon landscape was a Jeffersonian landscape.

The ideology of republicanism ideally promoted "heterosexuality" and a patriarchal gender system on the land and discouraged same-sex sexuality or, at the very least, broad social recognition of it. So firmly did even late-nineteenth-century Americans accept Jefferson's contention that the "corruption of morals" was impossible on the republican landscape that they also believed that homosexuality, what in their age they more aptly called "perversion" or "degeneracy," could not spring from or take root in their country. Even some Europeans agreed. For example, in the mid-1890s the German Max Nordau published the captivating book *Degeneration*, which concerned the widely felt belief that Europe had entered a period of decline in the fin de siècle. In his book, Nordau posed the query, "Why should Americans degenerate?" He answered rhetorically: "They have a new country, new opportunities, a boundless future, a restless . . . activity; their eyes are fixed upward, their impulses are toward better and higher things, their ambition is healthier. How can Americans be degenerate?"[20]

Eventually, American medical experts altered their opinions and accepted that homosexuality could very well occur on the western side of the Atlantic. But for some time they continued to resist the idea that it could be indigenous to rural America or to the West more generally. The physician James G. Kiernan, for example, noted that while it was true that the states of the Northwest Territory had deemed it necessary to enact laws against sodomy early in the nineteenth century, it was only because that sexual practice had been brought in by foreign "emigrants." Other medical experts associated "American" homosexuality with the city, in part because of the urban center's heavily immigrant population, but especially because of its environmental conditions. Pollution, tainted foods, and even the fast-paced nature of urban life "induced" it.[21]

Dr. James Weir, for example, declared that "large cities are the hotbeds and breeding places" of homosexual disorders such as "effemination" in the American male and "viraginity" in the female. For explanatory effect, and perhaps its shock value as well, Weir submitted to his readers one of his own patients, a "pronounced effeminant" whose condition could presumably be traced to life in a large city. The doctor reported that upon visiting this young, suffering man, his charge conducted him to his "boudoir," exhibited his "lingerie," and spoke in excessively delicate terms about one of his nightcaps that he claimed was a "perfect dream of beauty."[22]

The effeminacy diagnosed in Weir's male patient paralleled that which surfaced in Theodore Roosevelt in the early 1880s when he entered the rough-and-tumble world of New York politics. As the historian Gail Bederman has so well described, the more that the ideal Victorian gentleman Roosevelt asserted himself in the masculine realm of late-nineteenth-century statecraft, "the more his opponents derided his manhood. . . . They nicknamed him 'weakling,' 'Jane-Dandy,' 'Punkin-Lily,' and 'the exquisite Mr. Roosevelt.' They ridiculed his high voice, tight pants, and fancy clothing. Several began referring to him by the name of the well-known homosexual Oscar Wilde, and one actually alleged (in a less-than-veiled phallic allusion) that Roosevelt was 'given to sucking the knob of an ivory cane.'"[23]

Roosevelt lived during an era that witnessed significant alterations in American manhood. Shifts in the economic structure undermined the very Victorian notions of middle- and upper-class "manliness" with which he had been reared. This manliness—composed of a whole set of traits that included respectability, independence, honor, strong character, sexual restraint, morality, gentility, social responsibility, and tenderness—derived from the imperatives of entrepreneurial capitalism. They had less relevance in the emerging corporate order. Moreover, certain of these became interpreted as effeminate in nature, as Roosevelt soon learned. In response to shifting gender ideals brought about by alterations in the economic order, middle- and upper-class men sought new ways at the end of the nineteenth century to define their manhood, now increasingly referred to as "masculinity" instead of "manliness." One's masculinity became measured by one's action, vigor, physicality, aggressiveness, sexual assertiveness, and even violence.[24]

As homosexuality "appeared" in the late nineteenth century and was blamed on the degenerate or "over-civilized" city, Americans located its antidote where they long felt it likely lurked: in rural America, nature, the outdoors, and especially the wild American West. Henry Childs Merwin alluded to this inclination in his 1897 essay "On Being Civilized Too Much." Bowing deeply to the virtues associated with the republican landscape, he argued that those boys who leave the countryside for the city to take up positions in law, politics, medicine, and the ministry retain their "strength only by perpetually renewing . . . contact with Mother Earth." Those who fail to do this become "over-civilized," "effete," and "perverted." Just as Thomas Jefferson had feared for republicanism because slave masters did not toil on the land as did the yeomen, Merwin worried for the "human race" because "city people hire others to do for them" the tasks that country people do and that keep them "close to nature."[25]

As Roosevelt and other middle- and upper-class American men of his era understood it, masculinity and even the whole "human race" depended on environmental conditions opposite of what the city provided. In the early 1880s, then, Roosevelt left his effeminacy as far behind as possible when he fled to the invigorating American West. He purchased two cattle ranches in the shadow of the Black Hills and took up life as a cowboy. He developed incredible stamina by spending hours in the saddle, put on weight and grew muscular through ranching activities, and fell in love with the violent sport of big game hunting. Chided for his effeminacy only a few years before, it was through this western "strenuous life"—as Roosevelt would later refer to it—that he transformed himself into a popular symbol of the most masculine of men by the end of the nineteenth century. His love of the West and the character traits it supposedly instilled in American men (in particular Anglo-Saxon men) led him to conserve and preserve the region. In the late 1880s he founded the Boone and Crockett Club. As U.S. president he added millions of acres to the National Forest system, created dozens of wildlife refuges and national monuments, and strongly advocated national parks.[26]

In his political ideology, Roosevelt, like Jefferson, looked to the West for the salvation of the country. But Roosevelt was no Jeffersonian agrarian. Rather than celebrating the farmer, he venerated and emulated another early western America hero, one whom historians have called the "hunter." Whereas the yeoman was part of a collective, democratic process that established the Republic, the hunter, as Richard Slotkin has written, acted on his "own initiative, perhaps for the sake of the democratic *en masse* but without being bound by the constraints of moral or civic order which the social collective must observe." As a politician in the increasingly corporate age, Roosevelt felt that his aristocratic origins and his western masculinity placed him in a similar role as the "hunter," that is, a leader who looked out for the best interests of larger American society.[27]

Mount Rushmore sculptor Gutzon Borglum embraced Roosevelt's political vision at the same time that he clung to Jeffersonian republicanism. Like so many things, he blended the two. He looked to Jefferson's democratic society of the West to produce the strong individual who could become a forceful national leader, like Roosevelt, for the country that was growing increasingly complex and diverse in the late nineteenth and early twentieth centuries.[28] Similarly, Borglum admired Abraham Lincoln (he named a son in his honor) because he felt the sixteenth president to be an exemplar of this tradition. Lincoln had been born in the Daniel Boone country of Kentucky and reared on the Illinois prairies. As president he signed the Homestead Act. As the country's leader, moreover, he turned out to be its foremost preserver. It was Lincoln of the West, after all, who held the North and South together.

Ironically, the strong leader Lincoln had also carried on, while on the western prairies, a long-term, intimate, and romantic relationship with another man, Joshua Speed. The two shared a bed for almost four years. Serious historians have found it difficult to characterize the Lincoln-Speed relationship as "homosexual." Emotional and physical (though not necessarily sexual) intimacies between men commonly occurred through much of the nineteenth century before the invented ideas of heterosexuality and homosexuality stigmatized them. Little hard evidence exists to suggest that Lincoln and Speed had sexual relations. But the closeness that men of Lincoln's time were permitted allowed those who desired it to express their love for each other in sexual ways—at the same time both under and blind to the watchful gaze of society—which may very well have happened with Lincoln and Speed. Moreover, the degree of intimacy these two shared was somewhat unusual, and both men had ambivalent and even cold attitudes toward women throughout their lives and found sexual relations with them difficult.[29]

If not exactly in reality, then certainly in myths that most modern Americans want to believe in, the Lincoln-Speed relationship on the western prairies destabilizes the "heterosexual" republican landscape on which it occurred. But more than Lincoln and Speed undermines the traditional notions about sexuality and masculinity associated with rural America and the West. Many years ago Alfred Kinsey discovered that late-nineteenth- and early-twentieth-century teenage males in the "most isolated" farming areas engaged in a "considerable amount" of same-sex sexual activities. He also determined that those youths who lived in the West participated in such acts at rates higher even than their counterparts "in the smaller farm country of the Eastern United States." More notably, Kinsey revealed that "the highest frequencies of the homosexual" that his research team ever secured were "in particular rural communities in some of the more remote sections of the country." Specifically, he pointed to the western American communities of prospectors, lumbermen, cowboys, and ranchers—the very communities whose men Roosevelt regarded so highly because of their supposed masculine virtues. Indeed, Kinsey argued that these masculine virtues actually induced same-sex sexual activities. These "are virile" and "physically active" men, he claimed, "men who have faced the rigors of nature in the wild. They live on realities and on a minimum of theory. Such a background breeds the attitude that sex is sex, irrespective of the nature of the partner with whom the relation is had."[30]

The real private lives of Abraham Lincoln and his bed*fellow*, of Theodore Roosevelt and his cow*boys*, and of Jefferson and his yeo*men* undermine the sexual and gender expectations of the republican landscape of the West. So too does the private life even of George Washington, the most venerated of the Rushmore figures. Somewhat ineffective with women and also thwarted in an early love, Washington married slightly later in life. He did so to a woman who was a widow, a mother, his elder, and on whose own fortune he could depend. Contrary to republican dictates, Washington and Martha never had any children together. Some have made the metaphorical suggestion that Washington could not father his own children because he was too busy fathering a nation. More prosaically, it is proposed that a bout with smallpox during his younger years left him sterile. Gore Vidal's novel *Burr*, based in part on historical research, reveals talk in the late eighteenth century about Washington's sterility and connects it, in an allegorical way, to nature's possibilities and limits: "A mule stallion, as it were, whose unnatural progeny are these states. So at the end, not to the swift but to the infertile went the race." *Burr* also includes quips about what some people felt was Washington's feminine figure, a "broad . . . *derrière*" and the "hips, buttocks and bosom of a woman."[31]

Especially then do same-sex sexuality and male effeminacy lurk in the crevices of Rushmore. They destabilize the rocky slopes of that memorial and contribute to the mountain what Aldo Leopold might refer to as a "hidden meaning" or a "secret opinion." Historical memory has worked to mask these attributes in the faces of Rushmore. Thus the shrine of an idealized democracy is on the public level also the shrine of an idealized heterosexuality. Idealized democracy and heterosexuality reinforced each other, indeed depended on each other, in the social-political myth that grew up in early America long before Gutzon Borglum began work on Mount Rushmore in 1927. They were linked to the land and employed to inform and justify the way western expansion and settlement should be undertaken. In a circular sort of way, the land being expanded into provided the source itself for this political-sexual-gender system. When many of those who visit Rushmore gaze into the faces of the men who look out onto the western American landscape, conjured in them are these circular meanings and opinions. Circular meanings and opinions have been so hardened by myth that reality has found it difficult to penetrate them. Gutzon Borglum intended to chisel these onto Rushmore whose granite cliffs likewise defy erosive forces.

Borglum, however, never completed Rushmore as he originally intended. He died in 1941. Shortly thereafter, the all-consuming world war diverted men, money, and resources away from the faces of Washington, Jefferson, Roosevelt, and Lincoln. The events that occurred during the Great Depression when most of the work at Rushmore took place and the events that brought that work to an end—World War II—dramatically altered America's social landscape. Coincidentally, they also made the public meaning and the actual site of Mount Rushmore all the more critical in the postwar years to a country still experiencing extraordinary turmoil. The depression and World War II left the American family, the monogamous male-female couple, patriarchy, traditional gender roles, and heterosexuality in a seriously shaken condition. Years of poverty followed by years of abundance; a birth rate that during the depression dropped below replacement levels; the collapse of the single-family housing industry along with the stock market; high rates of mobility pulling families apart as individual members searched the country for jobs; New Deal programs that took young men from their homes in America's eastern cities and placed them in work camps in the West; millions of men and women leaving home for military training and then heading overseas to fight wars, many never to return; women who left home for jobs in war industries and found a new sense of independence; children placed in day care facilities or left to their own devices; spiraling rates of juvenile delinquency and the appearance of victory girls; the arrival of large numbers of single men and women on military bases and in port cities; and the incredible growth of gay and lesbian consciousness and community in the military—all these Great Depression–World War II era developments, in the heterosexist view, weakened the traditional American family, violated the way children should be raised, undermined patriarchy, and threatened the monogamous male-female relationship.[32]

As the United States attempted to recover normalcy after the war, it is no surprise that an exaggerated emphasis was placed on heterosexist values as a way to weave the country together again. The entire baby-boom culture espoused marriage, monogamy, reproduction, nuclear families, single-family dwellings, child and baby care, fathers who were breadwinners, and mothers who remained home as domestics. Concomitantly, homosexuality emerged as the greatest menace to distinct masculine and feminine genders, to the fragile family and its children, and to heterosexuality generally. A homosexual panic enveloped the country at the social level at the very time that communism emerged as the primary threat to the American state. The two became linked in the American consciousness.[33]

And they did so in a particularly noticeable way on the slopes of Mount Rushmore in Alfred Hitchcock's critically and popularly acclaimed 1959 film North by Northwest.[34] Although directed by a Briton, it was an American, Ernest Lehman, who wrote the story. It is based on a complicated plot of mistaken identity in which a private citizen, Roger Thornhill (Cary Grant), representatives of the federal government, including the head of the "Intelligence Agency," known only as "Professor" (Leo G. Carroll), and a steamy double agent, Eve Kendall (Eva Marie Saint), chase and are pursued by a communist spy ring. Its leader, Phillip Van Damme (James Mason), has been spiriting microfilms of top secrets out of the country for some time. Kendall poses as his lady friend. Van Damme is assisted by a trusted aid, Leonard (Martin Landau), who is, notably, a homosexual with certain effeminate characteristics.[35] The story begins in New York City and heads roughly "north by northwest" to Chicago and even to Lincoln's Illinois prairies. It concludes at Mount Rushmore where Van Damme maintains a secret hideaway and air service that whisks him in and out of the country.

The government's attempt to infiltrate and uncover the details of the spy ring encompasses only half the plot. The other is the passionate and by 1950s standards erotic romance that develops between Kendall and Thornhill. After about ninety minutes of suspense, the lust and love that the two have developed for each other are jeopardized by the need for Kendall's continued secrecy about her double agent status and by the fact that Van Damme has been trying to dispatch Thornhill, whom he mistakenly believes is an Intelligence Agency detective. But their affair is saved when the Professor helps Kendall and Thornhill reunite at the base of Rushmore. In this most American setting that combines nature, democratic images, the Intelligence Agency, and the National Park Service, the threatened heterosexual romance is saved.

But the reunion is presently broken up when the Professor explains that the United States is losing the Cold War and Kendall must return to Van Damme to learn more about his spy network. Thornhill resists this news, but a burly National Park ranger drops him in his tracks. Recovered from the shellacking, that evening while secured away in an area hospital Thornhill easily gives the Intelligence Agency the slip (no wonder America is losing the Cold War) and tracks Kendall to Van Damme's mountain retreat above Rushmore.

Here is where the film reaches its exciting climax, literally. The homosexual Leonard reveals to Van Damme that his "woman's intuition" led him to unearth Kendall's double agent status. Angry and deflated, Van Damme implies that he will dispatch Kendall that night by pushing her from the plane as he departs the country. At this point, Thornhill secretly arrives, overhears Van Damme and Leonard, and gets word to Kendall that she is in trouble. The two protagonists make off on foot—Kendall in a pair of sexy heels—carrying the microfilm of top secrets. Their path takes them through the night air to the top of Rushmore with the menacing Leonard in hot pursuit. After Thornhill and Kendall precariously descend to the base of Washington and Jefferson, Leonard overtakes them, grabs the microfilm from Kendall's hands, and then pushes her over the precipice. Kendall just catches the ledge with one hand when Thornhill, who is likewise scarcely holding on, barely grabs her free hand with his. The scene boldly exposes on the slopes of Rushmore the full force of the era's fears about the homosexual menace to heterosexual love and coupling. As the heteronarrative literally dangles by a thread, Thornhill begs the lurking Leonard to help him and Kendall. But the homosexual instead wickedly uses his foot to crush Thornhill's grasping fingers, thereby hoping to quicken the demise of a heterosexuality that scarcely clings to the slopes of America's Shrine of Democracy and barely holds a beleaguered country together.

But across the way at the summit of Rushmore, the Professor and National Park officials have arrived. In an incredible show of western marksmanship, from this distance and with pistols, the park rangers dispatch the homosexual who, as he tumbles from the Shrine of Democracy, drops the microfilm, thus saving the American state. Meanwhile, Thornhill and Kendall still struggle for survival. The former encourages the latter, who screams that she cannot make it, with the words, "Come on. I've got you." This precarious Rushmore setting is cleverly fused with a scene of a private cabin on a train—the place where Thornhill's and Kendall's romance first began earlier in the film. Simultaneously, Thornhill's words "Come on" at Rushmore blend into "Come along, Mrs. Thornhill" as he lifts Eve directly off the face of Rushmore and into a nuptial berth. Homosexuality is finally vanquished as heterosexual love is consummated (appropriately for familial values, after marriage), as the train carrying Thornhill and Kendall rushes headfirst into a mountain tunnel.

To broader American society in the post–World War II era, communism and homosexuality presented the greatest threats to the country's cherished and interlinked political, sexual, and gender values. Rushmore, however, contained within itself reaffirming, long celebrated, and idealized meanings and opinions about a system that connects republicanism, heterosexuality, and patriarchy as well as distinctly separate masculine and feminine genders. Its slippery slopes made it impossible for Leonard, his sexuality, and his gender deviance to gain a firm foothold. It is not surprising, then, that Americans looked to Rushmore in the 1950s for reassurance. There and at that time America's historically prevalent heteronormative narrative of the (publicly) heterosexually masculine Cary Grant and the sultry feminine Eva Marie Saint could vanquish homosexuality and effeminate males. Yet Mount Rushmore where this scene played out is a cultural creation never completed by Borglum as he originally intended. Some have suggested that Rushmore's unfinished condition symbolizes America's unfinished character. This condition, therefore, leaves open the possibility that the hidden meanings and secret opinions dwelling in the less told parts of Lincoln's, Roosevelt's, Jefferson's, and Washington's lives and times might someday be more fully accepted and commemorated. At that time, Mount Rushmore may very well provide the source for a seismic shift in Americans' thinking about both their social and natural landscapes.

NOTES

I wish to thank my colleague Ron Hatzenbuehler for his thoughtful sugges-
tions and for generously sharing his expertise on Thomas Jefferson.

1. Aldo Leopold, "Thinking Like a Mountain," in *A Sand County Almanac
and Sketches Here and There* (New York: Oxford University Press, 1949), 129–33;
Ronald Rees, "The Scenery Cult: Changing Landscape Tastes over Three Centuries," *Landscape* 19 (May 1975): 39–47, and "The Taste for Mountain Scenery,"
History Today 25 (1975): 305–12.

2. U.S. Department of the Interior, National Park Service, *Mount Rushmore
National Memorial* (Washington, D.C.: Government Printing Office, 1998).

3. Rex Alan Smith, *The Carving of Mount Rushmore* (New York: Abbeville
Press, 1985), 25–27, 129; Doane Robinson, "Inception and Development of the
Rushmore Idea," *Black Hills Engineer* 18, no. 4 (November 1930): 334–35.

4. Badger Clark, "The Mountain That Had Its Face Lifted," in *The Black
Hills*, ed. Roderick Peattie (New York: Vanguard, 1952), 225; Smith, *Carving*,
130–31.

5. Quoted in Albert Boime, *The Magisterial Gaze* (Washington, D.C.: Smithsonian Institution Press, 1991), 161–62, as referenced by Kenneth R. Olwig, "Reinventing Common Nature: Yosemite and Mount Rushmore–A Meandering Tale of
a Double Nature," in *Uncommon Ground: Rethinking the Human Place in Nature*, ed.
William Cronon (New York: W. W. Norton, 1996), 398.

6. Gutzon Borglum, "The Political Importance and the Art Character of the
National Memorial at Mount Rushmore," *Black Hills Engineer* 18, no. 4 (November 1930): 288–89.

7. Cleophas C. O'Harra, "The Black Hills, the Birthplace of the Americas,"
Black Hills Engineer 18, no. 4 (November 1930): 301.

8. Thomas Jefferson, *Notes on the State of Virginia*, ed. William Peden (New
York: W. W. Norton, 1954, 1982), 164–65.

9. See Walker Rumble, "Gutzon Borglum: Mount Rushmore and the American Tradition," *Pacific Northwest Quarterly* 59, no. 3 (July 1968): 121–27.

10. Jefferson, *Notes*, 84–85, n. 1, query 19, 292.

11. Barbra Murray and Brian Duffy, "Jefferson's Secret Life," *U.S. News and
World Report*, November 9, 1998, 58–63; Jan Ellen Lewis and Peter S. Onuf, *Sally
Hemings and Thomas Jefferson: History, Memory, and Civic Culture* (Charlottesville:
University Press of Virginia, 1999); "Thomas Jefferson and Sally Hemings Re-
dux," *William and Mary Quarterly* 57, no. 1 (January 2000): 121–210.

12. Jefferson, *Notes*, 143, 163; Peter S. Onuf, *Jefferson's Empire: The Language of
American Nationhood* (Charlottesville: University Press of Virginia, 2000), 147–88,
and "Every Generation Is an 'Independent Nation': Colonization, Miscegenation,
and the Fate of Jefferson's Children," *William and Mary Quarterly* 57, no. 1 (January 2000): 153–70; Ron Hatzenbuehler, "'I Tremble for My Country': Thomas Jefferson as Gentry Reformer in Virginia, 1770–1826," unpublished.

13. I have commented on this topic in my earlier work, "Sexuality, Gender,
and Identity in Great Plains History and Myth," *Great Plains Quarterly* 18, no. 4
(Fall 1998): 327–40.

14. Virginia J. Scharff, "My Head and My Heart: Jefferson's View of Woman's Place, 1771–1789," paper written at the University of Arizona, Tucson, 1984.

15. Jefferson, *Notes*, 165.

16. Dorothy O. Johansen, *Empire of the Columbia: A History of the Pacific Northwest*, 2d ed. (New York: Harper and Row, 1967), 231.

17. Peter Boag, *Environment and Experience: Settlement Culture in Nineteenth-Century Oregon* (Berkeley: University of California Press, 1992), 116; Johansen, *Empire of the Columbia*, 232; Vernon Carstenson, ed., *The Public Lands: Studies in the History of the Public Domain* (Madison: University of Wisconsin Press, 1968), xxv.

18. This and the next paragraph are derived from evidence that I presented in my earlier work, *Environment and Experience*, 120, 122, 125, 158–59.

19. Vera Norwood, *Made from this Earth: American Women and Nature* (Chapel Hill: University of North Carolina Press, 1984); Annette Kolodny, *The Land before Her: Fantasy and Experience of the American Frontiers, 1630–1860* (Chapel Hill: University of North Carolina Press, 1984), and *The Lay of the Land: Metaphor as Experience and History in American Life and Letters* (Chapel Hill: University of North Carolina Press, 1975).

20. The Nordau quotation is in James G. Kiernan, "Are Americans Degenerates? A Critique of Nordau's Recent Change of View," *Alienist and Neurologist* 18, no. 3 (October 1896): 446 (Kiernan actually takes the opposite view and argues that Nordau's theory can appropriately be applied to the United States).

21. James G. Kiernan, "Increase of American Inversion," *The Urologic and Cutaneous Review* 20, no. 1 (January 1916): 44; "Viraginity and Effemination," *Journal of Urology and Sexology* 15, no. 4 (April 1919): 187–88; John C. Burnham, "Early References to Homosexual Communities in American Medical Writings," *Medical Aspects of Human Sexuality* 7, no. 8 (1973): 41; Kiernan, "Increase of American Inversion," 44–46; Alfred C. Kinsey, Wardell B. Pomeroy, and Clyde E. Martin, *Sexual Behavior in the Human Male* (Philadelphia: W. B. Saunders, 1948), 455–57.

22. "Viraginity and Effemination," 187–88.

23. Gail Bederman, *Manliness and Civilization: A Cultural History of Gender and Race in the United States, 1880–1917* (Chicago: University of Chicago Press, 1995), 170.

24. Ibid., 17–19, 170–96; E. Anthony Rotundo, *American Manhood: Transformations in Masculinity from the Revolution to the Modern Era* (New York: Basic Books, 1993).

25. Henry Childs Merwin, "On Being Civilized Too Much," *Atlantic Monthly*, June 1897, 838, 839.

26. Bederman, *Manliness*, 170–96; David G. McCullough, *Mornings on Horseback* (New York: Simon and Schuster, 1981); Paul Russell Cutright, *Theodore Roosevelt: The Making of a Conservationist* (Urbana: University of Illinois Press, 1985); Michael L. Collins, *That Damned Cowboy: Theodore Roosevelt and the American West, 1883–1898* (New York: Peter Lang, 1989); Roderick Nash, *Wilderness and the American Mind*, 3d ed. (New Haven, Conn.: Yale University Press, 1982), 149–53; Richard Slotkin, *Gunfighter Nation: The Myth of the Frontier in Twentieth-Century America* (New York: Atheneum, 1992), 29–62.

27. Slotkin, *Gunfighter Nation*, 29–62.

28. Rumble, "Gutzon Borglum," 125.

29. Jonathan Ned Katz, *Love Stories: Sex between Men before Homosexuality* (Chicago: University of Chicago Press, 2001), 3–25.

30. Kinsey, *Sexual Behavior in the Human Male*, 455–57.

31. Gore Vidal, *Burr: A Novel* (New York: Random House, 1973, New York: Vintage, 2000), 6, 23, 26, 40; Frederic Fox, "Pater Patriea as Pater Familias," *American Heritage* 14, no. 3 (April 1963): 32–37, 100–102; John E. Ferling, *The First Men: A Life of George Washington* (Knoxville: University of Tennessee Press, 1988).

32. On various of these issues, see John D'Emilio and Estelle B. Freedman, *Intimate Matters: A History of Sexuality in America* (New York: Harper and Row, 1988); Beth Bailey, *Sex in the Heartland* (Cambridge, Mass.: Harvard University Press, 1999); Robert S. Lynd and Helen Merrell Lynd, *Middletown in Transition: A Study of Cultural Conflicts* (New York: Harcourt Brace Jovanovich, 1937); Richard R. Lingeman, *Don't You Know There's a War On? The American Home Front, 1941–1945* (New York: G. P. Putnam's Sons, 1970); William M. Tuttle Jr., *"Daddy's Gone to War": The Second World War in the Lives of America's Children* (New York: Oxford University Press, 1993); Glen H. Elder, *Children of the Great Depression: Social Change in Life Experience* (Chicago: University of Chicago Press, 1974).

33. John D'Emilio, "The Homosexual Menace: The Politics of Sexuality in Cold War America," in Kathy Peiss and Christina Simmons, eds., with Robert A. Padgug, *Passion and Power: Sexuality in History* (Philadelphia: Temple University Press, 1989), 226–40; John D'Emilio, *Sexual Politics, Sexual Communities: The Making of a Homosexual Minority in the United States, 1940–1970* (Chicago: University of Chicago Press, 1983), 40–53; Estelle B. Freedman, "'Uncontrolled Desires': The Response to the Sexual Psychopath, 1920–1960," in Peiss, Simmons, and Padgug, *Passion and Power*, 199–225; George Chauncey Jr., "The Postwar Sex Crime Panic," in *True Stories from the American Past*, ed. William Graebner (New York: McGraw-Hill, 1993), 167–78; John Howard, "The Library, the Park, and the Pervert: Public Space and Homosexual Encounter in Post–World War II Atlanta," in *Carryin' on in the Lesbian and Gay South*, ed. John Howard (New York: New York University Press, 1997), 107–31; Randolph William Baxter, "'Eradicating This Menace': Homophobia and Anti-communism in Congress, 1947–1954" (Ph.D. diss., University of California, Irvine, 1999); David K. Johnson, "The Lavender Scare: Gays and Lesbians in the Federal Civil Service, 1945–1975" (Ph.D. diss., Northwestern University, 2000); K. A. Cuordileone, "'Politics in an Age of Anxiety': Cold War Political Culture and the Crisis in American Masculinity, 1949–1960," *Journal of American History* 87, no. 2 (2000): 515–45.

34. *North by Northwest*, directed by Alfred Hitchcock and written by Ernest Lehman, Metro-Goldwyn-Meyer, 1959.

35. For years, speculation existed as to whether or not Leonard is indeed a homosexual, but the film's writer Ernest Lehman has verified this fact and explained that even early audiences understood this reality. See *Destination Hitchcock: The Making of North by Northwest*, produced and directed by Peter Fitzgerald, Turner Entertainment and Warner Home Video, 2000, and Ernest Lehman's running commentary to *North by Northwest* on the same DVD. Vito Russo, *The Celluloid Closet: Homosexuality in the Movies*, rev. ed. (New York: Harper and Row, 1987), 94, makes a brief reference to Leonard's sexuality.

PART II: BODIES

CHAPTER FOUR

Scaling New Heights:
Heroic Firemen, Gender, and the
Urban Environment, 1875–1900

Mark Tebeau

On a cold morning in January 1882, in the midst of a blinding snowstorm, an alarm bell clanged in the firehouse of Ladder Company Number 1 of New York City. Awakened by the bell, the company converged upon a scene that would "never be forgotten by those who witnessed it." Firefighters discovered the five-story Old World Building, with its brick exterior and wood interior, almost completely engulfed; even worse, dozens of people were trapped, dangling in windows on the fourth and fifth floors as flames and smoke shot up into the sky around them. A second, third, and then a general alarm—the "three sixes"—followed in rapid succession bringing nearly thirty engine and truck companies to the scene. A crowd that gathered to watch the carnage quickly swelled to more than five thousand as firefighters struggled against the clock to tame the environment run amok and rescue those trapped by the blaze. The *New York Times* reported: "Terror-stricken faces of men and women peered down through the smoke upon the thousands of their fellow-creatures below, stretching out their hands for aid and shrieking loudly for rescue. The mingled smoke and flames gave to the face an unearthly hue, and the shrieks, mingled with the roar of the fire and the hoarse calling of the firemen, came to the ears of the surging crowd below like voices from the tomb."[1]

Firefighters quickly mounted rescue attempts, even as they began to battle the blaze itself. Low water pressure, worsening weather, and especially the network of wires surrounding the building hampered their work. Forced to use relatively short ladders, firemen often found themselves just short of those people trapped in the building's top stories. In the heat of the moment, firefighters, like John Rooney of Hook and Ladder Company Number 10, performed daring rescues. As Rooney maneuvered

Adapted from a chapter in Mark Tebeau, *Eating Smoke: Fire in Urban America, 1800–1950* (Johns Hopkins University Press, 2003).

to save a woman trapped on the fifth floor, he instructed the men of his company to raise the ladder on which he precariously perched. An additional six feet of height brought him within striking distance. As he swayed back and forth on the ladder's top rung, Rooney asked the woman to lean downward; with a swoop of his arms and intricate balancing he pulled her to safety.

Firemen John Horan and Henry Murray climbed a twenty-five-foot ladder carrying an additional ten-foot section of ladder. They extended the smaller ladder from the top of the twenty-five-foot ladder to reach a fifth floor window. Horan then entered the smoking windows of the fifth floor, hugging the ground on his hands and knees, searching for survivors. He found four men disoriented and face down in the building interior. He revived the despondent and choking victims and led them to the window. Finally, along with Murray, Horan shuttled the men down the chain of ladders.

The struggle to control the fire continued well after the last rescue had been performed. Firefighters slowly worked their way into the building's interior, toward the base of the flames, pulling down dangerously teetering walls. Over the next days, firefighters found twelve victims in the smoldering ruins, although their heroism in saving as many as a hundred trapped citizens was not soon forgotten. In the ensuing months, the men of Hook and Ladder Company Number 10 received accolades from a crowd of over two thousand during a public church service sponsored by the congregation where one of the rescued women worshipped. The New York Fire Department also honored several of the firefighters, placing the names of Rooney, Horan, Murray, and others on its Roll of Merit. Rooney received the NYFD's coveted Bennett Medal, given yearly by the department to a firefighter who demonstrated unusual courage in saving a life.[2]

The heroics of Rooney and his fellow firemen at the Old World blaze vividly illustrate the challenge involved in providing fire safety in American cities. As part of much broader societal efforts to create safety and order, the battle to control fire provides insight into how understandings of gender and nature intersected in the construction of urban America. Even as fire fueled rapid development, it threatened the physical and social integrity of America's landscapes, as cities exploded across the nation. On the eve of the Civil War, less than 20 percent of Americans lived in cities, but by 1920 more than half dwelled in urban places. During this period of unprecedented expansion, no other danger jeopardized the entirety of the city-building process—human life, property, or the dreams of city boosters—in such a sweeping or intense fashion. In the last decades of the nineteenth century, there seemed to be no reliable solution to the problem, as conflagrations routinely swept through cities. Building laws had not yet become pervasive or systematic, and the financially unstable in-dustry struggled as hundreds of companies went bankrupt because they were unable to pay claims. Yet, despite the threat, fire served as mass en-tertainment. Stories of blazes filled newspapers and became the subject of theatrical performances. By century's end, one of Thomas Edison's earli-est films depicted the drama of the burning of Coney Island. It would not be until well into the twentieth century that the danger of sweeping blazes, much less fire more broadly, diminished.[3]

Firefighters first took leadership in this elemental struggle early in the nineteenth century when the problem intensified. New, more aggressive firefighting techniques can be dated to 1803, when volunteer firefighters in Philadelphia transformed urban fire protection. In a move that was widely imitated, the men of the Philadelphia Hose Company confronted the emerging threat of fire by adopting specialized technologies and organi-zational forms to control the elements run amok. The first half of the nine-teenth century witnessed two significant struggles among volunteer firefighters. On the one hand, firefighters worked to identify the bound-aries of their service, balancing the interests of their ethnic, political, or ge-ographic community against those of the company, other men fighting fires, and the polity. On the other hand, they refined their work techniques, tools, and organization, seeking to upgrade their efficiency. Although ur-ban fire companies sowed the seeds of change, the notion of cohesive, city-wide fire departments did not emerge until after midcentury.[4]

Beginning in the 1850s, volunteer firefighters formally began and led the process of transforming their avocation into an occupation and of cre-ating urban fire departments. For the first time, firefighters understood that their duties and identities as men who protected the social order transcended their connections to localized communities and individual fire companies (that had been based in geography, demographics, or cul-ture). As firefighters carved out a niche for themselves in a public sphere increasingly dominated by particularized interests, they gradually rede-fined their work and the boundaries of their service. Only after the 1870s did firefighters begin to prioritize heroic action—like that displayed by Rooney, Horan, and Murray—as a rationale for their "calling." Thus, dur-ing a century-long and gradual process, firefighters first carved out a functional niche within cities, organized work routines, and finally dis-tinguished themselves as a class of individuals according to their occu-pation. However, it would not be until the waning decades of the nineteenth century that firemen became "Heroes Who Fight Fire," to bor-row a phrase from urban journalist Jacob Riis.[5]

Why did it take so long for firefighters to become popular heroes? I argue that firefighters became professional heroes and transformed them-selves into icons of public safety late in the nineteenth century because of the manner in which they confronted changing built and cultural landscapes. Firefighters reorganized their work in two important and related ways: they altered their firefighting strategies in terms of an ongoing dialogue with the ever-changing built environment, and they established work practices and narratives of action that magnified their role as virile men, protecting women and children.[6]

Both gender and the environment played critical roles in how firefighters became professionals, but central to this struggle was fire itself. In nineteenth-century American cities, fire revealed nature in many complex forms: nature transformed into buildings, consumer products, and wealth; nature as fire feeding off wood, air, and the altered landscape of urban America; nature in the form of water redirected to dampen blazes, coursing through the veins of the urban infrastructure that was often likened to a biological system; nature in the form of soft bodies vulnerable to the elements as was represented by the stories of women and children endangered by fire; nature in the form of hard, muscular, and athletic bodies of firemen who confronted fire even though their individual and collective bodies sometimes failed to contain the ravaging elements. Firefighters understood well the physical and cultural dimensions of their struggle, and they transformed it into a grand drama between man and nature. More important, firefighters placed themselves at the center of this epic struggle. In the process, they not only performed harrowing rescues and authored narratives of manhood in action, but also constructed the boundaries of their occupation as they became icons of safety. [7]

Firefighters understood well that urban landscapes were composed of natural materials that had been recast into physical structures and an infrastructure. Likewise, they understood that the urban environment possessed no single regimen of danger but a host of risks, which changed in each dynamic array of buildings and with each fire and circumstance. Indeed, in 1873, when leading firefighters established the National Association of Fire Engineers (NAFE), this sensitive reading of the landscape was expressed as a fundamental tenet. The first professional organization established by firefighters, NAFE linked particular modes of building practice to the broader environmental structure of North America and argued that the "tinder box style of construction so universally practiced" was a problem of national character. Building upon the work histories of its membership, NAFE recognized that the shifting structure of the urban (fire) environment produced different, if not entirely new, dangers to urban residents. Cities grew taller and denser even as they spread over larger areas in the decades following the Civil War. As a result, the organization claimed that the threat posed by fire both intensified and changed. The structure of cities constituted diverse environments in which danger and safety varied. Blazes charred the top stories of tall buildings, smoldered in basements, burned more hotly, and caused walls to topple. Firefighters experienced the shifting dangers viscerally and developed their identities in relation to their changing work environments.[8]

Firefighters noted how subtle changes in building structure produced wildly different fire environments, and they discovered that new spatial arrangements complicated their labor and altered fire risk. For instance, NAFE examined urban fire risk and the landscape in a remarkably detailed manner. Along with other nascent professionals, fire engineers explored the many different aspects of the relation between fire and particular structural features of the urban environment, including the dangers posed by construction materials inside and outside buildings, aesthetic detailing, openings within and outside buildings, and firewalls. The organization gave special consideration to the increasing height of cities and area (square footage) of buildings. Fire engineers repeatedly argued that the height and area of buildings outstripped the ability of fire departments to reach fires at such heights. In 1887, New York City's fire chief reported to NAFE, "We find mammoth structures being steadily erected to a height that the longest portable ladders fail to reach, and to which the most improved pumping machinery fails to deliver effective streams of water. . . . Even those constructed of slow-burning, or so-called fire-proof materials, are liable to be seriously damaged or even destroyed by intense heat from the burning contents, where water, the only known combatant of open fires cannot be applied." The expansion of building height and area aided the spread of fires because they developed uncommonly high heat (which so-called "slow-burning" construction sometimes exacerbated) that made extinguishing them all but impossible. High heat also facilitated the fire's spread to adjoining structures, even those as far as sixty feet away—sometimes beyond the width of a street. Moreover, unless buildings had properly constructed "anchoring" walls, they were liable to collapse, thus spreading fire to adjoining structures. NAFE even remained skeptical of so-called "fire-proof" construction, arguing that building technologies altered danger but did not eradicate it.[9]

By studying the landscape in such detail and by understanding how the natural materials that composed the urban environment produced complex regimens of risk, firefighters established their expertise. They also sought greater authority over the process of city building and demanded changes in building practices in order to create greater safety or, at least, to produce spaces that were more easily susceptible to firefighters' interventions. From NAFE's initial meetings, reducing fire hazards in the landscape became a topic of intense, recurring, and increasingly detailed discussion. The organization took the lead in advocating systematic safety in urban areas, and it both developed and promoted a national municipal building code more than two decades before the insurance industry successfully disseminated the first comprehensive building code. As early as 1876, again in 1884, and repeatedly through the 1890s, NAFE transformed its discussions of environmental dangers into increasingly exhaustive recommendations for building, including design provisions that prevented the spread of fire and provided for human safety. Most proposals required that fire escapes be provided in buildings of two or more stories in which workers were employed above the second floor. Significantly, firefighters also wanted to alter the urban fire protective infrastructure to gain an advantage in the war against fire. For instance, NAFE recommended improving water delivery: expanded urban water systems, "standpipes" for large structures, and special hose fittings like so-called "siamese connections," which forced water from two hose lines through a single nozzle. Just as improved water systems could help firefighters to overcome impediments faced in larger buildings, alterations to the infrastructure also enhanced their effectiveness.[10]

Although firefighters' attempts to frame a systematic building code failed, they adopted strident rhetoric of reform, which they cast explicitly in terms of class and gender. In the 1880s and 1890s, for instance, firefighters advanced their arguments for elevated status as professionals most forcefully when they contrasted themselves with builders and fire insurers, whose view of fire danger as an economic problem conflicted with NAFE's sense of the human toll of fire risk. In particular, the organization distinguished firefighters' commitment to public service from the acquisitive capitalism of American builders and insurers, illuminating the failures of the fire insurance industry to provide a meaningful degree of safety to policyholders. Firefighters often turned the insurers' own rhetoric against them. As late as 1894, for instance, American fire underwriters remained unconcerned about public fire safety, often claiming it was not their responsibility. The insurers' job, paraphrasing the National Board of Fire Underwriters (NBFU), was to make profit out of conflagration, to figure them, and to assess them to the public. This apparent lack of concern about human safety in the face of profit offended NAFE, which was especially critical of "carelessness." It reported that "firemen's lives, which are exposed to danger every moment from the time a signal is received until they return to quarters, should not be thus placed in jeopardy because careless or dishonest men hold indemnity from insurance companies." The organization's critique called into question popular representations of middling men as prudent and disciplined, as promoters of order and regularity. According to firefighters, laissez-faire marketplace and rationalized business practices were failing to discipline the American environment. NAFE, then, questioned the very founda-

tions of middle-class manhood, suggesting that true public safety resulted only from the manliness of firemen.[11]

If firefighters sought authority by questioning the manhood of capi-
talists, their identities as men and firemen drew primarily from their actual struggle to contain fire. Firemen's sense of their manliness developed
along a continuum between the changing landscape and the work techniques that they pioneered to deal with the problem of fire. Moreover, as
they shifted their strategies, firemen often faced more intense hazards
and constructed new identities. For example, the danger of urban fire
changed after the Civil War, when cities grew taller and more densely
populated and structures were more robust though not less flammable.
Even so, the risks faced by firemen changed only when they became more
aggressive in confronting fires—when they penetrated deeper into burning buildings to extinguish fires. When firemen began, for the first time,
to value "getting to the seat of the fire," their work moved from the outside—pumping engines and directing hose streams—to the inside of
buildings. Riis describes the ethos that had developed in the NYFD by the
1890s: "New York firemen have a proud saying that they 'fight fire from
the inside.' It means unhesitating courage, prompt sacrifice, and victory
gained all in one." In point of fact, however, this strategy for battling
blazes had emerged in the occupation and made its way into urban fire
departments as early as the 1870s, when newly developed manuals emphasized the importance of fighting fire up close, urging firemen to take
action from a position "as near the fire as the heat and condition of the
building will permit." Company foremen were told to place "pipemen"
strategically, in such "position that water will strike directly upon burning materials." This aggressiveness engendered a host of new work techniques and tools, such as hooks, ladders, axes, and other equipment—
which, as they became routinely used, helped firefighters to distinguish
themselves from their predecessors.[12]

If such tools helped firefighters to organize their labor, they also allowed them to identify and to confront another natural enemy in their
struggle to contain fire. Smoke became almost a singular concern, even an
obsession, of firefighters. To confront this natural consequence of fire,
firemen adopted the strategy of ventilating buildings with axes, hooks,
and other deconstruction tools that removed smoke and heat from structures, thus allowing firefighters to enter buildings more deeply. Not only
did this method help them to locate and extinguish fires more quickly,
but it also made possible the rescue of innocents disoriented in the dense
smoke that accompanied blazes. Smoke itself became a defining aspect of
firefighters' culture, in some ways as profoundly as fire itself. As Jacob
Riis explains, "The fire is the enemy; but he can fight that, once he reaches
it with something of a chance. The smoke kills without giving him a show

to fight back. Long practice toughens him against it, until he learns the trick of 'eating the smoke.'" By the twentieth century, "eating smoke" had become a central marker of a firefighter's prowess as a fireman.[13]

As eating smoke and quashing blazes at close quarters entered the lexicon of firefighters, lifesaving activities, like those for which Rooney won the Bennett Medal, became especially valued. More important, firefighters institutionalized the tools and techniques connected to these new strategies into the organization and infrastructure of their departments. For instance, as early as 1874, NAFE urged fire departments to add more "truck companies," which brought equipment, such as hooks and ladders, as well as other tools and additional hoses to fires. Such companies became increasingly necessary as the physical environment was transformed; according to NAFE, "the constantly increasing height to which buildings are now carried requires a radical change in this respect, to bring the departments up to their former comparative standard of efficiency." The organization argued that all towns should have at least one truck company and that cities with populations greater than twenty-five thousand should have two such companies. It recommended that each truck carry eight ladders, eight short hooks, and axes as well as fire extinguishers.

In 1877, the publisher of the influential *Fireman's Journal* recommended organizing fire departments into "battalions" composed of two "truck" companies for every three "engine" companies. The proliferation of these new ladder skills paralleled the growing emphasis that firefighters placed on battling fire at close range, and both practices had been institutionalized in fire departments across the country by the twentieth century. For instance, in the St. Louis Fire Department, the ratio of engine companies to hook and ladder companies declined from 10 to 1 in 1870 to 5 to 1 in 1880 to almost 3 to 1 in 1900. In American urban centers with populations greater than thirty thousand—those cities most likely to have many tall or especially large buildings or both—the ratio of pumping apparatus to ladder apparatus had declined to nearly 2 to 1 by 1917. The shift was significant; the fact that ladders became standard equipment signified that firefighters had altered their practice in light of changing work environments as the nature of the fire danger shifted.[14]

Recasting firefighting organizations also entailed the transformation of the individual and collective bodies of firefighters. According to the National Association of Fire Engineers, firemen possessed a host of physical and mental attributes. These included the "inventive genius, tireless devotion, ceaseless watchfulness, unfailing wisdom, strength and endurance to show that we are able, in God's strength to meet every instrument of destruction with superior skill, alacrity and tact, until . . . fire shall no longer be a terror to mankind." As Jacob Riis describes, "Firemen are athletes as a matter of course. They have to be, or they could not hold

CARRYING A MAN DOWN THE "ROOF-LINE."

By the turn of the century, climbing skills and lifesaving procedures were a part of firefighter culture and were displayed on the pages of early occupational manuals. As experienced firefighters taught novices the ropes, they also instructed them in the lore and values of their calling, thus transforming raw recruits into firemen. (Illustration from Charles A. Hill, *Fighting a Fire*, 1898)

their places for a week, even if they could get into them at all. The mere
handling of the scaling ladders, which, light though they seem, weigh
from sixteen to forty pounds, requires unusual strength." The physical
prowess demanded of firefighters was evident on the pages of firefighting manuals and in the discussions of fire engineers as well as in the work
activities of firefighting itself. If not all firemen possessed them universally, firefighting required a host of physical characteristics including
dexterity, strength, technique, teamwork, and precision. The work of the
fire department, according to NAFE, demanded firemen with "the skill
necessary . . . to reach dizzy heights."

Perhaps the most significant innovation occurred in St. Louis in 1877,
when Christian Hoell developed the "pompier corps" following the city's
devastating Southern Hotel fire. Using scaling ladders, a special climbing
belt, climbing techniques, and rope, pompier corps could carry hoses to a
"commanding position" or save lives. The pompier corps captured the
imagination of firefighters and departments nationwide. NAFE promoted pompier techniques, and they flourished when Christian Hoell received several months' leave to train firefighters in cities across the nation
and to write a pamphlet on the technique. He even made his way to New
York City, at the request of the NYFD, shortly after the Old World blaze.
Importantly, Hoell's story—and that of so many firemen-inventors who
developed new work tools and strategies on the job—underscores the
connection between firefighters' mental acuity and physical skills. In fact,
the ability to implement new techniques and equipment "invented" by
firemen could not have occurred without the ability to master an array of
physical skills.[15]

A firefighter could have all the physical skills in the world, but according to his fellows and the popular press, firefighting depended upon
attributes of character. NAFE especially recognized the importance of
character as an intangible when it considered strategies to preserve "that
mental vigor, that intellectual keenness, without which man cannot vie to
deeds of bravery, without which he is unreliable." Whatever its particular components, whether "nerves of steel" and "coolness and courage,"
as Jacob Riis puts it, fighting fires was not an occupation for everyone. Between 5 and 10 percent of firefighters in New York washed out of the department during the initial service period, a number born out by
quantitative research on the careers of firemen in Philadelphia and St.
Louis. Firemen had to survive, physically and emotionally, those first few
brushes with fire (not to mention the culture of individual firehouses). As
Riis describes, "The first experience of a room full of smothering smoke,
with the fire roaring overhead, is generally sufficient to convince the
timid that the service is not for him. No cowards are dismissed from the
department, for the reason that none get into it." However they described

the character traits so critical to their profession, firefighters believed that
these attributes were vital to the betterment of men throughout the nation. Indeed, fire engineers fashioned themselves as "representative men
engaged in one of the grandest professions in the land." As sober and efficient firemen, as well as "good husbands" and "good fathers," fire engineers believe that they influenced the moral character of their fellow
urban residents better than "ten ministers."[16]

Although the rhetoric of firefighters sometimes suggested that attributes possessed by them were innate to some men and not to others,
firemen were made, not born. Indeed, the National Association of Fire
Engineers repeatedly emphasized training and drilling as a way to keep
firefighters' physical skills and character attributes honed to do battle
with fire. Training firemen kept them focused; it allowed fire department
leaders to answer NAFE's concerns about firefighters' technical and
physical competence: "Do we keep our men up to the line of progress
with the machinery?" By disciplining themselves, firefighters kept themselves ready to do battle. As Jacob Riis describes, "Against that possibility [of losing his head] the severe drill in the school of instruction is the
barrier." Extensive training regimens and the recommended use of mili-
tary-style drill were features of most training manuals, of discussions
among fire engineers, and of fire departments in the last three decades of
the nineteenth century. And by the 1910s, training schools began to appear in individual departments. Indeed, departments discovered that
lack of "thorough and systematic drill in the different branches of the fire
service" rendered advances in firefighting equipment useless. NAFE
noted that "when the extension ladders were first introduced, it was almost impossible to get men enough around a seventy-foot ladder to raise
it in any reasonable time and with safety."[17]

The link between the shifting urban environment and firemen's conception of the manliness so central to their story found its clearest expression in the heroic narratives about firefighters that began to appear
regularly in the 1870s and 1880s. To the degree that gender is constructed
in a relationship between male and female, narratives of firefighting
heroism underscored the point that firefighters were men. Firefighters
also seemed intuitively aware of the metaphorical dimensions of their
struggle to contain nature. In fact, they placed themselves at the center of
a grand drama. They moved their battle against fire from outside of
buildings to inside them, and they adopted strategies that stressed saving
lives rather than property. Indeed, when the environment went amok,
firemen not only preserved the urban industrial order but also prioritized
human life, especially for women and children. As Isaac Meserve recommended in his firefighting manual published at the behest of NAFE, "Always give precedence to women and children in rescuing lives."

Although in practice firefighters saved all sorts of people, in the popular press firemen saved women, children, and helpless men, often middling office workers trapped in tall buildings. With bodies and nerves of steel, they saved those who lacked such qualities. Firefighters' male identity became clearly delineated. Of equal importance, if such accounts underscored gender differences, they also emphasized firefighters' power over both women and nature. At the same time, firemen became cultural icons. The narrative and image of the fireman rushing from a burning building carrying a young child or a damsel in distress became the symbol of the occupation and the basis for firefighters' claims to professionalism. Firefighters had transformed their understanding of the environment and their manhood into a calling; they had become professional heroes.[18]

To understand the degree to which firemen constructed their manhood, one needs only to look at how they also conceived their occupation as the exclusive domain of white men. Indeed, as firefighters controlled nature, affirming their manliness, they also asserted their white racial superiority as the basis for their manhood. Firefighters' occupational culture drew upon the racial stereotyping common to late-nineteenth-century society and defined heroism as the exclusive domain of white men. One set of particularly demeaning caricatures of African Americans appeared in firefighting imagery during the 1880s. Currier and Ives, which had produced the heroic print series *The American Fireman* and *Life of a Fireman*, issued nearly 550 comics during the firm's seventy-five-year history. Approximately half of those prints belong to a subcategory known as the "Darktown Comics." One set, titled *The Darktown Fire Brigade*, derided the notion that African Americans could serve as effective firefighters and infantilized them as simpletons, incapable of skilled labor or coherent action. In particular, the prints depicted African Americans as bungling circus clowns incapable of using the tools—hooks and ladders—that were so crucial to urban firefighters' professional identity. The point could not have been lost on urban and rural audiences throughout the nation. Accustomed to epic narratives in which white male firefighters endangered life and limb to save trapped women and children, such prints argued that African Americans lacked the physical and mental dexterity to perform complex tasks routinely executed by pompier corps of heroic firemen.[19]

Ultimately, as they negotiated simultaneously the complexities of nature and gender, firemen constructed themselves as heroes. In the process, they set out the boundaries of their occupation, even claiming status as professionals in an effort to empower themselves as skilled workers, men, and public servants. If this epic struggle against the elements pitted men against nature—in its many forms—it centered on firefighters' knowledge of and conversations with dynamic urban landscape. As firemen trained

HARPER'S WEEKLY

A JOURNAL OF CIVILIZATION

VOL. XVII.—No. 841.] NEW YORK, SATURDAY, FEBRUARY 8, 1873.

In the 1870s, firefighters came to emphasize saving lives as a central organizing principle for their nascent occupation. Laboring in increasingly dangerous built landscapes, firefighters adopted work strategies that put them at greater risk. These new tools and techniques—including those necessary to perform rescues—were dramatized in the press, which captured firefighters into the popular imagination as heroes. (*Harper's Journal of Civilization*, February 8, 1873. Courtesy Hall of Flame, Phoenix, Arizona) and developed skills that would help them to fight fire in close quarters, they penetrated buildings to throw water directly on the base of a fire and manipulated the built environment to gain an advantage in their battles. Fire departments acquired new equipment, especially ladder trucks, and demanded that firemen practice physical dexterity, climbing, and ladder technique. In the process, firefighters discovered a new rationale for their service and reconstructed their occupation around matters of human safety. Although this revision involved advocating fire prevention, it was heroic rescues that captured the popular imagination. Saving the lives of people trapped in tall buildings, endangered by the changing urban landscape, became the raison d'être of firefighting labor. Firemen became icons, whose manhood reassured urban residents and brought order to chaotic American cities.

NOTES

I wish to thank Virginia Scharff and Nancy Jackson for their close reading and insights, which pushed me to think more critically about nature and gender.

1. *New York Times,* February 1 and 2, 1882.
2. Ibid. Paul Hashagen, *A Distant Fire: A History of FDNY Heroes* (Dover, N.H.: DMC Associates 1995), 32–38.
3. The classic history of fire, albeit set in rural America, is Stephen J. Pyne, *Fire in America: A Cultural History of Wildland and Rural Fire* (Princeton, N.J.: Princeton University Press, 1982); on fire in American life, see Margaret Hindle Hazen and Robert M. Hazen, *Keepers of the Flame: The Role of Fire in American Culture, 1775–1925* (Princeton, N.J.: Princeton University Press, 1992); on conflagration, see, for instance, Christine Meisner Rosen, *The Limits of Power: Great Fires and the Process of City Growth in America* (New York: Cambridge University Press, 1986), Carl Smith, *Urban Disorder and the Shape of Belief: The Great Chicago Fire, the Haymarket Bomb, and the Model Town of Pullman* (Chicago: University of Chicago Press, 1995), and David D. Dana, *The Fireman: The Fire Department of the United States* (Boston: E. O. Libby, 1858): 358–65; on Edison's films, see Andrea Stulman Dennett and Nina Warnke, "Disaster Spectacles at the Turn of the Century," *Film History* 4, no. 2 (1990): 101–11; for statistics on fire, I examined *Statistical Abstracts of the United States* (Washington, D.C.: Department of Commerce), 1879 through 1960.
4. This chapter is based on arguments contained in my forthcoming book, *Eating Smoke: Fire in Urban America, 1800–1950* (Baltimore, MD: Johns Hopkins University Press, 2003); on the history of firefighting, see Bruce Laurie, "Fire Companies and Gangs in Southwark," in *The Peoples of Philadelphia,* ed. Allen F. Davis and Mark Haller (Philadelphia: Temple University Press, 1973), 71–87, Amy Greenberg, *Cause For Alarm: The Volunteer Fire Department in the Nineteenth-Century City* (Princeton, N.J.: Princeton University Press, 1998), Paul Ditzel, *Fire Engines, Fire Fighters* (New York: Crown, 1976), Rebecca Zurier, *The American*

Firehouse: An Architectural and Social History (New York: Abbeville Press, 1982), Miriam Lee Kaprow, "Magical Work: Firefighters in New York," *Human Organization* 50, no. 1 (Spring 1991): 97–103, and Robert McCarl, *The District of Columbia Fire Fighters' Project: A Case Study in Occupational Folklife* (Washington, D.C.: Smithsonian Institution Press, 1985).

5. Jacob Riis, "Heroes Who Fight Fire," *Century Magazine* 55, no. 4 (February 1898): 483–97.

6. For a provocative and engaging analysis of the imagery of heroic firemen that places them in the context of the nineteenth-century "crisis of manhood" but not their nineteenth-century work environments, see Robyn Cooper, "The Fireman: Immaculate Manhood," *Journal of Popular Culture* 28, no. 4 (Spring 1995): 139–71.

7. The notion of boundaries for occupations comes from Andrew Abbott, *The System of Professions: An Essay on the Division of Expert Labor* (Chicago: University of Chicago Press, 1988); on occupation and profession in American history, see Burton J. Bledstein, *The Culture of Professionalism: The Middle Class and the Development of American Higher Education* (New York: W. W. Norton, 1978), Barbara Melosh, *"The Physician's Hand": Work Culture and Conflict in American Nursing* (Philadelphia: Temple University Press, 1982), and Susan Porter Benson, *Counter Cultures: Saleswomen, Managers, and Customers in American Department Stores, 1890–1940* (Urbana: University of Illinois Press, 1986).

8. Quotation from *Proceedings of the National Association of Fire Engineers (NAFE), 1884,* 19; on the history of the association and their first meeting, see Donald M. O'Brien, *"A Century of Progress through Service": The Centennial History of the International Association of Fire Chiefs* (International Association of Fire Chiefs, 1973); *First National Convention of Fire Engineers, 1873*; on the changing structure of cities, see for instance, *Proceedings of the NAFE, 1887,* 18–20, and *Proceedings of the NAFE, 1892,* 44ff.

9. Quotation from *Proceedings of the NAFE, 1887,* 20; for more on building construction and building laws, see *Proceedings of the NAFE, 1874,* 10–12, 16–17, 21–25, *Proceedings of the NAFE, 1875,* 32–33, *Proceedings of the NAFE, 1876,* 11–15, *Proceedings of the NAFE, 1880,* 38–56, *Proceedings of the NAFE, 1882,* 16–39, *Proceedings of the NAFE, 1883,* 15–19, 24–25, 27–28, 33ff, *Proceedings of the NAFE, 1887,* 20–26, 29–46, *Proceedings of the NAFE, 1889,* 35–50, 59–67, *Proceedings of the NAFE, 1892,* 44–56, and *Proceedings of the NAFE, 1894,* 82–91.

10. Firefighters "produced space"; that is, they created identity in direct relationship to the physical spaces in which they worked. For a discussion of the relationship between physical and mental space, see Henri Lefebvre, *The Production of Space* (Cambridge, Mass.: Blackwell, 1994; originally published in French, 1974, trans. Donald Nicholson-Smith). On the evolution of building code recommendations by NAFE, see, for instance, *Proceedings of the NAFE, 1874,* 10–13, *Proceedings of the NAFE, 1876,* 11–15, *Proceedings of the NAFE, 1877,* 10, *Proceedings of the NAFE, 1882,* 44, *Proceedings of the NAFE, 1884,* 18–32, and *Proceedings of the NAFE, 1891,* 26–27, 61–67, 150–151; on water systems, see, for example, *Proceedings of the NAFE, 1875,* 33–35, *Proceedings of the NAFE, 1877,* 14–19, *Proceedings of the NAFE, 1880,* 25ff, *Proceedings of the NAFE, 1882,* 46–47, 49–50, *Proceedings of the NAFE,*

1883, 33–35, 36ff, *Proceedings of the NAFE, 1894,* 148–149, *Proceedings of the NAFE, 1874,* 19–20, and *Proceedings of the NAFE, 1875,* 33–35; on so-called "Siamese" couplings, see *Proceedings of the NAFE, 1877,* 8–9, 20–26, and *Proceedings of the NAFE, 1889,* 35–58.

11. Quotation from *Proceedings of the NAFE, 1892,* 75. Firefighters often criticized underwriters; see, for instance, *Proceedings of the NAFE, 1883,* 13–19, *Proceedings of the NAFE, 1887,* 29–35, *Proceedings of the NAFE, 1892,* 35, 75–76, and *Proceedings of the NAFE, 1894,* 96–104; on the fire insurance industry and its priorities in this period, see Tebeau, *Eating Smoke,* especially chap. 5, *Proceedings of the NAFE, 1894,* 97–101, and Harry Chase Brearly, *Fifty Years a Civilizing Force: The History of the National Board of Fire Underwriters* (New York: Frederick Stokes, 1916), 79–80.

12. Quotations from Riis, "Heroes," 492; William C. Lewis, *A Manual for Volunteer and Paid Fire Organizations* (New York: Fred J. Miller, 1877), 11–12.

13. Riis, "Heroes," 490; on "ventilating" fires, see, for instance, *Proceedings of the NAFE, 1892,* 67–73, and Charles T. Hill, *Fighting a Fire* (New York: Century, 1898).

14. Quotation from *Proceedings of the NAFE, 1874,* 18–19; Lewis, *A Manual,* 8; for data on truck companies in the St. Louis Fire Department, see, for instance, St. Louis Firemen's Pension Fund, *"Justifiably Proud": The St. Louis Fire Department* (St. Louis, Mo.: Walsworth, 1978), 82–101; for national data on truck companies, see U.S. Department of Commerce, *Statistics of Fire Departments of Cities Having a Population over 30,000—1917* (Washington, D.C.: Government Printing Office, 1918), table 10.

15. Quotations from *Proceedings of the NAFE, 1880,* 14; Riis, "Heroes," 486; *Proceedings of the NAFE, 1884,* 111; on pompier techniques, including visuals, see Hill, *Fighting a Fire,* 36–62, *Proceedings of the NAFE, 1880,* 76, and *Proceedings of the NAFE, 1882,* 45; on Chris Hoell, see Tebeau, *Eating Smoke,* introduction, chap. 6, *Evening Chronicle,* August 10–12, 1877, *Fireman's Herald* 24 (November 24, 1892), "The Chicago Training School," *Fire and Water* 6 (1889): 62, 87, *Fire and Water* 18 (1895): 477, St. Louis Firemen's Fund, *History of the St. Louis Fire Department* (1914), 178, *Proceedings of the NAFE, 1887,* 65, *Proceedings of the NAFE, 1888,* 87, and Hashagen, *A Distant Fire,* 39–40.

16. Quotations from *Proceedings of the NAFE, 1880,* 12; Riis, "Heroes," 488; *Proceedings of the NAFE, 1885,* 17–18.

17. Quotations from *Proceedings of the NAFE, 1880,* 12; Riis, "Heroes," 486; *Proceedings of the NAFE, 1887,* 66; on drilling more broadly, see also the discussions of training schools and their evolution in *Proceedings of the NAFE, 1887,* 65–66, 78–79, *Proceedings of the NAFE, 1888,* 86–89, *Proceedings of the NAFE, 1920,* entire, especially 155–56, Lewis, *A Manual,* Andrew Isaac Meserve, *The Fireman's Hand-Book and Drill Manual* (Chicago: Stromberg, Allen, 1889), Hill, *Fighting a Fire,* John Kenlon, *Fires and Fire-Fighters* (New York: George H. Doran, 1913), New York Fire and Water Engineering Department, *The New York Fire College Course* (New York: Fire and Water Engineering Department, 1920), and Department of Commerce, *Statistics of Fire Departments,* table 10.

18. Quotation from Meserve, *The Fireman's Hand-Book,* 69; for further dis-

cussion of these images, and for side-by-side contrasts, see respectively Tebeau, *Eating Smoke,* chap. 6, and Cooper, "The Fireman," 139–71.

19. The discussion of Currier and Ives relies on Karin C. C. Dalton, "Currier and Ives's Darktown Comics: Ridicule and Race," presented at *Democratic Vistas: The Prints of Currier and Ives, A Symposium,* Museum of New York City, May 2, 1992; to compare the classic Currier and Ives firefighting prints with the "darktown" series, see, for instance, Louis Mauer, *The American Fireman: Prompt to the Rescue* (New York: Currier and Ives, Lithograph, 1858), and Thomas Worth, *The Darktown Fire Brigade—to the Rescue!* (New York: Currier and Ives, Lithograph, 1884); on whiteness, see David Roediger, *Wages of Whiteness: Race and the Making of the American Working Class* (New York: Verso Press, 1993).

CHAPTER FIVE

"New Men in Body and Soul": The Civilian Conservation Corps and the Transformation of Male Bodies and the Body Politic

Bryant Simon

Think about the shirtless men pictured here. They are symbols of the Civilian Conversation Corps, the New Deal program that provided unemployed young men with work out in the country. These fair-skinned, broad-shouldered men are tall, muscular, and powerful. Busy at work, they look out on a bright future. Clearly, these men are romantic figures. But of course they are not real. They are inventions, the projections of an ideal. What was this ideal? What do these men stand for? Why do they look like they do? What do these men and their bodies tell us about the politics of the people who invented them?

Before answering these questions, a little background is required on the Civilian Conservation Corps (CCC): The CCC was President Franklin D. Roosevelt's "pet project," his favorite New Deal program. Formed in the spring of 1933, following FDR's promise to the nation in his inaugural address of "action now," the "tree army" rapidly assembled. By the first day of summer, 250,000 largely unemployed, mostly white and unmarried young men between the ages of seventeen and twenty-five were working in CCC camps located far from urban centers. By the time Congress pulled the funding on the project nine years later, 2,670,000 men from big cities, small towns, and farm communities all over the country had completed stints, ranging from six months to a year, as "soil soldiers." During this period, the CCC left its mark on the nation's landscape. Enrollees installed 89,000 miles of telephone line, built 126,000 miles of roads and trails, constructed millions of erosion control dams,

From Bryant Simon, "'New Men in Body and Soul': The Civilian Conservation Corps and the Transformation of Male Bodies and the Body Politic," in *Gender and the Southern Body Politic*, edited by Nancy Bercaw (2000). Reprinted courtesy of the University Press of Mississippi.

"Spirit of CCC," circa 1934–1935. (Franklin D. Roosevelt Library,
Hyde Park, New York)

planted 1.3 billion trees, erected 3,470 water towers, and spent over 6 million hours fighting forest fires.[1]

Administered by the War Department, the Labor Department, the
Department of Interior, and the Department of Agriculture, the CCC
reached into virtually every corner of the nation.[2] Along the way, it won
the praises of politicians and editorial writers, bankers and steelworkers,

mothers and wives. Local leaders and state officials lauded the CCC for providing much-needed jobs for unemployed young men and putting money into the pockets of financially strapped consumers. Conservationists celebrated the New Deal agency's efforts to protect the environment. So popular was the CCC that even longtime South Carolina senator Ellison "Cotton Ed" Smith, who hated just about everything about the New Deal and who *Time* magazine once dubbed a "conscientious objector to the Twentieth Century," liked the program.[3]

Yet middle-class promoters of the New Deal agency talked about more than trees and the environment, relief and patronage, when they talked about the CCC. [4] Projecting their own fears of social division, radicalism, and emasculation onto the tree corps, they imagined the CCC as a way to restore the nation's flagging manhood and virility, which meant talking about the body. Few discussions about the CCC, in fact, did not include some mention (or picture) of manhood, masculinity, and the physical body. President Roosevelt himself declared that the agency's most valuable contribution to the nation was its work in turning boys into men.[5] The second of the CCC's two directors, James J. McEntee, wrote a book about the New Deal agency entitled *Now They Are Men*, in which he boasted that the CCC molded "idle boys" into "sturdy young men."[6] Referring to what he called the sociological side of the agency, an army colonel claimed, "It is our aim to send you men home as better citizens . . . men better physically, better mentally for having joined the CCC —men with clear eyes and renewed or new-born confidence in themselves; men with high morale and superb esprit . . . in fact, new men in body and soul."[7]

Focusing on the idea of turning boys into men and re-creating manhood "in body and soul," this chapter examines how the white, educated supporters of the tree corps envisioned, and in a sense sold, the CCC. This, then, is a story about middle-class men and their hopes and fears for the nation. Buried between the lines of their CCC sales pitches were clues to their anxieties about chaos, decadence, industrialization, and the cities. Displaying a surprising lack of self-consciousness, they also made plain their views about male bodies as public spaces.

Most New Dealers regarded healthy male bodies, particularly young male bodies, as symbolic of the nation's manhood, virility, and energy.[8] Physically weak men, they believed, weakened the nation. With this connection buried in their minds, reformers seized on the CCC as a way to "beef up" male bodies and strengthen the state. Examining the language and images used to promote the agency, therefore, lays bare many broadly held middle-class ideas about health and the physical body, reform and the body politic in the first half of the twentieth century.

CCC backers tailored the tree corps to fit their ideas about masculinity and male bodies. As a new bourgeois culture took shape in the nineteenth century, the physical body became less important to ideas about manhood than it had been in aristocratic Europe where men dueled to prove themselves.[9] Crafting its own aesthetic, the emerging middle class emphasized character and self-restraint as the essential characteristics of manhood. Civilized men, they insisted, controlled their impulses. This discipline over their own urges, in turn, gave them the right to dominate others. Yet as the nineteenth century gave way to the twentieth century and aggressive nationalism, social Darwinism, and imperialism gripped the public imagination, some middle-class Americans nervously started to talk about overcivilized. They feared that the "best" men, college men, educated men, had grown too cultured, too genteel, too soft, and too effeminate to lead. Seeking refinement and civilization, young men, some critics further charged, had drifted away from their competitive, brutish, physical natures.[10] Men, quite simply, had paid too much attention to their minds and allowed their bodies to go to waste. Many wondered how physically weak men—sissies, stuffed shirts, she-men, and molly-coddles, in the vernacular of the early twentieth century—could protect the nation?[11]

Looking to remake their soft arms and tired legs, in the early part of the twentieth century, middle-class men embarked on a loosely coordinated public fitness campaign. Holding up muscle man Charles Atlas as the model of masculinity, they emphasized appearance as well as good character as essential ingredients to manhood. A righteous man was a strong and muscular man. Trading in books for barbells and the classics for football, men dedicated themselves to toning their bodies ahead of their minds. By the end of World War I, the strong muscular man was celebrated in film and advertisements as the ideal man. Yet more than appearance mattered. Viewing the world as an organic whole, middle-class Americans considered outward beauty to be a clear sign of inner righteousness, not just self-indulgence. The discipline and dedication needed to sculpt the perfect body was, CCC backers seemed to believe, the same discipline and dedication needed to create the perfect citizen.

Teddy Roosevelt embodied the new vision of manhood and nation. Every schoolboy in America in the first decades of the twentieth century knew the Rough Rider's story. Raised by a doting mother in a wealthy, quite civilized household, well-read and well-mannered young Teddy epitomized "genteel culture." But physically, he was pale and skinny and grew up to be a "sickly, delicate" child who suffered from all kinds of ailments including asthma, nearsightedness, and just plain clumsiness. Riding on a train one day, he met a few not so well-read or -bred boys. Like only kids can do, they teased Teddy to the point of torturing him, but he was too weak to defend himself. The bitter taste of this humiliation pushed Roosevelt down his own personal road to Damascus. He started to go to Wood's Gymnasium every day. Soon the "frail child" filled out. Strong and muscular, he headed out West, rode across the badlands of South Dakota, beat up a few barroom toughs, and led the charge up San Juan hill. National glory, wide-open spaces, and powerful bodies were now forever linked.[12]

Not only did a nation need strong men like Teddy Roosevelt to prosper and defend itself, it also had to be unified. Middle-class Americans, however, sensed all kinds of troubling divisions swirling around them in the early twentieth century. They were particularly unsettled by immigrants, especially those who they thought of as living crammed into the ghettoes and slums of the nation's industrial cities. Middle-class people heard foreign accents and saw old-world fashions as disconcerting reminders of fractures in the body politic, of people who placed ethnic bonds ahead of national loyalty. In the packed and noisy immigrant enclaves of the cities, they feared that foreign men gathered at late-night meetings to read Marx, map out violent strikes, and plot revolution. And everywhere in these neighborhoods they saw darker skins and darker bodies. All these differences—the sounds, shapes, smells, and politics of the city—fueled middle-class anxieties about social divisions and the explosive potential of these divisions to tear the country apart. America, they believed, was white, Protestant, and English-speaking. Immigrants, at least European ones, could assimilate, but only by becoming like middle-class white people. That meant talking like them, acting like them, dressing like them, and looking like them. Until immigrants remade themselves, they stuck out to middle-class men as a pressing problem, as something that desperately needed attention.

The onslaught of the Great Depression heightened middle-class concerns. With jobs hard to find, they fretted that not-quite-white Poles would fight with not-quite-white Irish or that not-quite-white Italians might go after not-quite-white Jews. Worse yet, those communists, socialists, and militant trade unionists holding clandestine late-night meetings might find new recruits for their nefarious campaigns to destroy white middle-class society. (Strangely—or maybe not so strangely—reformers never said a word about Anglo uprisings.)

Still, not everyone worried about the immediate ruptures of revolution. Some feared that unemployed city kids spent too much time on street corners, "bumming around" or trying to "pick up girls," rather than attending 4-H or Boy Scout meetings, learning how to cooperate and work with others.[13] Fraternity man Russell A. Beam, for instance, voiced his apprehensions about the nation's future. He worried that the youth of America had become, in his words, "individualists," self-centered people who resisted "seeking to establish relationships with others." Alarmed about what he saw around him, Beam wondered whether a divided nation could rally to meet a military crisis, or any other crisis, for that matter.[14]

Beam and others envisioned the CCC as a way to heal the rifts in American society. Under capable leadership—supporters always made this distinction—they imagined the CCC as a citizenship training school teaching lessons of thrift, sobriety, discipline, and respect for private property to the wayward children of immigrants.[15] Once again, agency supporters never talked about Anglos. Apparently, middle-class reformers thought that these white people already knew, either by birth or training, what citizenship entailed. By bringing Poles, Slavs, Jews, Irish, and Italians together to work for a common cause, the camps, boosters promised, would erase troubling ethnic differences. Backers' racialized conceptions of the world also shaped the CCC. Only white and ethnic European manhood concerned camp officials; these were the only people they wanted to transform into new men "in body and soul." Despite clearly spelled out sanctions against discrimination in the organization's original charter, CCC camps, like other New Deal programs, remained, for the most part, segregated. African Americans found it harder to get into the CCC than whites did, and when they did gain entrance, administrators usually assigned them to inferior camps in out-of-the-way places. Obviously, agency officials were not worried about bolstering African-American manhood or healing the nation's racial divide. [16]

Despite these racial biases, supporters touted the CCC as a way to mold new American men—white men—dedicated to the nation ahead of neighborhood, region, or religious group. Colonel Alva J. Brasted, chief of chaplains of the U.S. Army, predicted that the CCC would "instill the right character" in enrollees. "Christ," he wrote, "mingled with the common people. He talked and ate and lived with them. The man of character fits into his environment in God's way, and both the military service and the C.C.C. provide the chance to affect right relationships with one's fellowman."[17] An agency veteran from Ohio claimed that the CCC broke down "strong and ardent sectionalism." "Poles, Slovaks, Italians, Hungarians," he added with enthusiasm, "all are discovering the broad basic brotherhood that welds us all together. They are finding a new pride in saying, 'We are *Americans!*'"[18] Yet another CCC veteran remembered, tying together sociability and manhood, that "it was a wonderful thing for us. . . . It taught us to get along with one another. It made men out of boys."[19]

One thing that men supposedly did—something that boys did not do—was fight wars, but not all men were born soldiers. The CCC, supporters pledged, could help in this area by teaching the nation's youth the virtues of national service. With copies of William James's "The Moral Equivalent of War" stuck in their breast pockets, CCC backers designed the tree corps as a kind nonmilitary military training school.[20] Stressing the lessons of cooperation, citizenship, and service, it would get young men ready for military battle. The CCC's capacity to shape boys into soldiers took on added significance after Hilter's forces pushed their way into Czechoslovakia and later invaded Poland. With war raging across Europe, CCC supporters increasingly described the organization in explicit military tones. One official bragged that it taught young men how to obey orders. An agency pamphlet, published in 1941 and subtitled *Contributing to the National Defense,* declared, "While helping conserve the natural resources of the Nation [CCC enrollees] have received instruction in military training—the thing most difficult to teach a recruit." As always, there was an emphasis on the physical body. Aware of middle-class notions about the body as well as their fears of disorder, Director James McEntee insisted in 1940 that "the Corps" has "toughened" recruits "physically, taught them work skills, improved their morale, and taught them love and respect for their country and government."[21]

With war looming and the economy in the doldrums, gritty and gray industrial cities with their swarms of dark-skinned, possibly radical immigrants stood out to the middle-class Protestant majority as the principal threat to the nation's ability to prepare for war and pave the way to prosperity. Mixed with their fears of ethnic strife and working-class disorder, CCC boosters worried about the insidious influence of urban space on the nation's young men. Along the teeming streets of New York, Philadelphia, and Chicago, young men, they thought, drifted into corruption and decadence. Just about every piece of CCC promotional literature featured a passage or two describing how the tree army snatched kids from the poolrooms and beer parlors of urban ghettoes, reformed them, and turned them into productive citizens and soldiers. Describing what the CCC did, the editors of the *Forestry News Digest* wrote, "Taking the men from city streets, poor food, insufficient clothing and unventilated and unsanitary living quarters and putting them out in the open, the fine pure air of the forest, feeding them plentifully, clothing them comfortably, housing them serviceably, in addition to exercising them with seven hours work a day is making new men physically of these boys."[22] Highlighting the same theme of redemption, Monogram Pictures produced a feature film in 1935 that told the story of "an incipient gangster in the CCC and his reform in this organization."[23]

Telling a similar story to mark the CCC's fiftieth anniversary, Joseph Toltin recalled that in 1936 he was unemployed. Without anything to do, he wasted his time wandering the streets of Cleveland. One afternoon he found a set of keys and used them to open a local grocery store that was closed. A policeman caught and arrested him. A judge gave him the choice of going to reform school for thirty days or joining the CCC for the standard enlistment of six months. Rescued from the streets, Toltin went to the CCC, reenlisted twice, and eventually earned a high school equivalency degree.[24]

Toltin's story was no doubt true, but it was also part of the myth of the agency.[25] Most CCC boys were not city kids like he was or "incipient gangsters" or, in the words of another observer, "sharp-faced products of big cit[y] slums."[26] More than half of all CCC enrollees, in fact, came from small towns and farms, and the organization's recruitment rules generally barred felons from serving in the tree camps. Still, the city and urban space served as meaningful tropes in the packaging of the CCC.[27]

Agency backers looked at the city through overlapping, and somewhat clouded, lenses. Like others, they marveled at the architectural, artistic, and industrial accomplishments showcased in the nation's urban areas. But people like President Roosevelt also thought that the nation was "overcommitted to urban living" and that city life served as a breeding ground for vice and corruption.[28] Deluged in schools and newspapers with a steady steam of urban criticism from Lincoln Steffens, Ida Turbell, Jacob Riis, Upton Sinclair, Theodore Dresier, Mark Sullivan, Stephen Crane, and Charles F. Russell, New Dealers saw the city as a diseased and decadent environment that poisoned and weakened young men.[29]

Environment, in fact, was a key concept for CCC officials. Like an earlier generation of reformers, New Dealers associated the urban poor with drink, filth, idleness, and radicalism. But Depression-era activists saw these vices as symptoms rather than causes of poverty. The poor were poor, in other words, not because they drank; they drank because they were poor. Barred from well-paying jobs and crammed into stuffy one-room tenements, the poor, the reformers further believed, inevitably would be degraded and seek escape in the cheap amusements offered by bars, poolrooms, street corners, and tacky music halls. Over time, the character of these urban denizens would only get worse. Men and women raised in the chaotic environment of city slums would eventually "degenerate" into nonproductive citizens, unworthy soldiers, and possibly even threats to the government. This theory of urban degeneracy undergirded New Dealers' ideas about the CCC.[30]

CCC supporters did not regard degeneracy as a metaphor; they meant it as something that quite literally happened. For them, overexposure to the city was a kind of disease that infected the body. Sophisticated diagnostic equipment was not needed to identify the illness. The proof was in the body. City kids—the hapless by-products of "urban degeneracy"—were pale, thin, and soft. They had rotten teeth and narrow chests.

All of these things were important clues to CCC officials who generally considered physical appearance to be a direct reflection of moral character.[31] The outwardly ugly were inwardly dangerous. They were sly, untrustworthy men who in the politically charged world of the reformers jeopardized the health of the state.[32]

Molding new citizens, therefore, meant inoculating young men against the degenerative diseases of the cities. Like most Americans educated in the Teddy Roosevelt school of morality, CCC officials believed that life "lived in close communion with beneficent nature" possessed "a wholesomeness and integrity impossible for the depraved populations of the cities."[33] Not surprisingly, their view of nature, wilderness, and the outdoors was also gendered. CCC backers imagined these places as wholesome, pure sources of male "virility and toughness." With these ideas in mind, agency leaders deliberately located the tree camps far from urban slums. They wanted to get vulnerable, impressionable young men off beguiling city streets. Let them breathe clean, fresh air. Let them work outside with their hands digging dirt and planting trees.[34] And let them sleep under the stars. The combination of fresh air and exhausting labor, CCC officials boldly predicted, would eradicate the infection of the city. Six months in the wilderness would, New Deal leaders also thought, strengthen teenaged city boys, flush the tenements out of their systems, and transform them from scrawny, unattractive revolutionaries and criminals into proud, dutiful men.[35]

More than just the pernicious effects of urban space frightened CCC supporters. They also worried about the volatile mixture of urban slums and unemployment. Again, when New Dealers thought of unemployment, they also thought about manhood and male bodies. They feared that joblessness not only sapped the strength of the economy and eroded purchasing power but also devastated young men for years to come, maybe even forever. Most American men in the 1930s linked work to masculinity. Quite simply, self-respecting men worked. When they didn't work, they were not men, but lazy and slothful social parasites. Urging Congress to fund the CCC in 1933, President Roosevelt warned of the "threat of enforced idleness to spiritual and moral stability." Several years later, CCC Director McEntee labeled youth unemployment "human erosion."[36]

Without work or the hope of ever getting a job, young men, Roosevelt, McEntee, and others believed, lost their self-respect and sense of manhood. Some young men, they feared, had in 1933 already been unemployed so long that they forgot what constituted an honest day's work. Many had become angry and sullen. They spent too much time hanging out on street corners, robbing and stealing, or aimlessly riding the rails. Lacking the manly self-respect that came with having a job, the

"The Cottonwood Anniversary CCC." (Franklin D. Roosevelt Library, Hyde Park, New York)

unemployed represented raw recruits for mischievous revolutionaries. Unless something was done, and done quickly, CCC backers warned, unemployed city kids would become "hostile to the economic and social system" and, more ominous still, "the type of sansculottes who are the first gust of the revolutionary storm."[37]

Arriving in the nick of time, the CCC promised to quell the threat of revolution by giving the jobless work, and not just any kind of work but work outside in the wholesome, pure wilderness. "The greatest achievement of the CCC," crowed one camp administrator, "has not been the preservation of material things such as forests, timber-lands, etc., but the preservation of American ManHood [sic]."[38] Still preserving "American ManHood," CCC supporters argued, required not just jobs and fresh country air but also rebuilding male bodies.

CCC backers repeatedly described the bodies of enrollees before they entered the camps. Chaos, urban decadence, and chronic unemployment, they suggested, attacked male bodies like some out-of-control contagion, leaving muscles "soft and untrained."[39] Chroniclers of camp life started their stories with descriptions of wiry, hollow-chested, and ragged young men standing in line on the first day of service waiting for fatigues. They looked to one commentator like "the threat of tuberculosis hover[ed] over them." Again appearance mattered to middle-class men; it was a clear window into character. These sickly boys hardly looked like real men.[40] Unmanly men troubled CCC leaders. They glanced at small, thin men with rotting teeth and saw potential threats to the state.[41] In order to eliminate the specter of rebellion, of sanscoulettes swarming through the streets of Washington D.C., government officials developed a wide range of programs to transform—deradicalize and tame—young men by transforming their bodies.

"Very few physically weak men," the skipper from a Pulaski, New York, CCC camp asserted, "ever succeed." "It takes a healthy body," he continued, "a clear eye, a strong constitution to stand the strain of managing a big business or runing [sic] a state or nation."[42] With the goal of sculpting young male bodies into the shapes of corporate managers, tough-minded soldiers, and future politicians, CCC administrators initially sent new recruits to conditioning camps for two weeks of hiking and calisthenics.[43] From there, the boys were transferred to rural forest camps where they performed taxing manual labor outdoors for eight hours a day. Thinking of Teddy Roosevelt, CCC leaders wanted the warm sun to bronze the pale skin of Bowery boys, making them look and feel healthier and more handsome. Proud of their new bodies, according to one rather eroticized report, after a few weeks, soil soldiers "bared their backs to the sun and worked without shirts."[44]

Thinking again of Teddy Roosevelt, CCC leaders made the "strenuous life" a central part of the camp routine. National administrators ordered local officials to set up daily exercise programs. Each morning, CCC enrollees spent ten to thirty minutes, usually outside, stretching, running, and doing jumping jacks and push-ups. Even leisure in the camps was organized around the body and the open air. CCC outfits included a wide range of extracurricular sports and gymnastics programs. Camp leaders encouraged—some even insisted on—broad participation in athletic competitions, especially team sports.[45] Sports, CCC officials believed, would help to mold strong, muscular, virile young men. Camp administrations pushed the enrollees into sports not just to build up their arms and legs, but also because they were convinced that baseball and football fostered "certain militaristic tendencies" needed to succeed in business and war.[46]

Education was another feature of camp life. Enrollees took classes in American history, civics, grammar, letter writing, etiquette, auto mechanics, aviation, map making, and fish culture.[47] CCC schools also included detailed lessons in personal hygiene. Experts came in each week to lecture on the correct ways to cut fingernails, bathe, and brush teeth. "Look around you," one health official instructed campers, "and note the fellow who is neat, hair combed, and whose clothes are clean, and well kept, and there you will find the fellow who has personal pride."[48]

Finally, CCC outposts fed enrollees "three square meals a day." Calculating how best to fatten up city kids, officials prescribed a daily diet of 4,000 to 4,500 calories—almost twice the daily recommended diet of today. One CCC veteran remembered that camp leaders punished enrollees who left any food, even a bite, on their plates.[49] Food also played a part in the CCC's military preparedness campaign. When New Dealers set up the tree corps, they were, no doubt, thinking of the undernourished bodies of World War I recruits. If another war broke out, CCC leaders vowed to do their part, serving endless meals of meatloaf, mash potatoes, and gravy, to make sure that the nation's young men were physically fit and sturdy enough to fight.

With so much of the program geared toward changing male bodies, CCC supporters measured the success of the agency quite literally by the pound. From California to Florida, camp leaders wrote to the CCC national newspaper, *Happy Days,* boasting about their outfits. They bragged about forest recovery, firefighting missions, and tree planting campaigns, but mostly they talked about weight gain. Virtually every CCC story included a description of how men filled out in the camps. A California CCC leader, Captain R. R. Haley, gushed in the fall of 1933 that "Co. 857 has gained a ton since enrolling." He continued: "A total of 177 men jumped in aggregate weight in three months from 25,156 pounds to 26,777 pounds."

Carl Abbot of Choctaw, Oklahoma, was perhaps the camp's greatest success story. Arriving weighing only 125 pounds, he put on 20 pounds in three short months. Bravo, cheered Captain Haley. New England men, another source enthusiastically reported, gained on average 7½ pounds during their tours of duty with the CCC. Yet another camp leader recounted that enrollees put on "at least five pounds." "The increases," he argued, "are attributable, partly, to the variety of health-building goods in the mess and the benefits of clear sunshine and invigorating air."[50] Feeling the pressure to get bigger and worried that he was not gaining enough weight fast enough, one nervous soil soldier wrote his girl friend, "I hope I'm not too thin for you."[51] In a poem entitled "Seconds," a camper lamely rhymed about the virtues of gaining weight:

> O mother dear did you, hear
>   The news that's going 'round
> Another mess-kit's empty
>   And I've gained another pound
>
> They give me all the toughest jobs
>   They work me soon and late,
> I've worn out twenty brush hooks
>   I've hiked through half the state.
>
> I've blistered in the burning sun
>   In rainstorms I've been drowned,
> But when I smelled the cook-tent
>   I gain another pound.
>
> My pants that went twice 'round my waist
>   And met me coming back,
> Are now so tight that when I bend
>   I wait to hear them crack.[52]

Like the poet, national leaders also pointed to bigger bodies as evidence of the New Deal's success. Each year the director of the CCC in his annual report mentioned how much weight the men had gained over the past twelve months.[53] Speaking before a congressional committee deliberating over whether or not to make the CCC a permanent government agency, the original director, Robert Fechner, bragged, "First of all, it gives them good personal habits, and through proper food . . . makes them into fine physical specimens."[54] In his 1959 New Deal tribute, historian Arthur Schlesinger Jr. concluded his glowing appraisal of the CCC quoting an enrollee, who beamed, "I weighed about 160 pounds when I went there, and when I left I was 190 about. It made a man of me all right."[55]

CCC supporters presented more than statistics about weight gain to trumpet the organization's contributions to America. They developed, probably out of necessity, a whole iconography to celebrate the agency. By the 1930s, seeing was believing in America. Statistics were one thing, but to get people to embrace change, to know it was real and recognize its impact, they had to see it. Tuned into this visual culture, CCC officials created a narrative of still frames to tout the organization's accomplishments.[56] Remarkably, these images rarely depicted long rows of new trees or shiny water towers or cleverly conceived dams. Instead, they were almost always portraits of male bodies, and they told a melodramatic before-and-after story.

Usually the drama opened with a picture of a city kid whose body has been devastated by urban vice. Gray and grizzled, the figure is sometimes slumped over, other times leaning up against a streetlight smoking a cigarette. His eyes are downcast. Dressed in a dark, heavy coat, his body is entirely covered, as if he is afraid or embarrassed to reveal his frail frame and pale skin. Flash to the next scene. After six months of three square meals a day, jumping jacks, football games, and hard work in the fresh country air, a new man takes shape. Looking a lot like Charles Atlas, the hero of the CCC stands erect. Stripped to the waist, he confidently looks out on the future. He is tall and muscular. His broad, contoured shoulders narrow down from his smooth, hairless, powerful chest to a thin waist. He has a chiseled face, perfect teeth, and a strong prominent square jaw. Even swinging an ax in the hot summer sun, the CCC man is unmistakably neat and clean.

For his time and place, the CCC man was the flawless man, a perfect representation of the middle-class ideal of masculinity. "A century ago," the historian T. J. Jackson Lears wrote in 1981, "the stout midriff was a sign of mature success in life." Yet by the 1930s, society no longer celebrated portly models of conspicuous wealth and gaudy excess. Nor did it praise the cultured and civilized man who neglected his body. By the New Deal era, the ideal male was defined by his physicality. He was younger, not older; his body was powerful and strong, yet still lean and sinewy.[57]

To middle-class promoters of the CCC, the appearance and form of this body, its positioning, stance, and posture, resolved all the tensions that they detected around them. Viewing the world as they did as an organic whole, the outward beauty of the male figure conveyed his inner righteousness. The determination needed to sculpt the perfect body was, CCC backers believed, the same determination needed to create the perfect citizen-soldier. By the 1930s, the image of man, including the CCC man, took on its perhaps inevitable military dimensions. Given what reformers thought about healthy bodies and a healthy society, they instructed men to hone their bodies not simply to put themselves on display but also for the higher calling of flag and country. Committed to sacrifice and heroism, the perfect man put the soldierly values of the nation ahead of his individual or group desires.

At the same time, this well-toned, muscular young man was clearly not overcivilized or incapable of manly action. His bulky arms, solid legs, and barrel-shaped chest paid tribute to the harmony between body and soul but also to the masculine capacity for brutality. The CCC man's taut body suggested his potential as a warrior and soldier capable of well-channeled fury.

The CCC pictures and posters also celebrated manly labor.[58] Framed clutching an ax or shovel, the shirtless man was always busy at work. This active image addressed yet another middle-class fear. Depression-era narratives are filled with stories, told from a patriarchal perspective, of men who lost their land or job. Displaced as the breadwinner, these beaten men idly stand by as women take over households and turn traditional gender roles upside down.[59] If the private world of the home was in turmoil, then middle-class Americans were certain that the public world of the state would be in trouble. The mythical CCC man, however, was virile, powerful, and in control. Clearly, he had put a stop to "human erosion," fought off the degenerative diseases of the city and unemployment, and learned the value of labor. And just as clearly, he was not emasculated by the devastating economic forces of the depression. To the contrary, the pictures show a handsome, brawny man simultaneously subduing and coexisting with nature.

Of course, there are empty spaces and gaps in the pictures. Most striking, women are nowhere to be seen in the visual narratives. In part, these images reflect the fact that women were generally blocked from participating in the CCC.[60] Yet their absence also figuratively suggests that the tree soldiers—perhaps all men—could be independent from women and still be a complete man. In this male homo-social setting, men live in a world where women cannot control them, humiliate them, or disgrace them. It is a fantasy world where men apparently do not need women.[61]

Again by saying nothing, CCC imagery also dealt with middle-class fears of the debilitating effects of unemployment and industrialization on male bodies. In other settings, middle-class commentators blamed the nation's growing dependence on machines for making men weak. A cartoon, for instance, in University of Chicago sociologist William F. Ogburn's influential 1935 book *You and Machines* pictures a man propping himself up with what are labeled "machine age crutches." He needs the support because, writes Ogburn, "[his] LEGS ATROPHIED BY MACHINE AGE!"[62] Convinced, just as the skipper from Pulaski was, that feeble men rarely prosper, CCC supporters once again looked to the redemptive powers of nature and work.

Cool, fresh air without a factory chimney in sight would cure young men of the ruinous effects of dependence on machines. Getting boys out of crowded cities and away from assembly lines and into the woods would, moreover, build up their arms and legs. Strong men would, in turn, strengthen the nation. Each CCC picture portrays a mighty young man working outside in the fresh air. Far from the factories and the constant supervision of management, he is working at his own pace, to his own rhythm. Like the strong men depicted in other forms of New Deal public art, the figure of the manly CCC worker embodied, in historian Barbara Melosh's words, "the nostalgia for an imagined past of individual dignity lost in the world of rationalized work and impersonal bureaucracy."[63]

While honoring manly individualism, the CCC images simultaneously held up the ideal of a single, collective national identity.[64] When pictured together, the "soil soldiers" are harmoniously working toward a common goal. Neither their bodies nor their faces reveal a hint of uneasiness, friction, or division. That's because all of the bodies look exactly alike. Conveying a unified vision of American masculinity, the CCC pictures visually attempt to wipe away ethnic, regional, racial, and class divisions. They venerate a single Anglo ideal. Because all the images are virtually the same, they further suggest a consensus—maybe a forced consensus—on the masculine ideal, one that visually resolves the ethnic and class conflicts that so deeply disturbed middle-class white Americans in the 1930s. The pictures reassured these jittery men that American manhood had been saved, America had been saved.

Obviously, the male bodies displayed by the CCC in the 1930s bear a striking resemblance to the male bodies displayed in Nazi Germany, Stalinist Russia, and other industrial nations at the same time. Noting the similarity among these images is not to say, however, that the New Deal was a quasi-fascist or proto-Stalinist movement. Rather, they suggest that all these societies celebrated the same image of man—muscular, tanned, shirtless, strong-jawed. Yet each grafted its own social and political ideals onto this strikingly similar man. The image, to put it another way, was the same, but the politics were quite different.

Still, there is one conspicuous similarity between the linkage of politics and masculinity in the United States, Germany, the Soviet Union, and other European nations in the 1930s. Blurring, perhaps even obliterating, the lines between the public and the private, politicians in all of these countries, to quote George L. Mosse, "idealized masculinity as the foundation of the nation and society."[65] What's more, in each of these nations, masculinity was thought to be conveyed through the body. Healthy men were the foundation of a strong state. With these crucial concepts in mind, policymakers saw male bodies quite naturally, that is without really thinking about it, as legitimate, indeed vital, sites of state action.[66]

Bodies were, in other words, public property, and as such, they fell under the realm of the state. In fact, in a largely unexamined aspect of twentieth-century reform, social engineers repeatedly contended that maintaining social order required not only tinkering with the economy or

"Activities Build Men," circa 1934–1935. (Franklin D. Roosevelt Library, Hyde Park, New York)

bolstering patriarchy or introducing welfare reforms but also remaking male bodies. Only by transforming the shape and size of men, they trusted, could they create stability, and this was the fundamental goal of all state actors everywhere in the first half of the twentieth century. State actors also wanted to make sure that the nation was prepared to fight. Healthy bodies, like those featured on posters in the United States, Germany, and the Soviet Union in the 1930s, stood for the strength and determination that a nation needed to wage war. And war was on the minds of everyone in those tense years.

The image of the CCC man, however, is not just a vision from the past. He still lives. Just look at a Calvin Klein advertisement or an episode of Beverly Hills 90210. There is the CCC man, the hero of the tree camps. He is still shirtless and in jeans, strong and muscular, clean-cut and square-jawed. He is still here, but there are key differences between the image of man in the 1930s and today. Gone are the ax and shovel, the sweat and the earth. The new model man in magazines and on television is not working nor is he looking out to a promising future. Rather, he is staring at you with a wry smile, daring you, calling on you, begging you to gaze back at him. No longer the property of the state, he is the product of Madison Avenue and he sells himself as a private fantasy rather than the public icon of a healthy nation. That's what makes the new shirtless man so different from the older shirtless man. Now he is stands in the service of consumption, not politics.

NOTES

1. For overviews of the CCC, see "The Civilian Conservation Corps," *American Conservation,* 2, printed materials, CCC Vertical File, Franklin D. Roosevelt Library, Hyde Park, N.Y. (herein cited as FDRL); T. H. Watkins, *The Great Depression: America in the 1930s* (Boston: Little, Brown, 1993), 131; and Robert S. McElvaine, *The Great Depression: America, 1929–1941* (New York: Times Books, 1984), 154–55.

2. For a succinct explanation of the structure of the CCC and the roles of various agencies in its administration, see Watkins, *The Great Depression,* 130.

3. *Time,* August 7, 1944, 18. On the CCC, see Anthony J. Badger, *The New Deal: The Depression Years, 1933–1940* (New York: Hill and Wang, 1989), 174.

4. For the standard institutional account of the CCC, see John A. Salmond, *The Civilian Conservation Corps, 1933–1942: A New Deal Case Study* (Durham, N.C.: Duke University Press, 1967).

5. "Message from the President of the United States to the Members of the Civilian Conservation Corps Read over the National Broadcasting Company Red Network," April 17, 1936, Official File 268, Folder—March–June 1937, FDRL.

6. James J. McEntee, *Now They Are Men: The Story of the CCC* (Washington, D.C.: Government Printing Office, 1940), 58.

7. *Happy Days,* August 19, 1933.

8. For more about masculinity and the body in the larger context, see George L. Mosse, *Fallen Soldiers: Reshaping the Memory of the World Wars* (New York: Oxford University Press, 1990), esp. 73.

9. For an examination of changing European conceptions of manhood, see Robert A. Nye, *Masculinity and Male Codes of Honor in Modern France* (New York: Oxford University Press, 1993).

10. On the fears of overcivilization and changing conceptions of manhood,

see E. Anthony Rotundo, *American Manhood: Transformations in Masculinity from the Revolution to the Modern Era* (New York: Basic Books, 1993); Gail Bederman, *Manliness and Civilization: A Cultural History of Gender and Race in the United States, 1880–1917* (Chicago: University of Chicago Press, 1995), 10–15; and George Chauncey, *Gay New York: Gender, Urban Culture, and the Making of the Gay Male World, 1890–1940* (New York: Basic Books, 1994), 111–22.

11. Chauncey, *Gay New York,* 111–14.

12. On TR's transformation, see Theodore Roosevelt, *Theodore Roosevelt: An Autobiography* (New York: Charles Scribner's Sons, 1913). See also, Richard Slotkin, "Nostalgia and Progress: Theodore Roosevelt's Myth of the Frontier," *American Quarterly* 33 (Winter 1981): 608–37; Arnaldo Testi, "The Gender of Reform Politics: Theodore Roosevelt and the Culture of Masculinity," *Journal of American History* 81 (March 1995): 1515–18; Bederman, *Manliness and Civilization,* 170–215; Chauncey, *Gay New York,* 113–14; and J. Anthony Lukas, *Big Trouble* (New York: Simon and Schuster, 1997), 386.

13. See Kenneth Holland and Frank Ernest Hill, *Youth in the CCC* (Washington, D.C.: American Council on Education, 1942), 205.

14. Russell A. Beam, "Counseling for Adjustment and Rehabilitation," *Phi Delta Kappa* 19 (May 1937): 338, Folder—Education in CCC, printed materials, CCC Vertical File, FDRL.

15. Quite explicitly, CCC educational programs attempted to teach students "character and citizenship training" (Holland and Hill, *Youth in the CCC,* 158). For the most insightful account of the CCC as a citizenship training ground, see Eric B. Gorham, *National Service, Citizenship, and Political Education* (Albany: State University of New York Press, 1992), 130–40.

16. Salmond, *The Civilian Conservation Corps,* 88–101, and Harvard Sitkoff, *A New Deal for Blacks: The Emergence of Civil Rights as a National Issue—The Depression Decade* (New York: Oxford University Press, 1978), 74–75.

17. Col. Alva J. Brasted, chief of chaplains, U.S. Army, *Character Building Agencies* (Fort Leavenworth, Kans.: Command and General Staff Press, 1936), Folder—General CCC Pamphlet, Re—Introduction, FDRL.

18. James W. Danner to FDR, September 21, 1936, PPF File, FDRL (Robby Cohen pointed out this source to me).

19. Michael Kernan, "Back to the Land: CCC Alumni Reunite on Skyline Drive," *Washington Post,* April 6, 1988, Folder—Virginia, CCC Vertical File, FDRL.

20. On the importance of James's essay to the conception of the CCC, see Leslie Alexander Lacy, *The Soil Soldiers: The Civilian Conservation Corps in the Great Depression* (Radnor, Pa.: Chilton, 1976), 17–18. In fact, one CCC camp was named after James; see Jack J. Preiss, *Camp William James* (Norwich, Vt.: Argo Books, 1978).

21. In order, these references to the CCC and war come from Robert Fechner's testimony before the U.S. Congress, House Committee on Labor, *To Make the Civilian Conservation Corps a Permanent Agency,* February 9, 23, 24, 1939, 9; *Civilian Conservation Corps: Contributing to the National Defense* (1941), pamphlets, Eleanor Roosevelt Papers, Folder—U.S. Civilian Conservation Corps, FDRL; and James McEntee, *The CCC and National Defense* (1940), Folder—American Forestry Association Publications, CCC Vertical File, printed materials, FDRL. See also the chapter entitled "Workers for Defense" in Holland and Hill, *Youth in the CCC,* 182–89.

22. The *Forestry News Digest* (this journal was published by the American Tree Association; this particular issue was labeled a "Special CCC Edition"), July 1933, Folder—American Forestry Association Publications, Vertical Files, FDRL. See also Helen Mabel Walker, *The CCC through the Eyes of 272 Boys: A Summary of the Reactions of 272 Cleveland Boys to Their Experience in the Civilian Conservation Corps* (Cleveland: Western Reserve University Press, 1938), 12, 22–23, 27–28, and *Happy Days*, August 12, 1933.

23. Guy D. McKinney to William Hassett, June 4, 1937, Official File 268, Folder—March–June 1937, FDRL.

24. David Schwab, "CCC Alumni Recall the Hard Times and FDR's Fast, 'Creative' Response," *Sunday Star-Ledger*, April 24, 1983, Folder—CCC 50th Anniversary, printed materials, CCC Vertical File, FDRL.

25. According to one survey done in 1937, only 16 percent of CCC recruits were from "large" cities; see Holland and Hill, *Youth in the CCC*, 83. One CCC enrollee addressed this issue in 1935. In an open letter, he wrote: "What about rescinding some of those press notices about the CCC boys ALL being anemic, undernourished bums before they came into the C.C.C. [*sic*] I've never been a bum and I've never been undernourished, but I did need a job—and thanks to FDR I got one and I'm proud of it" (Boys of Company 1699 CCC, Richland Center, WI to FDR, May 25, 1934; attached is the *Weekly Journal* 1 [May 25, 1934], Official File 268, Civilian Conservation Corps, Box 11, Folder—CCC Periodicals, 1933, FDRL). Again, the reality of the situation often contradicted the CCC's self-generated mythology. To cite another example, recruits were usually portrayed as poor, uneducated urbanites rescued from the vices of the city, but according to one survey, more than half of the enrollees in fact came from families that owned their own homes and most had completed the tenth grade; Walker, *The CCC through the Eyes of 272 Boys*, 13, 16.

26. James W. Danner to FDR, September 21, 1936, PPF File, FDRL.

27. Scholars have repeated, almost verbatim, this view of the city and the country in their own accounts of the CCC. For instance, in his recent book on the 1930s, T. H. Watkins writes, "The CCC at its best took some young men out of the urban tangle of hopelessness . . . [and] . . . introduced them to the intricacies and healing joy of the outdoors" (*The Great Depression*, 131).

28. For FDR's view of the city, see Arthur Schlesinger Jr., *The Age of Roosevelt: The Coming of the New Deal* (Boston: Houghton Mifflin, 1988), 319–20, and Lacy, *The Soil Soldiers*, 18.

29. Teddy Roosevelt, for example, was influenced by this stream of urban literature. What's more, he obviously influenced Franklin Roosevelt's thinking. On TR, see George Mowry, *The Era of Theodore Roosevelt and the Birth of Modern America, 1900–1912* (New York: Harper, 1958), 60–61, 65.

30. On the idea of "urban degeneracy," see Gareth Stedman Jones, *Outcast London: A Study in the Relationship between Classes in Victorian Society* (Oxford, Eng.: Clarendon Press, 1971), 127–30, 285–87. See also Max Nordau, *Degeneration* (1892; reprint, Lincoln: University of Nebraska Press, 1968. On similar ideas about the sources and impact of poverty in the United States, see William F. Ogburn, *You and Machines* (Washington, D.C.: National Capital Press, 1934), 33. Historians have looked at this connection; see Robert Bremner, *From the Depths: The Discovery of*

Poverty in the United States (New York: New York University Press, 1956, 1992). See, finally, from the CCC William L. Talbott, "The New Challenge: Twentieth Century Pioneers," *The Builder* (November 1934), Official File 268, Box 12, Folder—CCC Periodicals, 1935, FDRL.

31. See, for example, Beam, "Counseling for Adjustment and Rehabilitation."

32. For a broader discussion of this organic conception of the world, which linked physical appearance with the intellectual and emotional health, see George L. Mosse, *The Image of Man: The Creation of Modern Masculinity* (New York: Oxford University Press, 1996).

33. Richard Hofstadter made this observation about nature in *Age of Reform: From Bryan to F.D.R.* (New York: Knopf, 1955). He is quoted by Salmond, *The Civilian Conservation Corps*, 104.

34. Some people, like Georgia congressman Robert Ramspeak, assumed that the deleterious effects of the city and the redemptive aspects of nature were obvious—so obvious that they required no explanation; see his comments in House Committee on Labor, *To Make the Civilian Conservation Corps a Permanent Agency*, 34–35.

35. Roderick Nash, *Wilderness and the American Mind* (New Haven, Conn.: Yale University Press, 1967), 145, 153. For more on ideas about nature, see Simon Schama, *Landscape and Memory* (New York: Knopf, 1995). See a discussion of Jacob Riis's views of the world in David Leviatin's introduction to Riis, *How the Other Half Lives: Studies among the Tenements of New York* (Boston: Bedford Books, 1996), 20–21. The editorial "City Men Win," talks about how urban boys are transformed in the camps; *Happy Days*, September 30, 1933. See also the comments by a CCC enrollee in Lacy, *Soil Soldiers*, 126. For more on the purifying view of nature in the CCC, see Salmond, *The Civilian Conservation Corps*, 108.

36. McEntee, *Now They Are Men*, 10, 58. For more on Roosevelt's view, see Donald Day, *Franklin D. Roosevelt's Own Story* (Boston: Little, Brown, 1951), 166.

37. Lacy, *Soil Soldiers*, 20, and James Lasswell, "Shovels and Guns: The CCC in Action," (1935), in Folder—CCC Pamphlets, printed materials, CCC Vertical File, FDRL.

38. Talbott, "The New Challenge: Twentieth Century Pioneers."

39. Enrollees of Company 1261, T.V.A. Camp 20, Clouds, Tennessee, "The Program of the C. C. C. in the United States," *The Cloud Gazer* (June 23, 1934): 2, Official File 268, Box 11, Folder 1933, FDRL; Captain Francis V. Fitzgerald, "The President Prescribes," *The Quartermaster Review* (July–August 1933): 10, printed materials, CCC Vertical File, FDRL. See also *Happy Days*, September 16, 1933.

40. Enrollees of Company 1261, "The Program of the C. C. C. in the United States"; *Happy Days*, August 5, 1933.

41. Similarly, homosexual men, who of course many people believed could be identified just by looking at them, were also typically characterized as a threat to the state; Chauncey, *Gay New York*, 8–9.

42. "The Skipper Says," *The Weekly Blabber* (January 11, 1935): 3, Official File 268, Box 12, Folder—CCC Periodicals, 1935, FDRL.

43. On the conditioning camps, see Jack Irby Hayes Jr., "South Carolina and the New Deal, 1932–1938" (Ph.D. diss., University of South Carolina, 1972), 265.

44. Hoyt, *We Can Take It*, 57.

45. See *Happy Days*, September 30, 1933; Salmond, *Civilian Conservation Corps*, 137, 139; Holland and Hill, *Youth in the CCC*, 202–4; and Lacy, *The Soil Soldiers*, 133, 178. For a broader discussion of exercise, see Mosse, *The Image of Man*, 109. There was criticism, however, from some quarters that the sports were reserved for the best athletes, leaving others on the sidelines. See Holland and Hill, *Youth in the CCC*, 204–5, and Walker, *The CCC through the Eyes of 272 Boys*, 47–48.

46. On the importance of team sports, see Steven A. Riess, "Sport and the Redefinition of American Middle-Class Masculinity, 1840–1900," in *Major Problems in American Sport History*, ed. Steven A. Riess (Boston: Houghton Mifflin, 1997), 197–98, and Harvey Green, *Fit for America: Health, Fitness, Sport, and American Society* (New York: Pantheon, 1986), 233.

47. See a list of the kinds of classes offered in Clarence Riley Aydelott, "Facts Concerning Enrollees, Advisers, and the Educational Program in the CCC Camps of Missouri" (Ph.D. diss., University of Missouri, 1936), 80–83.

48. See, for example, Charles C. Bucyzinski, "Your Health: Mouth Hygiene," *Northlander* 9 (June 1936): 4, 7, 16, Folder—Michigan, printed materials, CCC Vertical File, FDRL. See also the recollections of CCC members in Michael Kernan, "Back to the Land," *Washington Post*, April 6, 1983, Folder—Virginia, printed materials, CCC Vertical File, FDRL, and Holland and Hill, *Youth in the CCC*, 195–98.

49. Quartermaster Corps Subsistence School, "Subsistence Menus and Recipes for Feeding 100 Men for One Month," Folder—CCC Menus, printed materials, CCC Vertical File, FDRL, and Holland and Hill, *Youth in the CCC*, 58. See also Hayes, "South Carolina and the New Deal, " 267. Not surprisingly, there was considerable rancor over the food, and several camps had food strikes. For more on food protests, see Walker, *The CCC through the Eyes of 272 Boys*, 29. For the larger context on the American diet, see Harvey Levenstein, *Paradox of Plenty: A Social History of Eating in Modern America* (New York: Oxford University Press, 1993). The last story was related to me by Jane Barrasso, who had talked to her father who was in the CCC.

50. On weight gain, see *Happy Days*, September 30, November 21, 1933, and *The Forestry News Digest* (August 1933): 12, Folder—American Forestry Association Publications, Vertical Files, FDRL. See also Walker, *The CCC through the Eyes of 272 Boys*, 29; Holland and Hill, *Youth in the CCC*, 191; Perry Merrill, *Roosevelt's Forest Army: A History of the Civilian Conservation Corps, 1933–1942* (Montpelier, Vt.: P. H. Merrill, 1981), 73, 102; and Mrs. Ella L. Parent to FDR, August 26, 1933, Official File 268, Folder—Misc., September–October, 1933, FDRL.

51. Lacy, *The Soil Soldiers*, 33.

52. *Happy Days*, August 26, 1933.

53. Salmond, *Civilian Conservation Corps*, 129.

54. Statement of Robert Fechner, House Committee on Labor, *To Make the Civilian Conservation Corps a Permanent Agency*, 3.

55. Schlesinger, *The Age of Roosevelt*, 339.

56. Not surprisingly, CCC supporters also developed written narratives to pay tribute to the agency's impact on individual lives. See, for instance, Holland and Hill, *Youth in the CCC*, 1–6.

57. T. J. Jackson Lears, *No Place of Grace: Antimodernism and the Transformation*

of American Culture, 1880–1920 (New York: Pantheon Books, 1981), 4. See also Green, Fit for America.

58. Interestingly, it is usually the middle class who celebrate work. Although certainly recognizing the necessity of work, working-class writers and artists rarely celebrate work itself. More often, they talk about time away from work. See, for instance, the songs of Bruce Springsteen; Jim Cullen, Born in the U.S.A: Bruce Springsteen and the American Tradition (New York: Harper Collins, 1997), 102–08.

59. For discussions of family relations during the Great Depression, see Ruth Shonle Cavan and Katerine Howland Ranck, The Family and the Depression: A Study of One Hundred Chicago Families (Chicago: University of Chicago Press, 1938); E. Wight Bakke, Citizens without Work (New Haven, Conn.: Yale University Press, 1940); and Mirra Komarovsky, The Unemployed Man and His Family (New York: Dryden Press, 1940). Think also here of the role of Ma Joad in John Steinbeck, The Grapes of Wrath (New York: Viking Press, 1939). See how a CCC chronicler deals with this link between the work of the relief agency and the Depression-era crisis of masculinity in Lacy, The Soil Soldiers, 7.

60. The Federal Emergency Relief Administration did set up a few "She-She-She Camps" for women. On this subject, see Joyce L. Kornbluh, "The She-She-She Camps: An Experiment in Living and Learning, 1934–1937," in Sisterhood and Solidarity: Workers' Education for Women, 1914–1984, ed. Joyce L. Kornbluh and Mary Frederickson (Philadelphia: Temple University Press, 1984), 255–83.

61. For some ideas on this fantasy, see Klaus Theweleit, Male Fantasies, vol. 1, Women, Floods, Bodies, History (Minneapolis: University of Minneapolis Press, 1987).

62. Ogburn, You and Machines, 3.

63. Barbara Melosh, Engendering Culture: Manhood and Womanhood in New Deal Public Art and Theater (Washington, D.C.: Smithsonian Institution Press, 1991), 92.

64. Ibid., 83.

65. George L. Mosse, Nationalism and Sexuality: Middle-Class Morality and Sexual Norms in Modern Europe (New York: H. Fertig, 1985), 17.

66. For more on this important point, see Eric Gorham, "The Ambiguous Practices of the Civilian Conservation Corps," Social History 17 (May 1992): 229–49. Gorham's article, like this chapter, has obviously been influenced by Michel Foucault. See, in particular, Foucault, Discipline and Punishment (New York: Pantheon, 1977), and The History of Sexuality (New York: Pantheon, 1978).

CHAPTER SIX

Voices from the *Spring:* *Silent Spring* and the Ecological Turn in American Health

Maril Hazlett

In September 1959, a married couple named Boberg moved into their dream home next door to an apple orchard in Poughkeepsie, New York. In October 1962, after repeated exposures to the orchard's regimen of pesticide sprays, Mrs. Boberg described her sufferings in a letter to scientist Rachel Carson, who had just published *Silent Spring*, a controversial bestseller about pesticides.

"The symptoms vary with the chemical used," Mrs. Boberg wrote. "I may come down with an excruciating headache, stiff neck, and the inability to keep food down. I may have a sinus condition, or a tingling that jars the nerves. Most often there is an incessant itching, a soreness that penetrates deep inside, and the swelling of various parts of my body. . . . I have reached a point where I can sense sprayed produce in a store. My hands tingle when they touch it, and blisters develop. These can spread to other areas." The Bobergs complained repeatedly to the orchard owners, but to no avail. Mr. Boberg then notified his local health department.[1]

"From all the information so far," the county official wrote back, "it is impossible to consider your wife's allergy a public health problem at this time. Allergies to insecticides are extremely rare and although your wife's condition does constitute a major individual health problem, it does not come within the scope of our program."[2]

Furious, Mr. Boberg fired back: "You described my wife's reaction to insecticide sprays as being a 'rare allergy.' I think she is unusually sensitive to air-borne poisons which affect all people in this area, whether they realize it or not. Her case is like that of the proverbial canary in the coal mine. . . . It isn't a case of the canary being 'allergic' to the poison gas." Finally, with no other alternative in sight, the Bobergs filed suit against the growers.[3]

From our perspective today, it seems reasonable to assume that Mrs. Boberg probably did suffer either a severe allergic reaction or complications from an acute case of pesticide poisoning. These instances were comparatively rare, as Carson had acknowledged in her book. However, for Carson, the Bobergs, and even for the general public, such acute illnesses were still very significant. They were warning signs of the potential— but yet unknown— long-term effects of pesticides on human health.[4]

The reception of *Silent Spring,* then, represented an important turning point in American ideas about nature. In the text, Carson investigated the effects of chemical pesticides on wildlife and human health. Summarizing the scattered scientific research, she built a damning case against the carelessness of the chemical industries and agribusiness and the lax government regulation of pesticides. The impact of *Silent Spring* extended far beyond the controversy that lasted from its publication in 1962 to Carson's death from breast cancer in 1964; many scholars have credited *Silent Spring* with inspiring the contemporary environmental movement. As the fears and experiences of Mrs. Boberg show, human health was a crucial, motivating concern in this new environmental era. If Mrs. Boberg's sufferings were those of a canary in a coal mine, issues of human health in the controversy over *Silent Spring* also provided a test case for the newly shaping agendas of environmentalism as well.[5]

In an increasingly troubled (and chemical) postwar world, human health and pesticides sharply reminded Americans that it was also possible to know nature through the body.[6] From poisoning to cancer, such intimate cellular truths were very frightening. On this larger scale, the controversy over *Silent Spring* and the rise of environmentalism reveal an important and overlooked historical development: an ecological turn in American health. Readers of *Silent Spring* who took the ecological turn experienced a simultaneous shift in their perceptions and physical awarenesses of the natural world. Carson's work forced many people to acknowledge the penetration of industrial toxins into not only their environment but their flesh, and thus to redefine their very ideas of health according to the context of their surroundings. Through the initially intimate, individual medium of the ecological turn, many readers then reconfigured bodies, consciousness, and the natural world into a radical new cultural critique.

What exactly was the ecological turn, and how did it take place? First, the ecological turn began in people's growing experience or recognition of their bodies as ecological entities. Inextricably embedded within the unpredictable natural world, human flesh would eventually, even inevitably, manifest the environment's ills. In letters and responses to *Silent Spring,* many of Carson's readers used fears about pesticides and human health to describe a world where, in the physical body at least, humans and nature were inseparable; pesticide residues flowed as easily through human arteries as river veins. Such an ecological understanding of human bodies revealed as artificial the boundaries between nature and culture, between humans and their environment. Moreover, this realization was based on what historian Conevery Bolton has called people's common sense of lived experience.[7] And in the postwar world, such common sense increasingly stood in opposition to the treacherous knowledge of scientific experts.

Physical, ecological awareness led to a second step in the ecological turn. Many of Carson's readers—mostly members of the general public, but even scientists and doctors—then used this commonsense idea of vulnerable, ecological bodies to challenge postwar directions of science and technology. In a letter to an Ohio paper, for example, citizen John Wolf linked the debate over human health and pesticides to other contemporary health concerns: fluoridation, aminotriazole residues in cranberries, and thalidomide. He especially criticized scientists: "Scientific specialists CAN be wrong . . . the rest of us need not apologize for questioning and mistrusting their decisions, especially when they seem to go against our common sense, instincts, and experiences."[8] The debate over human health and pesticides became one way to criticize the scientists who, believing they could control nature, had unleashed unpredictable, even atomic forces on the postwar world. In contrast, some people had begun to see nature itself as an unstable and mysterious entity, beyond any experts' complete knowledge or control.

The ecological turn in American health established an alternative environmental ethic that could account for such volatility. In a perilous world, why take risks with human health, either today's or that of future generations? The ecological turn's challenge to science was based not only on the standard of common sense. It also incorporated a larger sense of an ethical community. Members of this community all inhabited fragile ecological bodies; thus they all shared inalienable rights to hold science and technology accountable for unwanted chemical invasions of their flesh. Already growing visible in the 1950s during debates over fallout and food additives, the controversy over *Silent Spring* and synthetic pesticides exploded the ecological turn in American health into the public discourse.[9]

Obviously, this radical critique had great potential to affect environmental decision-making and policy. Yet the initial legislative reaction was quite limited. Congress did not even outlaw DDT until 1972. After the publication of *Silent Spring*, pesticide production and profits continued to rise. Many of the chemicals that Carson discussed are still produced in the United States and abroad. Others she could have barely dreamed of flood our environment today. With so much potential, why did the ecological turn result in so little tangible political and industrial change?[10]

Because even as this ecological turn began its shift, its body-sensitive understandings of nature became problematically entangled in and limited by traditional notions of gender. Ecological bodies still existed in a context where gender influenced, complicated, and translated the realms of the material and corporeal. Particularly in the backlash against *Silent Spring*, the chemical companies, scientists, and government officials used narrow interpretations of traditional gender roles to criticize or limit the implications of Carson's work. Interestingly, many of Carson's ideas, as well as the ecological turn itself, pointed toward not only a fluid, unstable nature but also to a more complicated world where gender—and thus many traditional relations of power—could potentially be transcended as well. Frightened of (or ferociously trying to eliminate or both) this disquieting possibility, a combination of forces among industry and science used traditional interpretations of gender to marginalize and limit the effects of the ecological turn.

The following story of the controversy over *Silent Spring* and the splintering of the ecological turn, however, left us an especially important lesson. The complicated processes of knowing nature through gender change greatly when the human body enters the equation.

BACKGROUND

On one level, human communities have always understood that their bodies are intimately connected to the surrounding environment. In Western culture, however, this basic understanding of the body has also coexisted with another, opposite strain of thought developed by philosophers and religious thinkers. Over the years, these different groups came to agree on one major assumption: that the needs and experiences of the physical body existed in sharp opposition to the powers of the mind. This mind/body duality, feminist thinkers have more recently argued, corresponded to similar dualities between male and female, reason and emotion, subject and object, even culture and nature; they also noted that each opposition incorporated a hierarchy where the first quality stands as superior to the second.[11]

This type of thinking about the body came to shape the dominant premises of Western culture, including the enterprise of contemporary science.[12] The very ability to reason was perceived as coming from denial of the mind's physical connection with the flesh. Linda Martin Alcoff has pointed out that "needless to say, it was men who could hope to transcend the realm of the body, with its everyday commitments, its pedestrian passions, and its emotions shadowing the route to the Real. Women . . . more regularly reminded of their fleshly limitations, could never ascend to the plane of the universal."[13]

Thus, men and masculinity became identified with the mind, women and femininity with the body, the realm of the irrational, emotional, intuitive—and the permeable. In reproduction, menstruation, and intercourse, women's physical bodies seemed to ooze and bleed especially easily through social boundaries, always reminding of and threatening to merge again the carefully separated realms of human and nature. Woman-flesh symbolized unpredictable flux, transformation, and exchange: the blurring of boundaries between inside and out, even order and chaos.[14] When the ecological turn presumed a body whose boundaries were loose, easily permeable, and vulnerable to outside invasions, it thus connected long-standing, negative, and undeniably feminine images with issues of human health and pesticides.

At the time of the ecological turn, ideas about the human body carried enormous baggage. Associated with women, nature, and the feminine, the flesh shared their erratic, mutable, and devalued connotations. Severed from men, culture, and rational thought, the body also existed outside the stable, culturally sanctioned processes of reasoning. Such ideas about the human body also served as the basis for traditional stereotypes about gender. They seemed to explain women's subordination to men as well as social mores that dictated women should be safely confined to the private realms of home and children and excluded from the public.

Leakages through barriers of body, sex, or gender thus were signs of a dangerous instability. Combined associations of bodily suffering, penetration, and contamination with the feminine also demeaned anyone who experienced unwanted fleshly invasions. Carson, for example—as an unmarried female scientist, who pointed out that no one's flesh was invulnerable to toxic contamination and who eventually died of breast cancer —broke all the rules.

In contrast, the masculine world of scientific reasoning believed that progress meant the ability to hold human bodies separate from and superior to the environment by virtue of scientific and medical technology. For example, during the mid–twentieth century, exploding postwar chemical technologies spread toxic residues—radioactive fallout, strange new food additives and dyes, pollution of all kinds, the dangerous drug of thalidomide, and so on—throughout human surroundings. Many scientists argued that tests had proved that many of these frightening substances could not possibly pose threats to human health; in essence, the powers of scientific minds could transcend the accumulations of toxins in human bodies. Increasingly, however, a dissatisfied and fearful public (several of them, just as Mrs. Boberg did, having experienced reactions to these substances), fearing the apparent rise in cancer or simply believing that enough poisons released into the environment would eventually cause health problems, began to challenge these assertions.[15]

In many ways, the ecological turn introduced a resurgence of belief in the long-standing idea that human bodies were inextricably connected to their environment. As far as its understanding of "ecological," however, this turn also explored new terrain. As there existed two competing strains of thought about the body, two opposing ideas divided ecology as well. Ecology, the science that studied the interactions of organisms in the context of the natural world, itself had a long history. Donald Worster argued that Western thought, especially with the rise of industrialization, conceived of nature through two conflicting understandings: the holistic, biocentric, sentimental, romantic, even mystical, wanting to coexist with nature; or the mechanized, utilitarian, rational, and scientific, wanting to dominate it.[16]

By the time of *Silent Spring*, this clash had both invigorated and almost threatened to tear apart the discipline. Was an ecological system a stable balance of various quantifiable components, or was it a fluid, unpredictable world of complex disturbances and interruptions? Scientific specialists could not agree. Worster pointed out, however, that the debate now extended past the confines of science and into popular discourse. Crucially, Carson had made the arguments and images of ecology accessible to the general public.[17]

An anonymous letter to a Texas paper proved this connection in commenting on the controversy over *Silent Spring:* "It stands to reason that when these poisons are sprayed on our fields of vegetables and our fields of grain that they are eventually washed into our streams of water. These poisons are not broken down and dispersed through filtration. Eventually they reach us in our drinking water, and our system retains the poisons, and it only takes a small percentage to make us ill, and when we keep consuming this poison, it eventually kills us."[18]

Such a popular understanding of ecology reached beyond the dichotomy between sentimental and mechanical ways of understanding nature. For many readers of *Silent Spring*, limited scientific knowledge did not justify dismissing people's health questions as irrational or mystical. Rather, in a world divided by the mind/body dualism, the ecological turn meant reaching beyond this dichotomy for new understandings, bringing together again humans and their environment.[19] A turn from science and toward common sense, a turn from expert knowledge and toward individual understandings: in the middle of the twentieth century, the ecological turn mounted a powerful challenge to technology. Understanding and also experiencing one's own physical health as an intimate, lived state embedded in the natural world gave many people the strength to challenge the monopoly of medicine and science on explanations of nature and the body.

SILENT SPRING

After the success of her best-seller *The Sea Around Us* (1950), scientist and writer Rachel Carson quit her job as editor of publications for the U.S.

Fish and Wildlife Service. Writing full-time, she next published the like-wise successful *Edge of the Sea* (1955). Carson's unique writing style merged scientific information with the observations of a naturalist. Beauti-fully, she combined expert with everyday knowledge and earned a de-voted following of readers.[20]

For many years, however, Carson had also worried about the dangers of pesticides. After World War II, synthetic chemicals developed for war-fare found release into the domestic markets. The chlorinated hydrocarbon DDT was one such product; the family of organic phosphates (malathion, parathion, and so on) was another. Carson knew that wildlife biologists feared the effects of pesticides on animal populations, and she was also fa-miliar with the increasing evidence of pesticides' dangers to human health. Already committed to various book projects, Carson tried to get other writers interested in working on the pesticide issue, but with no luck. Fi-nally, in 1958, she committed to the pesticide project herself. What was meant to be only a short book dragged on into a four-year ordeal. The writ-ing of *Silent Spring* was lengthened especially by Carson's various health problems, including in 1960 her diagnosis with breast cancer.[21]

One of the hallmarks of *Silent Spring* was Carson's meticulous re-search. Although she was the first to synthesize the widely scattered lit-erature on pesticides, Carson was not the only one investigating problems with environmental toxins. General concerns over chemical contaminants in the environment—food additives, pollution, dyes, harm-ful drugs, as well as concerns over pesticides—already pervaded Ameri-can society. William Longgood's *Poisons in Your Food* (1960) and Lewis Herber's *Our Synthetic Environment* (1962) also expressed these fears. Popular magazines likewise rumbled nervously over new chemical anx-ieties.[22]

In a climate of such widespread apprehension, however, *Silent Spring* emerged to hold center stage. The issue of pesticides focused a larger de-bate about chemicals in the postwar world. What made *Silent Spring* stand out? Like the rest, Carson also predicted fearful dangers. "For the first time in the history of the world," she wrote, "every human being is now subjected to contact with dangerous chemicals, from the moment of conception until death." However, she offered new answers, based on ecological principles, as to exactly how the dangers occurred. Humans were also vulnerable components in the mysterious webs of natural processes, viscerally connected to water, air, soil, and wildlife. Pesticide residues permeated just as easily through boundaries of human flesh, and the chain of life conducted accumulating levels of poisons to human bodies balanced precariously at the top.[23]

Ecologically, then, humans and nature were not separate, but inte-grated and equal before the pervasive forces of chemical contamination.

Carson's message held a potentially radical challenge to postwar consumer society where increasingly, industries depended on various chemicals to create cheap, attractive, and plentiful products. Science and industry, Carson argued, should ultimately be accountable to basic ecological truths, such as the shared vulnerability of both nature and human flesh. And so far, these powers had miserably failed this responsibility. "I do contend," she wrote, "that we have put poisonous and biologically potent chemicals indiscriminately into the hands of persons largely or wholly ignorant of their potentials for harm . . . that we have allowed these chemicals to be used with little or no advance investigation of their effect on soil, water, wildlife, and man himself."[24]

Such a charge, no matter how she tried to qualify its implications by saying that she supported the careful use of chemical sprays, directly questioned all the presumptions of mid-twentieth-century industrialized society, where concerns about profit were at least equal to worries about public health. In July 1962, as soon as the *New Yorker* published the first of three installments of an abridged *Silent Spring,* the controversy exploded. By the time Houghton Mifflin released the hardcover version the following September, debates still raged. Members of the public, scientists, doctors, and representatives of the media, chemical companies, and government all fought passionately for or against Carson's case.[25]

Some voices, however, were heard more loudly than others. The conflicts among professionals—doctors, scientists, industry experts, government, and the media—dominated the discussion and drowned out the public. These vocal and contentious experts, however, did agree on one point. They assumed that their role was to sort through the "true" facts about human health and pesticides and defuse what even some of Carson's supporters referred to as the public's "emotionalism," a quality her detractors called (among other things) "hysteria." Within the gendered context of this debate over pesticides and human health, such accusations of emotionalism and hysteria were especially significant. They suggested an assumption, even on the part of supportive experts, that chaos resulted from bringing fluid, vulnerable bodies—bodies bound up not only in ecology but also in sex and gender—into the public sphere and the environmental policymaking process.

Similar beliefs about the feminine connections between body and hysteria were also long-standing. The root of the Greek word "hysteria" is *hyster-,* which means "womb." Ancient Greeks believed that hysteria was the condition of a "wandering womb," where essentially a woman not having enough sex or babies (and therefore not assimilating appropriately into the patriarchal order) became distraught and irrational. No equivalent condition existed to describe emotional outbursts in men, though one could surmise that the very use of the term might have reflected some strong emotion on the part of the critics. Tracing the history of hysteria, women's historians have noted that the phrase has consistently been used as an excuse to "discredit women's political protest" as well as unpopular protests in general.[26]

Attempts to discredit Carson and *Silent Spring* as emotional and hysterical also drew upon a long legacy of gender inequality. Invoking traditional ideas about gender, chemical companies and their supporters tried to maintain their own power. A world where women existed as the private, contained keepers of children and the home was also a world where, ideally, industry was free to pursue production and profit, with only limited attention to worrisome concerns of health and the environment. The ecological turn, with its assumption that all humans inhabited vulnerable, fragile, ecological bodies, threatened to destabilize this architecture of gender and power.

ECOLOGICAL BODIES

The ecological turn thus began by disordering traditional understandings of gender through proposing a fluid idea of nature and broadening the category of who could legitimately care about interior, intimate, bodily concerns. The turn sprang from the exact seam in the individual where mind and body met. Mrs. Boberg first felt the effects of the pesticides in her body, then experienced a change in her conscious awareness of the world. Others felt the ecological turn first in a visceral, changing awareness of the world around them and then feared for the fragility of their flesh.

Judging from many readers' reactions to *Silent Spring*, this new awareness abounded among men and women alike. Some wrote of organic home vegetable gardens contaminated with pesticides spread by careless neighbors or by overhead spray planes. Others mourned beloved pets dead or seriously ill after pesticide exposure. Still others fretted over a housewife's groceries and the neighborhood children doused by dense clouds from spray trucks on patrol through a residential neighborhood. And again, some wrote of seemingly too many neighbors in one small area stricken with cancer in a two- to three-year period. One man also noted an acquaintance's son who developed aplastic anemia and died within three weeks after the family started using a certain brand of insect repellent.[27]

Pesticides appeared to pose the gravest dangers to the private sphere: the circles of family and community and the immediate habitat of vulnerable, ecological bodies. But the threats in the home originated in the public terrain of industrial production. John C. Burnham has noted that in the middle of the twentieth century, at the same time as the rise of environmentalism, the meaning of "poison" shifted. Originally, people perceived poisons as the products of nature—venomous insects, animals, or toxic plants—administered by villainous or suicidal humans. With the increasingly dangerous and skyrocketing usage of synthetic chemicals, especially in the home, Americans began to perceive man-made toxic agents as the major threats.[28]

These private dangers also represented very public concerns. As Sandra L. Showalter of Chicago observed in a letter to Rachel Carson, "I have noticed that in my city, there are almost no birds in areas which formerly used to flourish with them. Also, the ever-increasing rate at which cancer is growing, and the fact that we may be aggravating, if not directly causing this cancer ourselves, must be explored."[29] In a small Connecticut paper, Grace Lee Kenyon also wrote: "I do say that 'pizen is pizen' no matter how fancy the name nor how big the profit to the manufacturer and the sprayer, so let common sense be your guide. Anything strong enough to kill a bug cannot be anything but harmful to the human 'tummy'! And, no matter what they tell you, anything sprayed from the sky falls alike on the just and the unjust!"[30]

From birds to cancer, from bugs to the human "tummy," common sense told both Showalter and Kenyon that poisons—chemical pesticides—knew no boundaries in ecological or even cultural systems. For these two women, humans and nature stood on equal footing before the toxins that permeated the environment. Within this framework, science and technology could no longer hold humans separate from or superior to the nonhuman natural world. The logic of the ecological turn was based on this commonsense understanding of a vulnerable, permeable body as the crucial link between humans and nature. Moreover, it not only blurred traditional distinctions between private and public concerns but also threatened to make private fears for health and the body the highest priority.

And apparently, more women than men responded positively to *Silent Spring*, offering their opinions on pesticides and human health either to Carson or to some arm of the media.[31] In their various responses, women often identified themselves either by their usually female group memberships or by their traditional gender roles. They mention belonging to garden clubs, reading groups, Audubon societies, and peace groups; above all, they refer to their roles as wives, mothers, daughters, and housewives. Vera Norwood has also suggested that many of Carson's female supporters understood ecology and the natural environment as extensions of the feminine domain of the home.[32]

Contemporary observers noted this pattern as well. In a California paper, one headline read: "Authorities Assure Housewives No Need to Fear Pesticide Use."[33] The *Weyerhauser News* published an open letter to a Washington housewife who wrote to them after reading *Silent Spring*.[34] And the business columnist for a Virginia paper, bemoaning all this fuss about pesticides, predicted that "after the women's clubs get through reading Miss Carson's book, [the local health department] will be under increasing pressure to act."[35] Certainly, both Carson's female supporters and other contemporary observers understood women's protests against pesticides as generating from a long tradition of female reform movements. These movements were anchored in the private sphere, in concerns of motherhood and domesticity.[36]

In taking the ecological turn, however, Carson's female supporters used an old tradition in a threatening new way. Only on the surface was their link with long-standing female gender roles traditional. Mrs. Ann E. Wissler, president of the San Bernardino Valley Audubon Society, simply argued that "pesticide manufacturers making billions from their poisons should be the ones required to prove that there are no dangers from eating mixtures of poison residues at every meal."[37] According to Mrs. Wissler, experts in government and industry, not the bodies of the public, should bear the burden of establishing the long-term effects of these chemical pesticides. This logic, however, challenged the entire premise of industrial production, which assumed that all consumers tacitly agreed to accept such risks. Moreover, it transformed the vulnerable, ecological body into a source of public power instead of an isolated female problem.

In their essentially radical critiques of pesticide manufacturing and their belief in nature as a fluid, unpredictable entity of mostly unknown processes, Mrs. Wissler and many other women threatened the relations of domination that ordered the postwar world. Feminine and masculine, private and public, nature and culture, body and mind: all the submissive elements now seemed poised to become equals, maybe even take precedence. Certainly, these women believed they had the power to unsettle the relationship between the active act of production and the passive act of consumption. As Mrs. Miriam Zuger told Rachel Carson, "As a doctor's wife and mother I view the small type on all purchases with a great concern."[38] For Mrs. Zuger as well as many other women, everyday household decisions were important political actions on behalf of the environment.[39]

In the debate over human health and pesticides, these women experienced the connections between nature and female gender roles as, to some extent, empowering. They drew on the strengths of the traditional categories in order to challenge the systems of power that maintained such narrow boundaries. In doing so, these women also drew upon an old vision of nature in a new way; they argued that a volatile, unpredictable nature deserved respect, not domination. No better symbol of this empowerment exists than Carson herself. In the postpublication battle, she drew on the support of many women's organizations, groups that like-wise believed that human relations with nature defied traditional social categories, gender among them. The consequences for entrenched power structures of manufacturing and even government were frightening; taken to its logical conclusion, the ecological turn could make many so-cial hierarchies all but irrelevant.

Further evidence of the transcendent power of the ecological turn comes from the reactions of men. Fears for vulnerable, ecological bodies broadened the category of who could legitimately care about intimate corporeal concerns. Even though more women than men appear to have responded in support of *Silent Spring*, that difference is still slight.[40] Many men reacted along the same lines as Arthur A. MacConochie, a resident of Norfolk, Virginia. Only a few months after the publication of *Silent Spring*, his community found itself embroiled in controversy over a diel-drin aerial spraying campaign.[41]

"From the recent information supplied us," MacConochie wrote in a passionate letter to the editor of the *Virginian-Pilot*, "it seems as if we are going to have four and one-half tons of poison dumped on us, whether we like it or not. At the moment, there is no precise information on the ar-eas to be dieldrin-ized. Therefore, I do not know whether the family cat runs a risk of being murdered, not to mention the attendant risk to my children; or whether we have to wait for the dieldrin to reach us by . . . the slow percolation of groundwater." He ended his argument with a heartfelt plea: "There is just an outside chance that we will someday have a 'silent spring'—not a mere birdless one—but one without the sound of children."[42]

A man's voice raised against the powers that be, begging for clemency on behalf of his children: Arthur MacConochie and many other men feared for the safety of their families, feared the penetration of pes-ticides into the intimate enclosures of their everyday private lives. Con-cerns about health and the environment had the potential to unite men and women. Yet even as the ecological turn empowered people to seek common ground on the basis of their shared vulnerability in the face of unpleasant ecological truths about pesticides, traditional gender roles worked to limit this changing awareness. The biased lens of gender still problematically distorted ideas of body and nature. Men who took the ecological turn found themselves in conflict with a dominant ideal of masculinity.

What does it mean for a man to have a vulnerable body? Porous, penetrable flesh is in fact presumed to be a source of shame. Part of the dominant masculine ideal, Michael Kimmel has noted, incorporates bod-ies that are "impenetrable, impervious to outside threat"; an important hallmark of masculinity is control over one's body, self, and boundaries.

Moreover, masculinity is defined above all to the degree that it can distance itself from the feminine. Men in the postwar world already walked a fine line of gender identity. As head of the household, their presence was important to the home; however, this patriarchal power also depended on observing the proper masculine distance from domestic, feminine concerns: not helping too much with the dishes, only making baby formula on Sundays, and so on. The foil for this masculine, breadwinning yet nurturing American father was his submissive wife, who embodied the ultimate in feminine domesticity.[43]

Voices such as Arthur MacConochie's thus bespoke gender trouble. In the postwar ideology of traditional gender roles, men—and the realm of acceptable masculine behavior—were most strongly identified with life outside the home, not with private, bodily, and seemingly feminine concerns. For men to speak of home, health, children, nature, and vulnerable bodies was to voice a historically feminine protest. And in comparison to the group connections and networks linking the voices of women, most men's objections to pesticides echoed in hollow isolation. Identified primarily with the public sphere—industrial interests, scientific research, and governmental oversight—men's strictly defined roles of fatherhood and husbanding worked against, rather than for, men's antitoxic activism.[44]

In other ways, traditional gender roles also limited the potential of the ecological turn. Certainly, the controversy offered new voices and visions for women. However, women were almost completely absent elsewhere in the debate, such as in the conflicts between doctors, scientists, and members of government and industry. During the postwar period, women had begun to integrate into the workforce in greater and greater numbers, but few had the potential to influence policy decisions.[45]

In addition, the act of connecting pesticides and human health with private concerns and a female tradition of reform had serious limitations as well. Historically, women's protest traditions equated feminine gender behavior with the biological equipment necessary to bear children. In questioning the use of pesticides, some women also apologized for this maternal identity. As Hesta Forster explained to Carson, "After all, I am only a housewife, and even though I have always been avidly interested in all forms of life, I have felt it rather arrogant of me to voice my opinion." Other women, however, used maternity as a reason to speak out. In the words of Mrs. George Hilliard, "Maybe it is impractical and stupid, but I am concerned for my children's children, if we as a race can survive under such unfavorable odds as prevail today."[46]

Women's concerns for nature and for future generations: arrogant? impractical and stupid? Although the maternal tradition of protest did empower some women to speak out on behalf of the environment, apparently it also distanced and—we can only guess—perhaps silenced others. And maternalism could be turned against women as well, including Carson herself. Most historians credit former secretary of agriculture Ezra Taft Benson with first voicing the oft-repeated remark about Carson, wondering "why a spinster with no children [is] so concerned about genetics."[47]

The ecological turn thus both empowered and limited public reactions to Carson's book, as it simultaneously both destabilized and remained confined by popular gender ideologies. And in the rising backlash, chemical companies and other institutions effectively seized upon very narrow understandings of gender to fight against Rachel Carson and *Silent Spring*.

BACKLASH

This backlash against *Silent Spring* came from many different elements in postwar society: chemical companies, businesses and industry leaders, scientists, and members of government and the media. Importantly, dissident voices—Carson supporters—also appeared in each of these sectors. However, they remained unable to persuade her attackers. Interestingly, her defenders' failure, as well as the strength of Carson's detractors, arose from common underlying assumptions. Most believed in the dominant role of man in nature and the fixed boundaries of the human body and, accordingly, in basically untroubled, unproblematic connections between human health and the environment. Fundamentally, all participants in the backlash united around the legitimacy of a masculine-identified scientific expertise, where the powers of the mind dominated nature and human bodies. In common, they rejected the historically feminine concerns about human health that united much of the support for *Silent Spring*.

Central to the backlash, of course, was the chemical industry, in particular the producers of pesticides. At the publication of *Silent Spring*, the fast-growing business of pesticide production already earned $300–480 million per year. The profits of the vastly larger chemical industry reached over $23 billion. Manufacturers were greatly concerned about the controversy over *Silent Spring*. The fate of pesticides would serve as a test case for all the chemical products currently flooding domestic markets: to what extent would the public support an industrial system in which private profit either triumphed over concerns for public health or succeeded in strictly narrowing the definition of public health concerns?[48]

The pesticide industry's main lobbying group, the National Agricultural Chemicals Association (NACA), and various pesticide manufacturers—including Monsanto, Stauffer, Velsicol, and American Cyanamid—took the lead in the industry's responses to *Silent Spring*. The NACA alone devoted at least $250,000 to the public relations effort. The total spent on anti-Carson propaganda is all but incalculable, considering the reach of chemical manufacturers throughout postwar society. Corporate public relations efforts flooded the media with thousands of press releases, which in turn generated vast amounts of print and radio coverage telling the chemical companies' "side of the story."[49]

What tale did the pesticide manufacturers tell? In their view, pesticides gave life, not took it away. According to food industry lobbyist Dr. Frederick J. Stare (the bulk of the food industry used pesticide-raised produce, and food processors were very concerned about public reactions to *Silent Spring*), "So far, through the broad application of a brilliant technology which includes the wide use of agricultural chemicals, man has managed to stave off starvation, disease, and social and political unrest in many parts of the world."[50] An unsigned editorial in the *American Vegetable Grower* put the case against Carson baldly, declaring that in America, our "food supply [is the] safest in the world and our people enjoy the longest life span," and that the conflict over *Silent Spring* was between "scientific agriculture and those who would turn back the day to when the human being was at the mercy of the environment."[51]

To support this story of the powers of pesticides, the chemical and food industries also invoked a popular, triumphant, and undeniably masculine reading of history, fundamentally based on the need to dominate nature. Dr. William J. Darby, a major figure in the fight against Carson, insisted that any talk of accommodating rather than dominating nature represented "passive" and "pessimistic" philosophies. He believed such attitudes boded "an end of all human progress, reversion to a passive social state devoid of technology, scientific medicine, agriculture, sanitation, or education. It means disease, epidemics, starvation, misery, and suffering incomparable and intolerable to modern man. Indeed, social, educational, and scientific development is prefaced on the conviction that man's lot will be and is being improved by . . . an increased ability to control or mold those forces responsible for man's suffering, misery, and deprivation."[52]

In Darby's vision, man's role in civilization and human progress was in essence the individual hero's struggle in a constant battle against nature. Through hard work and ingenious technology, man conquered and reconquered the unruly environment. Nature lurked as a dangerous opponent threatening from the outside; certainly, heroic man did not experience nature as an intimate companion within. Questioning this explanation, let alone eliminating or limiting the production of pesticides, threatened all of American progress. The best response to *Silent Spring*, Carson's attackers in the pesticide sector advised, was to downplay the "emotional" public reaction and to emphasize man's ongoing need to control nature. For that matter, the heart of the backlash also recognized the need to control Rachel Carson. One headline from *Chemical and Engineering News* proclaiming "Silence, Miss Carson" made this point emphatically clear.[53]

Dominating nature, controlling emotion, and silencing an unruly woman: These goals in turn were linked to fostering the narrowest possible definition of pesticides' dangers to public health. In the view of most industry spokesmen, a chemically increased food supply warded off starvation and epidemic diseases, the only potential health problems worth taking seriously. Carson and her supporters had raised questions about the connections between gradual accumulations of toxic chemicals in human tissue and the rising rates of cancer, but chemical producers responded that health problems with pesticides were the faults of individuals who accidentally or deliberately misused them. Most of these misuses allegedly took place in the home and garden, the domain of women. The chemical and food industries charged that any other interpretation, including questions about cancer, represented uninformed and hysterical scare-mongering.[54]

Not all who opposed Carson were quite so vituperative. However, many other scientists, including government experts, did agree with the extremists' fundamental assumptions about science, if not their intemperate rhetoric. For example, many scientists disagreed with *Silent Spring*'s basic premise that humans and nature were not separate. In a largely supportive article, a professor of biology still noted that the "weakest part of *Silent Spring* is the note on which it ends. 'The control of nature,' we are told, 'is a phrase conceived in arrogance, born of the Neanderthal age of biology,' caveman stuff. Yet controlling nature is precisely what man has been doing since he discovered the use of fire. His ability to do so is one of the chief things setting him apart from the beasts." To lose this distinction evidently threatened the very scientific enterprise.[55]

And in the framework of science, the idea of dominating nature was again linked to a gender hierarchy. As historian of science Evelyn Fox Keller has explained, there exists a "deeply rooted popular mythology that casts objectivity, reason, and mind as male, and subjectivity, feeling, and nature as female."[56] In this context, it becomes more understandable how even those scientists who might agree with some of Carson's arguments regarding pesticides also feared her writing and felt that the responses to her work were too "emotional." Likewise, their praise of her "beautiful writing" undermined her scientific credibility. Such faint praise linked her with the isolated feminine world of beauty rather than acknowledging her standing to criticize the world of capital, knowledge, and power.[57]

In effect, such assessments represented the masculine world of science slamming the door on Carson and her supporters as well as on visions of a fluid natural world and vulnerable ecological bodies. Scientists distanced themselves from the discourse of the ecological turn in order to protect what they believed was the basis of their own cultural authority. Controlling bodies, controlling nature, and distancing themselves from a public discourse associated with any hint of the feminine, as the debate over *Silent Spring* so clearly was: the biased premises behind the dominant ideal of masculinity shaped not only the extremes of industry rhetoric but also the supposedly more objective inquiries of science.

Such a reaction, so concerned with redrawing strict boundaries around categories at the basis of social order and power, rooted itself in not only a limited, static, and traditional view of feminine, but of the masculine as well. On the whole, the framework of industry and science agreed that to bring vulnerable, ecological bodies into public debates, or to even reconsider the relentless conquest of nature, was to invite chaos. Successfully, through hierarchical understandings of gender, they managed to associate the public reaction to *Silent Spring* with the forces of social disorder. And as the conflict over Carson's book raged on, science and industry also succeeded in controlling the terms of the government policy debate over pesticides.[58]

Central to this effort was the role of scientific expertise in narrowing the question of how pesticides might cause problems for public health. In the experts' discussions about human health and pesticides, an abstract norm of the body repeatedly appears, an image of an ideal body understood through statistics and laboratory studies. The superior knowledge of science and technology carefully patrolled the boundaries of this stable flesh, separating it from the unstable processes of nature. At the U.S. Senate hearings on pesticides, the chemical industry hammered home this not only narrow but also gendered interpretation of the body. "You're never going to satisfy organic gardeners or emotional women in garden clubs," one agricultural expert told a reporter.[59]

Unpredictable chemical effects, differences in individuals' symptoms, the unknown ecological interactions between humans and their immediate habitat—all the commonsense lessons from sufferers such as Mrs. Boberg posited a body-nature connection that somehow transcended and complicated traditional forms of gender. In comparison, the experts' body did not admit the individual, nature-connected insights of the ecological turn as a valid form of knowledge. Rather, it defaulted to the abstract norm of a healthy body as understood through scientific expertise, with all the weight of cultural legitimacy and history behind it. In expert debates, the issue was reduced to a question of how soon science could accurately evaluate the effects of toxic residues in human tissues, not whether such residues should penetrate the flesh at all. "Miss Carson is talking about health effects that will take years to answer," one consultant for Shell Chemical Company told the Senate hearings. "In the meantime, we'd have to cut off food for people around the world. These peddlers of fear are going to feast on the famine of the world—literally."[60]

LESSONS FROM THE TURN

In the ecological turn, knowing nature not only through gender but also through a gender written uneasily over a fluid, permeable, ecological body pointed to a world where human cultural orders were at best transient and unstable. Potentially, in either the sudden death of atomic warfare or the slow death of cancer, human worlds (and their hierarchical, divided societies) might even become obsolete. Against such physical dangers, the divisions between culture and nature, between masculine and feminine, between other seemingly settled opposites, stood as comparatively feeble human obsoletes, products of culture and history rather than immutable natural orders. If such once-concrete categories and relations were unstable, what other assumptions might rip free?

The controversy over *Silent Spring*, revealing as it did the already ongoing shift of the ecological turn, was in truth a radical historical moment. Ecological understandings of human health burst into the mainstream consciousness, and through the ecological turn, a powerful, albeit marginalized, new environmental ethic did begin to take shape. In the context of the early 1960s, the problematically fluid, ecological image of the body did limit the degree of this ecological turn and marginalized its impact. Nonetheless, potentially positive signs of slippage in these confining gender identities and ideas of nature were everywhere as well: men concerned about their own vulnerable bodies, pleading on behalf of their children; women claiming that ecology, not biology, was to some extent destiny for us all; and men and women agreeing that this time, Adam not only ate, but grew, the poisoned apple. Perhaps the realization that all humans inhabit ecological bodies still holds the possibility of shifting other confining cultural boundaries as well as redrawing larger human relationships with nature.

NOTES

For funding and support, thanks to the University of Kansas, Linda Hall Library of Science, Technology, and Engineering, the Woodrow Wilson Foundation, and the Kranzberg Fellowship Committee of the Society for the History of Technology. For comments and guidance, thanks to Kevin Armitage, Lisa Bitel, Conevery Bolton, Lisa Brady, Tara Lynne Clapp, Brian Allen Drake, Nancy Scott Jackson, Nancy Langston, Linda Lear, Peter Mancall, Carolyn Merchant, Dale Nimz, Adam Rome, Virginia Scharff, Brian Trigg, and Donald Worster and to participants in the Hall Center Nature and Culture Seminars and American Society for Environmental History (ASEH) conference sessions, all of whom generously commented on the material.

1. Mrs. Charles Boberg to Rachel Carson (hereafter cited as RC), October 8, 1962, Rachel Carson Papers, Beinecke Rare Book and Manuscript Library of Yale University (hereafter cited as RCP/BLYU). Later she also contacted J. I. Rodale and Robert Rodale, publishers of *Organic Gardening and Farming (OGF)*, to publicize her ordeal; see Mrs. Charles Boberg to editor, *OGF* 10, no. 3 (March 1963): 16–17; Robert Rodale, "People against Poisons," *OGF* 10, no. 4 (April 1963): 27–29.

2. Lewis E. Patrie, M.D., health commissioner, Duchess County Department of Health, Poughkeepsie, N.Y., September 13, 1962, RCP/BLYU.

3. Quote from Charles P. Boberg, to Lewis E. Patrie, M.D., September 24, 1962, and Charles P. Boberg to Dr. Clarence Targwell, U.S. Public Health Service, November 2, 1963, both in RCP/BLYU.

4. Rachel Carson, *Silent Spring* (New York: Houghton Mifflin, 1962).

5. Information on the debate over *Silent Spring* comes from the following scholarship: Linda Lear, *Rachel Carson: Witness for Nature* (New York: Henry Holt, 1997); Lawrence Buell, "Toxic Discourse," *Critical Inquiry* 24, no. 3 (1998): 639–66; Paul Brooks, *The House of Life: Rachel Carson at Work* (Boston: Houghton Mifflin, 1972); H. Patricia Hynes, *The Recurring Silent Spring* (New York: Pergamon Press, 1989); Craig Waddell, ed., *And No Birds Sing: Rhetorical Analyses of Rachel Carson's Silent Spring* (Carbondale: Southern Illinois University Press, 2000); Frank Graham Jr., *Since Silent Spring* (Boston: Houghton Mifflin, 1970); Thomas Dunlap, *DDT: Science, Citizens, and Public Policy* (Princeton, N.J.: Princeton University Press, 1981); Robert Gottlieb, *Forcing the Spring: The Transformation of the American Environmental Movement* (Washington, D.C.: Island Press, 1993); and Stephen Fox, *The American Conservation Movement: John Muir and His Legacy* (Madison: University of Wisconsin Press, 1981).

6. As Carolyn Merchant has written: "Consciousness as a way of knowing nature . . . is broader than the mind alone. It encompasses knowing through the body, all the senses working together—feelings, volitions, and thought" (*Earthcare: Women and the Environment* [New York: Routledge, 1995], xxi). The quote continues: "Representations of material reality are socially constructed from a real, material world by real bodies, mediated through local modes of production and reproduction (such as indigenous systems, colonialism, and capitalism)."

7. Thanks to Conevery Bolton for her presentations at the University of Kansas and at the ASEH conference. Also see Conevery Bolton, "'The Health of the Country': Body and Environment in the Making of the American West, 1800–1860" (Ph.D. diss., Harvard University, 1998).

8. John Wolf to editor, the *Sun*, Springfield, Ohio, February 18, 1963, RCP/BLYU.

9. On fallout, see Ralph H. Lutts, "Chemical Fallout: *Silent Spring*, Radioactive Fallout, and the Environmental Movement," in Waddell, *And No Birds Sing*, 17–41. On food additive controversies, see Harvey Levenstein, *Paradox of*

Plenty: A Social History of Eating in America (Oxford: Oxford University Press, 1993), 131–43; on connections between food additive scares and environmentalism, see my forthcoming dissertation, "Voices from the Spring: *Silent Spring* and the Ecological Turn in American Health."

10. Edmund Russell, *War and Nature: Fighting Humans and Insects with Chemicals from World War I to* Silent Spring (Cambridge: Cambridge University Press, 2001); Theo Colburn, Diane Dumanoski, and John Peterson Myers, *Our Stolen Future* (New York: Penguin Group, 1996, 1997); Sandra Steingraber, *Living Downstream: An Ecologist Looks at Cancer and the Environment* (Reading, Mass.: Perseus Books, 1997); John Wargo, *Our Children's Toxic Legacy: How Science and Law Fail to Protect Us from Pesticides,* 2d ed. (New Haven, Conn.: Yale University Press, 1998).

11. On early understandings of the body, see Peter Brown, *The Body and Society: Men, Women, and Sexual Renunciation in Early Christianity* (New York: Columbia University Press, 1988); Caroline Walker Bynum, *Holy Feast and Holy Fast: The Religious Significance of Food to Medieval Women* (Berkeley: University of California Press, 1987); Joan Cadden, *Meanings of Sex Difference in the Middle Ages: Medicine, Science, and Culture* (Cambridge: Cambridge University Press, 1993); and Sarah Kay and Miri Rubin, eds., *Framing Medieval Bodies* (Manchester: Manchester University Press, 1994). On feminist thought on the body, see Linda Martin Alcoff, "Feminist Theory and Social Science," in *BodySpace,* ed. Nancy Duncan (New York: Routledge, 1996), 13–27; Donna Haraway, "A Manifesto for Cyborgs: Science, Technology, and Socialist Feminism in the 1980s," in *Feminist Social Thought: A Reader,* ed. Diana Tietjens Meyers (New York: Routledge, 1997), 502–31, and "Situated Knowledges: The Science Question in Feminism and the Privilege of Partial Perspective," *Feminist Studies* 14, no. 3 (Fall 1988): 575–99; and Janet Price and Margrit Shildrick, "Openings on the Body: A Critical Introduction," in *Feminist Theory and the Body: A Reader,* ed. Price and Shildrick (New York: Routledge, 1999), 1–14. For crucial foundations on this thought, see Simone de Beauvoir, *The Second Sex,* trans. H. M. Parshley (New York: Alfred A. Knopf, 1952, 1980; Random House, Vintage Books edition, 1989); Rosemary Radford Ruether, "New Woman and New Earth: Women, Ecology, and Social Revolution," in *New Woman, New Earth: Sexist Ideologies and Human Liberation,* ed. Ruether (New York: Seabury Press, 1975; Boston: Beacon Press, 1995), 186–211; and Carolyn Merchant, *The Death of Nature: Women, Ecology, and the Scientific Revolution* (San Francisco: Harper Collins, 1980, 1990).

12. Evelyn Fox Keller, *Reflections on Gender and Science* (New Haven, Conn.: Yale University Press, 1985).

13. Alcoff, "Feminist Theory and Social Science," in Duncan, *BodySpace,* 15.

14. Ecofeminist critiques have long pointed out that the linked cultural concepts of the feminine, bodies, biological sex, and nature are often all devalued accordingly. Generally, ecofeminist scholarship provides the backbone for many of the ideas in this chapter, including the works of the following: Merchant, *Earthcare;* Susan Griffin, *The Eros of Everyday Life: Essays on Ecology, Gender, and Society* (New York: Anchor Books, 1995); Mary Mellor, ed., *Feminism and Ecology* (New York: New York University Press, 1997); Karen J. Warren, ed., *Ecofeminism: Women, Culture, and Nature* (Bloomington: Indiana University Press, 1997); and Ruether, "New Woman and New Earth: Women, Ecology, and Social Revolution," in *New Woman, New Earth.*

15. For a discussion of scientists who argued that radioactive fallout and various toxic residues in food and the environment were safe, see Howard Ball, *Justice Downwind: America's Atomic Testing Program in the 1950s* (New York: Oxford University Press, 1986), 102–27; Philip L. Fradkin, *Fallout: An American Nuclear Tragedy* (Tucson: University of Arizona Press, 1989); and Levenstein, *Paradox of Plenty*, 101–18, 160–77. On a dissatisfied public, see Marston Bates, "It's a Big, Big, Synthetic World," *New York Times Magazine*, November 18, 1962, 54, 59, 60, 69, and "Do You Know What You're Eating, Drinking, Breathing?" *U.S. News and World Report* 48, no. 11 (March 14, 1960): 57–58, 60.

16. Donald Worster, *Nature's Economy: A History of Ecological Ideas*, 2d ed. (Cambridge: Cambridge University Press, 1985).

17. Ibid., 342–87.

18. "Concerned" to editor, the *Caller,* Corpus Christi, Tex., June 11, 1963, RCP/BLYU.

19. The controversy over *Silent Spring* was not the first time that such a clash between the ideas of ecology, gender, and the body had occurred, at least in the history of American industrialization. Historians have tended to treat the rise of the early nineteenth- and twentieth-century conservation and preservation movements as separate from the simultaneous development of industrial hygiene and sanitarianism, or municipal housekeeping. These movements, however, did connect on a deep level; in that time of rapidly changing, even destabilizing, culture and technology, people also struggled to reintegrate with their environment through alternative understandings of the body. See Christopher Sellers, *Hazards of the Job: From Industrial Disease to Environmental Health Science* (Chapel Hill: University of North Carolina Press, 1997); Suellen Hoy, *Chasing Dirt: The American Pursuit of Cleanliness* (New York: Oxford University Press, 1995); and Robert Gottlieb, *Forcing the Spring: The Transformation of the American Environmental Movement* (Washington, D.C.: Island Press, 1993). See also Merchant, "Earthcare: Women and the American Environmental Movement," in *Earthcare*, 139–66, and H. Patricia Hynes, "Ellen Swallow, Lois Gibbs, and Rachel Carson: Catalysts of the American Environmental Movement," *Women's Studies International Forum* 8, no. 4 (1985): 291–98. It would remain for *Silent Spring* and the ecological turn to bring the physical dimension of the human-nature connection roaring back, if only for a short time, to the forefront of American thought.

20. The following summary owes especially to Lear, *Witness for Nature*, and Graham, *Since* Silent Spring.

21. On the history of the postwar rise of chemical pesticides, see Russell, *War and Nature;* Dunlap, *DDT: Scientists, Citizens, and Public Policy;* Christopher J. Bosso, *Pesticides and Politics: The Life Cycle of a Public Issue* (Pittsburgh, Pa.: University of Pittsburgh Press, 1987); and Paolo Palladino, *Entomology, Ecology, and Agriculture: The Making of Scientific Careers in North America, 1885–1985* (Amsterdam: Harwood Academic Publishers, 1996).

22. William Longgood, *Poisons in Your Food* (New York: Simon and Schuster, 1960); Lewis Herber (Murray Bookchin), *Our Synthetic Environment* (New York: Alfred A. Knopf, 1962); Bates, "It's a Big, Big, Synthetic World," and "Do You Know What You're Eating, Drinking, Breathing?"

23. Carson, *Silent Spring,* 15.

24. Ibid., 12–13.

25. For an overview of the controversy, see Graham, *Since* Silent Spring.

26. Marilyn A. Katz, "Daughters of Demeter: Women in Ancient Greece," in *Becoming Visible: Women in European History*, 3d ed., ed. Renate Bridenthal et al. (Boston: Houghton Mifflin, 1998), 47–75, 63; Elaine Showalter, *Hystories: Hysterical Epidemics and Modern Media* (New York: Columbia University Press, 1997), 10.

27. Mrs. Gerhard H. Roberts to editor, *Suffolk County News*, Sayville, N.Y., December 13, 1962; Edith G. Kellam to editor, *Virginian-Pilot*, Norfolk, Va., January 27, 1963; William Palmer Taylor to editor, *Chemical Engineering*, New York, N.Y., November 26, 1962, all in RCP/BLYU. See also Elizabeth Lorrimer to RC, undated; anonymous letter signed "Worried," to editor, *Tarentum News*, Tarentum, Pa., November 16, 1962 (reasoning from dead animals and vegetation as consequences of pesticide use to the potential effects on her own health, arguing that we should never use chemical pesticides because they are too strong); Mrs. Robert Jones to editor, *Dallas News*, October 15, 1962; Mrs. Robert Visel to editor, the *Pantagraph*, Bloomington, Ill., August 17, 1962 (pointing out that the public is not in fact all that healthy even with an increased food supply—cancer, heart disease, and so forth); Grace Lee Kenyon to editor, the *Mirror*, Altoona, Pa., January 9, 1963: "To the thoughtful housewife, who is forced to use a kit of burglar tools to remove the contents of the modern food container, it would appear that our authorities have her health and welfare very much at heart. However, a glance at spraying statistics shows something very different!"; and Mrs. Thomas W. French to Board of Health, Middletown, N.J. Township, reprinted as letter to the editor in *Red Bank Register*, Red Bank, N.J., July 7, 1963, all in RCP/BLYU. Another letter contains an interesting reference not to organic pesticides but to the arsenical pesticides commonly used prior to the postwar use of organophosphates, regarding arsenic problems "in the well at Twin Oaks School and in private wells, and a woman . . . sick with arsenic poisoning. What is the connection between these alarming findings and the use of chemical sprays on fruit trees and other plants in our area?" (Norman D. Sundberg to editor, *Register-Guard*, Eugene, Ore., October 10, 1962). On pesticide poisoning problems prior to *Silent Spring*, see James Whorton, *Before* Silent Spring: *Pesticides and Public Health in Pre-DDT America* (Princeton, N.J.: Princeton University Press, 1974).

28. John C. Burnham, "How the Discovery of Accidental Childhood Poisoning Contributed to the Development of Environmentalism in the United States," *Environmental History Review* 19, no. 3 (1995): 57–81.

29. Sandra L. Showalter to RC, August 8, 1963; see also Annie Laurie Spencer to RC, April 7, 1964, both in RCP/BLYU.

30. Grace Lee Kenyon to editor, *Bristol Press*, Bristol, Conn., January 28, 1963, RCP/BLYU.

31. Lear, *Witness for Nature*, 435, also observes that more women than men appear to have written letters to the editor regarding *Silent Spring*.

32. Vera Norwood, *Made from This Earth: American Women and Nature* (Chapel Hill: University of North Carolina Press, 1993), 143–71, and "The Nature of Knowing: Rachel Carson and the American Environment," *Signs* 12 (Summer 1987): 740–61. For other observations on the gendered dimensions of the debate over *Silent Spring*, see Lear, *Rachel Carson*; Hynes, *The Recurring Silent Spring*; and

Doris Z. Fleischer, "*Silent Spring:* Personal Synthesis of Two Cultures," *Bulletin of Science, Technology, and Society* 13, no. 4 (1993): 200–202.

33. *Humboldt Times,* Eureka, Calif., November 3, 1962, "Authorities Assure Housewives No Need to Fear Pesticide Use"; also see Bob Hartley, the *Journal,* East St. Louis, Ill., January 13, 1963, "Battle Rages over Use of Insecticide Poisons," (reporting increased phone calls after the publication of *Silent Spring,* especially from housewives), both in RCP/BLYU.

34. As reported in an editorial in the *Agricultural Chemicals* issue of June 1963, RCP/BLYU.

35. Elmer Roessner, "Business Today" column, *News-Record,* Harrisonburg, Va., October 3, 1962, RCP/BLYU. Another especially rude editorial from the *Gazette* in Emporia, Kans., scoffs that garden club women go to "club meetings to learn how to boss their husbands around the yard." It also rants on about the controversy over pesticides and Rachel Carson: "A woman, of course, started the whole thing" (Editorial, "What to Do about Bugs," RCP/BLYU).

36. For the history of women and gender in the 1950s and early 1960s, see the following works: Linda Kerber, Alice Kessler-Harris, and Kathryn Kish Sklar, eds., *U.S. History as Women's History: New Feminist Essays* (Chapel Hill: University of North Carolina Press, 1995); Lynn Y. Weiner, "Reconstructing Motherhood: The La Leche League in Postwar America," *Journal of American History* 80, no. 4 (March 1994): 1357–81; Blanche Linden-Ward and Carol Hurd Green, *American Women in the 1960s: Changing the Future* (New York: Maxwell Macmillan International, 1993); Elaine Tyler May, *Homeward Bound: American Families in the Cold War Era* (New York: Basic Books, 1988); Joanne Meyerowitz, ed., *Not June Cleaver: Women and Gender in Postwar America, 1945–1960* (Philadelphia: Temple University Press, 1994); Ruth Rosen, *The World Split Open: How the Modern Women's Movement Changed America* (New York: Penguin Books, 2000); Amy Swerdlow, *Women Strike for Peace: Traditional Motherhood and Radical Politics in the 1960s* (Chicago: University of Chicago Press, 1993); Sara Evans, *Personal Politics: The Roots of Women's Liberation in the Civil Rights Movement and the New Left* (New York: Free Press, 1979); Daniel Horowitz, *Betty Friedan and the Making of the Feminist Mystique: The American Left, the Cold War, and Modern Feminism* (Amherst: University of Massachusetts Press, 1998); and Betty Friedan, *The Feminine Mystique* (New York: Dell Publishing, 1962).

37. Mrs. Ann E. Wissler, president, San Bernadino Valley Audubon Society, to editor, the *Caller,* Corpus Christi, Tex., November 14, 1962, RCP/BLYU.

38. Miriam (Mrs. Bernard) Zuger to RC, July 2, 1962; Mrs. M. E. Herr to RC, September 1, 1962, both in RCP/BLYU.

39. On women and consumption, see Ruether, "New Woman and New Earth," 196–204.

40. Certainly not all women agreed with Rachel Carson; women attack her as well. See, for example, Flora Perales to editor, the *Caller,* Corpus Christi, Tex., November 10, 1962, and Mrs. Neil Quirin, *Des Moines Register,* Des Moines, Iowa, May 27, 1963, both in RCP/BLYU.

41. Arthur A. MacConochie to editor, *Virginian-Pilot,* Norfolk, Va., January 8, 1963, RCP/BLYU.

42. Ibid.

43. Michael Kimmel, *Manhood in America: A Cultural History* (New York: Free Press, 1996), viii, ix–x, 223–58.

44. Also on masculinity in the postwar era, see Barbara Ehrenreich, *The Hearts of Men: American Dreams and the Flight from Commitment* (New York: Anchor Books, 1984). For studies of masculinity generally, see Michael S. Kimmel, "Masculinity as Homophobia: Fear, Shame, and Silence in the Construction of Gender Identity," in *Theorizing Masculinities*, ed. Harry Brod and Michael Kaufman (Thousand Oaks, Calif.: Sage Publications, 1994), 119–41; Mairtin Mac an Ghail, "Introduction," in *Understanding Masculinities: Social Relations and Cultural Arenas*, ed. Harry Brod and Michael Kaufman (Philadelphia: Open University Press, 1996), 1–13; Nigel Edley and Margaret Wetherall, "Masculinity, Power and Identity," in *Understanding Masculinities*, 97–113; and David H. Morgan, "Theater of War: Combat, the Military, and Masculinities," in *Theorizing Masculinities*, 165–82.

45. Susan M. Hartman, "Women's Employment and the Domestic Ideal in the Early Cold War Years," in Meyerowitz, *Not June Cleaver*, 84–100. On women in science, see Margaret W. Rossiter, *Women Scientists in America: Before Affirmative Action, 1940–1972* (Baltimore: Johns Hopkins University Press, 1995), and Londa Schiebinger, *Has Feminism Changed Science?* (Cambridge, Mass.: Harvard University Press, 1999).

46. Hesta Forster to RC, February 28, 1964; Mrs. George Hilliard to RC, August 13, 1962, both in RCP/BLYU.

47. As quoted in Lear, *Witness for Nature*, 429.

48. "Lawn, Garden Chemicals Line Up for Market: Sales Expected," *Chemical and Engineering News* 40, no. 7 (February 12, 1962). The numbers for sales depended on the trade journal reporting and their definition of the sector. See Lawrence Lessing, "The Great American Scientists: The Chemists," *Fortune* 61, no. 4 (April 1960): 131–35, 266.

49. The NACA published portions of their press releases and tracking in their monthly journal, the *NACA News and Pesticide Review*; see especially vol. 21, no. 1 (October 1962): 11, 14–15, and vol. 21, no. 2 (December 1962): 13 (reporting the distribution of over 5,300 news stories). The industry also sponsored panels and meetings all over the country, especially in agricultural areas and at trade shows, gatherings that were heavily loaded with university professors who received research funds from chemical companies. See Gillis Morgan, "On Farm Products: Chemical Firm Heads Speak at Meet Here," *Journal*, Montgomery, Ala. (February 19, 1963), and "Opinions of *Silent Spring* Given at Trade Show," *Tribune*, Hornell, N.Y. (January 19, 1963), both in RCP/BLYU. See also Sheldon Rampton and John Stauber, "Silencing Spring: Corporate Propaganda and the Takeover of the Environmental Movement," in *Reclaiming the Environmental Debate: The Politics of Health in a Toxic Culture*, ed. Richard Hofrichter (Cambridge, Mass.: MIT Press, 2000), 157–75.

50. Frederick J. Stare, "On *Silent Spring*," *Nutrition Reviews* 21, no. 1 (January 1963): 1–4.

51. Unsigned editorial, "The Rachel Carson Book," *American Vegetable Grower* (October 1962).

52. Dr. William J. Darby, "Silence, Miss Carson," *Chemical and Engineering News* 40, no. 40 (October 1, 1962): 60–62.

53. Ibid.

54. "Pesticides: The Price for Progress," *Time* 80, no. 13 (September 28, 1962): 45–46, 48; "For Many a Spring," *Time* 83, no. 17 (April 24, 1964): 73; Gordon Tullock, "Of Mites and Men," *National Review* (November 20, 1962): 398–99; Howard Earle, "Pesticides: Facts, Not Fear," *Today's Health* 41, no. 2 (February 1963): 19–20, 23, 58–60; "If You Didn't Have Poison Sprays," *U.S. News and World Report* 54, no. 22 (June 3, 1963): 74–75; "A Life in Nature," *Newsweek* 60, no. 6 (April 27, 1964): 95; "Insecticides: Hiss of Doom?" *Newsweek* 60, no. 6 (August 6, 1962): 55.

55. On negative reactions to Carson and her supporters as "emotional," see Pat Field, "UT Professor Calls New Book 'One-Sided,'" the *Journal*, Knoxville, Tenn., February 2, 1963 ("one-sided, over-emotional, hysterical"), Edwin Diamond, "The Myth of the 'Pesticide Menace,'" *Saturday Evening Post*, Philadelphia, September 28, 1963 (calling *Silent Spring* "emotional, alarmist"), John K. Newell, science column, "'Silent Spring' Sure to Kick up a Fuss," *Express-News*, San Antonio, Tex., September 23, 1962 (regarding "emotional" tone of *Silent Spring*), Darby, "Silence, Miss Carson," 60–62, and quote from Gardner B. Moment, professor of biology, Goucher College, comment in *Sunday Sun* (no location preserved), October 7, 1962, all in RCP/BLYU. See also Dr. William M. Clay, chairman, Department of Biology, University of Louisville, a pro-Rachel supporter, who gave the "other side" of the story first: "Has not industrialized technology established the supremacy of man over nature? The mightiest streams have been dammed, dark forests cleared and replaced by teeming cities, black plague and tuberculosis are so controlled that more and more people live on into senile old age, to die ultimately of other causes. Only rarely is a warning voice raised" ("Is Man Poisoning Himself in Battle against Bugs?" *Courier-Journal*, Louisville, Ky., September 23, 1962). For an example of this positive yet "reserved" response, see William Vogt, "On Man the Destroyer," *Natural History* (January 1963): 3–5 ("Miss Carson is, alas, all too vulnerable to attack because of a tendency to attack and an occasional, uncritical acceptance of data").

56. Keller, *Reflections on Gender and Science*, 6–7. In further thinking through questions of science, technology, and gender, see Evelyn Fox Keller, "Gender and Science: Origin, History and Politics," *Osiris* 10 (1995): 27–38; Londa Schiebinger, *Has Feminism Changed Science?* (Cambridge, Mass.: Harvard University Press, 1999), and "Creating Sustainable Science," *Osiris* 12 (1997): 201–16; Carroll Pursell, "The Construction of Masculinity and Technology," *Polhem* 11 (1993): 206–19; and Nina E. Lerman, Arwen Palmer Mohun, and Ruth Oldenziel, "Versatile Tools: Gender Analysis and the History of Technology," *Technology and Culture* 38, no. 1 (January 1997): 1–8, and "The Shoulders We Stand On and the View from Here: Historiography and Directions for Research," ibid., 9–30.

57. I. L. Baldwin, "Chemicals and Pests," *Science* (September 16, 1962): 1043; "Interview with Dr. Byron T. Shaw, Administrator, U.S. Agricultural Research Service," *U.S. News and World Report* 53, no. 2 (November 26, 1962): 86–94.

58. "After the Wiesner Report . . . Feeling Little Pain," *Business Week* (May 25, 1963): 36.

59. As quoted in Graham, *Since Silent Spring*, 88. Industry ideas of health, body, and environment focused especially on the concept of safe "tolerances" for toxic substances, arrived at through laboratory animal testing. See George C.

Decker, "Pros and Cons of Pests, Pest Control, and Pesticides," *NACA News and Pesticide Review (NAC NPR)* 20, no. 6 (August 1962): 3–12, and "Six Million Years and a Million Dollars in Tests for Safety," *NAC NPR* 20, no. 5 (June 1962): 3–6. Interestingly, this same line of argument often denied that the disastrous effects of wildlife on humans might have any implications for concerns over human health; "Facts on the Use of Pesticides," *NAC NPR* 21, no. 2 (December 1962): 8–10. The epitome of the scientific endorsement of this view of the body came from Dr. Wayland Hayes Jr., chief of toxicology at the U.S. Public Health Service; see Hayes et al., "Storage of DDT and DDE in People with Different Degrees of Exposure to DDT," *A.M.A. Archives of Industrial Health* 18 (November 1958): 398–406; Lear, *Witness for Nature,* 334–35.

60. As quoted in Graham, *Since* Silent Spring, 88.

CHAPTER SEVEN

Gender Transformed: Endocrine Disruptors in the Environment

Nancy Langston

In the late 1970s, anglers in England began reporting that they were catching bizarre fish—rainbow trout that seemed to be partly male and partly female. Perplexed, a biologist from Brunel University named John Sumpter went out to investigate these reports of what the media called "sexually confused fish."[1] He discovered that the trout were males that had indeed developed female characters, and he found that the best places to find these gender-bending fish were near sewage plants, in the lagoons and pools just below the discharge outlets for treated waste. The obvious question occurred to him: could anything in the sewage effluent be affecting the masculinity of the fish?

Sumpter, with the help of fellow Brunel University biologist Charles R. Tyler and researchers from the Ministry of Agriculture, Fisheries, and Food, found male fish that were producing elevated levels of vitellogenin, a protein responsible for making egg yolks in female fish. Male fish possess a gene that can produce vitellogenin when triggered by estrogen, but ordinarily males lack enough estrogen—a female sex hormone—to trigger this gene. To test whether sewage treatment plants had anything to do with the elevated levels of vitellogenin in the male fish blood, the scientists took healthy male trout raised in captivity, put them in cages, and placed them for three weeks near the discharge points of thirty different sewage treatment plants. Soon those males began producing vitellogenin, just like females.[2]

Some of the scientists suspected that industrial chemicals such as nonylphenols—breakdown products of detergents, pesticides, and cosmetics—might be responsible for feminizing the males. But initial studies failed to support this hypothesis. They wondered next if the problem might stem from birth control pills. Estrogens from contraceptives, they reasoned, might not be completely breaking down in the women's bodies or in the sewer treatment process, so those estrogens might be ending up in the effluent and somehow stimulating males to become females.

Lab experiments showed that ethynylestradiol, the main estrogenic compound in birth control pills, could indeed stimulate male fish to produce female proteins, even when concentrations were as low as one nanogram per liter of water. But the scientists could not initially find ethynylestradiol in the rivers at levels their instruments could detect.[3] Other researchers suspected that the male fishes' problems might stem from something even stranger: during certain times of their menstrual cycles, women's urine is brimming with estrogen. Perhaps this urine was powerful enough so that, even after being diluted and treated, it could alter the natural world. Could hormones in women's urine—whether of natural or synthetic origin—be feminizing male fish?

Sumpter's results suggested several disturbing things. First, we might be poisoning wildlife with chemicals that alter their hormonal systems, sometimes even transforming them from one gender to another—transformations that could harm their ability to successfully reproduce and thus threaten their survival. Second, some researchers suspected that what was happening to the fish might also happen to humans. And third, the results suggested that industrial chemicals were not the only potential problem: our private bodily functions might also be altering gender in the environment.[4]

On the most basic level, we tend to assume that what happens inside our bodies is a personal matter. When we take those pills, those cups of coffee, those birth control hormones, we assume that they're disappearing into the black box of our innermost bodies. Yet those chemicals, both natural and unnatural, don't end with us; they come out, get flushed down the toilet, and make it through our septic tanks or sewer systems into the waters we share with other creatures. In many places now, water carrying our bodily effluents may form more than half the flow in a summer stream. And remnants from our bodily wastes may be changing the nature of gender, turning male fish into female fish and female fish into male fish—and potentially affecting human development as well.

In this chapter, I will examine some transformations in the biological constructions of gender since the 1930s.[5] To do this, I will look at two sets of changes. First, I will examine changes in the levels of natural sex hormones in women's bodies, changes stimulated in part by larger societal transformations. Second, I will examine what are called endocrine disruptors, the industrial pollutants that mimic female sex hormones and disrupt the endocrine systems that control the biological expression of gender in wildlife as well as people.

Endocrine disruptors connect environmental histories of the body with environmental histories of wild places and wild animals.[6] What we eat, what we drink, what we excrete, how we procreate: these are at the core of our animal selves. Our bodies are how we're most natural, but now they're also how we're most industrialized, since our bodies are where our industrial chemicals are coming back to haunt us. As strange as it may seem, even our pee has become hazardous waste, capable of turning male fish into quasi-females. In this chapter I will explore what endocrine disruptors might mean for the nature of gender and for our relationships with the environment.

The more researchers looked, the more they found that the waters of Britain, Europe, and America were laden with chemicals excreted in people's urine and that these chemicals could be causing widespread reproductive impairment in males from many different species. For example, scientists in Minnesota found male carp and walleyes in the effluent of sewage plants that weren't making sperm but were producing high quantities of vitellogenin instead.[7] Other studies in the Great Lakes region found male white perch that had become intersex—part male, part female, and completely uninterested in sex.[8] Urine, researchers found, could contain over sixty different synthetic chemicals, not to mention plenty of natural hormones as well.[9] It turns out that our pee is doused with poisons—metabolites from the breakdown of birth control pills, caffeine from all the coffee and Mountain Dew we're quaffing, remnants from the aspirin and Tylenol and anticholesterol drugs we use to stanch the pain of our modern ailments. These chemicals in sewage effluent seemed to be altering the action of hormones during development, with potentially profound effects on the fetus.[10]

Industrial chemicals as well as sewage effluents were also implicated in gender switches. Students on a biology field trip in Florida noticed that every single mosquitofish they found seemed to be a male, for each had a gonopodium—an anal fin that males use for copulation. But many of these "males" turned out to be pregnant, and the students found that all the females in this stretch of the creek had been masculinized. The problem, biologist W. Mike Howell learned, was that wastes from pulp and paper mills were contaminated with chemicals that acted like androgens, male sex hormones that trigger the production of testosterone.[11] Females from other fish species also became masculinized when exposed to pulp mill wastes; killifish and sailfin mollys developed fins resembling gonopodia, becoming extremely aggressive as well. In one researcher's words, female killifish stopped acting like normal, well-behaved females and instead became "like little sharks."[12] Bluegill sunfish, American eels, Swedish eelpouts—all these fish became masculinized in the presence of pulp mill waste in streams across the world.

Gender confusion wasn't limited to fish. Male alligators exposed to DDT in Florida's Lake Apopka had abnormally small penises. They were just one-half to one-third the normal size, too small to function, and these males also seemed to have ovaries, while the females produced abnormal eggs.[13] Two-thirds of male Florida panthers—an endangered species whose total population only numbered thirty to fifty individuals in 1994—were found to have cryptorchidism, a condition in which the testes doesn't descend, much less produce normal sperm. These male panthers are producing twice as much estrogen as testosterone, while normal male panthers do the reverse. In some western rivers, male Chinook salmon have undergone sex-reversal; many of the fish that look like females are actually males that have suffered a hormonal emasculation. Prothonotary warblers in Alabama, sea turtles in Georgia, mink and otters around the Great Lakes—all show reproductive malformations.[14]

The list of recent gender transformations in wildlife can go on and on: female Great Lakes gulls and terns that try to mate with other females instead of with males. "Gulls in these colonies show excessive chick mortality, birth defects, and skewed sex ratios, with an excess of females."[15] Male Atlantic cod and winter flounder that show reduced testosterone levels, hampering reproduction. Female Atlantic croakers (a kind of fish) that aren't growing normal ovaries. Male porpoises that don't have enough testosterone to reproduce. Polar bears on the Arctic island of Svarlbard that are hermaphrodites, which is not something one normally sees in a polar bear.[16] In perhaps the most disturbing example of gender switches, Gerald A. LeBlanc of North Carolina State University in Raleigh found that over one hundred species of marine snails were experiencing something known as imposex, a pollution-induced masculinization. Females developed a huge malformed penis that blocked their release of eggs. They swelled up with eggs that couldn't get out and then they died.[17]

By the 1990s, researchers noticed that it wasn't only wildlife that were showing difficulties with their reproductive health. Increasing numbers of people were as well. As with panthers, the incidence of cryptorchidism (undescended testicles) in British men doubled in two decades. In the three decades since 1970, American boys appear to have become increasingly likely to develop severe hypospadias, a birth defect of the penis.[18] Testicular cancer has increased in many industrialized countries. For example, in Denmark, the incidence of testicular cancer has more than tripled since World War II, while in the United States, the incidence increased by 51 percent between 1973 and 1995. Similar increases are occurring in other Scandinavian countries and in Scotland.[19]

Since the 1950s, sperm counts in some (but not all) regions across the world have declined significantly.[20] Men in many industrial nations are showing increases in prostate cancer; for example, a 1999 review found that men in the United States in 1994 had "about a three- to four-fold risk of being diagnosed with prostate cancer compared with their fathers."[21] Much of this increase in the number of diagnosed cases was probably due to better screening tests, but researchers were nonetheless concerned that actual incidence was also increasing for unexplained reasons. Studies suggest that, across the United States and Puerto Rico, many girls are developing breasts at younger ages.[22] Other research on women's reproductive health shows an increase in the incidence of misshapen wombs, infertility, endometriosis, fibroids, breast cancer, and ovarian cancer since the 1950s.[23]

What, if anything, connects all these bizarre problems with gender and reproductive health? Are there any links between human and wildlife problems? Possibly; many researchers now believe these changes may stem from the consequences of fetal events—namely, imbalances in sex hormones during fetal development. Since the 1950s, we may have been changing the biological basis of gender by filling the world's waters with synthetic chemicals that alter the balance of sex hormones controlling the biological development of gender. Hundreds of the synthetic chemicals we started dumping into the environment since World War II—PCBs, DDT and other pesticides, dioxins, many compounds in plastics—disrupt the action of natural sex hormones, particularly on the fetus. Endocrine disruptors don't just shut down the endocrine system: they can actually fool it into "accepting new instructions that distort the natural development of the organism."[24]

These estrogen-disrupting chemicals are not rare; some of them are among the most common synthetic chemicals in production. We now live submerged in a sea of estrogens, some natural and some synthetic. These estrogens affect men as well as women, wildlife as well as humans. Tracing the pathways of that estrogen—its naturalness and its unnaturalness—can illuminate an environmental history of gender.

The Greeks called the main female sex hormone "estrogen" because it produced the state of "estrus," when a female goes into heat. Estrus, in turn, derives from the Greek word *oistros*, which means "frenzy," or a woman driven wild.[25] Estrogen, like other hormones, is a chemical produced by the body that regulates the body's growth and development. Hormones are messengers that create a complex signaling system (called the endocrine system) that tells the body what to produce, where, and when. Sex hormones tell the developing fetus to develop a penis or not, as the case may be. Sex hormones tell a boy's testicles to descend, a girl's breasts to develop, a woman's ovaries to grow eggs. They control what makes us female and what makes us male.

Postmodernists like to imagine that gender is culturally constructed, and clearly cultural forces do shape the expression of gender differences in our society. But gender is also profoundly biological. Hormones control the biological construction of gender, and now hormone mimics may control the biological deconstruction of gender as well. To complicate matters, cultural constructions influence the biological constructions of gender because behavior, social interactions, and expectations can all change the ways our bodies produce sex hormones. On a more direct level as well, culture alters the biological control of gender differences because many of the chemicals our culture produces have powerful effects on hormonal functions.

Sex hormones link wildlife and humans, wild places and human places, because we share our hormonal systems with animals. Surprisingly, the same chemical can act like a hormone in an alligator, a fish, a panther, and a woman. For 300 million years of evolutionary history, the hormonal system has been remarkably conserved, the reproductive endocrinologist Frederick vom Saal argues, because "it's so critical to life. So if a chemical can disrupt the endocrine system by acting as an estrogen in a fish, for instance, the likelihood is that it will do that in humans. Endocrine disruption in fish has to be a concern with regard to human health. Not just mice, not just birds or reptiles, it's all of them. They're all sentinels for our health because these chemicals are in all likelihood operating on systems that we all share."[26] The fact that we share our hormonal systems with other vertebrates means that what happens out in wild places also happens within our bodies. For example, the PCBs dumped in the Hudson River decades ago may well be stimulating tumors in women's wombs and breasts to swell. It is within our bodies that we are most vulnerable to the pollutants we think we've disposed of.

HOW HORMONES WORK: CREATING GENDER

Normal development of a creature, from egg to adult, is controlled by the balance between hormones. Tiny changes in this balance signal growth, sexual differentiation, and other critical functions from the control of blood sugar and metabolism to brain development to the growth and function of reproductive systems. The endocrine system, like the nervous system, is a communication network that regulates all functions of the body. Glands within the body secrete chemical messengers—hormones—which travel through the bloodstream until they encounter cells with specific target receptors. Each hormone has a unique shape that fits the shape of the receptor protein at the target cell; imagine the hormone as your key and the receptor protein as the lock in your door. But hormones are also flexible: a given receptor protein may exist on different cells in different organs, so that the body can use the same hormone to perform radically different functions in different tissues. Hormones act slowly (compared, say, to the nervous system, the other communication network in the body), and their effects persist in the body for long periods of time (again, compared to the nervous system, whose effects are very rapid and very short). Most important, the endocrine system is designed so that incredibly tiny amounts of a chemical (on the order of molecules) can produce enormous changes in the body.[27]

For example, consider estrogen (which isn't just one chemical, but several, including estradiol, estrone, and estriol). Estrogen, like the male androgens, is a steroid, meaning a fat soluble hormone derived from cholesterol. Several locations within the female body can make estrogen—even our fat cells do as we age—but the ovaries are the most important site for estrogen production. Estrogens help develop gender in the fetus, tell a girl's body to begin developing breasts and hairy armpits, tell the breasts to prepare for lactation, regulate changes during menstruation, increase libido, protect the heart, and help bones to grow denser. Too many estrogens at the wrong time, however, are a problem: they stimulate the replication of cancer cells, tell tumors in women's uteruses to grow, and derail normal male development.

After the ovaries release a molecule of estrogen, it travels through the blood until it encounters receptors at the breast (or any of a number of organs). The estrogen molecule passes within the breast cell and binds to a receptor protein inside that cell, which triggers a change in the shape of that receptor protein. This receptor-estrogen complex enters the cell's nucleus and binds to the DNA, which causes a change in the gene's expression and changes in the cell's activity—for example, telling the breast to start growing.[28]

What keeps estrogen from going wild in the body, from growing breasts the size of houses, for example? First, the body controls the production of hormones by having the pituitary gland produce other hormones that signal the ovaries to regulate their secretion of estrogen. Certain proteins, such as sex hormone binding globulin, circulate within the bloodstream, binding to loose estrogen in the blood and keeping it from acting on target cells. For estrogen to function correctly in the body, it needs to be in a certain ratio with other sex hormones: the androgens or male sex hormones (which are also present in females but in lower quantities, just as estrogens are present in males, at low quantities). Often it's not the absolute quantity of estrogen that matters, but instead the ratio between estrogen and androgen, or the change in the amount of estrogen, that signals genes to get to work.[29]

Estrogen receptors are everywhere in a woman's body (and a man's too): in breast cells, the uterus, the ovaries, bone cells, hair cells, blood vessels, liver, kidneys, eyes, and even a man's prostrate. To complicate matters, hormone receptors don't come in just one shape. Some hormone receptors are very specific, allowing only a single configuration of a molecule to fit. Other receptors are much less choosy. Using language that is extraordinarily gendered, cellular biologists call estrogen receptors "womb-like" because they have "wobble"—they are flexible and accommodating. Or, as some male biologists put it, estrogen receptors have a "promiscuous" pouch that welcomes lots of different chemicals.[30] Cells don't need to hear from real estrogens; anything that binds to their estrogen receptors can have estrogenic effects, switching on cellular processes just as if a normal estrogen molecule had bound. And this method is how many synthetic chemicals seem to disrupt the endocrine system: they bind to estrogen receptors, fooling the body into thinking it has received a message from a real estrogen molecule.

Estrogen and other sex hormones control gender in fundamental ways, beginning with telling certain fetal tissues to turn into structures that are either male or female.[31] About six weeks into a pregnancy, sex determination begins. The developing fetus is extremely sensitive at this point to confused signals from synthetic chemicals. For example, in the male fetus, Sertoli cells direct the development and descent of the testes, control the development of germ cells, and control the cells that secrete the hormones responsible for masculinization. Turning on too many estrogen receptors in the developing fetus could reduce the multiplication of Sertoli cells and fix their numbers at very low levels. This result could also affect descent of the testes and the development of urethra, setting into motion events that might lead to birth defects and testicular cancer.[32] The obvious question, however, is this: since natural estrogen occurs in very high levels in a pregnant woman, why isn't her own estrogen confusing the development of her sons? The answer seems to be that most of a pregnant woman's natural estrogen is tied up by something called "sex hormone binding globulin" (SHGB), a protein that protects the fetus from the mother's high hormone levels. Synthetic estrogen-mimicking chemicals are not tied up by SHGB, making them potentially more powerful at lower doses than a woman's own estrogen.[33]

Normal sexual development depends upon getting the right hormonal signals at the right time in the fetus. If there is a tiny shift in the balance between hormones, a fetus might end up with the wrong number of digits, seriously confused genitalia, a uterus that's shaped wrong, a reproductive tract that cannot function, an immune system that later in life will turn against itself, and testicles or breasts that are programmed to develop cancer years down the road.[34] Yet those effects might not be detected for many decades because problems that start in the womb's environment may not emerge until puberty or adulthood.

CHANGES IN SEX HORMONES

In the last fifty years, American women have been exposed to increasing levels of estrogen, not just from synthetic sources but also from our body's own natural estrogen. Throughout much of history, women of reproductive age were likely to have been pregnant or lactating for a greater percentage of their reproductive years than is now typically the case. We put off pregnancies, or else we don't ever get pregnant; we start our periods earlier, and we go into menopause later than our ancestors, which means that many women now have from 355 to 450 menstrual cycles during their lives. In earlier generations, many women may have averaged far fewer. As we get exposed to more menstrual cycles, we get exposed to more estrogen.[35] Hormone replacement therapy can also bring more estrogen into women's bodies, as do most birth control pills.

Obesity rates in America have increased over the past fifty years, which increases estrogen levels, since fat cells produce estrogen from circulating adrenal hormones. Our diets contain more estrogen than they did half a century ago, especially through meat and dairy products. Changes in dairy production mean that cows are now often pregnant while they're being milked. This determinant leads to higher levels of natural bovine estrogen in that milk, since pregnant cows have more estrogen. Changes in diet during the last half century have also altered the ways women metabolize their own estrogen: the more fat and protein in a woman's diet, the more she recycles her own estrogens in her gut, in effect eating them twice. Drinking alcohol leads to higher levels of estrogens as well, because the liver is important in breaking down and excreting estrogen. When a woman drinks more than about fourteen drinks a week, the liver can no longer break down estrogen effectively, leading to higher estrogen levels in the body.[36]

Not only do women have their own estrogens to contend with; since World War II, women have had to deal with ever-increasing sources of synthetic estrogens and estrogen mimics. Although women's bodies produce natural estrogens and women also eat phytoestrogens (estrogens from plant sources) in their food, synthetic estrogen mimics differ from both. Synthetic estrogen mimics tend to be flexible molecules that can bend into many shapes and fit into many different cellular receptors, which means they can play havoc with the body's endocrine system. Unlike natural estrogen, estrogen mimics rarely bind with sex hormone binding globulin, so while they may at first be present in much lower levels than our own estrogen, their effective concentration can soon be much higher. Unlike natural estrogens, many synthetic estrogen mimics such as PCBs cannot be easily broken down by the body. During pregnancy and breast-feeding, these synthetic chemicals can be released, only to enter the fetus or the child. At other times, synthetic estrogen mimics accumulate in a woman's fatty tissues: breasts, ovaries, and brains.[37]

DES

The first signs that synthetic hormones might disrupt development came with DES daughters. In a huge, uncontrolled experiment, over five million women during the 1950s and 1960s were given DES, a potent synthetic estrogen, to prevent miscarriages. After years of increasing problems with the children of DES mothers, researchers in the 1970s finally starting connecting their problems with the hormones given to their mothers. Ironically, the 1930s researchers had known that DES caused cancer in lab animals, yet these studies were ignored when the FDA approved DES for pregnant women in 1947. Why? And why were people so slow to consider that treating millions of women with a synthetic, untested hormone might be a bad idea? Examining these questions will illuminate how our problems with endocrine disruptors have developed.[38]

DES is notable because it is the only large experiment done on estrogenic chemicals with human subjects. DES was not a perfect experiment, of course, because it was not designed as one: few follow-up studies were done on the children of DES mothers, and many women had no idea they were even being given DES during their pregnancies. Most of the doctors who prescribed DES had retired by the time its effects were being recognized, so those patients have never been followed. Nevertheless, it has become a model for the "long-term effects possible from in-utero exposure to an endocrine disruptor."[39] What happened with DES illustrates both the effects that synthetic hormones can have on people and the dangers of our culture's assumptions that people are so different from animals that animal experiments need not apply to humans.

In 1938, an English biochemist named Edward Charles Dodds first synthesized estrogen, creating diethylstilbestrol, or DES. Dodds's work showed that hormonal function in people and animals could be induced by synthetic substances—something no one had been certain was possible, even though now it seems obvious to those of us who have grown up in the age of the contraceptive pill. After Dodds's discovery (which he never patented), DES was manufactured quite cheaply from coal tar derivatives, soon becoming available under more than four hundred different trade names. (Since the drug was prescribed under so many trade names, most women never knew they had been given DES. Today, at least 64 percent of DES-exposed daughters do not know that their mothers had ever taken the drug.)[40]

When DES was first produced, people knew two things about it: it was extremely estrogenic, even more so than a woman's own estrogen, and it was highly carcinogenic in lab animals. Studies in the late 1930s showed that mice exposed in utero to DES developed breast cancer, while in 1939 and 1940, studies showed that mice exposed in utero to DES

sometimes developed liver cancer and were born with deformed reproductive organs.[41] Yet these experiments were ignored when the FDA approved the drug.

For centuries, doctors had tried to figure out how to prevent miscarriages. Suspecting that low levels of estrogen might be the problem, the
synthetic hormone DES was at first given only to pregnant women with
low estrogen levels and a history of miscarriage. A Harvard study published in 1947 suggested that the drug might reduce the risk of miscarriages, and FDA approval was given that year for use during pregnancy.
Only two early studies suggested that DES reduced the rates of miscarriages, and later, more careful studies showed the opposite. In 1953 and
1958, two reviews of the available research showed that DES slightly *increased* the risk of miscarriages, even though it was supposed to be decreasing miscarriages. Nevertheless, the drug continued to be prescribed.
DES was soon prescribed even for "normal" women "to make a normal
pregnancy more normal."[42] By 1957, the *Journal of Obstetrics and Gynecology* recommended it for all women to produce bigger and stronger babies.

Meanwhile, millions of people were being exposed to DES through
their diet. Beginning in the 1940s, DES was used in the United States as a
growth promoter in poultry, hogs, and cattle. Very high levels of DES
were soon being detected in poultry sold for human consumption—up to
one hundred times the concentrations necessary to cause breast cancer in
mice. When exposed male agricultural workers suffered sterility, impo-
tence, and breast growth, the FDA banned its use in chicken and lambs in
1959, while allowing its use in cattle feed to continue and allowing it to
be promoted as a wonder drug for pregnancy.[43]

Given these findings, why didn't scientists ask whether DES might
cause problems for the developing fetus? Until very recently, scientists
and doctors had assumed the womb was inviolate and could not be affected by the outside world. People believed that the mother's placenta
provided a barrier, protecting the fetus from harm. This belief partly reflected available technology: until the invention of ultrasound in the
1970s, the fetus was hidden off in the womb. People could not visualize
the development of the fetus, so it was easy to assume the fetal environment was separate.[44]

In 1962, when thalidomide was found to cross the placental barrier
with profound effects on limb development, this belief that drugs could
not cross the placenta was finally disrupted. Yet concerns were still not
raised about DES. Thalidomide produced immediate, massive birth defects, while no birth defects were initially apparent with DES. Few doctors or researchers could comprehend that a hormone given during
pregnancy might have effects that would only emerge decades later
when the children of DES mothers reached adulthood.

By the late 1960s, some of the children born to mothers who had taken DES were becoming sexually mature. Problems began to appear in these children, but it wasn't until 1971, after Arthur Herbst at Harvard Medical School showed a relationship between DES use and rare vaginal cancers in daughters (clear cell adenocarcinoma), that researchers suspected DES might be a problem. By November 1971, twenty-one cases of a formerly extremely rare clear cell vaginal cancer were linked to DES use, and the FDA issued an alert advising against the use of DES during pregnancy.[45]

Ensuing research revealed that only about 1 percent of the daughters developed vaginal cancers linked to DES, but nearly 90 percent of DES daughters have experienced reproductive tract problems, including menstrual irregularities and infertility.[46] For example, half of DES daughters have fertility problems, well above the rate of the general population. Sons of DES mothers have higher rates of undescended testicles, cysts of the reproductive tract, low sperm counts, and testicular cancer, while both sons and daughters showed depressed immune systems, higher rates of depression, and lowered libido. As these findings emerged, the FDA began trying to withdraw the chemical from use, but this action proved extremely difficult. In 1972, the FDA withdrew all approval for animal uses, but it took five years of litigation before the courts upheld this ban on the use of DES in animals.

At the peak of its use in the 1960s, DES was given to five million pregnant women and to nearly thirty million cattle, which means millions of people consumed meat tainted with artificial estrogen.[47] The press usually depicts DES as simply an individual woman's concern (like so many other things that affect women's health). The message is: ask your mother if she used DES, and if the answer is yes, then worry. DES is rarely portrayed as a larger environmental concern. But DES is an environmental exposure issue as well, since through food and waste from feedlots, and possibly through women's urine, the chemical entered the environment at large, exposing wildlife as well as women.

In the early 1970s, the toxicologist John McLachlan became concerned about the effects of DES in the food supply. He began studying its effects on development in mice, trying to find out if animal models could replicate the effects seen in daughters of DES mothers. Much to everyone's surprise, he showed just that: DES-exposed female mice had increased rates of vaginal cancer, and exposed male mice exhibited reduced fertility, undescended or stunted testicles, and genital tumors.[48] Work on the effects of DES on mice also showed that the artificial estrogen was feminizing male mice at the molecular level: male mice exposed prenatally to DES would express female proteins in the reproductive systems later in life, a result that at the time seemed astonishing. These findings, and McLachlan's concern about DES in animals, stimulated his growing concern that estrogenic substances in the environment might be affecting people. He first organized a symposium on estrogens in the environment in 1979, long before most people were concerned.[49] Yet, like most toxicologists, he was not fully aware of the wildlife research showing reproductive disorders. Moreover, his growing interest in endocrine disrupters isolated him within his own field.

One clear message from the DES story is that we should not assume that research on animals has no meaning for people. Yet our culture's unwillingness to believe that we are similar to animals may have been one of the biggest difficulties in creating a coherent response to endocrine disruptors. Many doctors and lawmakers are unwilling to believe that a compound's harmful effects on animals can be extrapolated to humans. As one of the leading researchers on endocrine disruptors, Dr. Frederick vom Saal, said, "Before DES was used on five million women in the U.S., it was clear from animal studies that DES would be damaging to fetuses. But we have this absolutely bizarre notion that humans are separate from the rest of life on Earth. You will hear physician after physician say, 'But that's an animal. What relevance does that have to humans?'"[50] Critics of the endocrine disrupter hypothesis argue that animal testing is not a perfect model for human effects, which is correct. Yet the irony is that animal testing probably *underestimates* the effects of estrogenic compounds on humans. Most common lab animals have been bred for large litter size and vigor, and these two qualities make them more resistant to the effects of estrogen.[51]

Although DES was still being prescribed to pregnant women, wildlife biologists were finding events in nature that resembled those induced by DES. In 1950, Howard Burlington and Verlus Frank Lindeman, two American biologists, showed that DDT could have estrogenic effects. Male chicks injected with a form of DDT had smaller testes (only 18 percent of normal size) and arrested development of secondary sexual characteristics compared to controls.[52] They looked like hens—in effect, they were chemically castrated. Other researchers showed that DDT could alter the formation of enzymes in the liver, which would then alter the formation and regulation of estrogen, progesterone, and testosterone, affecting reproduction.[53] Burlington and Lindeman urged researchers to further investigate these estrogenic effects of DDT, but their connections were not followed through by others.

Meanwhile, signs of reproductive trouble in wildlife populations exposed to DDT and PCBs were emerging. An early sign that environmental chemicals might impair endocrine function was the discovery in the 1950s that DDT, a persistent organochlorine pesticide, caused bald eagles

to lay eggs with thin shells. Reproduction in gull colonies heavily exposed to DDT began to decline in the late 1960s. Wildlife biologists observed that often two females, instead of a male and female, were sharing
nests, and the young in the colonies had "grossly feminized reproductive
organs."[54] In the 1960s, as Rachel Carson warned of the ecological effects
of pesticides and the links between humans and wildlife, scientists began
wondering why eagles, peregrine falcons, and similar birds were not reproducing. Carson singled out DDT as the likely culprit in eagle eradica-
tion and noted that "the insecticidal poison affects a generation once
removed from initial contact with it."[55] Few people, including Carson,
imagined that the problems might be hormonal in origin, yet in her insistence that wildlife effects had implications for humans, Carson's work
was central to the core of the endocrine disruption hypothesis.[56] But not
for three more decades, until a wildlife biologist named Theo Colborn
was studying problems with the Great Lakes, did anyone connect reproductive problems in wildlife to hormonal problems in people.

After finishing her Ph.D. in 1985, Theo Colborn took a position with
the Conservation Foundation examining wildlife responses to pollutants
in the Great Lakes. The Great Lakes have long been a trash can for industrial pollutants; DDT, PCBs, pesticides, and dioxins have all accumu-
lated in their waters. About one-fifth of American industry and one-half
of Canadian industry are located along the Great Lakes or tributary
streams, making them a microcosm for problems with pollutants in industrial society.

Colborn found no shortage of wildlife problems in the Great Lakes
region, but few consistent patterns. Some studies suggested elevated
rates of cancer in certain species; other studies showed impaired fetal development, while others revealed changes in behavior. Little seemed to
tie these results together.

Research by Frederick vom Saal had shown that developing fetuses
could be extraordinarily sensitive to tiny differences in the amount of
hormones in the fetal environment. Vom Saal noticed that female mice
from the same litter—mice that were genetically identical to each other—
showed dramatic differences in size and aggression. He discovered that
womb position had a powerful influence on a female mouse's adult behavior. Certain positions within the womb were more exposed to androgens, bathing the mouse fetus in a few more molecules of sex hormones
at certain critical stages of growth. In maturity, those mice were much
more aggressive, slower to mature, and more "masculine"—all because
of parts-per-trillion differences in hormones within the womb.[57]

Vom Saal's work made Colborn wonder if the disparate effects she
was seeing in Great Lakes species might be linked by problems with fetal development. If vom Saal had shown that tiny amounts of hormones

could lead to great effects later in life for laboratory animals, might the same be true for wildlife? Might synthetic chemicals be disrupting the endocrine system in developing fetuses? In 1989, when Colborn heard Dick Peterson describe "the changes in the development of male rat pups exposed prenatally to very low doses of dioxin—the same changes vom Saal described in male mice that developed between two females—she knew that endocrine disruption was not just a product of her imagination."[58] Colborn proposed a unified explanation to explain the myriad problems she observed in Great Lakes wildlife. She hypothesized that certain synthetic chemicals in the Great Lakes were mimicking estrogen, thus disrupting the action of sex hormones on fetal development and leading to problems in reproduction and behavior later in life.[59]

Although many in the scientific community were initially critical of Colborn's hypothesis that synthetic chemicals could mimic estrogen, it turns out that Charles Dodd, the inventor of DES, had found some support for this idea in the 1930s. Yet in the excitement that greeted his synthesis of estrogen, his work on the estrogenic effects of other chemicals had been overlooked. From 1933 to 1938, a series of journal articles from Dodd's laboratory reported that certain chemicals seemed to induce estrogenic responses in animal tests. As early as January 1933, having studied the chemical properties of ovarian hormones, he had foreseen that synthetic compounds could indeed act like estrogens, writing , "It seems likely that a whole group of substances of related chemical constitution will be found to have estrus-exciting properties."

The next month, Dodd wrote to the journal *Nature* that "because cell proliferation which characterizes the estrus state is in some respects reminiscent of the early stages of a malignant growth, we have sought a correlation between substances having estrogenic action and those having carcinogenic properties." He had found that two potent carcinogens had estrogenic activity as well, a result that he believed was "striking" since no scientific model explained how one compound could create such different types of biological activity—estrogenic and carcinogenic.[60] Among the compounds that showed estrogenic activity in Dodd's early studies were ones that had two phenol groups, what he called the diphenyls. Today, this class of compounds is called the biphenyls and includes many of the most problematic endocrine disruptors: DES, bisphenol-A, and many PCBs.

Other warnings that estrogens could cause serious problems emerged as early as the 1930s, but these warnings were largely ignored in the rush to synthesize new chemicals. For example, during the 1930s, a French chemist showed that estrogen exposure could induce breast cancer in male mice. Doctors recognized that if women had their ovaries removed and thus weren't exposed to estrogen, they rarely developed breast cancer—in retrospect, a clear suggestion that estrogen could lead to cancer, so synthetic estrogens might be problematic.[61]

Half a century later, in 1987, Professors Ana Soto and Carlos Sonnenschein at Tufts University discovered the first hints that extremely common synthetic substances—plastics—might be leaching chemicals that could cause estrogen-like responses. Soto and Sonnenschein were examining how estrogens can make breast cancer cells multiply. They used a special line of breast cancer cells, isolated and grown in a lab, for their research; these cells will only grow in the presence of estrogens. Suddenly something went wrong with their work. Breast cancer cell cultures started growing and dividing on their own, even before the experiments had started, when nobody had added anything to them. Soto assumed someone in the lab had been careless and had contaminated the clean cells; then she thought someone in the lab had simply made a mistake and added estrogen to the wrong cell lines.

Eventually, she realized no one in the lab had made a mistake. The problem was in the new plastic tubes: something from these tubes was leaching into their cultures and stimulating the growth of breast cancer cells. The manufacturer had changed the formulation of the tubes without telling anyone, and those sterile tubes were leaching something that acted like an estrogen. This development astonished Soto and Sonnenschein because they knew of no one who had reported estrogens leaching out of plastics. Everyone, including the manufacturers, assumed plastics were inert.

The problem turned out to be something called nonylphenol, a chemical widely used in industry and domestic products such as paints, detergents, oils, toiletries, and agrochemicals (ironically, this was one of the chemicals that Dodd in the 1930s had reported to possess estrogenic properties). Nonylphenols are just one in a larger class of related chemical compounds called alkylphenols, many of which turn out to be weakly estrogenic, making breast cancer cells multiply in lab cultures. In Britain alone, twenty thousand tons of these chemicals are used a year, and a third of these end up in our rivers and lakes at concentrations of fifty micrograms per liter—levels higher than those that induce cancer cell responses in the lab.[62]

Similar problems with other plastics emerged in the early 1990s. During the effort to create artificial estrogens in the 1930s, researchers had first synthesized bisphenol-A (one of the chemicals Dodd noted "excited estrus" in his lab animals.)[63] Not as powerful as DES, bisphenol-A was ignored until researchers realized that, when polymerized, it formed a useful plastic known as polycarbonate. Polycarbonate is now used for numerous common items: plastic baby bottles, water bottles, dental sealants, coatings for the inside of food cans. Unfortunately, bisphenol-A leaches out of those products, ending up in food, children's teeth, and in wildlife at concentrations higher than the levels that induce estrogenic responses in lab animals. For example, in one study in Spain, scientists showed that, in fourteen out of twenty cans, food contained bisphenol-A in amounts high enough to make breast cancer cells divide. Seventy percent of cans showed estrogenicity.[64]

In the past decade, most children's teeth in America have been sealed with cavity-retarding dental sealants, which consist of a solution containing high concentrations of bisphenol-A. During and right after the procedure, levels of the chemical in the saliva were found to be very high; even six months after treatment, bisphenol-A was still leaching into saliva. The sealants wear down after about five years, which means they are getting chewed and some, presumably, are being swallowed.[65] Are these levels high enough to cause problems for children as their reproductive systems are developing? No one knows. But no one knows if they are safe, either. Dentists have filled children's mouths with estrogenic compounds at concentrations high enough to induce cancer in the lab, yet the FDA has never required tests to see if these compounds are safe for children.[66] The American Dental Association's written response to this finding was that it was "interesting." But they refused to change their recommendation that all children get their teeth sealed, writing that "the biological implication of this observation needs to be further elucidated. . . . The ADA cannot at this time draw definitive conclusions from this [study's] observation."[67]

The ADA is right that more research needs to be done before we can say the estrogenic substances leaching into children from dental sealants harm them. But does that mean it's fine to continue business as usual, in the absence of evidence that shows the compounds are safe? Although the FDA requires pharmaceutical manufacturers to show that their drugs do not cause harm, no such requirement exists for other chemicals. Chemicals are assumed safe until proven to cause harm in humans—but the problem is that is nearly impossible to do this, since it is considered unethical to test potentially toxic compounds on human fetuses.

Animal experiments show that prenatal exposure to bisphenol-A causes mice to enter puberty earlier and to weigh 20 percent more than normal (how ironic if Americans turn out to be getting fatter not just because we exercise less and eat more fast food, but also because we had prenatal exposure to endocrine disrupters).[68] Japanese researchers recently demonstrated that the placenta does not act as a barrier to bisphenol-A. In only twenty minutes, maternally ingested bisphenol-A reached maximum concentration in the fetuses of lab rats.[69]

Vom Saal's early work on the low-level effects of hormones had stimulated Theo Colborn to develop the endocrine disruptor hypothesis. Recently, vom Saal showed that extremely low levels of bisphenol-A—the levels found in our background, our levels of "normal" exposure—could induce potent responses. These are levels thought completely trivial by traditional toxicology. These are the background levels experienced by most of us living our normal lives in the normal world, not the levels of those living near a toxic waste dump. As *Our Stolen Future*'s Web site states, "Vom Saal's work shows that every day levels matter."[70]

A third group of chemicals used in making plastics that leach estrogenic compounds are phthalates. These are incredibly common substances, perhaps the most abundant synthetic compounds in the environment. Phthalates are oily solvents that make plastics flexible but strong. Since phthalates need to be flexible, that means the molecules can't be too rigidly locked together, for flexibility requires molecules that slide over each other. But that lack of molecular rigidity also means they leach out easily.[71] Phthalates keep your car dashboard from cracking and your nail polish from splintering; they allow plastic wrap to be shaped around food. They help cosmetics absorb quickly into your skin, so they are added to shampoos, skin creams, sunscreens—all the stuff we smear on our skin to stay pretty. In fact, as ABC News reported, loopholes in federal laws allow cosmetics manufacturers to put unlimited amounts of industrial chemicals such as phthalates into personal care products without any testing for adverse health effects.[72]

Phthalates are in all of us. In March 2001, the U.S. Centers for Disease Control recently released the results of its first study of the levels of twenty-seven chemicals found within American bodies. Researchers found phthalates in nearly every person they examined (out of 3,800 people drawn from healthy individuals around the country with no special exposure to toxic substances).[73] The highest concentrations came from certain phthalates (such as di-ethyl phthalate) used in toiletries like bar soaps, perfumes, and shampoos, perhaps because direct skin contact increases body burden. Some of the highest concentrations were in women of childbearing age—not the results anyone wanted to find, since fetal exposure is likely to be the riskiest.[74] These levels were much higher than scientific models and a government panel had predicted just six months earlier.

In mice, phthalates "undermine the masculinity of mice exposed during lactation and weaning, creating individuals with both male and female sexual (intersex) characteristics."[75] They do this by blocking the action of male sex hormones as they program sexual development. A team of Environmental Protection Agency researchers led by L. Earl Gray Jr. gave phthalates to female rats from weaning through lactation at doses of two hundred to one thousand milligrams per kilogram of body weight (levels similar to those that people are exposed to). The sons of these rats produced far less testosterone than normal, and some males lacked a testicle.[76] Another team of researchers from an industry group known as the Chemical Industry Institute of Toxicology found developmental defects in male rodents whose mothers were given as little as one hundred milligrams of phthalate per kilogram of body weight. The chemical halved testosterone production in the fetus while leading to testicular tumors when the animals became adults.[77]

What do these results mean for people? Nobody knows yet; connecting human problems to phlatate exposure is an exercise in correlation, not causation. For example, consider early puberty. One recent study indicates that in Puerto Rico, girls who show premature breast development have significantly elevated phthalate levels compared to other girls.[78] Puerto Rico has the highest incidence of premature breast development ever reported, and 70 percent of girls studied have significantly high levels of phthalates. As the authors of this study wrote, "Some organic pollutants, including pesticides and some plasticizers, can disrupt normal sexual development in wildlife, and many of these have been widely used in Puerto Rico."[79] Another study on these Puerto Rican girls indicated that those who had consumed DES in meat developed large breasts at an early age and had other signs of precocious puberty.[80]

Yet another study (this time in North Carolina) showed that the higher the level of prenatal exposure to PCBs, the earlier puberty occurred in the girls, while a study in Michigan found a correlation between PCBs and early onset of menstruation.[81] A Belgian study showed that immigrant girls with precocious puberty had higher levels of DDE (a metabolite of DDT) in their blood.[82] Such correlations suggest that estrogen mimics might contribute to premature puberty, but correlations are not proof of a causal relationship. Proving that an observed trend in human health is real turns out to be very difficult, for we lack good data on when girls entered puberty in the early twentieth century. Moreover, even with good historical records, it is nearly impossible to prove causation with correlations.

Recent research has found that some girls—particularly African-American and Latina girls—are developing breasts and pubic hair much younger than in past generations, a trend that may be linked to estrogen exposure (although the source of those estrogens is not clear). In 1997, Marcia Herman-Giddens's data on 17,707 American girls suggested that girls were developing breasts and pubic hair on average as much as a year earlier than expected based on historical data (data that were not of the best quality). Not only did the average age of puberty (as measured by those two indices) appear to be decreasing, but significant numbers of girls were maturing sexually long before the average. By age eight, 48 percent of black girls and almost 15 percent of white girls were showing signs of sexual development.; 3 percent of African-American girls had begun to develop breasts by the age of three.[83]

Why would some girls be entering puberty earlier? Some of the changes may be due to changes in diet, which as mentioned earlier have led to increased estrogen exposure. Some of the changes may be due to increases in obesity, which is correlated with increased estrogen in the body (as well as with increased leptin, a hormone that is also linked with the onset of puberty).[84] Some of the changes may be due to synthetic estrogen mimics in the environment, while others may be due to social factors such as increased exposure to sexual stimuli in the culture, which might trigger a girl's body to begin puberty early. Although the science on people is uncertain, animal experiments do show that exposure to estrogen mimics reduces the age of puberty, suggesting the same might be true in girls. For example, a recent experiment reported in *Nature* showed that pregnant mice exposed to bisphenol-A at "a dose equivalent to that typically found in the environment" had daughters who entered puberty early.[85]

What do we do with this research? How do we think about women's health from a historical perspective in a world where chemical contamination may be changing fundamentally the biological nature of what makes us female? Women's bodies are biologically different from men's bodies; sexual differentiation is not just a cultural construction. Yet the biological differences between men and women are also shaped by culture and by cultural expectation.[86] For example, consider sexual size dimorphism, which is a measure of the size differences between men and women. Male humans are, on average, larger than female humans. Yet these differences, while partly biological, are also shaped by culture. The degree of difference in size predicted by biological factors is much smaller than the actual difference you observe in many segments of American culture. Why? Largely because societal pressures on women to diet increase the amount of sexual size dimorphism in white American culture. Expectations for women to be thin (or, in different cultures, to be fat) are clearly cultural constructions that can magnify the effects of genetic differences between men and women.[87]

Because women's bodies are biologically and culturally different from men's bodies, women react to endocrine disruptors differently than men do, and "women may be disproportionately affected by environmental pollution."[88] Or, as one government scientist put it, "Men's and women's bodies don't just look different—they also react differently to environmental agents."[89] Women manufacture more estrogen than men do, so they are exposed to more estrogen to start with. Women tend to carry more fat, and fat is where most endocrine disruptors are stored and can accumulate. Our ovaries and breasts have very high fat concentrations, making them especially vulnerable to endocrine disruptors. Because of pressures on white American women to diet, their weight tends to yo-yo more than men. "If toxicants stored in fat tissue are mobilized during [dieting], as some researchers have suggested, then this could be a significant factor in gender differences in responding to environmental factors."[90] Women retain higher levels of certain pollutants such as dioxin than men do, for reasons that aren't yet clear.[91] Women have smaller livers with less capacity for getting rid of toxic chemicals, and their livers are more susceptible to damage from alcohol, which in turn exposes them to more problems from endocrine disruptors.

Women's production of babies illustrates the tangled relationships between cultural and biological constructions of gender.[92] The timing and numbers of pregnancies are partly constrained by biology—two-year-old girls and ninety-year-old women don't get pregnant. But within those biological constraints, cultural forces shape whether a woman spends all her reproductive years pregnant or whether she spaces her pregnancies by choice. American women have fewer children than women at the turn of the century for reasons that are largely social and political, but biological factors related to chemical influences on fertility may also play a role.

Infertility appears to be increasing in American women (and in American men, but that is a different story). Part of this trend is probably tied to cultural changes: many women are delaying their first pregnancies, and older women are biologically less fertile. But infertility is also linked to chemical contaminants—causes that are environmental and political, not just personal. For example, women who eat fish from Lake Ontario (contaminated with PCBs) are less likely to conceive during a given menstrual cycle than those who eat less contaminated fish.[93] Women who eat more fish from Lake Michigan (again, contaminated with PCBs) are much more likely to have problems with their pregnancies, if they can even get pregnant.[94] Some phthalates clearly harm the ovaries in rodents; Barbara J. Davis, the leading researcher on ovarian toxicity, argues that "the effects of DEHP [a phthalate] could lead to infertility."[95]

Two increasingly important causes of female infertility in America are endometriosis and uterine fibroid tumors. Both are affected by exposure to estrogens (the body's own estrogens as well as synthetic estrogens).[96] And both problems have become far more common since the 1950s. Endometriosis, which sounds like something out of a Stephen King novel, occurs when endometrial tissue—the tissue that normally lines the uterus and gets shed during a period—grows outside the uterus and implants itself on the ovaries, fallopian tubes, bladder, bowel, or vagina. Endometriosis can often lead to infertility, and for unknown reasons it is increasing in industrialized nations. Anywhere from 10 to 15 percent of premenopausal women suffer from the disease. Belgium has the world's highest incidence; 60 to 80 percent of Belgian women who are infertile or have pelvic pain have endometriosis. Although the exact cause is unknown, we do know that many of the risk factors are related to estrogen exposure and so environmental estrogens may contribute.[97] For example, dioxin is a known estrogen mimic, and monkeys given dioxin have been shown to develop endometriosis. Belgian breast milk has some of the highest dioxin levels in the world, and some small studies have shown that dioxin levels are highest in women with endometriosis. Other studies, however, have not found that infertile women who had the disease had higher levels of dioxin in their blood than infertile women who didn't have it.[98]

Fibroids are another example of a condition often leading to infertility that may be related to endocrine disruptors.[99] The most common tumors in women are nonmalignant ones in the uterus called fibroids (or, more technically, uterine leiomyomas), which are clearly linked to estrogen exposure. Fibroids are the leading cause for hysterectomies—at least 550,000 American women a year have hysterectomies because of problems with them. Clinical studies show that these tumors are increasingly common. In one large study, 77 percent of women had fibroids growing in their uteruses (most of these tumors were subclinical—too small to cause problems), with the highest rates in African-American women.[100] Another study found that 73 percent of black women had uterine fibroids compared to 48 percent of white women.[101] Animal studies show that endocrine disruptors increase fibroid growth in rodents and monkeys, yet no human studies have been published that examine this potential link.[102]

The womb is an environment of its own, yet one that is linked to the outside world. The chemicals that a woman has been exposed to throughout her life—not just what she consumes while she's pregnant—reach her fetus, connecting one generation to the other. Pregnant women hope that if they don't take weird drugs like thalidomide or DES, their children will be fine. But chemical contamination is inside most women: 30 percent of pregnant women in one study had detectable levels of PCBs, DDT, and lindane and estrogenic compounds in their amniotic fluid, many at concentrations high enough to cause problems in lab animals.[103] And these background levels of chemicals could have effects on developing fetuses. For example, in Missouri, the state health department showed that children exposed to pesticides in the womb developed 600 percent more brain cancer than other children (which sounds terrible, but the levels were still extremely low). Using roach control chemicals during pregnancy led to a doubled risk of cancer in the child; using termite pesticides led to a 300 percent increase in brain cancer in the children. Yet the message that pregnant women shouldn't be using toxic chemicals is not getting out: the Missouri State Health Department found that 80 percent of pregnant women used pesticides while pregnant.[104]

Once a baby is born, problems don't stop there. Just about the only way for a woman to reduce her own body's burden of toxic chemicals is to breast-feed, since many of those toxic chemicals end up in breasts and only leave the woman's body within her breast milk. But there's an obvious problem here, since she's giving those toxic chemicals to her child. Breast milk is the food with the highest levels of PCBs and DDT and its metabolites such as DDEs (all endocrine disruptors).[105] In 1976, 99 percent of women's breast milk in America contained PCBs; a quarter had concentrations exceeding the legal limit (these concentrations have been declining since regulations reduced PCB use). The PCBs in breast milk can get into the children's blood; a 1998 study from the Netherlands showed that the blood of children who were breast-fed as infants had three times the levels of PCBs than children who weren't breast-fed.[106]

What do these levels mean for children? Nobody knows for sure. A long-term study of children in the Netherlands finds that background levels of prenatal PCB exposure experienced in the womb led to higher risk for childhood diseases, while "the latest study of the cohort of boys exposed in the womb to PCBs because of cooking oil contamination in Taiwan finds significant degradation in sperm quality in exposed individuals compared to their unexposed counterparts."[107] PCBs are labeled as a probable human carcinogen by the U.S. Environmental Protection Agency, while other studies show that they affect learning in both animals and humans. But could the levels found in breast milk harm children? The answer is unclear, since studies on postnatal exposure to PCBs in breast milk have been inconclusive. The National Institute for Environmental Health Sciences argues that breast milk, even when contaminated with PCBs and pesticides and other endocrine disruptors, is still better for the child than formula (especially given that both soy- and dairy-based formulas have their own sources of estrogens and estrogen mimics).[108]

Are endocrine disruptors a serious problem or not? Some of the central claims of the endocrine disruption hypothesis are now agreed upon by all scientists, even those from industry. Everyone agrees that wildlife exposed to certain synthetic chemicals demonstrate responses similar to those induced by sex hormones. They agree that lab studies show that synthetic chemicals can bind with and activate hormone receptors, resulting in gene expression. They agree that exposing pregnant mice to extremely low concentrations of certain synthetic chemicals—concentrations similar to those most people are exposed to—results in offspring with reproductive problems. They agree that some synthetic chemicals can make breast cancer cells multiply in culture. They agree that persistent organic chemicals build up in human tissue and are passed to the developing fetus and to the breast-feeding infant. They agree that many male fish and alligators exposed to industrial effluent show signs of feminization, a result also found in the lab when eggs are exposed to some synthetic chemicals.[109]

But people still disagree on a fundamental issue: what do these animal and lab studies mean for people? Do average people—those who don't work at toxic waste sites, for example—have anything to worry about? Can endocrine disruptors explain any of the apparent increases in infertility, reproductive cancers, birth defects, reduced sperm counts, or lowered ages of puberty? Or are endocrine disruptors present at such low levels that they are a trivial concern?

Circumstantial evidence is accumulating that supports the hypothesis that endocrine disruptors may be harming male reproductive health, while experimental studies have shown similar effects in laboratory animals. But you cannot ethically do these experiments on human fetuses to test whether the correlations between endocrine disruptors and reproductive disorders are real. Instead, we have to rely on epidemiology, which cannot always untangle confounding variables. Since we can't ethically do experiments on fetal exposure in humans, we need to rely on the weight of the evidence, rather than experimental proof, to form policy.[110] And this assumption is where reasonable people disagree.

In August 1999, the National Research Council (of the National Academy of Sciences) released its consensus report on endocrine disruption, a report commissioned in 1995 by the EPA and Congress.[111] The team of authors included independent scientists who are proponents of the hypothesis as well as those with strong ties to industry who are critics of it. After four years of review and debate, the team finally managed to agree that endocrine disruptors at high concentrations do affect human and wildlife health, yet they could not agree on the extent of harm caused by levels common in the environment. Moreover, they argued that their disagreements were not only due to gaps in scientific knowledge but also to major epistemologic differences on how one interprets data and draws conclusions. The consensus report stated: "Much of the division among committee members appears to stem from different views of how we come to know what we know. How we understand the natural world and how we decide among conflicting hypotheses about the natural world is the province of epistemology. Committee members seemed to differ on some basic epistemologic issues, which led to different interpretations and conclusions on the issues of hormonally active agents in the environment."[112]

The chemical industry's response to this report was to focus on the conclusion that no scientific certainty on human health effects had been established. Without certainty, the industry argued, endocrine disruption was not an issue for public health concern. As Myers argues, "This is a classic argument from industry spokespeople: that the absence of data proves safety. In reality, all it proves is ignorance. "[113] So, in the absence of firm proof, what should society do? Many in industry argue that we should do nothing until we have absolute proof. Others argue that such a response is unethical, for as the Boston Physicians for Social Responsibility stated, "We are engaged in a large global experiment. It involves widespread exposure of all species of plants and animals in diverse ecosystems to multiple manmade chemicals. . . . The limits of science and rigorous requirements for establishing causal proof often conspire with a perverse requirement for proving harm, rather than safety, to shape public policies which fail to ensure protection of public health and the environment."[114]

As individuals, what do we do with this uncertain information? As I write this, I pat my own fibroid-filled belly and wonder what connections there might possibly be between my own tumors and the sea of chemicals in which we've immersed ourselves. Like the vast majority of American women now, inside my uterus I have cells gone wild, cells that in the presence of estrogen mushroom into tumors beyond my control. When I drink my well water (tainted with atrazine, yet another endocrine disruptor), when I eat my plastic-wrapped cheese soaked in phthalates, when I paddle my kayak through the pesticide-laden waters of the nearby wildlife preserve, when I walk through my ordinary days, I wonder what strange world we've created for ourselves.

When I was writing this chapter, I spent a lot of time on the Sugar River, a little muddy river that runs through wildlife refuges and farmlands. For southern Wisconsin, this is a wild place. Herons rise up, hawks cry overhead, geese and cranes and mallards and wood ducks fly, raccoons and woodchucks and chipmunks and squirrels and coyotes hang out in the surrounding forest. Yet for all its wildness, the water is saturated with poisons. When I dip the paddle blade too deeply into the river, water runs over the shaft and down my wrists, and I can't help but wonder if I really want that water anywhere near my skin. I watch the herons and hawks and cranes around me and wonder how many pesticide residues end up in their body fat. Hunters motor their boats into the shallow backwaters, and solvents from their fuel tanks add to the chemical soup. Can any of this hurt us? Can any of it hurt the birds? Nobody really knows.

What we do know is that we're all in this together: the atrazine that gets sprayed on my neighbor's cornfield ends up in the river water, then in the fish, then in the herons and the raccoons that eat the fish—and it also ends up in my breasts, my belly, and my blood. What's out there in wildlife and wild places is also in our bodies. Just as Colborn connected studies of wildlife with studies of human bodies, endocrine disruptors connect environmental histories of the body with environmental histories of wild places and wild animals.

One of our culture's fondest illusions is that we can control our separation from nature: we can visit nature when we feel like it and live in a
human world the rest of the time. According to a commentator on National Public Radio, most Americans spend only fifteen minutes outside
each day. The rest of the time we drive in our cars, stare into our computer screens, watch our TVs, sit in our offices or schools, eat our phtha-
late-saturated suppers, and think the rest of the world is outside, staying
where it belongs. But that's not true. What is outside has come inside,
making itself at home in our testes, in our wombs, in our most private reproductive dysfunctions. The environment includes wild places and wild
things, but it also includes hair dye, golf courses, and ice cream—all full
of endocrine disruptors. Our most intimate reproductive environments,
the places that make us most female or most male, the places we are most
vulnerable and most natural, may have been hijacked by the residues of
our industrial world. This is a disturbing thought.

NOTES

1. For an example of the media response, see Elizabeth Smith, "Fibrocystic
Breast Diseases Provoked by Xenoestrogens Are Found in Everyday Synthetic
Materials," n.d., *http://www.fibrocystic.com/xeno.htm*. For the research, see S.
Jobling and J. Sumpter, "Detergent Components in Sewage Effluent Are Weakly
Oestrogenic to Fish: An In Vitro Study Using Rainbow Trout (*Onchorhynchus
mykiss*) Hepatocytes," *Aquatic Toxicology* 27 (1994): 361–72; S. Jobling, C. Tyler,
M. Nolan, and J. P. Sumpter, *The Identification of Oestrogenic Effects in Wild Fish*
(1998), Technical Report W119, Brunel University Environmental Agency Na-
tional Fish Health Laboratory; C. E. Purdom, P. A. Hardiman, V. J. Bye, N. C. Eno,
C. R. Tyler, and J. P. Sumpter, "Estrogenic Effects of Effluents from Sewage-Treat-
ment Works," *Chemistry and Ecology* 8 (1994): 275–85; and T. P. Rodgers-Gray,
S. Jobling, S. Morris, C. Kelly, S. Kirby, A. Janbakhsh, J. E. Harries, M. J. Waldock,
J. P. Sumpter, and C. R. Tyler," Long-Term Temporal Changes in the Estrogenic
Composition of Treated Sewage Effluent and Its Biological Effects on Fish," *Environmental Science and Technology* 34 (2000): 1521–28. For a useful overview of re-
search on sexual disruption in fish, see S. Jobling, M. Nolan, C. R. Tyler,
G. Brighty, and J. P. Sumpter, "Widespread Sexual Disruption in Wild Fish," *En-
vironmental Science and Technology* 32 (1998): 2498–2506.
2. J. P. Sumpter and S. Jobling, "Vitellogenesis as a Biomarker for Estrogenic
Contamination of the Aquatic Environment," *Environmental Health Perspectives*
103, Suppl. 7 (1995): 173–77; and J. E. Harries, D. A. Sheahan, S. Jobling,
P. Matthiessen, P. Neall, J. P. Sumpter, T. Tylor, and N. Zaman, "Estrogenic Activity in Five United Kingdom Rivers Detected by Measurement of Vitellogenesis in
Caged Male Trout," *Environmental Science and Toxicology* 16 (1997): 534–42.
3. J. Raloff, "The Gender Benders: Are Environmental 'Hormones' Emascu-
lating Wildlife?" *Science News* 145 (January 8, 1994): 24; online at *http://www.*

sciencenews.org/sn_edpik/ls_7.htm. This finding didn't rule out the possibility that ethynylestradiol was in the river at biologically active concentrations since their instruments weren't powerful enough to detect the chemicals. See C. Potera, "Forum," *Environmental Health Perspectives* 108 (October 2000): 108–10; online at *http://ehpnet1.niehs.nih.gov/docs/2000/108-10/forum.html#water.*

4. Both the scientific research and the popular writing on endocrine disruptors have exploded in recent years. The important popular work that brought general attention to the issue was Theo Colborn, Dianne Dumanoski, and John Peterson Myers, *Our Stolen Future: Are We Threatening Our Fertility, Intelligence, and Survival?* (New York: Plume, 1997). A scholarly examination of the origins of the hypothesis is Sheldon Krimsky, *Hormonal Chaos: The Scientific and Social Origins of the Environmental Endocrine Hypothesis* (Baltimore: Johns Hopkins University Press, 2000). An early scientific review article summarizing effects of endocrine disruptors is T. Colborn, F. S. vom Saal, and A. M. Soto, "Developmental Effects of Endocrine-Disrupting Chemicals in Wildlife and Humans," *Environmental Health Perspectives* 101 (1993): 378–84. For an overview of popular scientific journalism on endocrine disruptors, see Janet Raloff's series for *Science News,* including "Excreted Drugs: Something Looks Fishy," vol. 157 (January 22, 2000): 66; "Macho Waters: Some River Pollution Spawns Body-Altering Steroids," vol. 159 (January 6, 2001): 8–10; "Common Pollutants Undermine Masculinity," vol. 155 (April 3, 1999): 213; "Hormone Mimics Get Harder to Pigeonhole," vol. 151 (April 26, 1997): 254; "Sperm Changes Linked to Drinking Water," vol. 145 (February 26, 1997): 142; "Are Men Suffering from Prenatal or Childhood Exposures to 'Hormonal' Toxicants?" vol. 145 (Jan. 22, 1994): 56.

5. For a discussion of historical constructions of gender in earlier periods, see Londa Schiebinger, *Nature's Body: Gender in the Making of Modern Science* (Boston: Beacon Press, 1993); Thomas Laquer, *Making Sex: Body and Gender from the Greeks to Freud* (Cambridge, Mass.: Harvard University Press, 1990); and Joan Brumberg, *The Body Project: An Intimate History of American Girls* (New York: Random House, 1997).

6. For a discussion of the importance of considering the body in environmental history, see C. Sellers, "Thoreau's Body: Towards an Embodied Environmental History," *Environmental History* 4 (October 1999): 486–514.

7. L. C. Folmar, N. D. Denslow, V. Rao, M. Chow, A. D. Crain, J. Enblom, J. Marcino, and L. J. Guillette Jr., "Vitellogenin Induction and Reduced Serum Testosterone Concentrations in Feral Male Carp *(Cyprinus carpio)* Captured near a Major Metropolitan Sewage Treatment Plant," *Environmental Health Perspectives* 104 (1996): 1096–1101. For a comparison across five regions of the United States, see S. L. Goodbred, R. J. Gilliom, T. S. Gross, N. P. Denslow, W. L. Bryant, and T. R. Schoeb, *Reconnaissance of 17β-Estradiol, 11-Ketotestosterone, Vitellogenin, and Gonad Histopathology in Common Carp of United States Streams: Potential for Contaminant-Induced Endocrine Disruption,* U.S. Geological Survey Open-File Report 96-627.

8. Chris Metcalfe, "Sex and Sewage: Estrogenic Compounds in the Environment" (abstract, Geological Society of America annual meeting, 2001), *http://gsa.confex.com/gsa/2001AM/finalprogram/abstract_25760.htm;* reviewed in Raloff, "Excreted Drugs."

156   BODIES

9. C. G. Daughton and T. A. Ternes, "Pharmaceuticals and Personal Care Products in the Environment: Agents of Subtle Change?" *Environmental Health Perspectives* 107, Suppl. 6 (December 1999): 907–38.

10. Raloff, "Common Pollutants Undermine Masculinity."

11. For the story on the students, see Raloff, "Macho Waters." For the research, see R. A. Angus, H. McNatt, W. M. Howell, and S. D. Peoples, "Gonopodium Development in Normal and 11-Ketotestosterone–Treated Mosquitofish *(Gambusia affinis):* A Quantitative Study Using Computer Image Analysis," *General and Comparative Endocrinology* 123 (2001): 222–34; R. Jenkins, R. A. Angus, H. McNatt, W. M. Howell, J. A. Kemppainen, M. Kirk, and E. M. Wilson, "Identification of Androstenedione in a River Containing Paper Mill Effluent,"*Environmental Toxicology and Chemistry* 20 (2001): 1325–31; and K. R. Munkittrick, M. E. McMaster, L. H. McCarthy, M. R. Servos, and G. J. Van Der Kraak, "An Overview of Recent Studies on the Potential of Pulp Mill Effluents to Alter Reproductive Parameters in Fish," *Journal of Toxicology and Environmental Health,* Part B 1 (1998): 347–71 .

12. William P. Davis of the EPA, cited in Raloff, "Macho Waters."

13. L. H. Guillette Jr., T. S. Gross, G. R. Masson, J. M. Matter, H. F. Percival, and A. R. Woodward, "Developmental Abnormalities of the Gonad and Abnormal Sex Hormone Concentrations in Juvenile Alligators from Contaminated and Control Lakes in Florida," *Environmental Health Perspectives* 102 (1994): 680–88.

14. C. F. Facemire, T. S. Gross, and L. J. Guillette Jr., "Reproductive Impairment in the Florida Panther: Nature or Nurture?" *Environmental Health Perspectives* 103, Suppl. 4 (1995): 79–86. For work on salmon, see J. J. Nagler, J. Bouma, G. H. Thorgaard, and D. D. Dauble, "High Incidence of a Male-Specific Genetic Marker in Phenotypic Female Chinook Salmon from the Columbia River," *Environmental Health Perspectives* 109 (2001): 67–69. For a review, see J. Raloff, "Salmon Puzzle: Why Did Males Turn Female?" *Science News* 158 (December 23, 2000): 404–5, online at *http://www.sciencenews.org/20001223/fob2.asp,* and Raloff, "The Gender Benders."

15. T. Schettler, "Endocrine Disruptors: The State of the Science," Greater Boston Physicians for Social Responsibility (1997), online at *http://www.psr.org/tedfs.htm.*

16. This particular report was from the BBC, September 2000; cited at *Our Stolen Future's* Web site, written and maintained by John Peterson Myers. The Web site maintains abstracts on recent research and links to scientific journals; see *http://www.ourstolenfuture.org.*

17. Raloff, "Macho Waters." See also J. Oehlmann, U. Schulte-Oehlmann, M. Tillmann, and B. Markert, "Effects of Endocrine Disruptors on Prosobranch Snails (Mollusca: Gastropoda) in the Laboratory. Part I: Bisphenol-A and Octylphenol as Xenoestrogens," *Ecotoxicology* 9 (2001): 383–97; P. E. Gibbs, P. L. Pascoe, and G. W. Bryan, "Tributyltin-Induced Imposex in Stenoglossan Gastropods: Pathological Effects on the Female Reproductive System," *Comparative Biochemistry and Physiology* 100C (1991): 231–35; and G. A. LeBlanc, "Are Environmental Sentinels Signaling?" *Environmental Health Perspectives* 103 (1995), and "Steroid Hormone-Regulated Processes in Invertebrates and Their Susceptibility to Environmental Endocrine Disruption," in *Environmental Endocrine Disrupters:*

An Evolutionary Perspective, ed. L. H. Guillette Jr. and D. A. Crain (London: Taylor and Francis, 2000), 126–54.

18. For the CDC data that showed a doubling in the incidence of severe hypospadias, see L. J. Paulozzi, J. D. Erickson, and R. J. Jackson, "Hypospadias Trends in Two U.S. Surveillance Systems," *Pediatrics* 100 (1997): 831–34. For an analysis of international data that suggests that the increases may have been leveling off in many countries since 1985, see L. J. Paulozzi, "International Trends in Rates of Hypospadias and Cryptorchidism," *Environmental Health Perspectives* 107 (1999): 297–302. For an overview, see L. S. Baskin, K. Himes, and T. Colborn, "Hypospadias and Endocrine Disruption: Is There a Connection?" *Environmental Health Perspectives* 109 (2001): 1175–83.

19. Raloff, "Are Men Suffering from Prenatal or Childhood Exposures?" See R. García-Rodríguez, M. García-Martín, M. Nogueras-Ocaña, J. de Dios Luna-del-Castillo, M. Espigares García, N. Olea, and P. Lardelli-Claret, "Exposure to Pesticides and Cryptorchidism: Geographical Evidence of a Possible Association," *Environmental Health Perspectives* 104 (1996): 1090–95; J. M. McKiernan, T. W. Hensle, and H. Fisch, "Increasing Risk of Developing Testicular Cancer by Birth Cohort in the United States," *Dialogues in Pediatric Urology* 23 (2000): 7–8; R. Bergstrom, H.-O. Adami, M. Mohner, W. Zatonski, H. Storm, A. Ekhom, S. Tretli, L. Teppo, O. Akre, and T. Hakulinen, "Increase in Testicular Cancer Incidence in Six European Countries," *Journal of the National Cancer Institute* 88 (1996): 727–33; and J. Toppari, J. C. Larsen, P. Christiansen, A. Giwercman, P. Grandjean, L. J. Guillette Jr., B. Jégou, T. K. Jensen, P. Jouannet, N. Keiding, H. Leffers, J. A. McLachlan, O. Meyer, J. Müller, E. Rajpert-De Meyts, T. Scheike, R. Sharpe, J. Sumpter, and N. E. Skakkebaek, "Male Reproductive Health and Environmental Xenoestrogens," *Environmental Health Perspectives* 104, Suppl. 4 (1996): 741–806.

20. The literature on declines in sperm counts is large and contentious. For findings supporting the hypothesis that sperm counts are declining, see E. Carlsen, A. Giwercman, N. Keiding, and N. Skakkebaek, "Evidence for Decreasing Quality of Semen during the Past 50 Years," *British Medical Journal* 305 (1992): 609–13; S. H. Swan, E. P. Elkin, and L. Fenster, "Have Sperm Densities Declined? A Reanalysis of Global Trend Data," *Environmental Health Perspectives* 105 (1997): 1228–32; and S. H. Swan, E. P. Elkin, and L. Fenster,"The Question of Declining Sperm Density Revisited: An Analysis of 101 Studies Published 1934–1996," *Environmental Health Perspectives* 108 (2000): 961–66.

For findings supporting the alternate hypothesis that sperm counts are not declining (at least in some locations), see C. A. Paulsen, N. G. Berman, and C. Wang, "Data from Men in Greater Seattle Reveals No Downward Trend in Semen Quality: Further Evidence That Deterioration of Semen Quality Is Not Geographically Uniform," *Fertility and Sterility* 65 (1996): 1015–20; and H. Fisch, E. T. Goluboff, A. H. Olson, J. Feldshuh, S. J. Broder, and D. H. Barad, "Semen Analyses in 1,283 Men from the United States over a 25-year Period: No Decline in Quality," *Fertility and Sterility* 65 (1996): 1009–14.

21. G. E. Dinse, D. M. Umbach, A. J. Sasco, D. G. Hoel, and D. L. Davis, "Unexplained Increases in Cancer Incidence in the United States from 1975 to 1994," *Annual Review of Public Health* 20 (1996): 173–209.

22. For a review of conflicting evidence on changes in the timing of puberty,

158   BODIES

see D. Zuckerman, "When Little Girls Become Women: Early Onset of Puberty in Girls," *The Ribbon* 6 (2001); this is the newsletter for the Cornell University Program on Breast Cancer and Environmental Risk Factors in New York State; online at *http://www.cfe.cornell.edu/bcerf/Newsletter/general/v6i1/little.girls.cfm.*

23. M. E. Herman-Giddens, E. J. Slora, and R. C. Wasserman, "Secondary Sexual Characteristics and Menses in Young Girls Seen in Office Practice: A Study from the Pediatric Research in Office Settings Network," *Pediatrics* 99 (1997): 505–12; P. B. Kaplowitz, E. J. Slora, R. C. Wasserman, S. E. Pedlow, and M. E. Herman-Giddens, "Earlier Onset of Puberty in Girls: Relation to Increased Body Mass Index and Race," *Pediatrics* 108 (2001): 347–53. For a study showing that an endocrine disrupter advanced the age of puberty in laboratory mice, see K. L. Howdeshell, A. K. Hotchkiss, K. A. Thayer, J. G. Vandenbergh, and F. S. vom Saal, "Exposure to Bisphenol-A Advances Puberty," *Nature* 401 (1999): 763–64.

24. Krimsky, *Hormonal Chaos*, 2. For a list of currently known endocrine disrupters, see *http://www.ourstolenfuture.org/Basics/chemlist.htm.* For studies from the mid-1990s that review the data suggesting a common cause for reproductive problems, see R. Sharpe and N. E. Skakkebaek, "Are Oestrogens Involved in Falling Sperm Counts and Disorders of the Male Reproductive Tract?" *Lancet* 341 (1993): 1392–95; A. Giwercman, E. Carlsen, N. Keiding, and N. E. Skakkebaek, "Evidence for Increasing Incidence of Abnormalities of the Human Testis: A Review," *Environmental Health Perspectives* 101, Suppl. 2 (1993): 65–71; and E. Carlsen, A. Giwercman, N. Keiding, and N. E. Skakkebaek, "Declining Semen Quality and Increasing Incidence of Testicular Cancer: Is There a Common Cause?" *Environmental Health Perspectives* 103, Suppl. 7 (1995): 137–39.

25. D. Lindsey Berkson, *Hormone Deception: How Everyday Foods and Products Are Disrupting Your Hormones—and How to Protect Yourself and Your Family* (Chicago: Contemporary Books, 2000), xxii; Deborah Cadbury, *Altering Eden: The Feminization of Nature* (New York: St. Martin's Press, 1999), 41. For an exploration of the meanings of estrogen, both biological and cultural, see Natalie Angier, *Woman: An Intimate Geography* (New York: Houghton Mifflin, 1999).

26. Berkson, *Hormone Deception*, 16.

27. Mary W. Eubanks, "Focus," *Environmental Health Perspectives* 105 (May 1997): 5; online at *http://ehpnet1.niehs.nih.gov/docs/1997/105-5/focus.html.*

28. Ibid.

29. Berkson, *Hormone Deception*, 51.

30. Ibid., 48.

31. Raloff writes: "Gender—both its physical expression and its characteristic behavior—traces more to the relative concentrations of various sex hormones circulating in the body than to the mere existence of certain dominant ones. For example, women produce some androgens, or male hormones. Indeed, a woman's body synthesizes estrogens from androgens such as testosterone. Similarly, though estradiol is the animal kingdom's primary estrogen, or feminizing hormone, it plays important roles in both men and women. At no time does an imbalance of sex hormones produce more obvious results than during fetal development. Too much estrogen at the wrong moment can turn an organism with male genes into what to all outward appearances is a female. Similarly, an overabundance of androgens can produce the sex organs of a male

in a fetus with the genes to be female" ("Are Men Suffering from Prenatal or Childhood Exposures?").

32. Cadbury, *Altering Eden*, 36; Berkson, *Hormone Deception*, 43.

33. Cadbury, *Altering Eden*, 38.

34. Myers, "Contamination Threatens a Basic Reproductive Right." For example, see R. M. Sharpe, "Hormones and Testis Development and the Possible Adverse Effects of Environmental Chemicals," *Toxicology Letters* 120 (2001): 221–32.

35. Although it is impossible to know reproductive patterns from human evolutionary history, we can compare average numbers of menstrual cycles in current hunter-gatherer societies with current industrial societies. Researchers have found that American women experience approxiamably three times as many menstrual periods as women in foraging societies. For example, women in hunter-gatherer societies are about 16 years old at menarche, 19.5 years old at first birth, nurse for 3 to 4 years, average 5.9 live births, and have an average age at menopause of 47 years, with an average of 160 ovulations in their lifetime. In contrast, American women average 12.5 years old at menarche, 24 years old at first birth, nurse for an average of 3 months, average 1.8 live births, and average 50.5 years old at menopause, with an average of approximately 450 ovulations within their lifetime; data from S. B. Eaton, M. C. Pike, R. V. Short, N. C. Lee, J. Trussell, R. A. Hatcher, J. W. Wood, C. M. Worthman, N. G. Blurton Jones, M. J. Konner, K. R. Hill, R. Bailey, and A. M. Hurtado, "Women's Reproductive Cancers in Evolutionary Context," *Quarterly Review of Biology* 69 (1994): 353–67. See also B. Strassmann, "Menstrual Cycling and Breast Cancer: An Evolutionary Perspective," *Journal of Women's Health* 8 (1999): 193–202; and S. B. Eaton and S. B. Eaton III, "Breast Cancer in Evolutionary Context," in *Evolutionary Medicine*, ed. W. R. Trevathan, E. O. Smith, and J. J. McKenna (New York: Oxford University Press, 1999), 429–42. For a review of this controversial subject, see Rachel Bayer, "The Impact of Increased Menstruation Rates on Women's Health and Reproductive Cancers," (2001); online at *http://webpub.alleg.edu/employee/r/rmumme/FS101/ResearchPapers/RachelBayer.html.*

36. Cadbury, *Altering Eden*, 82–83; Berkson, *Hormone Deception*, 55.

37. Berkson, *Hormone Deception*, 29–30.

38. For a review of the scientific literature on DES effects, see R. M. Giusti, K. Iwamoto, and E. E. Hatch, "Diethylstilbestrol Revisited: A Review of the Long-Term Health Effects," *Annals of Internal Medicine* 122 (1995): 778–88.

39. Berkson, *Hormone Deception*, 63

40. Krimsky, *Hormonal Chaos*, 5, 9; Berkson, *Hormone Deception*, 65.

41. Krimsky, *Hormonal Chaos*, 9; Berkson, *Hormone Deception*, 63.

42. Berkson, *Hormone Deception*, 62–63.

43. Berkson, *Hormone Deception*, 67; Krimsky, *Hormonal Chaos*, 9–10.

44. Cadbury, *Altering Eden*, 48.

45. A. L. Herbst, and R. E. Scully, "Adenocarcinoma of the Vagina in Adolescence: A Report of 7 Cases Including 6 Clear-Cell Carcinomas (So-Called Mesonephromas)," *Cancer* 25 (1970): 745–47.

46. Editorial staff, "An Environment for Development," *Environmental Health Perspectives* 107 (September 1999). For recent research on second- and third-

generation DES effects, see R. H. Kaufman, E. Adam, E. E. Hatch, K. Noller, A. Herbst, J.R. Palmer, and R. N. Hoover, "Continued Follow-up of Pregnancy Outcomes in Diethylstilbestrol-Exposed Offspring," *Obstetrics and Gynecology* 96 (2000): 483–89; R. Newbold, "Cellular and Molecular Effects of Developmental Exposure to Diethylstilbestrol: Implications for Other Environmental Estrogens," *Environmental Health Perspectives* 103, Suppl. 7 (1995). R. R. Newbold, R. B. Hanson, W. N. Jefferson, B. C. Bullock, J. Haseman, and J. A. McLachlan, " Proliferative Lesions and Reproductive Tract Tumors in Male Descendants of Mice Exposed Developmentally to Diethylstilbestrol," *Carcinogenesis* 21 (2000): 1355–63; and R. R. Newbold, R. B. Hanson, W. N. Jefferson, B. C. Bullock, J. Haseman, and J. A. McLachlan, "Increased Tumors but Uncompromised Fertility in the Female Descendants of Mice Exposed Developmentally to Diethylstilbestrol," *Carcinogenesis* 19 (1998): 1655–63.

47. Krimsky, *Hormonal Chaos,* 10.

48. Eubanks, "Focus." For some of the early laboratory research on DES effects in mice, see J. A. McLachlan, R. Newbold, and B. Bullock, "Reproductive Tract Lesions in Male Mice Exposed Prenatally to Diethylstilbestrol," *Science* 190 (1975): 991–92; H. C. Shah and J. A. McLachlan, "The Fate of Diethylstilbestrol in the Pregnant Mouse," *Journal of Pharmacology and Experimental Therapeutics* 197 (1976): 687–96; J. A. McLachlan, "Prenatal Exposure of Dethylstilbestrol in Mice: Toxicological Studies," *Journal of Toxicology and Environmental Health* 2 (1977): 527–37; J. A. McLachlan, R. R. Newbold, and B. C. Bullock, "Long-term Effects on the Female Mouse Genital Tract Associated with Prenatal Exposure to Diethylstilbestrol," *Cancer Research* 40 (1980): 3988–99; J. C. Lamb IV, R. R. Newbold, and J. A. McLachlan, "Visualization by Light and Scanning Electron Microscopy of Reproductive Tract Lesions in Female Mice Treated In Utero with Diethylstilbestrol," *Cancer Research* 41 (1981): 4057–62; J. A. McLachlan, R. R. Newbold, H. C. Shah, M. Hogan, and R. L. Dixon, "Reduced Fertility in Female Mice Exposed Transplacentally to Diethylstilbestrol," *Fertility and Sterility* 38 (1982): 364–71; R. R. Newbold and J. A. McLachlan, "Vaginal Adenosis and Adenocarcinoma in Mice Transplacentally Exposed to Diethylstilbestrol," *Cancer Research* 42 (1982): 2003–11.

49. Editorial staff, "Extra Ingredients: Hormones in Food," *Environmental Health Perspectives* 102 (August 1994); Krimsky, *Hormonal Chaos,* 11, 13.

50 Berkson, *Hormone Deception,* 16.

51. Ibid., 15.

52. H. Burlington and V. F. Lindeman, "Effect of DOT on Testes and Secondary Sex Characteristics of White Leghorn Cockerels," *Society for Experimental Biology and Medicine Proceedings* 74 (1950).

53. R. M. Welch, W. Levin, K. Kuntzman, M. N. Jacobson, and A. H. Conney, "Effect of Halogenated Hydrocarbon Insecticides on the Metabolism and Uterotropic Action of Estrogens in Rats and Mice," *Toxicology and Applied Pharmacoloty* 19 (1971): 234–46; A. H. Conney, R. M. Welch, R. Kuntzman, and J. J. Burns, "Effects of Pesticides on Drug and Steroid Metabolism," *Pharmacological Therapy* 8 (1966): 2–8.

54. Editorial staff, "Extra Ingredients: Hormones in Food"; Raloff, "The Gender Benders."

55. Rachel Carson, *Silent Spring* (New York: Houghton Mifflin, 1962).

56. Krimsky, *Hormonal Chaos*, 6.

57. F. vom Saal and F. Bronson, "Sexual Characteristics of Adult Female Mice Are Correlated with Their Blood Testosterone Levels during Prenatal Development," *Science* 20 (1980): 597–99; F. vom Saal, "The Intrauterine Position Phenomenon: Effects on Physiology, Aggressive Behavior, and Population Dynamics in House Mice," in *Biological Perspectives on Aggression*, ed. K. Flannelly, R. Blanchard, and D. Blanchard, a special issue of *Progress in Clinical Biology Research* 169 (1984): 135–79; F. vom Saal, "Sexual Differentiation in Litter-Bearing Mammals: Influence of Sex of Adjacent Fetuses In Utero," *Journal of Animal Science* 67 (1989): 1824–40.

58. Personal communication, anonymous reviewer.

59. Krimsky, *Hormonal Chaos*, 4.

60. Cadbury, *Altering Eden*, postscript. See E. C. Dodds and W. Lawson, "Synthetic Estrogenic Agents without the Phenanthrene Nucleus," *Nature* 137 (1936): 996, and "Molecular Structure in Relation to Oestrogenic Activity: Compounds without a Phenanthrene Nucleus," *Proceedings of the Royal Society* B 125 (1938): 222–32.

61. Cadbury, *Altering Eden*, 43.

62. Ibid., 136. Soto describes this discovery in her untitled autobiographical essay in "in-cites," October 2001; *http://www.in-cites.com/papers/dr-ana-soto.html*. The research is reported in A. M. Soto, H. Justicia, J. W. Wray, and C. Sonnenschein, "P-Nonyl-Phenol: An Estrogenic Xenobiotic Released from 'Modified' Polystyrene," *Environmental Health Perspectives* 92 (1991): 167–73.

63. Dodds and Lawson, "Synthetic Estrogenic Agents," 996, and "Molecular Structure in Relation to Oestrogenic Activity," 222–32.

64. J. A. Brotons, M. F. Olea-Serrano, M. Villalobos, V. Pedraza, and N. Olea, "Xenoestrogens Released from Lacquer Coatings in Food Cans," *Environmental Health Perspectives* 103 (1995): 608–12. Another study (S. R. Howe, L. Borodinsky, and R. S. Lyon, "Potential Exposure to Bisphenol-A from Food-Contact Uses of Epoxy Can Coatings," *Journal of Coatings Technology* 70 [1997]: 69–74) found bisphenol-A migration from food cans into food at thirty-seven parts per billion. The chemical industry believes this level to be safe, while many environmental groups believe it to be unsafe, or at least not proven safe. For an industry perspective, see "Bisphenol-A Global Industry Group" at *http://www.bisphenol-a.org*. For conflicting claims about the low-dose health effects, see the industry's position at *http://www.bisphenol-a.org/new/051601.html*; *Our Stolen Future*'s position at *http://www.ourstolenfuture.org/NewScience/lowdose/lowdoseresults.htm*; and the National Toxicology Program's endocrine disrupters low-dose peer review interim report (which fails to find sufficient evidence in support of either position) at *http://ntp-server.niehs.nih.gov/htdocs/liason/LowDosePeerFinalRpt.pdf*.

65. N. Olea, R. Pulgar, P. Perez, F. Olea-Serrano, A. Rivas, A. Novillo-Fertrell, V. Pedraza, A. Soto, and C. Sonnenschein, "Estrogenicity of Resin-Based Composites and Sealants Used in Dentistry," *Environmental Health Perspectives* 104 (1996): 298–305. A response to this article can be found in Y. Imai, "Comments on 'Estrogenicity of Resin-Based Composites and Sealants Used in Dentistry,'" *Environmental Health Perspectives* 107 (1999): A290. The response to this response is N. Olea, "Comments on 'Estrogenicity of Resin-Based Composites and Sealants

162   BODIES

Used in Dentistry': Response," *Environmental Health Perspectives* 107 (1999): A290–92. See also Editorial staff, "Forum," *Environmental Health Perspectives* 104 (1996); online at *http://ehpnet1.niehs.nih.gov/docs/1996/104-4/forum.html#dental.* A study showing low-dose effects of bisphenol-A on mice is S. C. Nagel, F. S. vom Saal, K. A. Thayer, M. G. Dhar, M. Boechler, and W. V. Welshon, "Relative Binding Affinity–Serum Modified Access (RBA–SMA) Assay Predicts In Vivo Bioactivity of the Xenoestrogens Bisphenol-A and Octylphenol," *Environmental Health Perspectives* 105 (1997): 70–76.

    66. Myers, "Contamination threatens a basic reproductive right."

    67. Editorial staff, "Forum."

    68. K. Howdeshell, A. K. Hotchkiss, K. A. Thayer, J. G. Vandenbergh, and F. S. vom Saal, "Plastic Bisphenol-A Speeds Growth and Puberty," *Nature* 401 (1999): 762–64.

    69. H. Miyakoda, M. Tabata, S. Onodera, and K. Takeda, "Passage of Bisphenol-A into the Fetus of the Pregnant Rat," *Journal of Health Science* 45 (1999): 318–23; O. Takahashi and S Oishi, "Disposition of Orally Administered 2,2-Bis(4-hydroxyphenyl) propane (Bisphenol-A) in Pregnant Rats and the Placental Transfer to Fetuses," *Environmental Health Perspectives* 108 (2000): 931–35; J. Josephson, "Breaching the Placenta," *Environmental Health Perspectives* 108 (2000); online at *http://ehpnet1.niehs.nih.gov/docs/2000/108-10/ss.html#breaching.*

    70. Myers, *http://ourstolenfuture.org.* Frederick vom Saal recently found that bisphenol-A had measurable effects in laboratory experiments at levels thousands of times lower than previously thought. These low-dose effects challenge the adequacy of countless toxicity tests undertaken to establish standards. For years, the acceptable daily dose for bisphenol-A had been set at a no-effect level of fifty milligrams/kg, or fifty parts per million, based on data reported by the Society of Plastics Industry. Vom Saal, however, found effects at lower levels: at two parts per billion, twenty-five thousand times lower. When he fed pregnant mice bisphenol-A at two parts per billion (two micrograms per kg/day), their male sons had enlarged and hypersensitized prostates when they reached adulthood. An overview of this work can be found at *http://ourstolenfuture.org/NewScience.* The original research is S. C. Nagel et al., "Relative Binding Affinity–Serum Modified Access (RBA–SMA) Assay Predicts the Relative In Vivo Bioactivity," 70–76. See also C. Gupta, "Reproductive Malformation of the Male Offspring Following Maternal Exposure to Estrogenic Chemicals," *Proceedings of the Society for Experimental Biology and Medicine* 224 (2000): 61–68. See also C. M. Markey, E. H. Luque, M. Muñoz de Toro, C. Sonnenschein, and A. M. Soto, "In Utero Exposure to Bisphenol-A Alters the Development and Tissue Organization of the Mouse Mammary Gland," *Biology of Reproduction* 65 (2001): 1215–23.

    71. Cadbury, *Altering Eden,* 144, 155.

    72. *http://abcnews.go.com/sections/living/DailyNews/toxicpolish_dbp001128.html.*

    73. Centers for Disease Control and Prevention, *National Report on Human Exposure to Environmental Chemicals,* March 2001, Atlanta. The report can be found online at *http://www.cdc.gov/nceh/dls/report/Highlights.htm.*

    74. Bob Weinhold "Forum," *Environmental Health Perspectives* 109 (May 2001); online at *http://ehpnet1.niehs.nih.gov/docs/2001/109-5/forum.html#baby Forum; Washington Post,* March 21, 2001; online at *http://washingtonpost.com/ac2/wp-dyn.*

75. Myers, *http://www.ourstolenfuture.org/New/newstuff.htm.*

76. Gray's team reported the research in the following reports: E. L. Gray Jr. et al., "Administration of Potentially Antiandrogenic Pesticides (Procymidone, Linuron, Iprodione, Chlozolinate, p, p'-DDE, and Ketoconazole) and Toxic Substances (Dibutyl- and Diethylhexyl Phthalate, PCB 169, and Ethane Dimethane Sulphonate) during Sexual Differentiation Produces Diverse Profiles of Reproductive Malformations in the Male Rat," *Toxicology and Industrial Health* 15 (1999): 94, "Environmental Antiandrogens: Low Doses of the Fungicide Vinclozolin Alter Sexual Differentiation of the Male Rat," ibid., 48, and "The Estrogenic and Antiandrogenic Pesticide Methoxychlor Alters the Reproductive Tract and Behavior without Affecting Pituitary Size or LH and Prolactin Secretion in Male Rats," ibid., 37; cited in Raloff, "Common Pollutants Undermine Masculinity."

77. This work was cited in Raloff, "Common pollutants undermine masculinity," who reported on a series of papers given at the March 1999 meeting of the Society of Toxicology in New Orleans, including E. Mylchreest, and P. M. D. Foster, "Dose-Response for Altered Male Reproductive Development and Function Induced by Di(n-butyl) Phthalate," and M. Sar, E. Mylchreest, and P. M. D. Foster, "Di(n-butyl) Phthalate Induces Changes in Morphology and Androgen Receptor Levels in the Fetal Testis."

78. I. Colón, D. Caro, C. J. Bourdony, and O. Rosario, "Identification of Phthalate Esters in the Serum of Young Puerto Rican Girls with Premature Breast Development," *Environmental Health Perspectives* 108 (2000): 895–900.

79. Ibid.

80. Editorial staff, "Extra Ingredients: Hormones in Food.

81. H. M. Blanck, M. Marcus, P. E. Tolbert, C. Rubin, A. K. Henderson, V. S. Hertzberg, R. H. Zhang, and L Cameron, "Age at Menarche and Tanner Stage in Girls Exposed In Utero and Postnatally to Polybrominated Biphenyl," *Epidemiology* 11 (2000): 641–47; Berkson, *Hormone Deception,* 109.

82. M. Krstevska-Konstantinova, C. Charlier, M. Craen, M. Du Caju, C. Heinrichs, C. de Beaufort, G. Plomteux, and J. P. Bourguignon, "Sexual Precocity after Immigration from Developing Countries to Belgium: Evidence of Previous Exposure to Organochlorine Pesticides," *Human Reproduction* 16 (2001): 1020–26.

83. M. Herman-Giddens, E. J. Slora, R. C. Wasserman, C. J. Bourdony, M. V. Bhapkar, G. G. Koch, and C. H. Hasemeier, "Secondary Sexual Characteristics and Menses in Young Girls Seen in Office Practice: A Study from the Pediatric Research in Office Settings Network," *Pediatrics* 99 (1999): 505–12. See also *www. ourstolenfuture.org/NewScience/reproduction/Puberty/pubertydebate.htm.*

84. P. B. Kaplowitz, E. J. Slora, R. C. Wasserman, S. E. Pedlow, and M. E. Herman-Giddens, "Earlier Onset of Puberty in Girls: Relation to Increased Body Mass Index and Race," *Pediatrics* 108 (2001): 347–53.

85. K. L. Howdeshell, A. K. Hotchkiss, K. A. Thayer, J. G. Vandenbergh, F. S. vom Saal, "Environmental Toxins: Exposure to Bisphenol-A Advances Puberty," *Nature* 401 (1999): 763–64.

86. For fuller discussions of this point, see Deborah Blum, *Sex on the Brain: The Biological Differences between Men and Women* (New York: Viking, 1998), and Anne Fausto-Sterling, *Myths of Gender: Biological Theories about Women and Men* (New York: Basic Books, 1985).

164   BODIES

87. Brumberg, *The Body Project*; see also Laura Fraser, *Losing It: America's Obsession with Weight and the Industry That Feeds on It* (New York: Viking, 1996), 32–44.

88. Brandy E. Fisher, "Gender Matters," *Environmental Health Perspectives* 106 (1998); online at *http://ehpnet1.niehs.nih.gov/docs/1998/106-6/niehsnews.html*.

89. Editorial staff, "Working for Women's Health," *Environmental Health Perspectives* 108 (January 2000); online at *http://ehpnet1.niehs.nih.gov/docs/2000/108-1/niehsnews.html*, citing Barbara J. Davis, head of the Female Reproductive Pathology Group and now acting chief of the newly created Laboratory of Women's Health at the National Institute of Environmental Health Sciences (NIEHS).

90. Fisher, "Gender Matters."

91. Berkson, *Hormone Deception*, 146.

92. For a review that discusses the many difficulties researchers face when they try to test for relationships between human reproductve problems and environmental toxicants, see F. I. Sharara, D. B. Seifer, and J. A. Flaws, "Environmental Toxicants and Female Reproduction," *Fertility and Sterility* 70 (1998): 613–22, and a response from W. H. James, "Environmental Toxicants and Sex Ratios—Effects?" *Fertility and Sterility* 71 (1999): 775.

93. G. M. Buck, J. E. Vena, E. F. Schisterman, J. Dmochowski, P. Mendola, L. E. Sever, E. Fitzgerald, P. Kostyniak, H. Greizerstein, and J. Olson, "Parental Consumption of Contaminated Sport Fish from Lake Ontario and Predicted Fecundability," *Epidemiology* 11 (2000): 388–93; cited at Myers, *www.ourstolenfuture.org/NewScience/*.

94. Editorial staff, "Extra Ingredients: Hormones in Food."

95. Cited in Editorial staff, "Working for Women's Health."

96. Berkson, *Hormone Deception*, 148.

97. National Institute for Environmental Health Sciences, "Women's Health," Fact Sheet no. 10 (August 1997); online at *http://www.niehs.nih.gov/oc/factsheets/womens.htm*.

98. The studies that showed effects were P. R. Koninckx, P. Braet, S. H. Kennedy, and D. H. Barlow, "Dioxin Pollution and Endometriosis in Belgium," *Human Reproduction* 9 (1994): 1001–02; L. S. Birnbaum, "Developmental Effects of Dioxin," *Environmental Health Perspectives* 103, Suppl. 7 (1995): 89–94; and A. Gibbons, "Dioxin Tied to Endometriosis," *Science* 262 (1993): 1373. The studies that failed to find correlations were A. Pauwels, P. J. C. Schepens, T. D'Hooghe, L. Delbeke, M. Dhont, A. Brouwer, and J. Weyler, "The Risk of Endometriosis and Exposure to Dioxins and Polychlorinated Biphenyls: A Case-Control Study of Infertile Women," *Human Reproduction* 16 (2001): 2050–55, and G. Lebel et al., "Organochlorine Exposure and the Risk of Endometriosis," *Fertility and Sterility* 69 (1998): 221–28.

99. L. C. Hodges, D. S. Hunter, J. S. Bergerson, R. Fuchs-Young, and C. L. Walker, "An In Vivo/In Vitro Model to Assess Endocrine Disrupting Activity of Xenoestrogens in Uterine Leiomyoma," *Annals of the New York Academy of Sciences. Environmental Hormones: The Scientific Basis of Endocrine Disruption* 948 (2001): 100–111.

100. R. R. Newbold, R. P. DiAugustine, J. I. Risinger, J. I. Everitt, D. K. Walmer, E. C. Parrott, and D. Dixon, "Advances in Uterine Leiomyoma Research," *Environmental Health Perspectives* 108, Suppl. 5 (October 2000): 769–73.

101. National Institute for Environmental Health Sciences, "Disparities in Environmental Health," online at *http://www.niehs.nih.gov/oc/factsheets/disparity/thome.htm*.

102. D. S. Hunter, L. C. Hodges, P. K. Eagon, P. M. Vonier, R. Fuchs-Young, J. S. Bergerson, and C. L. Walker, "Influence of Exogenous Estrogen Receptor Ligands on Uterine Leiomyoma: Evidence from an In Vitro/In Vivo Animal Model for Uterine Fibroids," *Environmental Health Perspectives* 108, Suppl. 5 (2000): 829–34. For the research on monkeys, see S. Takayama, S. M. Sieber, D. W. Dalgard, U. P. Thorgeirsson, and R. H. Adamson, "Effects of Long-Term Oral Administration of DDT on Nonhuman Primates," *Journal of Cancer Research and Clinical Oncology* 125 (1999): 219–25, and L. Tomatis and J. Huff, "Evidence of Carcinogenicity of DDT in Nonhuman Primates," *Journal of Cancer Research and Clinical Oncology* 126 (2000): 246.

103. For example, see W. Foster, S. Chan, L. Platt, and C. Hughes, "Detection of Endocrine-Disrupting Chemicals in Samples of Second Trimester Human Amniotic Fluid," *Journal of Clinical Endocrinology and Metabolism* 85 (2000): 1.

104. J. R. Davis, R. C. Brownson, and R. Garcia, "Family Pesticide Use Suspected of Causing Child Cancers," *Archives of Environmental Contamination Toxicology* 24 (1993): 87–92. For an overview of the difficulties in establishing links between exposure to pesticides (or other synthetic chemicals) and fetal effects, see T. Nurminen, "The Epidemiologic Study of Birth Defects and Pesticides," *Epidemiology* 12 (2001): 145–46.

105. Berkson, *Hormone Deception*, 91. In Germany, studies showed that levels of PCBs were over 100 parts per billion; in Denmark, over 140 ppb; in Spain, over 250 ppb; see Cadbury, *Altering Eden*, 72. For some of the research on breast milk contamination, see K. Hooper and T. A. McDonald, "The PBDEs: An Emerging Environmental Challenge and Another Reason for Breast-Milk Monitoring Programs," *Environmental Health Perspectives* 108 (2000): 387–92; Kim Hooper, T. Chuvakova, G. Kazbekova, D. Hayward, A. Tulenova, M. X. Petreas, T. J. Wade, K. Benedict, Y. Y. Cheng, and J. Grassman, "Analysis of Breast Milk to Assess Exposure to Chlorinated Contaminants in Kazakhstan: Sources of 2,3,7,8-tetrachlorodibenzo-p-dioxin (TCDD) Exposures in an Agricultural Region of Southern Kazakhstan," *Environmental Health Perspectives* 107 (1999): 447–57; K. Hooper, "Breast Milk Monitoring Programs (BMMPs): World-wide Early Warning System for Polyhalogenated POPs and for Targeting Studies in Children's Environmental Health," *Environmental Health Perspectives* 107 (1999): 429–30; and K. Hooper, M. X. Petreas, T. Chuvakova, G. Kazbekova, N. Druz, G. Seminova, T. Sharmanov, D. Hayward, J. She, P. Visita, J. Winkler, M. McKinney, T. J. Wade, J. Grassman, and R. D. Stephens, "Analysis of Breast Milk to Assess Exposure to Chlorinated Contaminants in Kazakstan: High Levels of 2,3,7,8-tetrachlorodibenzo-p-dioxin (TCDD) in Agricultural Villages of Southern Kazakstan," *Environmental Health Perspectives* 106 (1998): 797–806.

106. Myers, *Our Stolen Future*; new research online at *http://www.ourstolenfuture.org/New/newstuff.htm#*. For a comparison between exposure through breast-feeding and long-term exposure through food, see S. Patandin, P. C. Dagnelie, P. G. H. Mulder, E. Op de Coul, J. E. van der Veen, N. Weisglas-Kuperus, and P. J. J. Sauer, "Dietary Exposure to Polychlorinated Biphenyls and

Dioxins from Infancy until Adulthood: A Comparison between Breast-feeding, Toddler, and Long-term Exposure," *Environmental Health Perspectives* 107 (1999).

107. Myers, *Our Stolen Future*; new research online at *http://www.ourstolenfuture.org/New/newstuff.htm#*.

108. J. S. LaKind, C. M. Berlin, and D. Q. Naiman, "Infant Exposure to Chemicals in Breast Milk in the United States: What We Need to Learn from a Breast Milk Monitoring Program," *Environmental Health Perspectives* 109 (2001).

109. Krimsky, *Hormonal Chaos*, 231.

110. Ibid., 232.

111. National Research Council, *Hormonally Active Agents in the Environment* (Washington, D.C.: National Academy of Sciences Press, 1999).

112. Ibid., 15. This section of the NRC report is a fascinating exploration of how different groups and individuals construct knowledge.

113. Myers, *Our Stolen Future*; online at *http://ourstolenfuture.org/Consensus/nrc.htm*.

114. Schettler, "Endocrine Disruptors."

PART III: CONSUMPTION

CHAPTER EIGHT

Putting Gender on the Table:
Food and the Family Life of Nature

Douglas C. Sackman

The world begins at a kitchen table. No matter what, we must eat to live.
The gifts of the earth are brought and prepared, set on the table. . . .
It is here that children are given instructions on what it means to be human.
 We make men at it, we make women.

—*Joy Harjo*[1]

MAKING SALMON, MAKING GENDER

From a young age, Yurok girls growing up along the Klamath River of
what would become California heard stories linking their ability to cook
to matrimonial success. In one myth, two girls, having been instructed on
the proper way to roast meat, cook up a meal that meets the approval of
an old man. "They must be good girls. I think my son had better marry
them," he decides.[2] Yurok culture assigned food preparation to women,
but women cooked up much more than food when they made their
meals. Male and female identities were expressed and maintained in
daily acts of consumption—along with the their culture's particular way
of relating to nature.

 If we could sit in on one of the two daily Yurok meals that were
served traditionally, we would begin to see how the seemingly simple act
of eating means so much more than basic caloric intake. Most likely, they
would be eating salmon. Each person would be carefully chewing a
mouthful at a time, and they would seem to be looking inward. In fact,
they would be conjuring images of wealth in their minds, imagining dentalium shells (which served as the local currency) "as large as a salmon."
The psychologist Erik Erikson, remarking on how the Yurok teach their
children restraint toward food and reverence for wealth, argued that this
education "later on allows the Yurok to think of wealth at any time in an
almost hallucinatory way." As male children grow up, it was "not only
his appetite for food which he learns to restrain for the sake of amassing
wealth, but also his sexual desires." Men "may sit in the sweat-lodge and

169

at the same time attempt to see in the river a dentalium shell as large as a salmon and try *not* to think of women."[3] But if they had consumed too many actual salmon in gluttonous fashion, their flabbiness would make them offensive to the river, offensive, ultimately, to salmon. And they wouldn't be able to enter the male-space of the sweat-lodge, for fatness was architecturally circumscribed: the only way into the lodge was through a narrow portal. To be a real man one had to control consumption.

It is impossible to understand Yurok behavior and attitudes toward food without considering two basic principles embedded in their views of nature: all of nature was alive, and this vital nature was watchful. No creature was more aware, more relentlessly vigilant, than the salmon (their word for which translates as "the food itself"). Lose the respect of the salmon, and the entire land would go barren.[4] Failure to wash one's hands or dispose of the bones in the proper way would offend the salmon. Menstruating women were forbidden to handle food (which gave them a respite from household chores during which they journeyed with other women to a "sacred moontime pond" in the mountains where they imagined seeing dentalium shells of their own).[5] As a conscious, powerful, and sensitive creature, the salmon ensured that gender would be prepared with every meal. At a Yurok dinner—the food having been carefully prepared by women so as not to offend, the men conjuring wealth and banishing women from their minds, the children being taught to discipline their appetites—family members at once consumed nature and became gendered.

Although the Yurok family's sense of kinship with the creatures they consumed is unusual, all kinds of American families make gender and identity when they consume nature as food. This chapter explores the way nature takes on a second life in the family circle by focusing on the intertwined consumption of nature and production of gender within two domains: the "farm family" of America's agrarian imagination and the "consumer family" that was rolled out in the early twentieth century. That culinary cliché "you are what you eat," with its nutritional determinism, overstates the case. But it is accurate to say that family members become who they are in part through the production, preparation, and consumption of nature as food. And in turning nature into food, families also put gender on the table.

THE FAMILY LIFE OF NATURE

Families do not appear out of thin air. They are human institutions forged of social, cultural, and natural materials. A family functions as a "procreative mechanism, a unit of economic production, a cultivator of cultural values, a relationship of power, and a means of social adaptation"[6] Families, of course, take on different forms in different times and places. Notions of kinship, like gender roles, are not biologically given. The elaborate anthropological lexicon of kinship, with terms for matrifocal, patrifocal, bride price, polygamy, polyandry, even fictive kin, will shake any belief in a "natural family."

Yet there is much that is natural about families. In their role as "a unit of economic production," for example, families are basically in the business of making a living off of the earth. Indirectly or directly, they shape parts of nature into forms that will be valuable to themselves or others. Farm families husband the earth, entering into an arrangement from which they derive their daily bread. But this relationship is no less true of families whose members work for wages: in factories as well as fields, nature is passed through human hands. Through exchanges that are more or less elaborate, nature in the form of food goes back into the bodies of human workers. It is consumed in myriad other ways has well, including the brick, mortar, timber, and hearthstone that families have used to make a home. And families fill their homes, and their lives, with objects imbued with cultural values but that ultimately come from nature.

If environmental history finds its main story at the place where nature and culture intersect, then the home should not fall outside of its purview. Yet the field has tended to look outside of city limits, and outside of suburban limits as well, to investigate agricultural or wilderness landscapes. The actors in environmental histories tend to be men situated in political or economic roles (e.g., the crusading preservationist or the despoiling capitalist).[7] Though some studies now have explored the connection between ideas of masculinity and wilderness, most works on the relationship of "man and nature" seldom consider the gender of their actors.[8] Rarer still is to see actors' interactions with nature as shaped by their involvement in family life. Bringing environmental history home means seeing how men, women, and children act in families as they interact with and consume nature. If we are to find nature at home, then we must expand the common definition of what counts as nature to include items found within four walls. Though we expect to find nature in the mountains, or in the country, or at least outside, investigating the relationship between nature and culture also properly takes us into the domestic sphere.

Inside the home of a modern American family, we might look hard and long for nature. Electronics will most likely be in abundance, including computers and televisions. But turn the television on, and you may see nature, usually embodied by a large alligator, cabled into the room on the Outdoor Life or Discovery channels. The house may have landscape paintings and photographs on the wall. Perhaps some houseplants. Uninvited organisms will, of course, abound, despite high standards of cleanliness—indeed, ones that hold up an antiseptic, sterile environment as ideal for the home.[9] There will be food in the cupboards and in the refrigerator. All of this will have been processed and wrapped up; milk or bread will most likely be stamped with a bucolic, country icon—cows in the pasture, barns, amber waves of grain. And we see fathers as ruddy farmers and smiling girls in a sundresses picking wildflowers. Of course, such pictures of family life close to nature mask the social and environmental realities of the modern dairy industry. Yet they capture and cultivate quite real desires: advertisers treat consumers of milk as members of families who imagine closeness with nature as a way of fulfilling familial togetherness.

The house is full of other stuff—microwaves and microfibers, loveseats and Monopoly games, magazines and newspapers, toys and baby products of all sizes and shape. We might regard these objects of consumption as doornail-dead commodities, the comatose hulls of nature's forms whose vital essences and connections have been stripped away. The environmentalist critique of consumerism often regards consumer objects as evidence of a destructive American materialism, walling families up in palaces of consumption and severing them from nature. Every thing bought and sold is seen as a blow to the earth. If one wishes to expose the loss that has attended consumerism, it makes sense to portray the products of ecosystems that have been razed and then remade as factories as a collection of meaningless junk.[10] Though such jeremiads against consumerism have their uses, they fail to appreciate the intricacies of buying behaviors and the complicated ways that families connect to nature as consumers.

Family identities are dependent on nature, though not always in ways that can be seen on the surface. It takes some work to uncover how all of this stuff is related to nature, and how living in the midst of it, American families are constantly wrapping themselves up in nature in order to be who and what they are. By tracing the path from farm or ranch to the kitchen table the connections between the household and the natural world can be recovered. In his magisterial work *Nature's Metropolis*, William Cronon has uncovered the routes through which the nature of the countryside passes into the culture of the city. He maps the traffic in meat from the plains and prairies, through the stockyards, "disassembly lines," and commodity markets of Chicago, and out to consumers across the country in the late nineteenth century. Knowledge of and contact with the animal that once lived and breathed has been severed by the modern meat industry. "The more people became accustomed to the attractively cut, carefully wrapped, cunningly displayed packages that

Swift had introduced," Cronon explains, "the more easily they could fail to remember that their purchase had once pulsed and breathed with a life much like their own."[11] The phrase "meat-market" has become synonymous with objectification, and rightly so. The reduction of living animals into interchangeable cuts "betokened a much deeper and subtler separation—the word 'alienation' is not too strong—from the act of killing and from nature itself."[12]

But some anthropologists argue that objects become animated and enculturated as they are consumed, that "commodities, like persons, have social lives."[13] The commodification of nature disenchants the natural world, to be sure; but the natural world can also be reanimated when it enters the human world. The use and consumption of objects connect people to nature, though often in ways they do not themselves recognize. Everything that families are—units of production, sources of reproduction, inculcators of values, relationships of affection—is intertwined with what nature becomes for them. Nature provides the raw materials for physical growth and yields symbolic resources as well, as when animal families are anthropomorphized to reflect human notions of proper family groups and gender roles in science, zoos, stories, or films like *Bambi*.[14] Nature is food and fiber for family life.

If in wilderness is the preservation of the world, as Thoreau said, we might add that in consumption is the preservation of social worlds. In all societies, goods have been used to define kinship and community as well as to create stability and meaning in an infinitely complex environment. The making of family consumers has involved not so much a severing of connections to nature as a transformation of those connections into a kind of "cultural capital." Turned into different forms of clothing, that cultural capital withdrawn from nature's bank can be spent to define gender roles within a society. Turned into an heirloom, a costume, a dowry, a holiday meal, or a plot of land, nature can be used to build and represent kinship and gender.

The anthropologist Claude Lévi-Strauss explored how humans categorize the world, how they separate the "raw" from the "cooked." Fire "mediate[s] the conjunction of the raw product and the human consumer . . . making sure that a natural creature is at one and the same time *cooked and socialized*."[15] Thus is the nature made fit, symbolically and physiologically, for human consumption. But who does the cooking is as significant as the cooking itself. The preparation and serving of food turns out to be good not only for feeding a family but also for teaching everyone in the family to play his or her proper role. Food, Lévi-Strauss revealed, is good for thinking; it is also good for gendering.[16]

Families cook themselves, but not under conditions of their own making. Outside influences and authorities play a large role in shaping what goes on in any kitchen and who works in what role. The economic conditions and normative prescriptions of family life affect how any particular family forms itself from nature's bounty. In the spread of the family farm—on the American landscape and in the American imagination—we can begin to trace the relationships among cultural norms, ecological and economic conditions, and the formation of gendered identities.

THE NATURE OF THE FAMILY FARM, REAL AND IMAGINED

Once upon time, popular memory has it, the American family was different than it is today. There was a little house, on the prairie or in the woods of New England. Father worked the soil, and male children lent a hand. The boys grew up to be American—self-reliant, productive, and handy. And they would be smart too, in a rough-hewn kind of way. Like Lincoln of lore, they would walk a mile to borrow a book, but they would know the honest value of work in nature as well. The girls would grow up to take after their mothers—strong and ethical, attending selflessly to the care of the garden, hearth, and home and, especially, to the men in their lives. They might harbor desires for baubles or fancy dresses, but deferred desire in favor of a homespun abundance.[17] This family produced—it grew wheat and other crops with family labor, and it spun and sewed. And this family reproduced—picturing the farmstead without children seems unnatural. The family grew what it ate, and as it ate it grew. But it did not consume, aside from the occasional sweet or store-bought dress.

One story of national identity makes these homesteading pilgrims both the genesis and ends of American democracy itself. As James Madison had it, "The class of citizens who provide at once their own food and their own raiment may be viewed as the most truly independent and happy . . . [and] the best basis of public liberty."[18] This family grows from the soil itself: its genius and character come through the taming of the wilderness. Domesticating nature is at once a domestic art, for ploughing, harvesting, and baking in the promised land make the family and the nation. Like paradise, this family is gone (indeed, it never quite existed), and yet the power of its imagery continues to fuel gender ideology and conceptions of the proper family structure. Even the other dominant image of American family life—the 1950s model—was fashioned partly out of images of the traditional homestead, with the lawn, for example, functioning as symbolic crops.[19] The farm family has one life in the realm of fiction, with its farmhouse located not on the actual American landscape but in the kingdom of myth.

Of course, there were, and continue to be, actual farm families making a living off of American soil; most Americans lived in the countryside until 1920. So how does the image constructed in the world of imagination compare to the actual life on the farm?[20] We can begin by pointing out some broad areas where the image diverges from common farm realities.

The farm family image pictures the relationship to nature as fundamentally harmonious. Children growing up on farms did form "pleasant memories" from their work gardening, hunting, and gathering food. As they grew up in a landscape from which they drew their subsistence, children also developed their very sense of self and identity.[21] Although it is true that farm families developed intimate relationships with the natural world on which they depended, the creation of an agricultural landscape also involves the domination and control of nature and often desperate struggle.[22] The bucolic portrait romanticizes work that was often backbreaking rather than body-building. And while working with farm animals may seem nice if you think all pigs act like Wilbur of *Charlotte's Web*, imagine the horror of a mother running back from the garden to her house to find a razorback's snout in her small son's mouth rooting for blood.[23]

The farm family of the imagination makes the male the *farmer* and the female the *farmwife*, which reduces the essential work women did on farms to an auxiliary position. The farm family appears to enjoy a cozy togetherness, but this picture erases the workings of patriarchal power with its rigid subordination of women and children. The image also cloaks the farm family in privacy, but such privacy was a luxury few farming families could ever afford. They needed their neighbors and their neighbors needed them to subsist. They also needed the government, which often secured titles to lands, forcefully usurped Indian claims and competition, and subsidized transportation and irrigation systems. Farms were rarely self-sufficient in the sense of growing and producing everything that they needed. If farm life was to be rich and wholesome and secure, farm families needed to rely on elaborate trade and social relationships, making production and consumption community, rather than strictly family, affairs.[24]

There were, of course, other families in America, residing in cities and earning their living by other means. Considering the place of those other families in the American family portrait—or, rather, their exclusion from it—allows us to see a second set of distortions. By privileging the image of the farm family, not only have Americans obscured their understanding of actual farm life, but they have also restricted their understanding of what counts as an American family. Immigrant families, for example, have not been considered central to American experience—their traditional family values were things to be ejected as they became

Americanized. Frederick Jackson Turner saw the countryside as a kind of magic barn of Americanization: in would go the European and out would come the hardy, democratic, liberty-loving American.[25] If the immigrants settled in the city, it was difficult for them to find a place in the national portraiture, perhaps because they didn't seem white enough.[26] But the countryside could confer this whiteness, cleansing away ethnic grit.[27] Whether they lived in the city or in the countryside, African Americans, Asian Americans, or Indians have been excluded from the homestead of American mythology. Mirroring the practices of post–World War II suburbs, the mythology of the American farm family has restrictive covenants in place that prevent Americans of color from moving in. If much has been invested in the image of the farmer and farmer's wife as embodiments of American manhood and feminine virtue, men and women of color have not been allowed to bank on it.[28]

The farm family image, with all of its inaccuracies, omissions, and exclusions, has played a large role in shaping the relationship between the model American family and nature in the twentieth century. It did so even though the key aspect of the farm family's identity—its role as producers working in a rural landscape—would be stripped from the new model of the American family. Its identity would be keyed to consumerism in urban and suburban landscapes. To situate this profound revolution in family values, we need to look back at the impact of the market revolution on farm families in the nineteenth century.

The birthplace of the (Euro)American farm family was twenty miles or more inland from the Atlantic seaboard or navigable rivers with their easy access to markets.[29] Carolyn Merchant suggests that the early colonial farmers lived in an "animate cosmos" not entirely unlike the Algonquians—or the Yurok in our opening family portrait. Conceiving of nature as an "animate mother," colonial farmers in the eighteenth century performed rituals to encourage nature to be generous with her gifts. Almanacs instructed farmers to work with the cycles of the moon and taught them to view nature as a "human writ large with whom the farmer had an intimate, personal relationship."[30] According to Merchant, the colonial family's relationship to nature was relational and mythical; nature left its imprint on the family, even as the New England farm family displaced Indians and modified nature to support its own needs for production and reproduction (social and biological) in the New World.

These farmers viewed "the world through the prism of family values."[31] Patriarchal family relations and a sexual division of labor defined the family farm and shaped its relations with the natural world. Fathers held the title to land and exercised authority over this household mode of production's labor force—that is, his wife and six to eight children. Men, women, and children worked the land, and as they did so, "the family gave symbolic meaning and emotional significance to subsistence activities."[32] The very space of the homestead was divided up into gendered zones of responsibility. Male "space radiated outward from the barn . . . [w]omen's domain radiated outward from the farmhouse kitchen."[33] Fathers were responsible for clearing fields, managing crops, attending to livestock, as well as hunting and fishing. From an early age, boys worked alongside their fathers and took over specific tasks as they grew older. Girls helped with their mother's mountain of work. As Charles Sellers points out, "While constantly pregnant or nursing infants for fifteen or twenty years, wives were responsible for the domestic interior, cooking, extensive food preparation, gardens, poultry, dairy animals, and the endless textile processes of carding, spinning, weaving, fulling, dying, quilting, sewing, and mending."[34] Labor itself—the work of bringing forth those astonishing numbers of babies—was an all-female affair. Midwives aided in these births, and many also served as the doctors of the countryside. To maintain a family's health, midwives (and wives) looked to nature, which "offered solutions to its own problems. Remedies for illness could be found in the earth, the animal world, and in the human body itself."[35]

However attractive this model of family life might seem to environmentalists, its mode of living was anything but sustainable. Its lack of sustainability had everything to do with how the family functioned on the farm. Merchant identifies a contradiction between the requirements for production and those of reproduction on the family farm. Because family labor was so crucial, family sizes were large, but children would need land of their own when they matured. This family's driving desire was not infinite accumulation; rather, it was to set up the next generation's males as independent freeholders and patriarchs and females as good wives and mothers. However much had been borrowed from Indians to make this world, more would be taken to keep it going ("free land explains American development," as Frederick Jackson Turner saw it). The desire to reproduce the family farm required ever more land and led to the adoption of commercial practices and, ultimately, a capitalist ethos. Farmers increasingly turned to intensive methods of farm management and sought out sources of cash that could be used to purchase new lands. Whether we see these as effective strategies for resisting capitalism or as capitulation to the new order, by the first decades of the nineteenth century, the farm family's role as producers for use and local exchange was being replaced by its role as producers for a market.[36] The ensuing world mechanized nature and split production along gender lines. Women became ensconced in a separate sphere of reproduction: they would be mothers and nurturers.

Attending and propitiating these changes was the collapse of household production and its replacement by factory production.[37] At the same time, an ideology of separate spheres was invented and refined. Although some women found love and reassurance in the homosocial world, they also found their opportunities and movement circumscribed as the "cult of true womanhood," a collection of refined traits, began to define the bounds of their identities. Men preserved for themselves the avenues of upward mobility in the emerging capitalist world; they would work in the business world and become the primary "breadwinners" of the family. While their menfolk advanced their family's interest in the grubby world of commerce, women were charged with raising children, attending to higher ideals, and making the home a "haven in a heartless world."

Though the separate spheres ideology and the cult of true womanhood were primarily artifacts of the middle class, society's dominant imagery increasingly disconnected women from productive work and etherealized womanhood. The "true woman" became light and purity. She was to stand above and apart from the grubby world of commerce and productive work in the soil. Yet, it was considered proper for a woman to have contact with nature in a carefully cultivated garden (and in the kitchen). In the garden, according to contemporary authorities, she could express her feminine virtues and see society's ideas about gender roles confirmed in the character of the plant and animal kingdoms. Sarah Cooper, for example, promoted the cultivation of native plants as a proper activity for women. She also celebrated the role of the farm family mother, contrasting her virtue to town girls who had become "wildly extravagant in their dress."

Approving of homemade clothes, Cooper wrote that "the home system is healthier and safer for the individual, in every way. Home, we may rest assured, will always be, as a rule, the best place for a woman; her labors and interests, should all centre there, whatever her sphere of life."[38] This affirmation of female domesticity was tightly woven with her affirmation of the "virtues of the bucolic American scene."[39] To Cooper, nature's virtues complemented, reinforced, and reflected human virtues. As Vera Norwood explains, "Cooper showed her female readers how a close observation of flowering plants taught the proper female virtues of modesty, constancy, and sisterhood. When she observed the birds, she found her family; when she looked at flowers, she saw images of the female sex."[40] Writing in 1840 in a popular magazine, Lydia Sigourney maintained that "the lessons learned among the works of Nature are of particular value in the present age. The restlessness and din of the railroad principle . . . and the spirit of accumulation . . . are modified by the sweet friendships of the plants."[41] Women were encouraged to use nature as a model and a resource with which to nurture children, balm the market wounds of their husbands, and build family harmony.

As the industrial revolution accelerated around the turn of the century, the family, as well as gender roles within it, would undergo substantial change. A new, national consumer market was invented to provide an outlet for myriad new products. However much the domestic sphere had been imagined as a refuge from the world of business, the commercial world came knocking on the door; it had goods to sell. In the first decades of the twentieth century, professional advertisers drove a cultural change that derailed the traditional ethos centered on production and propelled a new set of beliefs linking the good life to consumerism.[42]

Even farm families, looking through the catalogues of Montgomery Ward, would be drawn into the world of consumption. Though farm families often thought of themselves, and were represented by others, as moral bastions against a consumer-oriented culture, by the end of the nineteenth century most were interdependent with that world.[43] Yet rural Americans became ambivalent consumers. Many farm women, for example, eschewed store-bought goods in favor of the homemade bread or soup because the "family likes [it] better." Still, many farm women would join their urban and suburban counterparts who were increasingly attracted by the convenience of mass-marketed bread and other foodstuffs.[44]

MRS. CONSUMER IN THE NEW GARDEN OF EDEN

The family farm, whatever purposes it has come to serve as mythology, was ultimately grounded in a household mode of production that characterized agrarian society in the United States into the nineteenth century. The market revolution, with its components of commercialization, industrialization, and transportation advances, would pull the farm family in new directions, upsetting its economic basis and forcing family members to find their footing in a new landscape. For the middle class in urban or rural settings, ideas about breadwinning and homemaking would provide the ground rules for this new orientation. Men would go out into the public sphere to reap the opportunities of the market; no longer sowers of grain, they would become breadwinners. Women would become ensconced in the domestic sphere, where the household purportedly lost its importance as the center of economic production and instead became a zone women managed for the growth of children and the recuperation of husbands beaten down in the marketplace; instead of comanagers of household production, women would become "*house*wives"—married as much to a domestic ideology as they were to actual men. Having invested men with the power of earning money and delegitimized the economic aspirations of women, American society would witness profound changes in family life.

Since family labor was not needed on the farm, family size began to decline. By the early twentieth century, the dominant family pattern was beginning to bear little real resemblance to the farm family and would seem more and more to occupy the space of leisure. From this perspective, the work that women did cooking, cleaning, and rearing children came to be regarded as not work at all, but something akin to gardening for pleasure. Although it would not cease to be a unit of production and reproduction, the new "companionate family" would become ever more identified with consumption. Yet, the companionate family ideal would give mothers, fathers, and children much work to do as they secured wages and refashioned their identities to live up to the consumer model of family life. For this new model of family life, nature no longer served as the raw material for production. Instead, nature would be used as processed food, fashionable clothing, and scenic playgrounds to forge the family members' new identities as consumers.[45]

But the model farm family didn't get subsumed without a fight. The discourse about family life was fraught with anxieties about the loss of contact with nature in postfrontier, industrialized America. The plight of the farm family became a touchstone for these worries. President Theodore Roosevelt, believing that the "strengthening of country life is the strengthening of the whole nation,"[46] appointed a commission to study threats to the agrarian way of life. "It is especially important that whatever will serve to prepare country children for life on the farm, and whatever will brighten home life in the country and make it richer and more attractive for the mothers, wives and daughters of farmers should be done promptly, thoroughly and gladly," the president wrote. "There is no more important person, measured in influence upon the life of the nation, than the farmer's wife, no more important home than the country home, and it is of national importance to do the best we can for both."[47] When all was right in the rural home, the commission reported, "there are good gardens and attractive premises, and a sympathetic love of nature and of farm life on the part of the entire family."[48] Those who celebrated the rural family argued that "the farm home is a picture of family unity. The members of the farm work together, play together, share equal responsibilities about the home, whether it be the care of the flower garden, vegetable garden, dairy farm or whatnot."[49] A few sociologists celebrated the farm family as a "social organism" that exhibited a kind of organic unity, believing that it best reflected what they took to be the natural order.[50]

Although advertisers championed the modern, consumer family, they also sought to capitalize on nostalgia for the rural. In fact, some ardent supporters of the virtues of the "simple life" were also influential merchandisers and admen, including Edward Bok, the publisher of the first million-circulation mass magazine, the *Ladies' Home Journal*, John Wanamaker, the founder of one of the first truly wondrous department stores, James Webb Young, one of the most successful ad designers, and Henry Ford, who built a car empire but who also monumentalized preindustrial America with his Greenfield Village.[51] The products advertised in mass-circulation magazines such as the *Saturday Evening Post* or *Ladies' Home Journal* promised to bring the country to urban families and bring them into the country for therapeutic doses of the rural life without any need to give up the amenities and lifestyle of the city. Advertisers served up the farm family on a plate.[52]

Food was no longer the outcome of farm families' hard labor. Increasingly the product of "factories in the field" (as Carey McWilliams called them), mass-produced food was nonetheless advertised as if it had come from a rural idyll. Foods were symbolically charged with the splendor of nature so that the countryside could be imported into the home itself. The food industry had worked wonders with their products from the 1910s through the 1930s, stamping those products with new identities that called forth a vibrant palette of associations. But since the movement for pure food that culminated in Upton Sinclair's exposure of the stomach-turning operations of the meatpacking industry in *The Jungle* and the passage of the Pure Food and Drug Act in 1906, marketers of food felt the need to allay consumer skepticism and deliver products that seemed pure.

Food processors also had to contend with critics like Liberty Hyde Bailey, who served as chair of Roosevelt's Country Life Commission. Bailey argued that "danger may lie in any untruthfulness with which we use the raw materials of life."[53] For Bailey, the "adulteration" of foods was connected to "a staggering infidelity in the use of the good raw materials," which, in turn, threatened "vigor and good morals."[54] The distance from the "adulteration" of natural foods and adultery in a marriage was not that great in this discourse. Two-timing nature with such "infidelity" was thus a threat not just to good health but also to family values.

By highlighting the natural qualities of their foods, manufacturers sought to erase images of processing from the minds of their consumers and simultaneously reconnect them to their farm family roots (whether they were real or imagined) and to nature itself.[55] Nature somehow would go straight into the can of soup, not passing through human hands or sharp-bladed, dirty machinery. Heinz and Campbell's used images of ruddy fathers and young men bringing in tubs of tomatoes from a resplendent landscape—according to Heinz, a "place where the good green earth is bountiful." Campbell's assured consumers that their "plump, luscious tomatoes" were carefully inspected to assure that their soup would have "sparkle . . . gaiety . . . life . . . color . . . invigoration." Likewise, "every tomato Heinz uses is a beauty," and the harvest is a "picturesque procession . . . along the road to the Heinz kitchen. . . . Wagons carry colorful loads of Heinz 'aristocratic' tomatoes—the fresh morning dew still sparkling on their plump, rosy cheeks." There were no factory farms here, only tomatoes frolicking in the bucolic landscape as if they were country maidens.[56]

Just as true women were thought to have the power to redeem modern men, pure food would redeem modern America. Theodore Roosevelt and others worried that civilization had made Americans soft, even decadent. The frontier had closed, and the machine had enveloped America and Americans. To avoid falling off the ladder of progress, Americans had simply to partake of natural foods. For men, pure, unadulterated food could restore their manly vigor. For women, such foods could help them attain a new body image. In an advertisement for Bran Flakes, General Mills showed a svelte woman dressed in primitive furs: "To be slim and radiant," the ad instructed, "eat like a cave woman."[57]

Advertisers aimed at women, emphasizing the link between good and feminine virtue. They served up myriad assurances that by adopting new habits of consumption, women could at once be progressive and traditional. As Robert and Helen Lynd observed in their sociological study of the typical American community they called "Middletown" (aka Muncie, Indiana), through newspapers, billboards, and magazines such as *Good Housekeeping*, *Women's Home Companion*, and *Ladies' Home Journal*, "advertising pounds away at the habits of the Middletown housewife. Whole industries mobilize to impress a new dietary habit upon her."[58] Food products were portrayed as good for the woman and her family, indeed, essential to the proper growth of her children and the continued vitality and productiveness of the family's breadwinner. Armored with these perspectives, Mrs. Consumer (as the advertising field referred to its female customers) could resist criticism from traditionalists inside or outside her household and become a knowledgeable spokeswoman for the advertised foodstuffs that were at once new and natural.

The California Fruit Growers Exchange, the agricultural cooperative that launched the Sunkist trademark, showed particular genius with this theme.[59] California itself, through a long history of romantic representation in painting, literature, advertising, and endless booster tracts, had come to be associated with the vibrancy and grandeur of nature. Moreover, it had been depicted as a vast sanitarium, a place where bodies broken down by the ailments of modern living might go to recoup. Railroads and chambers of commerce told stories of individuals who had arrived in California weak and depleted but who had fully recovered under the sun's healing rays.[60] Sunkist salesmen became ambassadors of the Sunshine State, and oranges were embodiments of pure nature. Pictured in living color in their magazine ads, the oranges seemed almost real enough to touch. Readers were told, "*You* get them—in Nature's Germ Proof Package—as ripe and sweet and pure as if you plucked them yourself." Eat them and you could taste the sunshine. Squeeze them for an elixir of health.

Sunkist told different versions of the parable to men and women. Men were told that failing to eat oranges would make them susceptible to "acidosis," an enervating ailment that could very well lead to losing their edge at work. Women were hailed as "the health commissioner of the home." Presented with information on vitamin C and charts and diagrams showing the proper growth of children and the role of citrus in assuring healthy development, oranges became a basic ingredient for proper homemaking. Educating Mrs. Consumer about "vitamines" in the 1920s, Sunkist sought to confer on women an expertise about nutrition that would make them, the company hoped, into faithful customers by convincing them that oranges were essential to faithful homemaking. Sunkist purposely emphasized the health benefits to infants as a strategy to make the entire household into consumers. As one of Sunkist's advertising managers recalled, "In the first years we advertised orange juice for babies, the reason for that being that a mother will probably dip deeper into her budget to buy product that is good for her baby than she will for one that is good for herself or her husband."[61] Mother and father would pick up the habit as well, Sunkist hoped. The company also made sure to supply the housewife with a wealth of recipes for serving up citrus in original and pleasing ways.

Mrs. Consumer and her family often did not recognize that the act of consuming foods like oranges connected her to other women, the "Mrs. Producers" who packed those oranges for consumption. Many of the social and environmental relationships that consumers entered into by eating oranges were masked. After all, the advertising and the grocery store displays were designed to make her almost imagine that she had picked them herself. Sunkist's oranges were meant to embody the purity of nature, but the nature that made them—the landscapers of California—had been deeply transformed and regimented to create such products. The oranges themselves went through an elaborate processing from grove through packinghouse. Men picked oranges in the groves under exacting procedures of scientific management and then women performed the work of packing the oranges for market. These men and women made up families who, because of their Chinese, Japanese, Filipino, or Mexican heritage, were often barred from full membership in the body politic. Imagining that the oranges came straight from nature, unmediated by technology or human hands, consumers failed to see how oranges involved them in the lives of men in the groves and women workers in the packinghouses and with profoundly altered landscapes that were far removed from the Edenic purity of the copy.[62]

The rise of the consumer family would have been impossible without the supermarket. By the 1930s, chain grocery stores began replacing neighborhood stores, ushering in a revolution in how Americans purchased food. In a 1939 feature celebrating the "Parade of Progress of Nationally Advertised Grocery Products," the *Saturday Evening Post* highlighted these changes. It pictured a modern couple walking into the chain store they had become accustomed to but finding it transformed into an old-time neighborhood store. The clerk is rather ghostly, and when the wife asks him for oranges, he replies, "Oranges? We sell oranges only at Christmas time." The couple, with shocked looks on their faces, is further disappointed when they ask for tomato juice and a specific brand of coffee. Everything seems to be like it was back in the old days of "a few monotonous foods and long hours in the kitchen." What had happened to the new world, in which "food buying and food preparing are actually exciting!" [63]

By the 1950s, local communities of consumption were replaced with an imagined national community of consumers—all buying nationally advertised goods in supermarkets, all consuming nature's packaged bounty from across the country, all partaking in the American way of life.[64] In turn, the consumer family of the suburbs could become more detached from neighborhood communities, more insularly nuclear. Civic duty could be conflated with buying goods, as reflected in this 1947 headline from *Life*: "Family Status Must Improve: It Should Buy More for Itself to Better the Living of Others."[65] And buy they did: between 1946 and 1950, Americans purchased 20 million automobiles and 20 million refrigerators.[66] The routes bringing the family outside and the outside to the family were full of traffic by the 1950s, as those cars hit the road and those refrigerators were filled with goods.

The refrigerator was a domestic adjunct of the supermarket, though they were often marketed as a garden within the home. While canned goods promised that country life, vigor, and virtue had been packed within, homemakers found that they could can fresh foods by simply placing them in a new refrigerator. The Gibson, equally at home in green fields or in a new kitchen, could hold an entire garden's bounty and keep it all "farm-fresh." The refrigerator was a garden in and of itself, from which women would pluck the fruits of nature (and other "man-sized" foods) and present them on a platter to their smiling husbands.[67]

In a telling photograph appearing in *Better Living* (DuPont's employee magazine), one American family—the Czekalinskis—was pictured completely inside a refrigerated space. They are surrounded by a vast array of foods—apples from Washington, oranges and lemons from California (where DuPont fumigated orchards to please the consumer with fruit unblemished by insects), sugar from Hawaii, corn from the

Midwest, lettuce and tomatoes, chickens and other meats, dozens of eggs, rows and rows of bottled milk, and sacks and sacks of potatoes and Enriched Family Flour from Sunnyfield. All told, the Czekalinskis have spent $1,300 for nature's bounty, enough calories and vitamins to sustain this growing family for a year. Although there is no indication of the natural world from which this bounty comes, we are given a glimpse of the work that it takes to bring it all home—and it is assuredly women's work, for Mrs. Czekalinski has her hands on a shopping cart. There is an element of the old story in this still life, of how work in the American soil produces a rich bounty that fuels the moral and physical growth of the American family. But this mythology has been retooled for the consumer family and the containment culture of the Cold War: self-sufficiency and Americanization meant the ability to navigate a supermarket's aisles and the ownership of a modern kitchen. Everyone sports overcoats; it is proper cover for entering this cold locker chock-full of nature's goods—harvested, packaged, and arranged for easy consumption—in which the American family found itself by the 1950s.[68]

THINKING OUTSIDE THE ICE BOX?

Not everyone agreed that this kind of existence truly represented "better living." In the 1930s, Ralph and Mytle Borsodi, fleeing from the modern pace of life in New York, retreated upstate to what they would call an organic homestead. They felt that the modern American family was becoming alienated from nature. Rejecting the model of family life in which contact with nature would become only token—a contact with simulated or processed nature, not nature itself—the Borsodis went off into the country to put roots into the soil and reinvent the family as wholesome agrarian producers.

In *The Flight from the City* and other publications, Ralph fulminated against factories and mass-produced foodstuffs. Mass production had undermined "the economic foundations of the family" as agrarian producers and thereby "robbed men, women and children of their contact with the soil; their intimacy with the growing of animals, birds, vegetables, trees and flowers."[69] Writing in *Good Housekeeping*, Myrtle argued that women could be both more economically and more culturally productive by working in the home. Industrial production, she argued, had led to a division of the sexes so that men and women no longer worked together in the system of household production. Along with this change, the "money-making" of men in the public sphere replaced "home-making" as a valued activity. The home, in short, became economically irrelevant, and women's power and worth declined with that transformation.

To regain power, women should put small-scale electric technology to use in the home to produce for the home. She explained the various food items she produced on her "modernized version of the old homestead" —all more cheaply and efficiently than could be purchased on the market, she insisted.[70]

According to the Borsodis, the domestic production and consumption of food would lead to a healthier, happier, and more secure family life. Their back-to-the-land experiment was in part "a revolt against the kind of food with which mass production . . . provides the American consumer."[71] Eating "factory packed foodstuffs" would inexorably link them to "city life," producing the kind of malaise of which much advertising copy was made: "We lacked the zest of living which comes from real health and suffered all the minor and sometimes major ailments which come from too much excitement, too much artificial food, too much sedentary work. . . . our lives were barren of real beauty—the beauty which comes from the growth of the soil, from flowers and fruits."[72] For the Borsodis, only the productive work of transforming nature into a livelihood could build up strong and healthy families.

The Borsodis' back-to-the-land message reached a receptive audience among the back-to-the-landers of the 1960s and 1970s. Paul Goodman, in his preface to the 1972 reissue of *Flight from the City*, reported that the book "has become part of the hippie counter culture."[73] Having grown up on Wonder Bread, many young people now sought the mystery of growing their own food. They rejected the consumer model of family life and lit out for the territory to reinvent their lives, their families and their relationships to nature. Some would even challenge the traditional family form as they experimented with communal living and work relationships. The fact that most of these efforts became entangled and ultimately broken, like a wooden plough battling entrenched prairie grasses, should not keep us from recognizing the conditions and desires that animated the experiments. They showed that some American men and women became uncomfortable with the way that Madison Avenue had wrapped them up in nature. "And if anyone should be threatened by advertising, air pollution or the police," wrote the poet Gary Snyder, they should liberate themselves from "cars, houses, canned food."[74] Jack Kerouac's fictionalized version of Snyder continues the assault, envisioning a revolutionary cadre of rucksack-wearing "Dharma Bums refusing to subscribe to the general demand that they consume production and therefore have to work for the privilege of consuming, all that crap they didn't want anyway such as refrigerators, TV sets . . . certain hair oils and deodorants and general junk you finally always see a week later in the garbage anyway, all of them imprisoned in a system of work, produce, consume, work, produce, consume." The anticonsumer revolutionaries would go "up to the mountains to pray, making children laugh and old men glad, making young girls happy and old girls happier."[75]

If going to the mountains was an escape from consumerism, it was also, as Barbara Ehrenreich points out, a male escape from the family ideal of the 1950s.[76] For some, it was simply a flight from commitment. For others, it was the beginning of a commitment to an alternative family life—one that would be closer to nature and stand in opposition to the consumer model. Seeking to reinvent farm family life, the back-to-the-landers reoriented their relationship to nature. In doing so, however, they did not go back to some more pure or essential gender roles. Climbing a mountain, planting a garden, or baking bread from scratch were skills needed to earn the counterculture's merit badges, but, just as in main-stream society, there were different rewards and expectations for the boy and girl scouts. The rucksack revolutionaries may have challenged the consumer model of the American family, but they did not untie the knot binding the consumption of nature to the creation of gender.

In America, the family has always served as a primary incubator of gen-dered identity. As family members produce and consume, these identities grow: we become sons and daughters, brothers and sisters, husbands and wives, fathers and mothers. The family is an institution of biological and social reproduction. It is also a unit of production and consumption. In rural America until the twentieth century, the work of production and consumption within families was closely linked and balanced. Over the last century, the family's role as a unit of consumption has grown out of proportion to its other functions. Today, family members do not work in nature as they once did on the farm, but they still have daily contact with it as they make up their lives. Families have their breadwinners, those who bring home the bacon, those who put food on the table. Of course, this bacon and this bread are metaphorical: they stand in for wages. (This putting of food on the table is figurative as well, for it claims for male wage earners the actual work women have usually done.) At the super-market, "Mrs. Consumer" has exchanged these wages for these things. Buying, preparing, and eating this bread and bacon connects everyone to nature as well as their gender. Advertisers have shown us—mothers and fathers, sons and daughters—how to use their products in ways that will fulfill expectations for a wholesome and happy home life, setting the table at which we consume nature as food. That food at once fuels our bodies and shapes our identities.

In academe, it has become commonplace to think of gender as some-thing that is constructed. It is the cultural wrapping people put around nature's present, sex. First, we have our bodies. Then, after our society toned up our bodies to match expectations, we have our selves. But we should not simply conceive of our bodies as "nature" and our *selves* as "culture," for nature has been consumed congenitally to form our gendered identities. As we cook nature we also cook our selves. To fully understand human relationships to nature, we must put gender on the table, for "knowing nature" and "knowing gender" are epistemologies stewed in the same familial pot.

NOTES

1. Joy Harjo, "Perhaps the World Ends Here," in *Poetry of the American West*, ed. Alison Deming (New York: Columbia University Press, 1996), 284.

2. Edward Curtis, *The North American Indian*, vol. 13 (1923; reprint, New York, Johnson Reprint, 1970), 188.

3. Erik Erikson, "Observations on the Yurok: Childhood and World Image," *University of California Publications in Archeology and Ethnology* 35, no. 10 (1943): 286.

4. Robert Spott and Alfred Kroeber, "Yurok Narratives," *University of California Publications in Archeology and Ethnology* 35, no. 9 (1942): 175.

5. Thomas Buckley, "Menstruation and the Power of Yurok Women," in *Blood Magic: The Anthropology of Menstruation*, ed. Buckley Gottlieb and Alma Gottlieb (Berkeley: University of California Press, 1988), 196.

6. Elliott West, *The Way to the West: Essays on the Central Plains* (Albuquerque: University of New Mexico Press, 1995), 86.

7. See Virginia J. Scharff, "Man and Nature! Sex Secrets of Environmental History," in *Human/Nature: Biology, Culture, and Environmental History*, ed. John Herron and Andrew Kirk (Albuquerque: University of New Mexico Press, 1999), 31–48.

8. Annette Kolodny has looked at the influence of gender on perception and experience in American landscapes in *The Lay of the Land: Metaphor as Experience and History in American Life and Letters* (Chapel Hill: University of North Carolina Press, 1975), and *The Land before Her: Fantasy and Experience of the American Frontiers, 1630–1860* (Chapel Hill: University of North Carolina Press, 1984). The theme of masculinity and nature has yet to receive a full-scale treatment, but see William Cronon's discussion of masculinity, the frontier, and wilderness in "The Trouble with Wilderness: Or, Getting Back to the Wrong Nature," in *Uncommon Ground: Toward Reinventing Nature* (New York: Norton, 1995).

9. The sterile home environment is one of our culture's dominant images of cleanliness, while another is of "pristine" wilderness. The social and cultural history of cleanliness in the United States is traced in Suellen Hoy, *Chasing Dirt: The American Pursuit of Cleanliness* (New York: Oxford, 1995). For an anthropological look at the construction of cleanliness, see Mary Douglas, *Purity and Danger: An Analysis of Concepts of Pollution and Taboo* (London: Routledge, 1966).

10. For a nuanced exploration of nature consumption that avoids the simplifying righteousness of anticonsumerist polemics, see Jennifer Price, *Flight Maps: Adventures with Nature in Modern America* (New York: Basic Books, 1999), especially her chapter on the Nature Company, 167–206.

11. William Cronon, *Nature's Metropolis: Chicago and the Great West* (New York: Norton, 1991), 256.

12. Ibid., 212–13.

13. Arjun Appadurai, ed., *The Social Life of Things: Commodities in Cultural Perspective* (New York: Cambridge University Press, 1986), 3.

14. For scholarship exploring the human meanings projected on animal behavior, see Jennifer Wolch and Jody Emel, eds., *Animal Geographies: Place, Politics, and Identity in the Nature-Culture Borderlands* (New York: Verso, 1998); Arnold Arluke and Clinton Saunders, *Regarding Animals* (Philadelphia: Temple University Press, 1996); Lisa Mighetto, *Wild Animals and American Environmental Ethics* (Tucson: University of Arizona Press, 1991); and Donna Haraway, *Primate Visions: Gender, Race, and Nature in the World of Modern Science* (New York: Routledge, 1989).

15. Claude Lévi-Strauss, *The Raw and the Cooked*, trans. John Weightman and Doreen Weightman (New York: Harper and Row, 1969), 336.

16. For an anthropological understanding of goods and consumption that explains the important social work goods are made to accomplish, see Mary Douglas and Baron Isherwood, *The World of Goods: Towards an Anthropology of Consumption* (1979; reprint, New York: Routledge, 1996); for the notion of cultural capital, see Pierre Bordieu, *Distinctions: A Social Critique of the Judgment of Taste* (Cambridge, Mass.: Harvard University Press, 1984).

17. On spinning experience and mythology, see Laurel Ulrich, *The Age of Homespun: Objects and Stories in the Creation of an American Myth* (New York: Alfred A. Knopf, 2001).

18. Cited in James Henretta, "The Transition to Capitalism in America," in *The Transformation of Early American History: Society, Authority, and Ideology*, ed. James Henretta, Michael Kammen, and Stanley Katz (New York: Alfred Knopf, 1991), 226.

19. For a discussion of the functions of rural nostalgia, see Christopher Lasch, *The True and Only Heaven: Progress and Its Critics* (New York: Norton, 1991), 82–86.

20. A wealth of scholarship produced in the last generation helps answer that question, but it is perilous to compare the image with the reality of farm life, because that reality has varied considerably by time and place. A New England farm of the 1730s was different from one of the 1830s; a farm in Illinois in the 1880s was different from one in California at the same time.

21. Elliott West, "Children on the Plains Frontier," in *Small Worlds: Children and Adolescents in America, 1850–1950*, ed. Elliott West and Paula Petrick (Lawrence: University Press of Kansas, 1992), 34–35.

22. See Frieda Knobloch's excellent discussion of agriculture as an often violent form of domestication (of animals, plants, and land as well as laborers and women) and the "imperialist nostalgia" that identifies farming as "natural" rather than as a practice of dominating nature in *The Culture of Wilderness: Agriculture as Colonization in the American West* (Chapel Hill: University of North Carolina Press, 1996), esp. 49–78.

23. Luna Kellie, *A Prairie Populist: The Memoirs of Luna Kellie*, ed. Jane Taylor Nelsen (Iowa City: University of Iowa Press, 1992), 33.

24. On the difference between image and reality in family life, see Stephanie Coontz, *The Way We Never Were: American Families and the Nostalgia Gap* (New York: Basic Books, 1992).

25. Frederick Jackson Turner, "The Significance of the Frontier in American History" (1893), reprinted in *Rereading Frederick Jackson Turner* (New York: Henry Holt, 1994).

26. See Steven Mintz and Susan Kellog, *Domestic Revolutions: A Social History of American Family Life* (New York: Free Press, 1988), and Stephanie Coontz, *The Social Origins of Private Life: A History of American Families, 1600–1900* (London: Verso, 1988), for chapters on working-class families.

27. The construction of "whiteness" has received much scholarly attention recently. See, for example, Matthew Frye Jacobson, *Whiteness of a Different Color: European Immigrants and the Alchemy of Race* (Cambridge, Mass.: Harvard University Press, 1998).

28. For the imposition of agrarian ideology on Indian tribes and families, see David Lewis, *Neither Wolf Nor Dog: American Indians, Environment, and Agrarian Change* (New York: Oxford University Press, 1994). Also useful for understanding nineteenth-century attitudes toward Indian families is David Wallace Adams, *Education for Extinction: American Indians and the Boarding School Experience, 1875–1928* (Lawrence: University Press of Kansas, 1995). A romanticized version of a Mexican family appears in Helen Hunt Jackson, *Ramona* (1884; reprint, New York: Signet, 1988). On the economic and ideological forces aligned against Mexican-American families' adoption of the American dream, see Camille Guerin-Gonzalez, *Mexican Workers and American Dreams: Immigration, Repatriation, and California Farm Labor, 1900–1939* (New Brunswick, N.J.: Rutgers University Press, 1994). A good overview of the difficulties of Asian Americans in realizing the agrarian dream is Patricia Limerick, "Disorientation and Reorientation: The American Landscape Discovered from the West," *Journal of American History* 79 (December 1992): 1021–49. In reality, these groups all lived and worked in the American countryside, but their positions there were made more precarious, and their economic bargaining power diminished, because of a larger ideology that would preserve country life for white Americans. The imagery of rural America as a landscape in which whiteness is cultivated and protected is critical to understanding how race has shaped relationships to nature in America. One of the best investigations along these lines is Neil Foley, *The White Scourge: Mexicans, Blacks, and Poor Whites in Texas Cotton Culture* (Berkeley: University of California Press, 1997).

29. See Carolyn Merchant, *Ecological Revolutions: Nature, Gender, and Science in New England* (Chapel Hill: University of North Carolina Press, 1989), 149–50, and Richard Bushman, "Opening the American Countryside" in *The Transformation of Early American History*, 237–56, ed. Henretta, Kammen, and Katz.

30. Merchant, *Ecological Revolutions*, 139–45.

31. James Henretta, "Families and Farms: *Mentalité* in Pre-Industrial America," *William and Mary Quarterly*, 3d ser., 46 (1979): 32.

32. Ibid., 21.

33. Merchant, *Ecological Revolutions*, 167.

34. Charles Sellers, *The Market Revolution: Jacksonian America, 1815–1846* (New York: Oxford University Press, 1994), 9–10.

35. Laurel Thatcher Ulrich, *A Midwife's Tale: The Life of Martha Ballard, Based on Her Diary, 1785–1812* (New York: Vintage, 1990), 53. It is no wonder that colonial farm families so readily adopted the medicinal approaches of Algonquian Indians, for their European-derived folk beliefs in the curative properties of plants were compatible with Native American ethnomedicine. See Colin Calloway, *New Worlds for All: Indians, Europeans, and the Remaking of Early America* (Baltimore: Johns Hopkins University Press, 1997), 30–33.

36. Merchant, *Ecological Revolutions*, 145, 185–90.

37. See Sellers, *The Market Revolution*, and Christopher Clark, *The Roots of Rural Capitalism: Western Massachusetts, 1780–1860* (Ithaca, N.Y.: Cornell University Press, 1992).

38. Cooper, *Rural Hours*, 161–62, cited in Vera Norwood, *Made from This Earth: American Women and Nature* (Chapel Hill: University of North Carolina Press, 1993), 29.

39. Norwood, *Made from This Earth*, 30.

40. Ibid., 39.

41. Lydia Sigourney, "Horticulture," *Godey's* 21 (October 1840): 179, as cited in T. J. Jackson Lears, *Fables of Abundance: A Cultural History of Advertising in America* (New York: Basic Books, 1994), 428.

42. The literature on the rise of consumer culture is now vast. Key works include Roland Marchand, *Advertising the American Dream: Making Way for Modernity, 1920–1940* (Berkeley: University of California Press, 1985), Lears, *Fables of Abundance*, and William Leach, *Land of Desire: Merchants, Power, and the Rise of a New American Culture* (New York: Pantheon, 1993).

43. See Cronon, *Nature's Metropolis*.

44. Hal Barron, *Mixed Harvest: The Second Great Transformation in the Rural North, 1870–1930* (Chapel Hill: University of North Carolina Press, 1997), 172, 237–38. See also Mary Neth, *Preserving the Family Farm: Women, Community, and the Foundations of Agribusiness in the Midwest, 1900–1940* (Baltimore: Johns Hopkins University Press, 1995).

45. See Coontz, *The Social Origins of Private Life*, 349. It is important to note that work did not disappear with the advent of the consumer model of the American family; it was reoriented and intensified in other ways. See Ruth Schwartz Cowan, *More Work for Mother: The Ironies of Household Technology from the Open Hearth to the Microwave* (New York: Basic Books, 1983).

46. Theodore Roosevelt, "Introduction," in Commission on Country Life, *Report of the Commission on Country Life* (New York: Sturgis and Walton, 1917), 10.

47. Theodore Roosevelt, letter of appointment of the commission addressed to Liberty Hyde Bailey, August 10, 1908, in Commission on Country Life, *Report*, 44.

48. Ibid., 104.

49. Cited in Robert Griswold, *Fatherhood in America: A History* (New York: Basic Books, 1993), 27.

50. Ibid., 24.

51. For Bok, see David Shi, *The Simple Life: Plain Living and High Thinking in American Culture* (New York: Oxford University Press, 1985), and Jennifer Scanlon, *Inarticulate Longings: The Ladies' Home Journal, Gender, and the Promises of*

Consumer Culture (New York: Routledge, 1995); for Wanamaker, see William Leach, *Land of Desire: Merchants, Power, and the Rise of a New American Culture* (New York: Pantheon, 1993), 202–8; for Ford, see Roland Marchand, *Creating the Corporate Soul: The Rise of Public Relations and Corporate Imagery in American Big Business* (Berkeley: University of California Press, 1998), 207–211; Young, who owned a farm, filled his "diary" with celebrations of farm life, *The Diary of an Ad Man: The War Years, June 1, 1942–December 31, 1943* (Chicago: Advertising Publications, 1944).

52. Jürgen Habermas, as Wendy Kozol points out, argues that "capitalist societies 'feed parasitically on the remains of tradition,' such as religion and the patriarchal family" (Kozol, *Life's America: Family and Nation in Postwar Photojournalism* [Philadelphia: Temple University Press, 1994], 79).

53. Liberty Hyde Bailey, *The Holy Earth* (New York: Scribner's, 1915), 97–98.

54. Ibid., 100–101.

55. See also Susan Strasser's chapter on "The Politics of Packaged Products," in *Satisfaction Guaranteed: The Making of the American Mass Market* (New York: Pantheon, 1989), 252–85.

56. See Campbell's tomato soup advertisement in *American Magazine*, October 1934, 79, and Heinz advertisements in *Saturday Evening Post*, January 15, 1938, inside front cover, and *Life Magazine*, June 5, 1939.

57. Marchand, *Advertising the American Dream*, 224. Marchand explains the logic of the parable: "If Nature, in its instinctive wisdom, now sought to punish civilized mankind for its waywardness, then Civilization, in its own sophisticated wisdom, had found a way to regain Nature's intended gifts without sacrificing the fruits of progress" (p. 223).

58. Robert and Helen Lynd, *Middletown: A Study in Contemporary American Culture* (New York: Harcourt, Brace, 1929), 158. Several works trace the rise of mass-circulation magazines. See Richard Ohmann, *Selling Culture: Magazines, Markets, and Class at the Turn of the Century* (New York: Verso, 1996), Jan Cohn, *Creating America: George Horace Lorimer and the Saturday Evening Post* (Pittsburgh: University of Pittsburgh Press, 1989), and, for particular attention to gender, Helen Damon-Moore, *Magazines for the Millions: Gender and Commerce in the Ladies' Home Journal and the Saturday Evening Post, 1880–1910* (Albany: State University of New York Press, 1994), and Scanlon, *Inarticulate Longings*.

59. I explore Sunkist advertising in greater detail in *Orange Empire: California and the Fruits of Eden* (Berkeley: University of California Press, forthcoming).

60. See Richard Orsi, "Selling the Golden State: A Study of Boosterism in Nineteenth-Century California," (Ph.D. diss., University of Wisconsin, Madison, 1973).

61. Don Francisco, "The Story of Sunkist Advertising," typescript of a talk before the apprentice group of the J. Walter Thompson Company, December 9, 1948, in box 9, Powell Family Papers (Collection 230), Department of Special Collections, University Research Library, University of California, Los Angeles.

62. For discussions of workers and working conditions in the citrus industry, see Margo McBane, "The Role of Gender in Citrus Employment: A Case Study of Recruitment, Labor, and Housing Patterns at the Limoneira Company, 1893–1940," *California History* 74 (Spring 1995): 69–81; Douglas C. Sackman, "'Na-

ture's Workshop': The Work Environment and Workers' Bodies in California's Citrus Industry," *Environmental History* (January 2000): 27–53; and Gilbert González, *Labor and Community: Mexican Citrus Worker Villages in a Southern California County, 1900–1950* (Chicago: University of Illinois Press, 1994). The literature on California agricultural and environmental history is too vast to cite here; the classic work in the field that remains valuable is Carey McWilliams, *Factories in the Field: The Story of Migratory Farm Labor in California* (1939; reprint, Berkeley: University of California Press, 2000).

63. *Saturday Evening Post,* April 8, 1939, 68–69.

64. James Mayo, *The American Grocery Store: The Business Evolution of an Architectural Space* (Westport, Conn.: Greenwood Press, 1993), 87. The best social analysis of the displacement of independent groceries with chain stores can be found in Lizabeth Cohen, *Making a New Deal: Industrial Workers in Chicago, 1919–1939* (Cambridge: Cambridge University Press, 1990), 99–120.

65. *Life,* May 5, 1947, 27–33, as cited in Kozol, *Life's America,* 87.

66. Kozol, *Life's America,* 86.

67. The history of the refrigerator and its impact on the domestic work of women is traced in Susan Strasser, *Never Done: A History of American Housework* (New York: Pantheon Books, 1982) and Cowan, *More Work for Mother.*

68. See Elaine Tyler May, *Homeward Bound: American Families in the Cold War Era* (New York: Basic Books, 1998). For Americanization through the consumption of national brands, see Charles McGovern, "Consumption and Citizenship in the United States, 1900–1940," in *Getting and Spending: European and American Consumer Societies in the Twentieth Century,* ed. Susan Strasser, Charles McGovern, and Matthias Judt (Cambridge: Cambridge University Press, 1998), 37–58.

69. Ralph Borsodi, "One Way Out," *New Republic,* July 24, 1929, 253.

70. Myrtle Borsodi, "The New Woman Goes Home," *Good Housekeeping,* February 1937, 52–56.

71. Ralph Borsodi, *The Flight from the City: The Story of a New Way to Family Security* (New York: Harper and Brothers, 1933), 21.

72. Ibid., 1–2.

73. Paul Goodman, "Preface," *Flight from the City* (1933; reprint, New York: Harper Colophon, 1972), xi.

74. Gary Snyder, "Smoky the Bear Sutra" (1969); for his views on the family, see *Earth Household* (New York: New Directions, 1969), 103–112. Richard Cándida Smith illuminates Snyder's own back-to-the-land involvement in the context of new family ideals in *Utopia and Dissent: Art, Poetry, and Politics in California* (Berkeley: University of California Press, 1995).

75. Jack Kerouac, *The Dharma Bums* (1958; reprint, New York: Penguin, 1976), 97.

76. See Barbara Ehrenreich, *The Hearts of Men: American Dreams and the Flight from Commitment* (New York: Anchor, 1983), 52–67.

CHAPTER NINE

From Snow Bunnies to Shred Betties: Gender, Consumption, and the Skiing Landscape

Annie Gilbert Coleman

In the late 1990s, a singer/songwriter from New York City showed up at Mount Snow, Vermont, for a Women Only Snowboard Camp. "I'm on chairlift #8," remembered Amy Spence, "a borrowed snowboard dangling from my left foot, the bright April sun's warmth helping me temporarily forget my sore, wet, body." She glanced over at the shaggy boy beside her on the lift. "Rad sticker," he said, nodding and smiling at the message to "Ride Like a Girl" stuck to her board. "For a moment," she recounted, "I forget my age, my gender, my responsibilities," and she wondered how she appeared to the kid. "My blonde hair stuffed in under a hat, my face hidden under Oakleys, my body disguised by my baggy coat and pants. I could be any age, any gender. But I'm not. Here I am, a 29-year-old woman who, after only three days, is ready to trade in her world for the flight on a board. I am, as they say, stoked to be here."[1]

Spence's participation in this camp illustrated both the growth of snowboarding within the ski industry and the increasing popularity of women's camps, clinics, and equipment. Ski resorts and related businesses adopted snowboarding during the late 1980s after a period of some conflict and skepticism. By the mid-1990s, snowboarders bought 13 percent of all lift tickets sold, and 400,000 boarders, almost 20 percent of the total, were women.[2] By then, too, women skiers and boarders could buy equipment made especially for them and participate in lessons and clinics run by women for women at ski resorts across the country. The advent of women snowboarders like Spence happened after a sport that began as a young and male rebellion against the ski industry became incorporated into that industry and after marketers realized that women could be athletes as well as consumers of fashion. The consumption of clothing, equipment, and the landscape itself supported the growth of the ski industry after World War II, and efforts to keep business strong led the industry to adopt both women and snowboarders—groups it had marginalized in different ways—as their own.

Spence's snowboarding adventure raises bigger questions than how she came to be at Mount Snow, however. On her board, cloaked in baggy clothes, hat, and goggles, Spence transformed herself from singer/songwriter into the characteristic female snowboarder, the Shred Betty. She recalled the ultrafeminine skiing Snow Bunny but twisted it, replacing a placid fuzzy animal with a girl shredding, literally tearing up the slopes on her board. Spence participated in this image when she deemed being sore and wet as irritating and minor by-products of her main goal: flying down the mountain on a board. Despite her presence at a women-only camp, however, Spence's appearance and her shredding made her gender ambiguous. How, she seemed to be asking, does one actually "Ride Like a Girl"? And what does it mean when you do? Shred Betties' athletic riding and androgenous clothing, combined with the reaction of Spence's chairlift partner, suggest that to ride like a girl is to ride—and look—like a boy. Yet these girls and women know they are not boys and insist that appropriating male looks and athleticism does not compromise their gender identity. If the taunt "you throw like a girl" used to keep girls out of sports, the affirming call to ride like one has served to attract them.

As confusing as this motto is, riding like a girl clearly means something different from skiing like a girl. The Shred Betty has become a kind of stereotype for female snowboarders, but since the 1930s women skied under the shadow of a far more powerful image: the Snow Bunny. Dedicated to fashion, men, and socializing, Snow Bunnies flaunted their femininity. They decorated the slopes and ski lodges, drawing attention to their bodies as objects of beauty rather than instruments of mobility. Few actually fit this popular image, but the ski industry embraced it as a means to incorporate female consumers into the skiing landscape. Like the snowboarders to come, women skiers struggled to balance their femininity with the athleticism of their sport.

This story is not just about women on snowy mountains but about gender. Men and women constantly interacted in and around mountain resorts. Cultural understandings of both femininity and masculinity informed popular images of women on snow, defined the landscape, and created specifically gendered markets for men and women. Gendered relationships to the environment drove both the history of skiing and the ski industry. Defining the mountains as wild backdrops for physical adventure and conquest, skiers and resort advertisers associated skiing with masculinity. Yet the sport presented frequent opportunities to socialize, too. After World War II the ski industry crafted its mountain resorts as landscapes of both movement and consumption, selling adventure to men, fashion to women, and the après ski life to both. Skiers acting outside these constraints, however, along with changing notions of femininity, led an industry eager for customers to develop, expand, and define their landscapes in new ways. Snowboarders forced the industry to come to terms with a completely new group: young people who challenged skiing culture and defined board sports as almost exclusively male. However rebellious they thought they were, to resort developers, equipment manufacturers, and clothing designers, they still constituted a market. The result was the industry's ultimate incorporation of snowboarding—through urbanizing their mountain landscapes and marketing the sport to women as well as men—and the advent of the Shred Betty. This image, created largely by women, placed women's athleticism on equal terms with their femininity, identified them as consumers of mountains and equipment as much as clothing, and recognized that the thrill of flying down a mountain dissolved old gender boundaries.

Understanding the popularity of snow sports in America and the rise of the ski industry means figuring out why both men and women have enjoyed skiing so much. When Scandinavian immigrants introduced what we call Nordic skiing in the mid–nineteenth century, men and women skied up, down, and across mountain landscapes as a kind of labor and a form of recreation. The sport articulated a working-class masculinity when mail carriers, miners, and ranchers donned skis for work and play; it took on a differently gendered meaning when women practiced it.[3] Women in nineteenth-century mountain communities did errands, visited each other, and toured the area on skis fairly regularly, and their skiing acquired a meaning associated with female care for both the local community and the family. Their role as nurturers gave women some room to play. As historian John Allen observed, "In the [California] gold and silver camps social convention certainly continued to play its perceived role of civilizing society, yet it is clear when 'the beautiful' fell six feet deep that strenuous activity by women on skis was not condemned out-of-hand as un-sexing, non-womanly or simply not permitted. Indeed, skiing was a talent admired in both men and women."[4] This appreciation was the case in Colorado towns, as well. Photos from nineteenth-century mining towns throughout the state show women standing on their skis— dressed in long skirts—with pleasure and poise.[5]

Women continued to ski avidly in the East and West after the introduction of alpine or downhill skiing techniques in the 1920s and 1930s. They skied at small resorts a train ride away from the city, at the town rope tow with their local ski club members, at colleges with outing club members, at resorts such as Sun Valley and later Aspen, and in their backyards. Girls, young women, wives, and mothers graced the slopes, with and without male counterparts, increasingly after World War II when the ski industry began to grow. They took lessons, taught lessons, vacationed, and competed, supporting the industry through their consumption and fondness for the sport.

Downhill skiing appealed to both men and women largely because it requires balance as much as strength, grace as well as aggression, and it leads to introspection and calmness just as often as whoops of exhilaration. As one writer put it, skiing satisfies a primal urge for speed and thrills and also offers beauty in the "quiet grandeur of nature." He characterized the sport as "a synthesis which holds irresistible appeal for athlete, artist, poet, and philosopher."[6] In its eclectic mix of thrills and artistry, skiing appealed to a wide range of men and women. And since coordination counts more than strength, women could ski as fast, daringly, and beautifully as men. In choosing how to ski down the mountain—fast, slow, straight, or turny—each skier created a physical relationship to the landscape. Mood, skill level, and terrain had more to do with the nature of this relationship than gender, but plenty of people have viewed skiing down mountains in specifically gendered terms.

Men often interpreted this relationship as one of danger and conquest. They imagined the mountains as female and characterized skiing as a quintessentially masculine activity.[7] One man, in an effort to explain why skiers chose to race, concluded that "the great thrill in skiing rises from the mastery of the individual, unaided by mechanical means, over the forces of nature—her treacherous snows, her vast space—over the forces of gravity, over the pull of speed."[8]

Some writers pushed this theme of mastery over a feminine nature further, describing the sport in sexual terms.[9] An explicit if poorly written example appeared on the inside cover of a 1966 book, *See and Ski in Colorado*. The poem began:

> The mountain wears her ermine wrap today
> As heedlessly she rests on broken hills,
> Her heaving breasts thrust up from where she lay
> All night, unmindful of the piercing chills.

A buxom woman lying asleep in the cold, this mountain waited for fulfillment in the shape of skiers. "The waking mountain isn't long alone," the poem concluded, "for soon her flank's with flying snowmen sown."[10] Skiing and the physical act of sex, this author seems to be telling (presumably male) readers, are not so far apart. When Robert Redford's movie *Downhill Racer* (1969) came out, promoters employed similar imagery. The film's poster focused on a woman's upturned face, about to be kissed, imposed above a snowy landscape with a tiny downhill racer. As the man's mouth moves down upon the contours of her parted lips, so moves the skier down the mountain. The poster makes a frank argument that skiing really is all about going down. These examples raise interesting questions about how skiers have understood the relationship between gender and sexuality. Here, a feminized and sexualized landscape emphasizes the masculinity of the skier, making women skiing down the same mountain potentially subversive. [11]

Ski resorts alleviated some of this pressure in the way they organized mountain spaces. Categorizing trails by degree of difficulty marked certain terrains for experts, others for beginners, and the rest for intermediates. Slopes marked with a black diamond for "most difficult" promised adrenaline-filled adventure and demanded skill as well as confidence to descend. In image and practice, these trails represented masculine domain. Beginner slopes, however, coded with a green circle, welcomed the least experienced and most intimidated. Women could find a comfortable place here, on the part of the mountain usually referred to as "the bunny hill." Ski resorts inscribed gender onto their landscapes when they structured mountains this way, opening up some spaces to "bunnies" and blocking off others for "experts only."

Gender did more than inform the culture of mountain spaces, however; it also influenced the physical development of skiing environments. Blue intermediate slopes served male as well as female lift-ticket buyers, and with them ski area designers tended to emphasize the sensuality of skiing—a characteristic that women were presumed to appreciate as well as men. They chose ski area sites and cut trails in order to create particular feelings for skiers. "Variety is key," Chet Anderson, designer of Purgatory, explained. Good trails need steep and shallow pitches, room for cruising, and transitions between types of terrain. "That," he said, "is what can make it sensual."[12] A few designers became acknowledged masters. Friedl Pfeifer's trails on Aspen Mountain "had a rhythm you would feel [as you skied]," remembered racer Steve Knowlton.[13] One well-traveled ski instructor described Aspen as "really a very romantic mountain." "Friedl did a masterful job," he said. His trails "would turn a little bit and romance and turn a little bit and go down, and you could have a rest." Big resorts like Snowmass and Vail have more space, he continued, but "you don't feel like your blood is stirring up" there.[14] The most effective and popular trails fashioned a sensual relationship between skiers and the mountain, and designers knew it. Gender and sex, in other words, influenced the very shape of ski resort environments, which raises questions about how women skiers interpreted their sport.

Although the industry hoped to appeal to both male and female skiers with romantic imagery, women have tended to characterize their skiing less as an act of romance and more as an act of independence. In 1928, for instance, Marjorie Perry and her friend Elinor Eppich Kingery got off the train to Denver while it was delayed on the top of Rollins Pass and skied down along the tracks to Tolland, sixteen miles distant. "We could see three long switchbacks through the open timber and tiny Tolland far below," Marjorie Perry recalled. "We left the track and went straight down the hill, making big curves, with the perfect powdered snow swirling in the air."[15] For Perry, big curves and swirling snow were the sensual results of independent actions: leaving the train and donning skis. Beth Sinclair, who learned to ski as a girl in the late 1930s, said "the freedom and the speed" appealed to her. Fellow Aspen resident Cherie Oates, who took up the sport in the 1940s, also liked to ski downhill fast. "I'd be picking up pieces [of equipment and clothes] out of the trees [after a fall], I'd always be losing something," she said, "but there was just a real thrill about that, a real challenge . . . [and] a freedom that you're on your own power."[16] In their emphasis on freedom and movement, these descriptions implicitly acknowledge the social limitations imposed on women's behavior and reflect the ways in which skiing helped them move beyond those limits.

Physical movement through space, Virginia Scharff has argued, is historically associated with masculine power, making female mobility at once liberating and subversive.[17] Women's athleticism on the slopes, from the nineteenth century through the 1960s, could raise serious questions about their femininity.[18] One woman writing in 1936, for instance, questioned whether or not women should race competitively. She acknowledged the excitement, thrills, and "sense of fulfillment which the ordinary climb-lunch-and-run-down skier can never hope to enjoy," but questioned whether women could stand the physical strain of competition and characterized the German woman's team as "Amazons from beyond the Rhine." As a final piece of evidence she produced a photo of the U.S. women's national team and declared them unattractive. "Racing may endanger health and it may endanger bones," she concluded, "but unquestionably the greatest risk of all will be to one's femininity."[19] Commentators like this one got grumpy because skiing tended to subvert gender categories they held dear.

Women's athletic use of the environment, however, combined with more feminine behavior to leave most women skiers with their identities intact. Specifically, skiing provided women with opportunities to meet men, serving as a social occasion from the time that mountain towns hosted co-ed "snowshoe parties" in the nineteenth century.[20] During the 1930s, alpine skiing became associated with European resorts and their accompanying nightlife. Indeed, the German-language term for après-ski congeniality became central to skiers' vocabularies. "A skier loves company," a Colorado Mountain Club member wrote in 1938. "This is the root of the 'gemütlich[keit]' which is skiing's final justification."[21] In skiing, another author noted, there is "a large element of romance of the boy-meets-girl type, not to be overlooked."[22] This aspect of skiing defined mountains as a social space as well as athletic space and complicated the meanings attached to the sport.

Women negotiated this space through contrasting acts of consumption: by day they skied down mountains; by night they ate, drank, and danced in the town below. Moving from the slopes to the bar became common practice; consuming food, drink, and fashion indoors grew inextricably linked to consuming nature outdoors on skis. Throughout Colorado and the nation, men and women skiers shared stories of their day and relaxed together over drinks in clubhouses, restaurants, and hotels. Early skiers in Aspen frequented the Hotel Jerome, where they could drink highly alcoholic (and popular) "Aspen cruds." Arlberg Club members from Denver encouraged women to go skiing with them throughout the 1930s, even though they did not welcome female members until 1938, almost ten years after the club's inception. Some of those women, after marrying Arlberg men, skied no more.[23] These women transformed easily from socialites into skiers and back again once off the slopes. For them skiing enhanced their feminine identities and heterosexual goals rather than subverting them. In its manifestations as sexual conquest, sensual romance, physical freedom, and social scene, skiing could define men as commanding athletes or outdoorsmen and women skiers as independent athletes, romantic objects, or social beings. Alpine skiing offered women physical freedom and empowerment at the same time that it emphasized their roles as social beings and objects of beauty.[24] No matter what kind of woman you were or wanted to be, skiing could help you live that identity.

Why is it, then, that the Snow Bunny became such a strong and long-lasting stereotype of women skiers? The image appeared decades before Hugh Hefner introduced Playboy bunnies to the public. In 1931 the humor magazine *Judge* featured a woman on skis on its cover. She was artfully applying her makeup, more concerned with her appearance than the slope below. By 1939 this sort of woman had a name. In that year's *American Ski Annual,* one woman spoke out against the "Ski Rabbit," "a glamorous female whose main interest in the out of doors is to dazzle and not to ski."[25] The historical association between rabbits and feminine sex appeal remains clouded, yet it seems clear that this author both recognized and fueled the emerging stereotype of the Snow Bunny.

The Snow Bunny image served a number of important purposes, for skiers as well as the ski industry that took shape when ski resorts grew after World War II. First, in emphasizing women as social beings in search of husbands rather than as independent and possessing athletic mobility, the Snow Bunny image kept women skiers feminine. Even if they did enjoy the freedom inherent in flying down a mountain and sought it out

This 1931 magazine cover exemplified the early Snow Bunny. "Look before you leap" was good advice on early ski slopes for anyone, but some women applied it to the social aspects of the sport as well. (From Gary H. Schwartz, *The Art of Skiing, 1856–1936* [Tiburn, California: Wood River Publishing, 1989], 46)

regularly, they could avoid appearing too masculine by wearing the latest fashions and putting on some lipstick. And if many women did not identify with the Snow Bunny, others concerned with them acting outside the bounds of femininity could always claim that they did. For individuals and their observers, the Snow Bunny image allowed women to ski without transgressing accepted gender norms.

Second, the image appealed to a significant group of skiers—men. The Snow Bunny defined women skiers as objects of desire. Makeup and fashion drew attention to them as women seeking a strong, hopefully rich, male companion. Snow Bunnies highlighted the masculine identity of men who looked, came over for a chat, or offered an impromptu lesson. And in drawing attention to their beauty, Snow Bunnies adorned the landscape, festooning the mountain with the garb of gender. To the extent that men interpreted skiing as a metaphor for sexual conquest and Snow Bunnies proved amenable, they brought that metaphor to life.

In turning mountains into landscapes of display as well as athletic and social spaces, the stereotypical Snow Bunny served the ski industry in a third regard. She associated outdoor sport with female fashion consumption. In the 1920s, trying to unite skiing and fashion in consumers' minds, department stores offered an increasing array of outdoor clothing and equipment that promised to define the wearer as stylish and attractive. Stores like B. Altman effectively introduced alpine skiing to the American public by staging live ski shows in Boston and New York, and audiences were happy to see ski slopes as stages for fashion display. "Altho [sic] it had not been announced that a style show would be held in conjunction with the skiing," one reporter commented of a Denver event, "the brilliant display of sporting toggery was all of that, and caused many eyes to wander frequently from the tournament itself in the direction of some fair maid or matron."[26]

Magazine images depicting women skiers as impeccably dressed and made up appeared above text spouting "new spring fashions" and "exclusive style notes from Paris," the "luxurious smoothness" of a new Franklin automobile, or the seemingly incongruous slogan of Lucky cigarettes: "They taste better." In depicting women skiers as icons of beauty, the popular press emphasized women's role as consumers at the same time that it defined women skiers as passive objects of desire. In fact, the ability to purchase consumer goods helped establish these women as desirable. Snow Bunnies thus promoted two differently gendered ways of consuming the mountain landscape: through women's consumption of clothes and men's consumption of women.[27]

The rise of the ski industry depended on both notions. After World War II, Americans were eager to spend their money on recreation and leisure, and a number of war veterans helped them do so by building, developing, and running ski areas across the country.[28] Once ski resorts began to grow in the late 1940s and 1950s, members of the burgeoning ski industry (a group that included resort developers and marketers, clothing and equipment manufacturers, hotel and restaurant owners, and any number of store owners) did what they could to further increase people's spending. The image of the fashionable Snow Bunny served them well. In defining women as consumers and objects of consumption, it drew them into sport shops and attracted them to ski areas. In one 1946 ad, a photo of a beautiful woman appears over the text "Picard of White Stag *gives you glamour on the ski run.*"[29] The fashion column of that December's *Rocky Mountain Life* called to its women readers that "whether you be a mere Snow Bunny or an accomplished skiette, it's comme il faut to look the part." [30]

So while the beautiful beginner looking for men remained the classic stereotype, the Snow Bunny image encouraged observers to characterize all women skiers primarily as heterosocial and fashionable. In such a context, women's athleticism and skill posed less of a threat and could even add to the attraction. Gretchen Kunigk Fraser won the first gold medal for the United States in skiing at the 1948 Olympics, and Andrea Mead Lawrence won two gold medals in the 1952 Olympics. No one could call them Snow Bunnies; they were clearly out to win and they were more successful in international competition than the American men. In portraying their success, however, the press emphasized their womanliness as well as (if not more than) their athleticism. Photos showed their good looks, writers discussed their athletic accomplishments while mentioning they were happily married, and editors published articles after their alpine victories to congratulate them on their young children.[31]

While Fraser and Lawrence brought national attention to their skiing, the Snow Bunny kept hopping. *Sports Illustrated* used a photo of two "snow bunnies" to accompany an article on ski area development in 1955, and a cartoon in the same issue showed a woman skiing past a man while he pictured her in a bikini.[32] As the ski industry boomed, the image of the Snow Bunny continued to define an increasing number of women who could ski quite well and spent some time doing so. A 1958 article on Aspen described waitress Dianne Merrill as "typical of the pretty ex-collegians who spend winter in Aspen." The author described her as one of the girl ski bum set who "usually try the life for a year or two, then retire into marriage."[33] Her dedication to the sport, he implied, while significant, remained secondary to man-hunting.

By the mid-1960s, the ski industry supported two national magazines to bring its sport to the public and a trade magazine to help ski industry people improve their consumer base. Both used gender self-consciously to sell sex to men, ski clothes to women, and skiing to all. "Girls! Girls! Girls!"

one headline in a 1967 issue of *Ski* magazine exclaimed. "Quite frankly, we got tired of printing pictures of muscular male skiers," the text read. "So we are giving readers a break . . . by showing you a trio of the greatest girls we could find on skis. They ski on that well-known slope of the imagination: Availability Hill. All you have to do is ski by them and they follow you down, plop into the chairlift seat beside you. From there on, you simply have to breathe deep and keep looking masculine."[34]

By this time, the Snow Bunny stereotype was so strong that one marketer used it to his advantage by making fun of it. *Skiing Trade News* recommended the advertising approach one firm used in a campaign that featured a series of cartoons poking fun at skier stereotypes. A reclining beauty with a cast on her foot looks composed, and the text reads, "The Busted Bunny—crashed and burned on the beginner's slope. She now talks of gates and waxes and Jean Claude. And her gear from Streeter and Quarles somehow makes it all so."[35] The next year the same publication illustrated a different strategy. "Roffe [skiwear] Captures What Every Skier Wants," the headline read, accompanied by a photo of a man on horseback lassoing two women running through deep snow in ski outfits.[36] Assuming that "every skier" was male, this ad paradoxically used its message to sell women's skiwear. Women were supposed to define themselves as sex objects, one assumes, and admit that skiing was more about being captured by a man than actually skiing.

Women ski racers recognized the conflict between femininity and competition. During the 1930s, they solved the problem by skiing hard during the day and mingling with elite social crowds in the evening. Fraser and Lawrence allowed themselves to be characterized as tomboy types, a girl in pigtails, or a kid sister, playing for a while before retiring to become wives and mothers. By 1970 women confronted the tension between their gender identity and their athleticism more openly. "Women racers are women, first and foremost," 1968 Olympic gold medallist and *Ski* racing editor Nancy Greene wrote. "It's just that, in racing, they temporarily have to put skiing ahead of men. If this were understood, a lot of misconceptions about women who race could be cleared up." Greene argued that women skiers could be more than just Snow Bunnies. Although she bemoaned the fact that wealthy, blonde, and fashionable "racerchasers" steal away with members of the men's team at the end of the season, she insisted that women racers who are "tigers on the slopes" are also "ladies on the dance floor." During the season, however, racing must take priority over everything if you want to win, no matter who you are. Greene and her teammates refused to give up either their femininity ("picking their T-shirts and Levis for looks as well as duty, and always owning at least one swinging outfit") or their competitive career.[37] They wanted it all and said they deserved it.

By the time this photo appeared on *Ski* magazine's cover in 1960, the Snow Bunny was so prevalent that variations on the theme like this Snow Wolf began to appear. A friendly predator, she invited men to the slopes for all kinds of adventure. (*Ski*, March 1960. Reprinted with permission of *Ski* magazine. Photo by TK.)

By the 1970s, the Snow Bunny had outlived her usefulness to women skiers and to the industry. Pictures of beautiful and sexy women could still attract men to the slopes, and some women continued to value the social and sexual promise of skiing over the athletic, but the Snow Bunny had become a stereotype to laugh about or decry. The women's movement, Title IX, and Billie Jean King's victory over Bobby Riggs all encouraged women to celebrate and expand their athletic abilities rather than shrink them to fit an outdated feminine ideal. Moreover, many of the Snow Bunnies from the 1950s and 1960s had married and settled down. As they moved from the slopes to the kitchen, they shed their old identity—but not necessarily their interest in skiing. Fitness and sport grew as priorities for women in the 1970s at the same time that ski resorts sought more customers to help them pay the bills and finance expansions.

Women at home represented an important and untapped clientele, and the ski industry changed its marketing strategies accordingly. They began to address women not as shoppers but as skiers, redefining them as consumers of sport and equipment rather than fashion and adopting what could be called a feminist rhetoric. The industry served here as an accidental force for empowerment—their concern over the bottom line wound up encouraging women to ski, and to ski without men. As early as 1970, *Skiing Area News* commended Big Boulder ski area in Pennsylvania for the success of its Ladies' Day promotions, which targeted local housewives. "Women seem to learn faster when their husbands aren't around," the (female) ski school director said, "and since half the ski school staff is women, the local ladies are more comfortable taking lessons."[38] This approach worked because it treated women as skiers in their own right, separate from men and with their own strengths and weaknesses. Five years later, Elissa Slanger, an instructor at Squaw Valley, took these ideas further and designed a clinic specifically for women. Her Women's Way seminars took into account how skiers viewed themselves, how society viewed them, and each woman's sports history. Slanger treated women as female athletes with learning styles distinct from men and established a growing phenomenon in ski marketing.

By 1988 at least seven major ski resorts offered three- to five-day camps, clinics, or seminars exclusively by and for women.[39] Also in the 1980s, manufacturers began to design ski equipment specifically for women's bodies, and ski resorts promoted programs and facilities to accommodate children.[40] These changes treated women as more than dates or ornaments, and they learned to move through mountain landscapes as fast as they liked with no apology. Women exercised their power as a new kind of consumer, not just of fashion but also of sport and mountain landscapes. As women skied more, they demanded more space—an expansion of ski-scapes—and as they skied better, they opened up even the most difficult terrain to women as well as men. With their consumer dollars, fit bodies, and desire to ski hard, women in the 1970s and 1980s broke new gender ground and transformed mountain landscapes figuratively and literally. They undercut the power of the Snow Bunny through their spending and their skiing. They also gave birth to a new generation who challenged the old image head-on and ultimately declared it irrelevant.

Snowboarders developed a consumer culture that sought to upend the ski industry more broadly and in a distinctly different gendered manner. Originating largely from surf- and skateboard cultures in the 1970s, snowboarders attached their sport to a young, male counterculture that set skiers' teeth on edge.[41] Snowboarders first appeared at ski areas in the early 1980s, and they immediately consumed resort landscapes in challenging ways. They became notorious for cutting off skiers. They traveled in packs. They listened to the Beastie Boys. They wore telltale baggy pants and neglected to respect their elders. They "bonked," "jibbed," "tweaked," and rode "fakie"—acts that, among other things, included jumping over or actually riding something other than snow. And they were almost all young males. Snowboarders seemed to dismiss ski equipment, ski clothing, its co-ed social culture, and the older consumers who bought it all, and this attitude riled people up. In 1985 only 7 percent of U.S. ski resorts allowed snowboarding. Aspen and Keystone banned snowboarders from their slopes completely. [42] Animosity and even violence between skiers and boarders became expected. One running skier's joke went: "What's the difference between a Boarder and a catfish? One is a bottom-dwelling, disgusting, rejected muck sucker and the other is a fish."

The very characteristics that made snowboarding annoying to skiers were what made it cool, hip, and popular with young people. The skateboarders who originated "freestyle" and half-pipe snowboarding voiced an acutely countercultural attitude. "Skaters hated everyone," skate- and snowboarding magnate Tom Sims recalled. "'Everything Sucks' was the punk mantra that [skateboard magazine] Thrasher espoused and that was the modern skate culture in 1982."[43] Others turned to snowboarding as a specific critique of the ski industry. "Skiing was so elitist in the early '80s," said Chris Sanders, one of the founders of Avalanche Snowboards, "really cliquey, exclusive." According to snowboarding historian Susanna Howe, the Avalanche crew "was formed by amazing skiers who wanted to break out of the scene."[44] Jake Burton and his company in the East attracted ex–ski racers—"wildcards" of the sport, as Burton recalled.[45] Across the country groups of people looking for something different turned to snowboarding. "We'd get so much flack," pro boarder Jim Fulton remembered. "[Mt.] Baker was full of serious skiers and they'd yell at us 'Hey the ocean's that way!' or 'Get a boat to tow that thing' or 'Someday you'll be able to afford two!' All these little jabs. But as we got better and the equipment got better, it went from people heckling us to people being impressed and cheering us on."[46] A sport that, according to Howe, nurtured a set of values including rebelliousness, free-mindedness, subversion, and irony was about to go mainstream.[47]

By the late 1980s, snowboarding had grown to a point that the ski industry could not ignore. National contests early in the decade led to World Championships in 1987 and a World Cup circuit the next year. ABC and MTV covered the 1987 World Championship at Breckenridge, and by 1988 even *Skiing* magazine included an article about the sport, entitled "Shred Heads Go Mainstream."[48] By then, two snowboarding magazines (*ISM* and *Transworld Snowboarding*) graced newsstands, and a wave of new riders pushed snowboard sales for the 1987–1988 season to eighty thousand. [49]

Once snowboarders emerged as a significant market, the ski industry started to see them as a target rather than a problem. The editors of *Skiing* magazine began to test and evaluate snowboards in their annual buyer's guide issue in 1989. Ski resorts went out of their way to attract this fast-growing segment of the ski market, hiring snowboarding instructors, playing alternative music on area loudspeakers, and placing snowboarding ambassadors on mountains to answer questions and ease any residual acrimonious feelings. Entire sections of industry trade publications were dedicated to studying this economically significant market. By 1995 over 97 percent of U.S. ski areas allowed snowboarding, and boarders accounted for 13 percent of all lift tickets sold.[50]

Ski resorts had to do more than play the right music or hire instructors to attract snowboarders to their slopes, however; they had to change the physical resort landscape. Just as a gendered interpretation of skiing led designers to create sensual trails, snowboarding's connection to the young male world of skateboarding encouraged resort managers to make their mountains more urban. Skate- and snowboarding share an exhibitionist tradition of riding half-pipes that originated from skateboarders appropriating empty swimming pools to skate down and up the curved sides, doing tricks in the air as they turned to descend again. Other concrete landscapes offered similarly creative fodder for skateboarders, as they used sidewalks, steps, benches, and railings to jump, grab, spin, and slide (or grind) with their boards while their friends watched and waited for their turn. Snowboarders adopted skaters' tricks and sought snow-covered landscapes to try them out. This culture became such a large part of snowboarding that ski resorts took to building half-pipes and boarding parks out of snow, even buying expensive machinery designed specially to groom them, and incorporating metal railings and obstacles that mirrored concrete skate parks into snowy mountain resorts. In order to keep business booming, the ski industry introduced an explicitly urban motif to their landscapes and provided young male boarders with spaces to show off their expertise.

Women riders had a difficult time entering this gendered landscape in large numbers. Snowboarding seemed to grow from the top down—media coverage of professional riders drove growth in the recreational ranks—and the same seemed true for women riders. A few women rode on professional teams in the early 1980s, mainly as tokens. The media liked them because they were cute and were generally considered, snowboard historian Susanna Howe argues, "(a) brave to be out there riding with the guys, and (b) lucky to be included."[51] But a group of young pros who began riding later on in the 1980s helped create an image of women snowboarders that celebrated their athleticism, skill, ambition, and professionalism. These women found physical, psychological, and eventually financial empowerment in snowboarding, and through their involvement in the sport and the industry they united the act of shredding on a board with the athletic, aggressive, and female Shred Betty.[52]

Like women skiers, snowboarding women said they were drawn to the sport by the physical feelings of freedom. One half-pipe champion said the real fun of boarding was "play[ing] with the mountain." She was drawn to the "speed, flow . . . [that] makes you kind of fearless."[53] Another pro felt motivated by "how good it feels to accomplish something and how good it feels to fly through the air on your board."[54] When writer Susanna Howe tried the sport she said it changed her forever. "Speed, creativity, style, physical exhaustion, nature, fresh air, all of these things drew me in," she wrote. "It was absurd how fun it was."[55] And while they cited feelings similar to the exhilaration of skiing, many argued that boarding felt even better. One described it as "more effortless and graceful," and another said "even after years of ski racing I have never felt a sensation as powerful as this."[56]

As inheritors of the changes wrought by the women's movement and Title IX, furthermore, women boarders claimed their outdoor mobility and an active relationship to the mountains with more gusto than earlier generations of skiers could. When pro icon Michele Taggert described her first half-pipe contest back in the mid-1980s, she said, "You'd just b-line it and haul butt and go flying off this mound of snow and land in the flat and then go hauling toward the other mound of snow. I was a lunatic and it was a really good time."[57] Greta Gaines, 1992 Women's Extreme Snowboard Champion, advocated the sport and claimed it for women in even more colorful terms. "We want to have fun, not the quilting circle style of fun, but the real kick-ass, exhilarating meet-your-maker kind of fun, we want to ride hard, we want to play damn it and stop cheerleading."[58] These women, most of them professional riders, expressed their

Shannon Dunn riding her first pro-model board at Mt. Hood, 1994. Dunn's combination of androgynous looks, female identity, and big air characterized the Shred Betty, and her athleticism served as a model for male and female boarders. (From Susanna Howe, *Sick: A Cultural History of Snowboarding* (New York: St. Martin's Griffin, 1998), 127. Photo by Jeff Curtes.)

freedom by flying down mountains on snowboards and embodying the new image of the Shred Betty.

This image first took shape through riders such as Tina Basich, Michele Taggert, and Shannon Dunn, who merged their success in competitions with an increased role in the growing snowboard industry. By the 1990s, when they had established themselves as top competitors in a male-oriented sport, the ski industry was marketing to both women skiers and snowboarders. The combination opened the door for women boarders to move into the industry. Kemper and Sims came out with pro women's board models named for Basich and Dunn in 1994, which sold surprisingly well, and the two boarders took an active role in developing products for the fast-growing female market. The baggy, hip-hop–influenced clothing styles most boarders wore did not fit girls. Rather than reproduce boy's styles in smaller sizes for women, thereby reinforcing the male boarder stereotype and defining women boarders as masculine, Basich and Dunn launched a new clothing line in 1994 that emphasized femininity. "We called it Prom and wore prom dresses in the ads and made it all pastel colors," Basich recalled, but their goals were subversive. "We had to make fun of the whole girl thing," she said, "to get noticed as something different."[59]

Their next step was to juxtapose the "girl thing" with extreme ath-leticism, to combine women's consumption of fashion with their con-sumption of snowboarding landscapes. In 1994 Basich and Dunn attended a Big Air contest, one of the most extreme and male-dominated snowboarding venues. "They said 'no girls allowed,'" Basich remem-bered, but that only made them more determined. So they "went and put on all pink and pigtails" and proceeded to show that they could board just as well, and on the same big jump, as the men. They listened to the Beastie Boys "to get all amped up" and made the long hike to the top of the jump. Basich admits she was intimidated, but she did not hesitate. "I took three breaths," she said, "and then dropped."[60] The unusual combi-nation of girly looks, rap music, and fearless athleticism came together in the image of the Shred Betty that these women embodied and promoted. When they launched themselves off that big jump, they contested the masculinity of the space as well as their competitors' skills. Their simul-taneous consumption of feminine clothes, male snowboarding culture, and mountain landscapes seemed contradictory, but Basich, Dunn, and their cohorts removed the contradictions by turning the Shred Betty into a marketable image.

Dunn's and Basich's ironic girliness was important because it made everyone acknowledge their gender. They were not boys (though they could compete among them), and they wanted everyone to know it. This look attracted young women and girls to the sport in large numbers, but some—aware perhaps of the Snow Bunny that haunted women skiers—worried that it carried feminine images too far. Unwilling to use sex to sell product, especially to women, Dunn and Basich later started a new line of clothing based less on feminine looks and more on function. They were happy to see the girl craze die, and as boarding historian Susanna Howe put it, "soon, gender-identification seemed outdated."[61] Between women's actions on the mountain and this marketing switch, the Shred Betty image moved its focus to performance and grew more popular, il-lustrating the economic significance of women as consumers of sport.

By 1997, women's participation in snowboarding reached 30 percent, and women were the largest percentage of new boarders.[62] The ski in-dustry paid attention. *Skiing* magazine featured a woman boarder as early as 1991 and Shred Betties peppered the pages of the 1995 *Skiing for Women*. Ski resorts looked to attract female customers by hosting women's snowboarding camps and clinics.[63] Perhaps even more signifi-cant than the ski industry's attention to Shred Betties was women's par-ticipation in the growing snowboarding industry. By 1997 about twenty boarding clothing manufacturers catered to women, and female pros pro-moted their own signature boards, boots, clothes, and shoes.[64] A maga-zine created by and for women boarders called *Fresh and Tasty* hit the newsstands, Web sites later appeared with names like "Gurlz on Boards," and *Snowboard Life* did a feature on pro women riders (supported by an online article and an entire women's section called Circle Plus on their Web site). Women riders established new events such as Boarding for Breast Cancer and Wild Women and Women Only snowboarding camps. They gave the Shred Betty image some entrepreneurial energy from within the industry, and they did so quite self-consciously. They established an annual meeting in 1995 that grew from thirty-eight to one hundred in its second year, and they called it the Gathering of the Goddesses.[65] The result has been growing power and widespread respect for women riders within snowboarding culture and the ski industry, a Shred Betty image created by women for women, and the steady increase in people who want to ride like a girl.

The Snow Bunny and the Shred Betty have much to teach us about gender and environmental history. First, they illustrate the powerful ways skiers and snowboarders affect mountain landscapes through consumption. Their desires for sensual terrain or a half-pipe directly influenced how ski area designers built and expanded ski resort landscapes. The need for clothes, equipment, and lodging prompted the growth of restaurants, hotels, and retail stores at the mountain's base. As part of the larger tourist industry, ski resorts promoted consumption of the environment on a variety of levels, but sport acts as a kind of consumption, too. Skiers and boarders consumed resorts by moving through them, and their use of the mountains gave those mountains particular meaning. Lounging on beginner slopes created the bunny hill, for instance. By changing their behavior—showing up for Ladies' Day, conducting women-only clinics on expert terrain, or leaping off jumps while wearing pink and pigtails—they altered the social and cultural expectations attached to skiing landscapes and effectively redefined them. Skiers, snowboarders, and outdoor sports enthusiasts as a whole constitute an interesting set of historical agents worthy of environmental historians' attention.

Bunnies and Betties also show us how consumers, by becoming a significant market, can affect social as well as environmental change. Bunnies helped the ski industry attract a male market to the slopes at the same time that they became a market for ski fashion, resort shopping, and male skiers. When the ski industry needed more women to ski in order to keep profits up, however, it responded to changes in American society and helped define women as athletes instead of ornaments. Women's clinics reformed mountains when they taught pupils how to negotiate expert terrain on their own terms. Similarly, the industry promoted a new urban landscape and a new kind of feminism when it adopted the Shred Betty. Snowboarding's rebellious culture suddenly became appealing when millions of teenagers took it up, leading ski resorts to build new boarding parks and half-pipes on mountain resorts. Once a bastion of young males, snowboarding has more women than its skateboard and surfing brothers do because the ski industry recognized women as a significant market and sought them out. In order to attract them successfully, moreover, the industry made room for women in its ranks—promoting a Shred Betty image created largely by women, for women. As consumers, therefore, female skiers and snowboarders used the ski industry to affect the social landscape as well as the physical one, which leads us to a final lesson we can learn.

Consumption is a gendered activity, and the story of the Snow Bunny and the Shred Betty is all about the interaction between landscape and an unpredictable but consequential gendered market. The ski industry developed a culture and a landscape based on assumptions about gender that conflicted with the physical empowerment women experienced on the slopes. Few women, in other words, identified completely with the Snow Bunny image. They struggled to balance their femininity with their athleticism, and as soon as the industry recognized the scale of this conflict it embraced new images of women including the Shred Betty. In the 1990s, the industry adopted not only the physical changes necessary to incorporate snowboarding but also the social and cultural changes that reshaped how skiers and boarders consumed resort spaces. Pigtailed women swooping through half-pipes felt comfortable, and women like Amy Spence borrowed a snowboard and drove to Mt. Snow for the weekend. In her rise, the Shred Betty both depended upon and reshaped the ski industry and its mountain landscapes. To understand her is to appreciate how gender and landscape have constituted one another.

NOTES

Thanks to Nancy Scott Jackson, Virginia Scharff, and especially Jon T. Coleman.

1. Julia Carson, *A Ragged Mountain Press Woman's Guide to Snowboarding* (New York: McGraw-Hill, 1999), 3.

2. Deborah Frazier, "Ranks of Snowboarders Growing," *Rocky Mountain News,* February 13, 1994, 23A; Lisa Lytle, "Shred Fashion," *Boulder Sunday Camera,* January 21, 1996, 5C.

3. The masculine meanings behind skiing developed historically and are integral to the history of the sport in America. See Anne Gilbert Coleman, "Culture, Landscape, and the Making of the Colorado Ski Industry" (Ph.D. diss., University of Colorado, 1996), and Steven Reiss, "Sport and the Redefinition of Middle-Class Masculinity," *International Journal of the History of Sport* 8 (May 1991): 5–27.

4. E. John B. Allen, "Sierra 'Ladies' on Skis in Gold Rush California," *Journal of Sport History* 17 (Winter 1990): 347; Jim Wier, "The Beginning of Skiing in Grand County," *Grand County Historical Association* 4 (March 1988): 12.

5. Abbot Fay, *Ski Tracks in the Rockies: A Century of Colorado Skiing* (Evergreen, Colo.: Cordillera Press, 1984), 2, 5, 6; Jean Wren, *Steamboat Springs and the "Treacherous and Speedy Skee"* (Steamboat Springs, Colo.: Steamboat Pilot, 1972), 6.

6. John L. Frisbee, "Why Do We Ski?" *Ski* (November 1953): 36–37.

7. Characterizing the landscape as female and movement through it as a form of masculine conquest is not a new phenomenon. See Annette Kolody, *The Land before Her: Fantasy and Experience of the American Frontiers, 1630–1860* (Chapel Hill: University of North Carolina Press, 1984).

8. Dick Tompkins, "Much Ado about Nothing," *Trail and Timberline* 230 (January 1938): 3.

9. This phenomenon occurred mainly during and after the 1960s, when allusions to sex and women's bodies became more acceptable in popular culture.

10. Anonymous poem in Wallace L. LaBaw, *See and Ski in Colorado* (Broomfield, Colo.: Ingersoll Publications, 1966), 1.

11. Defining athletic activity as masculine is not new. See Susan K. Cahn, *Coming on Strong: Gender and Sexuality in Twentieth-Century Women's Sport* (Cambridge, Mass.: Harvard University Press, 1994), and Donald J. Mrozek, "The 'Amazon' and the American 'Lady': Sexual Fears of Women Athletes," and Allen Guttmann, "Sports and Eros," in *The New American Sport History: Recent Approaches and Perspectives*, ed. S. W. Pope (Urbana: University of Illinois Press, 1997), 198–222.

12. Chet Anderson, interview by the author, June 7, 1994, Durango, Colorado.

13. Steve Knowlton, from Beth Gage and George Gage, *Fire on the Mountain*, Gage and Gage Productions, Telluride, Colorado, 1995, videocassette; Charles Paterson, interview by the author, June 28, 1994, Aspen, Colorado, tape recording and transcript, Aspen Historical Society (hereafter cited as AHS), 10.

14. Jim Snobble, interview by the author, July 11, 1994, Aspen, Colorado, tape recording and transcript, AHS.

15. Janet Robertson, *The Magnificent Mountain Women: Adventures in the Colorado Rockies* (Lincoln: University of Nebraska Press, 1990), 43.

16. Elizabeth Oblock Sinclair, interview by the author, July 26, 1994, Aspen, Colorado, tape recording and transcript, AHS, 2; Cherie Gerbaz Oates, interview with the author, July 13, 1994, Aspen, Colorado, tape recording and transcript, AHS, 6.

17. Virginia J. Scharff, *Taking the Wheel: Women and the Coming of the Motor Age* (Albuquerque: University of New Mexico Press, 1991). Along similar lines, historians have characterized sport as maintaining the aura of a male preserve, at least until the 1970s. See Cahn, *Coming on Strong*.

18. Of course, gender norms changed throughout this time period. Generally speaking, though, athletic women have participated in sports at the risk of being seen as unfeminine or having their sexuality called into question. See Susan K. Cahn, Donald J. Mrozek, and Carroll Smith-Rosenberg, *Disorderly Conduct: Visions of Gender in Victorian America* (New York: Oxford University Press, 1985).

19. Helen Boughton-Leigh, "Racing for Women," *American Ski Annual* (1936–1937): 41, 45.

20. In Grand Lake, Colorado, an 1883 newspaper article noted that "coasting on snowshoes has taken the place of dancing parties," and in the 1880s Norwegian snowshoe parties became popular social events in Aspen, Tin Cup, White Pine, and Crystal as well. Wier, "The Beginning of Skiing in Grand County," 12, and Jack A. Benson, "Before Aspen and Vail: The Story of Recreational Skiing in Frontier Colorado," *Journal of the West* 22 (January 1983): 52, 57.

21. Dick Tompkins, "Much Ado about Nothing," *Trail and Timberline* 230 (January 1938): 3. Although certainly possible among a single-sex group of skiers, *gemütlichkeit* implied men and women socializing together. This connotation was especially true after the 1930s, when popularized Freudian psychology stigmatized same-sex relationships, the Great Depression shifted American society toward more conservative values, and even feminists cast themselves as more feminine, heterosexual, and social than before. Helen Lenskyj, *Out of Bounds: Women, Sport, and Sexuality* (Toronto: Women's Press, 1986), 73–74; see also Ellen Wiley Todd, "Art, the 'New Woman,' and Consumer Culture: Kenneth Hayes Miller and Reginald Marsh on Fourteenth Street, 1920–40," in *Gender and American History Since 1890*, ed. Barbara Melosh (New York: Routledge, 1993), 130–31.

22. John L. Frisbee, "Why Do We Ski?" *Ski* (November 1953): 19, 36.

23. Grand County Historical Association, *Winter Park: Colorado's Favorite for Fifty Years, 1940–1990* (Denver: Winter Park Recreation Association, 1989), 22.

24. Women's and gender historians note that the "New Woman" visible in the late nineteenth and early twentieth century changed in the 1920s and 1930s. Once referring to college-educated suffragists and Progressive reformers, by the 1920s the designation cut across class lines and included a variety of ways in which these women occupied public, urban, and modern spaces. By the 1930s, "new women" had set aside political demands for equality in exchange for lives that included interests outside the home as well as marriage and children. Such women enjoyed being chic, heterosexual, and feminine rather than political, and they focused on individual rather than collective goals. It is within this context that many women—particularly but not limited to upper-class women—embraced the sport of alpine skiing. See Todd, "Art, the 'New Woman,' and Consumer Culture," 130–32; see also Carroll Smith-Rosenberg and Nancy F. Cott, *The Grounding of Modern Feminism* (New Haven, Conn.: Yale University Press, 1987).

25. Neale Howard, "Junior Skiing for Girls," *American Ski Annual* (1939–1940): 93.

26. Eileen O'Connor,"Genesee Mountain Ski Tournament Proves to Be Winter Fashion Display," clipping, February 19, 1923, General Ski Collection, Grand County Historical Association, Hot Sulphur Springs, Colorado.

27. Feminist historians might argue whether this ability made women more or less powerful. As consumers, women in the 1920s and 1930s made important decisions that affected their own lives and influenced consumer culture generally. See Scharff, *Taking the Wheel*. Helen Lenskyj notes that by conforming to male-defined standards of beauty and heterosexual attractiveness, however, women competed with other women for the attraction and protection of men, thereby accepting a subordinate role in society; see *Out of Bounds*, 56.

28. There is much written on the Tenth Mountain Division and its impact on the American ski industry. For a brief introduction, see Jack Benson, "Skiing at Camp Hale: Mountain Troops during World War II," *Western Historical Quarterly* 15 (April 1984): 163–74, and the documentary film *Fire on the Mountain*, Gage and Gage Productions.

29. Daniels and Fisher advertisement, *Rocky Mountain Life* (March 1946): 21.

30. Jean Jolle, "For That Downhill Look," *Rocky Mountain Life* (December 1946): 27.

31. "Pat on the Back—Andrea Mead Lawrence," *Sports Illustrated*, December 19, 1955, 68; Luanne Pfeifer, *Gretchen's Gold: The Story of Gretchen Fraser* (Missoula, Mont.: Pictorial Histories Publishing, 1996), 82, 101, 108.

32. Ezra Bowen, "Skiing: A Builder's Year," *Sports Illustrated*, December 19, 1955, 48; untitled cartoon, 44.

33. Mort Lund, "Sophistication and Snow," *Sports Illustrated*, January 13, 1958, 38.

34. "Girls! Girls! Girls!" *Ski* 32 (December 1967): 74.

35. W. S., "Funny Ads," *Skiing Trade News* 6 (December 1969): 56.

36. Advertisement, *Skiing Trade News* 7 (Spring 1970): 34.

37. Nancy Greene, "The Woman Racer as a Woman," *Ski* 34 (January 1970): 57.

38. Rose Marie Cleese, "Building the Middle Week Throng," *Skiing Area News* 5 (Summer 1970): 23.

39. Sally Russell, "For Women Only," *Skiing* 41 (November 1988): 150, 153.

40. See, for example, Bard Glenne, "What's a Woman's Ski?" *Skiing* 38 (October 1985): 93, and Sally Russell, "Deals for Skiing Families," *Skiing* 38 (January 1986): 32. These changes reflected the growing number of women working within the ski industry as instructors, equipment designers, marketers, and magazine writers. See Russell, "For Women Only," and Janet Nelson, "The Trials of Jeannie Thoren," *Skiing* 44 (December 1991): 188, and "Pioneer Spirit," *Skiing for Women* 2 (Winter 1995): 88–92, for some examples.

41. See Susanna Howe, *Sick: A Cultural History of Snowboarding* (New York: St. Martin's Press, 1998).

42. Scott Turner, "Stick Speak," *Boulder Quarterly* (Ski Guide 1996): 10; Deborah Frazier, "Ranks of Snowboarders Growing," *Rocky Mountain News*, February 13, 1994, 23A. For a more recent analysis of snowboarder stereotypes and self-images, see Robert Kenneth Karsted, "The Growing Sport of Snowboarding: An Analysis of Popular Images, Perceptions, and Stereotypes" (master's thesis, University of Colorado, 1996).

43. Tom Sims, as quoted in Howe, *A Cultural History*, 29.

44. Ibid., 31–32.

45. Jake Burton, as quoted in ibid., 47.

46. Jim Fulton, as quoted in ibid., 24.

47. Ibid., 159.

48. Dana White, "Shred Heads Go Mainstream," *Skiing* 41 (September 1988): 82, 84, 222.

49. Bard Glenne, "How They Ride," *Skiing* 41 (January 1989): 62.

50. Turner, "Stick Speak," 10; Frazier, "Ranks of Snowboarders Growing."

51. Howe, *A Cultural History*, 119.

52. Shredding can refer to riding skate-, snow-, and surfboards. Of these three sports and cultures, snowboarding has proven the most accessible to women, so the Shred Betty image usually refers to female snowboarders.

53. Nicole Angelrath, as quoted in Carson, *A Ragged Mountain Press Woman's Guide to Snowboarding*, 19.

54. Megan Pischke, in Robyn Hakes, "Ladies Room: Insight into the Female Mind," *Snowboard Life*, November 20, 2000, 1, at *Snowboarding-Online.com*.

55. Howe, *A Cultural History*, x–xi.

56. Barrett Christy in Hakes, "Ladies Room," 13, and Betsy Shaw, as quoted in *A Ragged Mountain Press Woman's Guide to Snowboarding*, 11.

57. Michele Taggert, in Hakes, "Ladies Room," 18.

58. Greta Gaines, from Wild Women Snowboard Camps Web site, coach biography, at *www.wildwomencamps.com/coach%20bios/gretabiobody.html*.

59. Howe, *A Cultural History*, 121.

60. Ibid., 118.

61. Ibid., 125.

62. "The Girl's Gospel II," January 31, 1997, *Circle Plus*, at *Snowboarding-Online.com*.

63. Hollis Brooks, "Hey! Make Me Over!" *Skiing* 44 (November 1991): 192; Edwin McDowell, "Changing Skiing's Macho Image," *New York Times*, February 15, 1997, 35, 38.

64. Lisa Lytle, "Shred Fashion," *Sunday (Boulder) Camera*, January 21, 1997, 5C, 8C.

65. The meeting included women who worked in practically every aspect of the industry, including apparel, manufacturing, sales, media, and riders. For a report on the 1996 meeting, see Kathleen Gasperini, "A Gathering of the Goddesses II," January 20, 1996, *Circle Plus*, at *Snowboarding-Online.com*.

PART IV: POLITICS

CHAPTER TEN

"She Touched Fifty Million Lives": Gene Stratton-Porter and Nature Conservation

Amy Green

Gene Stratton-Porter and Theodore Roosevelt emerged at the turn of the century as the two giants of the conservation movement. In 1923, contemporary critic and author Grant Overton enthused that "each has swayed the millions; each, beyond all possible question, has influenced human lives."[1] Porter's actions on behalf of nature inspired her to educate the nation about the beauty and purpose of all wild creatures. She published some of the finest nature photography of the era. She wrote poetry, published books for children, authored innumerable articles, penned seven nature study books, and published twelve nature novels. Her best-selling nature novels—translated into fourteen languages—won her a national and international following and did the most to "sway" an estimated readership of fifty million.[2]

The connection between Porter and Roosevelt can also be located in their ideas about gender. Roosevelt's "strenuous life" espoused a regenerated masculinity, one that replaced effeteness with virility through an emphasis on bodily vigor and strength. Along similar lines, Porter's ideal woman embraced masculine-coded traits like bravery, physical prowess, and mental hardiness; she endorsed the rugged outdoor life as a path toward what we might term "muscular womanhood." Porter's muscular woman suppressed roles associated with "True Womanhood" while she rejected the more liberal attitudes and values of the "New Woman."

As an activist, Porter, a founding member of Isaak Walton League, joined national crusades and fought at the local level as well. Working to save undeveloped areas in Noble County, Indiana, in 1916, she publicly opposed a drainage project but failed to dissuade the county from reclaiming more farmable land. Still, defeat only motivated Porter to preserve some of the vegetation threatened by desiccated streambeds. Undertaking the formidable task of replanting native flora, her efforts have had an everlasting impact. Today, on a small piece of land in Northeastern Indiana, a heavily concentrated growth of vegetation survives—

the water hyacinths, arrowhead lilies, rosemary, and orchids Porter planted over eighty years ago.[3]

In this chapter I seek to posit three overlapping themes. First, it is of great consequence that for much of her life Porter's experiences in nature were unconstrained by gender norms. As a farm girl growing up in the post–Civil War era, she experienced an unusual degree of autonomy. Her freedom to explore the expanse of nature every day formed the seedbed of muscular womanhood. More at home in nature than anywhere else, Porter became fiercely independent, physically strong, and preternaturally connected to the wildlife around her. For her, nature and culture were coextensive; the traditional nature/culture dualism did not accord with her experiences.

Second, while not hemmed in by gender expectations during her childhood, Porter experienced the force of an established gender hierarchy in her adult life. Yet the muscular traits of cunning and prowess led her to compete on the same turf with men as a nature writer and field photographer. She maintained, as we will see, an unusual degree of control and power in her negotiations with magazine and book publishers. Yet, most historians have argued that Progressive Era women drew on existing gender norms to legitimize their actions in the political arena of conservation. Women invoked the tenets of moral motherhood, which dictated that such virtues as cooperation, nurturing, and restraint inhered in women through divine or natural causation; domesticity and ecological sensitivity, the scholarly literature suggests, appeared to go hand in hand.[4] The equation between domesticity and nature guardianship simply does not apply to Porter. She rejected domesticity and ignored gender dictates altogether.

Finally, Porter yearned for more than professional recognition in the field of conservation; she wanted to live the American dream. Although muscular womanhood liberated her from the constraints of domesticity, full independence meant economic self-sufficiency and the freedom to consume at will. To own wealth meant rejecting the more limited realm of economic activity afforded to most women and enjoying the status and power such riches conferred upon her. Porter adhered to the American myth of mobility. A staunch nativist, she rejected urban culture and promoted an agrarian utopia where purity and goodness issued forth from close-knit homogenous communities. Unconventional behavior did not always result in unconventional beliefs. For Porter, the preservation of nature and the preservation of the race were homologous. Echoing Theodore Roosevelt and Frederick Jackson Turner, nature would regenerate her overrefined sisters, preventing "racial" degeneracy.

In sum, the standard framing of the early environmental movement looks very different when we add Porter to the mix. The now immortalized battles between mountaineer John Muir and forester Gifford Pinchot, promoters of use and advocates of preservation, rendered the movement polarized and omitted those for whom the natural world was valued in more complex and contradictory ways. For example, Porter's contradictory impulse to sell the lumber and oil on her land—ruining habitats and leading to the loss of wildlife—as a way to capitalize her work in field photography only makes sense when studied through the lens of gender. When we consider her position as a woman with no formal education trying to make it in the male world of nature work, we find that Porter, and I imagine many others as well, attached more contradictory meanings to nature.

HOPEWELL FARM: GENDER AND CLASS AND THE MAKING OF GENE STRATTON-PORTER

Porter's knowledge of the natural world began in Wabash County, Indiana, a landscape that consisted mainly of family farms, including Hopewell Farm, her father's large homestead. Born Geneva Grace Stratton in 1863, Porter, the last of twelve children, was benignly neglected by her chronically ill mother. She spent her days roaming the farm environs alone or with her favorite brother. Not required to help her older sisters in the home, she enjoyed the freedom to enter a boy-coded world of outdoor, solitary adventure in nature.[5] A tolerant father and a relatively absent mother made it possible for Porter to cultivate physical hardiness, free spiritedness, and independence.

As long as she appeared at mealtime, Porter was permitted to run wild all day. She often spent entire days alone, beyond the farm's borders, or she might sleep on a patch of ground near the field while her father worked. Whenever she could, she traveled afield in search of her beloved birds. Her behavior took a strange turn when she started hearing sounds in nature, clearly inaudible to everyone else. Her disclosure might have robbed her of this solitary life in nature, especially when she began clambering atop the second-story beams of the barn to hammer out nature's "rhythms." Yet a doting father and a liberal doctor rescued her from confinement. When the local doctor could not make a diagnosis, he reminded Mark Stratton that his permissiveness had helped to create this creature of the woods and suggested that to restrain her now would be unfair. Her father followed the doctor's advice by blessing Porter's attachment to nature, viewing this special relationship and attunement as a gift from "God."[6] Whatever the explanation, she developed an exquisite, nonverbal attachment to nature.

On the other hand, while her childhood was nearly free of gender limits, it was not free from the burdens of impoverishment. She was acutely sensitive to the conditions of rural poverty, and her memories of being inadequately dressed and having to barter farm produce for much needed goods never diminished.[7] She recounted these times with bitterness and shame, happy that they were relegated to the past and that like Horatio Alger she had moved up in the world through hard work and good fortune. The two most formative experiences of childhood—mortification associated with want and exultation associated with nature—shaped the choices she made as an adult. Porter subscribed with equal zeal to the gospel of nature and the gospel of wealth. She would never give up on nature, but she wanted to distance herself as much as possible from the world of financial instability.

THE TREASURES OF THE LIMBERLOST: CONSERVATION AND COMMODIFICATION

Porter left rural poverty behind by making very practical decisions. First, she married in 1886, finding a husband with some local prestige. Undoubtedly, passion drew her to Charles Porter, the town druggist. A constant exchange of tender letters attests to their early romance.[8] However, it was also likely that the marriage, for Porter, was a pragmatic choice. Charles meant escape from probable fate as a farmwife and access to comforts denied to her as a child. Shortly after their first and only child Jeanette was born, Charles moved his family to Geneva, Indiana, in 1890. South and east of Geneva lay a relatively undeveloped stretch of land. The "bogs, streams, and virgin forest" would serve as a laboratory for Porter's nature study and also provide her with a dramatic landscape against which she plotted her best-selling novels, Freckles (1904) and Girl of the Limberlost (1909).[9]

Porter's phenomenally popular novels celebrated the natural beauty and diversity of swamp wildlife, but, ironically, the commercial development of the swamp itself launched her career as a naturalist. Soon after she and her husband moved to the Limberlost, a furniture company surveyed the swamp for its very valuable trees, including wild cherry, golden oak, black walnut, and hard maple. Other speculators soon discovered that the swamp harbored some promising oil deposits. The Porters welcomed this commercial development. The new roads built to harvest the swamp's resources would give Porter easy access into the Limberlost, facilitating her nature study work. And the Porters benefited in other ways too. Her husband took advantage of all this commercial activity and organized a bank, expanded the drugstore, built a hotel, bought a 365-acre farm, leased sixty profitable oil wells, and erected a fourteen-room "cabin" to which they moved in 1895.[10]

Eighteen ninety-five was a fortuitous year for Porter. First, she found herself occupying a capacious home, a bold statement about her economic ascent in the world. And during the same year, her husband and daughter presented her with a small box camera as a Christmas gift.[11] The camera served as fulcrum for Porter's path on which gender identity and nature experience constantly reinforced each other during her lifetime. First, by launching a career in wildlife photography, she intensified her immersion in nature. She lugged heavy photographic equipment into the swamp and bushwhacked into the most remote parts of these wetlands. Prolonged and strenuous contact with nature also meant further rejection of the separate spheres ideology, whether conscious or not. This rugged work required practical dress, and nothing could suit her needs better than a man's military attire. She traded in her gingham dress adorned with silk scarf and beads for durable field trousers, khaki shirt, and lace-up boots. Porter's dedication to conservation and her lifelong disregard for gender norms made her the target of criticism among the female population of Geneva. She never understood the scorn directed at her, believing all true women could enjoy the frills of town life and the delights of the swamp.

Porter was unflagging in her efforts to learn the techniques of wildlife photography. She first received recognition from outdoor magazines for her extraordinary talent in photographing live birds in situ. While other photographers relied on sleight of hand by using studio sets and stuffed birds, Porter dedicated her days to lying in swamps waiting for the bird to make its appearance at the right time for a usable shot. As the work became more strenuous and more dangerous, she did not retreat from her role as the swamp woman but continued down the path of muscular independence and career advancement.

Yet in 1913, the Limberlost was utterly overrun by development. The Porters, and other opportunists, commodified the resources of the area—especially its trees and oil deposits. This process, in addition to the drainage of the wetlands for more tillable land, destroyed habitats and spelled doom for much of the wildlife. Porter welcomed the financial windfall that the Limberlost provided, and their "modest" cabin was a stepping-stone to even more lavish homes. The Porters moved to the Sylvan Lake area in 1913 (more remote and farther north) where they built an even bigger twenty-room estate, named "Wildflower Woods."[12]

Although Porter's unquenchable desire for riches exhausted the Limberlost, she proved equally passionate in her efforts to preserve plant life in the areas surrounding her new home on Sylvan Lake. In this tract, densely bordered with trees, Porter embarked on a restoration project, fearing that the county's plans to drain the region would devastate all the native growth. She described her "frantic effort to establish in [her]

woods each species of . . . native wild flowers." And with little help from
others, she also rooted in the earth "more than five thousand trees, shrubs
and ferns," an American "Mother Earth" willing to suffer sunburn,
scratches, and the blisters of sumac poisoning for the sake of nature.
Porter not only preserved nature; she pursued the goals of a restoration
preservationist as well, spending countless hours replanting native
seedlings.[13]

Her dedication to planting and saving indigenous flowers from extinction resulted not from formal book learning or training in a specialized profession, but from the female tradition of gardening. The
garden—the woman's domain—was one place where Porter and her
mother connected. Mary Stratton taught Porter the finer points of plant
lore and demonstrated the importance of preservation by using her own
garden as a sanctuary for the transplantation of flowers threatened with
extinction.[14] Although most farm women necessarily raised vegetable
gardens adjacent to the house, many planted flowers as well. This gendered tradition, passed from mother to daughter, was the original source
of Porter's knowledge about wildflower preservation.

Her obsession with rescuing the plant world rendered her somewhat
oblivious to others, especially her husband Charles. Their move north to
Rome City required that Charles remain alone for the week in Geneva to
run his store, which began a slow but sure separation between the couple. Even the home at Wildflower Woods was not designed with Charles
in mind. As I will show, this large estate became an extension of nature itself, not a habitat that sufficiently met human needs, or a husband's
needs especially. To this end, the essentialist paradigm that draws an
equation between feminine refinement and the aesthetic use of flowers
inside or outside the home hardly applies to Porter. She redefined domesticity altogether.

REDEFINING DOMESTICITY: INSIDE/OUTSIDE

Porter's love for nature seemingly competed with her love for people, including her family. In this sense, she was a typical preservationist, often
attacked for loving nature too much and humanity too little. She explained that she was frequently "forced into the kitchen to attend to the
needs of [her] family in person," taking precious time away from her
work in the woods.[15] The more she immersed herself in nature, the more
her husband receded into the background. But Charles did serve as his
wife's field assistant. During one outing into the marsh, the Porters
looked for a black vulture nest, previously sighted by lumberjacks, men
in the process of destroying bird habitats, who discovered one of the rarer

species in the area and one that Porter longed to see. Charles accompanied her on these daily outings, and the pilgrimage was beset with difficulties. The Porters, according to a friend and early biographer, forced their way between "steaming, fetid pools," endured swarms of "gnats, flies, mosquitoes, poisonous insects," and watched fearfully for the ever-lurking rattlesnake. They "sank ankle deep at every step" and often fell when seemingly solid logs broke under them. After several weeks, their efforts were finally rewarded when they observed a downy hatchling take wing.[16] The sheer physical fortitude and fearlessness required for this endeavor underscore the role of gender in defining Porter's relationship to nature. Not only did she invert gender roles by displaying the traits of muscular womanhood, but she also inverted another gender paradigm of the period, the male naturalist relying on the assistance of his wife in the field, who, in turn, was grateful for her opportunity to spend time outdoors. In this instance, Charles played the secondary role of field assistant, while his wife directed the work and relished her time submersed in the marsh environment.

Porter strayed far from the model woman, mother, and wife. For example, Charles learned that if a caterpillar decided to lay its eggs on his favorite chair, then he must sit elsewhere. Their daughter Jeannette, though, shared her mother's enthusiasm for their nontraditional home in which meals were taken elsewhere so the cast-iron stove could serve as a habitat for guinea pigs and other animals. This home blurred the lines between inside and outside. Newly born moths could be found flying through the house to the adjacent conservatory where flowers were in abundance for feeding. Wounded birds took perch anywhere.[17] Porter's home was more than a sanctuary for wildlife. Here, the outside was not walled off by domestic living; instead animals and plants freely claimed the Sylvan Lake "cabin" as their habitat.

Domesticity took a backseat to her work as a naturalist. "I argued that if I kept my family so comfortable that they missed nothing from their usual routine, it was my right to do what I could toward furthering my personal ambitions," she recalled.[18] Porter was steadfastly ambitious, at times audacious, and always acquisitive, traits generally regarded as unfeminine. Driven to master field photography, she was quite delighted to use the family's wealth to secure state-of-the-art photographic equipment designed to her exact specifications. And she expressed confidence that her images of birds and moths might make her a living some day.

But she kept her ambition a secret, covertly sending "photographic and natural history hints" to the editors of *Recreation*.[19] Even when the magazine hired her in 1900 to take over the series "Camera Notes," she revealed nothing to her family. Her secrecy, then, must be understood in terms of gender just as her ambition makes sense when understood in the context of her atypical childhood. Most young and married women of the late nineteenth century knew better than to step out of place, challenging the husband's role as "bread winner" and pursuing their own path of economic self-sufficiency. Porter acted covertly to protect Charles's position as the nominal head of the family. Although Charles entered the marriage as her superior—a white male, born into a higher social class, and from a more urbane background—Porter would soon invert this relationship, claiming financial and personal independence and even fame and fortune.

FORMULA AND FORTUNE:
THE NATURALIST AND THE NOVELIST

In Porter's memory, the first earnings she received from *Recreation* in 1900 remained her greatest personal triumph.[20] The envelope containing her wages was quickly snatched from the mailbox and silently celebrated as the first step toward personal freedom. Despite an austere childhood, with limited formal education, she had made it as a career woman. She soon expressed dissatisfaction with her staff position at the magazine. Although she penned a few articles, she mainly dispensed picture-taking tips. Anxious to demonstrate her expertise as a naturalist, she jumped ship when the opportunity arose. Between 1901 and 1902, Porter wrote seven nature study pieces for *Outing*, and her *own photographs* accompanied each article.[21] When this exquisite camera work came to the attention of Edward Bok, editor of the mass-circulating *Ladies' Home Journal*, Porter was catapulted into the limelight.[22] In 1905, Bok published a six-month series of her nature study articles.[23] Typically, one or two photographs illustrated each article, though her piece on the beloved "Black Vulture" (in the August 1906 issue) merited six of Porter's artistic images (perhaps she hoped to convert her audience to the beauty and usefulness of the underappreciated carrion eater). Male conservationists' stories about bison and large elk transfixed their audiences with little prompting, drawing them to animals that embodied the traits ecologists term "charismatic megafauna." Their sheer size and regional exoticism lent them popularity when compared to seemingly more ordinary or objectionable creatures.[24]

Porter, on the other hand, dignified an ordinary bird whose large black feathers and scavenging ways most often provoked reactions of disgust and fear. In this way, she used the camera to encourage her audience to view nature differently, to shake their androcentric stereotypes, and to consider the ecological and aesthetic values of all animals. Such a move on Porter's part also upset gender expectations; a true lady would be "naturally" drawn to backyard songsters, playfully displaying flashes of bright color and symbols of life, not portents of death.

"The Hatchling!" Baby black vulture photographed by Gene Stratton-Porter. (Courtesy Gene Stratton-Porter State Historic Site, Rome City, Indiana)

As much as Porter wanted to continue writing nature study, such as her serialized article in *Ladies' Home Journal*, her first novel, published in 1903, won her an even larger fan following. She was inspired to write this novel after retrieving a dead cardinal from the side of the road, presumably shot by a man for target practice. *The Song of the Cardinal* established the never-fail Porter formula: nature teaches us how to be fully human, and in turn we learn the value of nature's denizens and dedicate ourselves to their protection. And her audience so happily consumed her formulaic plots, stock characters, and rural settings, that of the fifty-five books that sold over a million copies between 1895 and 1945, five were written by Gene Stratton-Porter.[25]

Porter's novels captured an audience of fifty million during her lifetime. She did as much or more than other crusaders to convert her audience to the conservation movement. Reminding her audience that killing life—human or animal—was a sin against "God," she explored with her readers the life cycle and habitats of common creatures. And the immediate success she enjoyed with *The Song of the Cardinal* had as much to do with the genre of sentimental fiction as it did with its animal subject. Sentimental fiction aimed at the heart, not the head, and as such had the power to change the sympathies of the reader. Porter did not want to be known primarily as a fiction writer, yet sentimental fiction was one of the few gender-appropriate vehicles through which women could produce culture, and through which she then could write about nature. In Porter's case, her publisher demanded that she work within this genre.

The profitability of her fiction would lead her directly to the coveted pot of gold, but she chafed at being typed as a female writer and relegated to the role of sentimental novelist by Doubleday, Page and Company. Wildlife photography and nonfiction had won Porter admiration as a conservationist and a naturalist, and this was the career path she would have chosen if she had the power to determine her fate. Nelson Doubleday, however, aware of Porter's profit-making potential, was eager to become the sole publisher of her novels. When she stubbornly resisted being pigeonholed as a fiction writer, Doubleday did not back down. Exclusive representation of Porter would also give the publishing house more prominence, a needed competitive edge. She finally signed a contract with the company when a compromise was struck that gave her some control over her career. The publishers agreed that for every sentimental novel she wrote, Porter could then write a book of nature study, alternating the genres on an annual basis.[26] The publisher's conditions were simple: always make sure there is a happy ending.[27] Her conditions were unspoken: these stories about hard knocks, hearts of gold, innocent love, and the rest would be heavily laced with nature study.

Porter made little distinction between her novels and her nature study books. For example, she maintained all along that her novels were nature study "sugar-coated with fiction."[28] Her ability to teach nature through the guise of the novel was indisputable. Even Porter's worst critics admitted that her evocation of nature was extraordinarily realistic and authoritative.[29] In *Freckles,* her passage on the Luna moth's emergence from its cocoon stands as a wonderful example of a nature study lesson inserted into a novel with no details left out for the sake of plot development. And when her character Freckles puzzled over the nesting patterns of turkey vultures, Porter explained how to find such nests by taking the reader through Freckles's trial and error efforts.[30]

THE "BIRD WOMAN" AND THE FLUID
BORDERS OF THE SELF: ANIMALS AND LADIES

In her two most popular works—*Freckles* and *Girl of the Limberlost*—Porter often gave center stage to a semiautobiographical character, a local naturalist who was known throughout the community as the "Bird Woman." As a conduit for Porter, the Bird Woman was the model nature study teacher, not only revealing to her young pupils the wonders of the natural world but also teaching techniques for preserving rare moths and photographing marsh birds. According to the narrator, the Bird Woman's tramping about the swamps, "staggering under a load of cameras and paraphernalia," did not diminish her qualities as a true lady.[31] In one scene, the Bird Woman appeared as a vision of elegance: "Her silks and laces trailed along the polished floors. The lights gleamed on her neck and arms and flashed from rare jewels." And yet, she described her fancy clothing as "war clothes." Her rigorous swamp expeditions did not compare, she teased the speechless Freckles, with the duties assigned to a proper hostess.

At another level, the very name "Bird Woman" suggests a boundary-less connection between women and animal. On the one hand, this designation may be a literary evocation of the female/nature equation and its grounding in essentialist ideas about women in nature. But given Porter's unconventional childhood, this "morphing" of the two—human and animal—takes on other meanings as well, an invocation of magical realism where the extraordinary overlaps with the ordinary in an entirely believable way. In literature, Porter recovered the child whose extra-auditory perceptions broke the barrier between human and nature, thus creating a persona who experienced the world beyond normal human limits. Although her universe drew deeply on Romantic dichotomies—Nature against and above the city—she, at the same time, collapsed other dichotomous arrangements determined by Judeo-Christian beliefs. In Porter's world, humans did not necessarily exist above animals, blessed with souls and singularly privileged with an afterlife. She blended the natural with the human, erasing assumptions about a divinely ordained pecking order. Porter reinforced the cultural boundaries and dichotomies that suited her and collapsed those that did not accord with her own experiences. The fluid or manifold personas of the Bird Woman at once satisfied Porter's imagination for a woman who could exist in many realms, often synchronously.

FROM CONSERVATION TO CASH:
USES OF NATURE IN *GIRL OF THE LIMBERLOST*

Porter's novels may have been a covert strategy on her part to deliver nature study lessons in an easily digested form, but the rags-to-riches formula was not simply window dressing; it was Porter's personal credo. And she freely interwove elements of her own success story into her novels and characters. For example, Elnora, in *Girl of the Limberlost* (1904), lived a spartan existence on a farm at the edge of a swamp. She and her mother survived by bartering farm produce for goods and barely got by from harvest to harvest. When Elnora's stinting mother would not give her daughter the money needed to attend high school, Elnora soon found a way to make the Limberlost pay for her education. A lady in town, she discovered, would pay a good price for rare moths, which was enough incentive to brave the treacherous swamp in search of these prized specimens. And Elnora netted moths and impaled them on specimen boards with feverish intensity; every properly mounted specimen brought her one step closer to earning book and tuition money for public school, one step closer to the culture and comforts of town life. Thus, the natural resources of the Limberlost, like moths and trees, provided Porter and her semifictional characters with start-up capital for their venture beyond home, beyond nature. To exchange nature for capital was no Faustian bargain. It was the American way; it made good business sense.

HOLLYWOOD MOGUL: THE PURITY CRUSADER AND THE TRUE LADY

Porter achieved the ultimate American dream—overseeing the film adaptation of her books. In 1917, Paramount Pictures produced *Freckles*, but Porter was displeased with the movie. Wanting more direct control over production was one inducement for her to leave Indiana for California. In addition, she had become bored with her routine at Wildflower Woods. Wrestling with boredom and ill health, Porter moved to Los Angeles in 1919, while Charles, as one biographer explains, "was left to his own devices." Not invited to join his wife, he moved into a Geneva boardinghouse.[32]

In dazzling Los Angeles, Porter began moving in important circles, striking up a friendship with renowned photographer Edward Curtis. She also was determined to fully explore the film medium. She observed the day-to-day operations of working on location with elaborate sets and colorful actors and eventually started her own film company, more evidence of the degree to which she controlled the production of culture by adopting male strategies of success, from outright ownership to production director.[33]

Spectacular success meant prominence in the media by the second decade of the twentieth century. Porter seized this opportunity to voice her opinions on social issues that she deemed matters of national concern. At the turn of the century, Porter decried the market in birds to supply the female fashion industry with decorative hats; by the 1920s she condemned cosmopolitan America outright and beseeched the government to enforce social purity.[34] She blamed all social ills on city life and its inhabitants and imagined a prefallen age of social stability. Like male professionals of her generation, once-country adults who had moved from farms into cosmopolitan settings, Porter espoused the Jeffersonian ideal and its emphasis on the beneficence of nature in shaping moral character. The country, however, was constituted as an exclusive realm, reserved for whites of Western European descent. Porter used her platform as the nation's nature emissary to speak out against the "evils" of the new social order. She was a nativist and a purity crusader, who openly maligned the Japanese living in California. She attacked social discontent and "bolshevism," linking these "evils" to working-class solidarity and ethnic immigration. Her nativist sentiments were rooted in a deep suspicion of the city—its heterogeneity, fast-paced life, impersonality, and especially its independent youth culture. As she stated unequivocally in one article, "I stand squarely for book censorship."[35] She wanted to sanitize cultural expression, hoping to stem the tide of "degeneracy" among youth, and she called "on our government to curb indecent literature."[36]

Porter particularly deplored literary realism, finding it too graphic for her taste and for the good of the country. Literary realism that sought to expose the exploitative working and living conditions of industrial life, and thus to frame poverty in terms of the environment rather than the individual, was too pessimistic and dangerously un-American for Porter's politics: "All of life is not lived in cities," she insisted. "All men and women do not fall." And "if good people are real too, why not make them the subject of literary works?"[37] In a rather naive and simplistic fashion, Porter blamed all social ills on the city and upheld country life as the key to social redemption. There was nothing particularly new about her articulation of this moral geography, and she was unrestrained on the subject: "My life has been fortunate in one glad way. I have lived mostly in the country and worked in the woods. For every bad man and woman I have ever known, I have met, lived with, and am intimately acquainted with an overwhelming number of thoroughly clean and decent people who still believe in God and cherish high ideals."[38]

For Porter, nature not only meant liberation from gender constraints, it also represented the place where "true" Americans dwelled, a classic articulation of agrarian nostalgia as a regressive response to rapid urbanization. And she turned to the film industry as a vehicle through which this American ideal could be transmitted to the masses. She celebrated the industry's potential to provide "sane, clean, educative and superbly beautiful pictures."[39] Just as she used her camera to preserve nature, Porter used moving film to convey and preserve a conservative social utopia. And with advances made in stage production—the use of indoor studios, the availability of newly designed props, and such—Porter found it far easier to simulate her version of reality.

Playbill for *Freckles*. (Courtesy Gene Stratton-Porter State Historic Site, Rome City, Indiana)

During her adult life, Porter experienced and fought against gender inequalities, but she saw no connection between gender inequities and other forms of social injustice. Her willingness to bend and even break gender dictates suggests that initially her contravention of traditional femininity was less intellectual and more visceral. Along with this inclination, Porter's terrible fear of impoverishment drove her to succeed independently rather than to risk reliance on others. Ironically, her success as a "true" American was facilitated by her very willfulness in undermining gender roles and establishing a place for herself among the American elite. Porter believed in the rags-to-riches myth; she promoted social homogeneity and participated in the bourgeois world of conspicuous consumption. For her, money and lineage (proving one's descent from Western European stock) quelled her status anxiety, an anxiety that propelled Porter to "muscle" herself into the male sphere of business and politics. And the natural world only benefited from the power she accrued over time. The conservationist continued to protect nature and the nativist sought to protect Americans by returning them to their "original homes"—nature, the countryside, the frontier.

A NEW MOSES: PORTER AS ROLE MODEL
FOR THE AMERICAN WOMAN

Gene Stratton-Porter became the voice of mainstream America because her widely read novels espousing traditional American values—hard work, good character, a reliable community, and a Western European lineage, were a sure recipe for individual success. It is no surprise that *McCall's* hired her in 1921 to speak to the women of America through a series of editorials entitled "Gene Stratton-Porter's Column." Ironically, she was given the formidable task of making "the American woman feel good about her role as housewife."[40] Porter was no feminist, but domestic values and domestic chores were low on her list of life's priorities. Yet, between 1922 and 1925, she wrote over thirty articles on such subjects as "The Good Old Institution of Home," "For the Newlyweds," and the "Division of Labor in the Home."[41] Since she never played the role of the ideal homemaker in her own life, we might conclude that she was simply pleasing an audience that helped make her rich and famous by establishing contact with them through this progenitor of the "Dear Abby" genre. But Porter never rejected outright the American cult of domesticity. Instead, she wanted to ensure that women did not embrace domesticity at the expense of nature, so she grafted muscular womanhood onto the true womanhood ideal. This approach meant warning her native-born sisters about the consequences of engaging in a "revolt against the forest." This "revolt," she claimed, "resulted in delicate women, narrowed minds, puny children, and extravagant living." She alleged alarm at the magnitude of the problem and feared that without redress the "entire fiber and morale of the nation" would weaken.[42]

Porter faced this impending national and racial tragedy by declaring herself fit to lead "women back to the forest," back to the wilderness to realize their full human potential. She also reasoned that because of her "inclinations, education and rearing," she was uniquely "equipped to be their Moses." Echoing Frederick Jackson Turner, Theodore Roosevelt, and John Muir, Porter-as-Moses would regenerate the American woman by leading her back to the past, away from "civilization" and its corrupting forces. Like other advocates of outdoor life, she wanted women to find physical and mental regeneration in the woods, not "regeneration through violence," but regeneration through restoration ecology. Porter never claimed to be a social renegade; rather she hoped to lead the American woman toward mental and physical fitness and away from dissolution.

At another level, her conflation of true womanhood with muscular womanhood served her personal need to normalize activities that often resulted in social ostracism. Porter grievously recounted a time when her peers at a vacation resort ridiculed her for fishing "in the rain one night" when she might "have attended a ball." Treated as an "outcast," and considered "half demented," Porter maintained that she was "blasted with scorn." Such scorn was not new to her, and the confusion and pain she felt persisted over the years.

IN SEARCH OF WILDLIFE:
REPRESENTATIONS OF PORTER IN NATURE

In nature, however, Porter more freely transgressed gender norms. Nature was home, her private space where her new-fashioned muscularity was unfettered by traditional femininity. Away from the limelight, her friend Edward Curtis captured Porter in her "natural" state. Well known for his elegiac images of Native Americans, Curtis's image of Gene Stratton-Porter was nothing like the conventional portraits for which she had posed from time to time throughout her life. Curtis shot Porter not as the "lady," but as the field naturalist; not in a studio, but in the out-of-doors, surrounded by large rough-surfaced boulders. Her uncovered head rose clearly above the boulder just behind her. Her khaki shirt was unbuttoned right above her breasts; one hand held a trowel, and the other a leather satchel for collecting. Her left foot pointed beyond the main boulder and rested on another flat rock below, revealing the intricately laced army boot reaching all the way to her knee. Curtis made Porter an extension of nature itself, her khaki uniform and worn brown boots blending into the scenery of rocks, trees, and marsh grasses. At the same time, she was bigger than life itself; Curtis did not minimize Porter's physical stature, and she looked gigantic, looming above seemingly colossal rocks.

Intentionally or not, Curtis inverted what was then a new idiom in landscape photography. Landscape photographer Timothy O'Sullivan was famous for representing the mammoth dimensions of western land formations. And to dramatize the meteoric size of a rock, O'Sullivan often placed a few men in the scene to provide a sense of scale, Lilliputian-sized humans sitting in a crevice along the rock's immense surface. But in Curtis's image, the crisply photographed rock is what provides scale, revealing the superhuman dimensions of Gene Stratton-Porter. She, not the rock, was the force of nature, breaking normative gender roles, serving her own material desires and professional goals, mentally and physically formidable, rugged, and unpredictable.

CONCLUSION: THE NEED FOR ALTERNATIVE STORIES

In 1924, Gene Stratton-Porter made a permanent move to Los Angeles. During the same year, she made plans to build a mansion, choosing a site

Gene Stratton-Porter in California, photographed by Edward Curtis. (Courtesy Gene Stratton-Porter State Historic Site, Rome City, Indiana)

between two canyons near present-day Beverly Hills. Her future palace would cover approximately eleven thousand square feet; it would include twenty-two rooms, servants' quarters above a four-car garage, fish ponds, a greenhouse, a tennis court, and separate quarters designed for Charles. But she never occupied this Bel-Air estate. On December 6, 1924, she died when her chauffeured Lincoln collided with a speeding streetcar.

By paying close attention to the specific contexts of women's lives—linking internal psychodynamics with external conditions—it is possible to find new stories about the relation between nature and gender. Porter was unlike her urban counterparts, bourgeois women whose newly won leisure time afforded them opportunities to go birding and camping. Born into the lower stratum of society and raised in the Midwest, Porter consciously used her talent as a naturalist to escape rural poverty. Her story allows us to begin to test some assumptions about American women and their relationship to nature in the late Victorian period.

Porter was both a nature zealot and an ardent materialist. Her successful efforts in preserving wildlife in parts of northeastern Indiana eventually led her to Hollywood, where she oversaw the film adaptation of her globally admired nature novels. The fact that Porter's obsession with nature and its preservation coincided with her pursuit of the ultimate American dream must be understood in the context of gender and class. She assailed the American woman for trading in the muscular resilience of pioneer living for the physical and moral impotency resulting from the indoor life. Yet in idealizing rural living and the pioneer past as a preserve of whiteness and moral correctness, Porter revealed her staunch nativism, for she perceived no tension between her rejections of a gender hierarchy and her impassioned intolerance of others.

Porter also exemplified the efforts of many women who appropriated the hegemonic male view to enhance their power in a world in which "Woman" and "Man" defined each other through ever more heightened opposition characteristics and activities. She not only manipulated the boundaries that contained her, but she also created a number of possible selves in the interstices of cultural and social arrangements, proving the malleability of even the most rigid boundaries. Writing for *McCall's*, Porter inhabited the true lady ideal, and in her fiction she conflated "muscularity" with traditional "femininity" and conjured up the "Bird Woman." Tracking vultures in the Limberlost and, in turn, tracked by Edward Curtis's lens, she more fully occupied the identity of muscular femininity.

And when she cloaked herself in the costume of a cross-dressing woman who was neither delicate, shapely, or modest, she opened the way for other women and men to take the work of conservation seriously, whatever the sacrifice. Her preservation work—handed down from mother to daughter—was at once gendered, yet also influenced by the time period when other female crusaders organized to protect wildlife, waterways, and forests through a multitude of women's organizations. One wonders how many patches of restored wildflowers might be found throughout the country and ultimately attributed to the work of women who will never be known or recognized for their attunement to the needs of nature.

Finally, for Porter, nature was not "out there," disturbing the conventional dualism—nature/culture—to which Americans were so attached. Nature was in her home, not in a cage or a tank, but right on her stove, the chairs, anywhere a moth or guinea pig might find suitable. Her embrace of wildlife was grounded in childhood and blurred the boundaries between self and nature such that she created in her novel characters like the "Bird Woman" and the "Swamp Angel." Her evocations of nature were grounded in an intimacy with her subject and in acquired knowledge that inspired fifty million readers both to know and to love this world.

NOTES

1. Judith Reick Long, *Gene Stratton-Porter: Novelist and Naturalist* (Indianapolis: Indiana Historical Society, 1990), 1; Long located this tribute to Porter in Grant Overton, *American Nights Entertainment* (New York: D. Appleton, 1923), 287. For a thorough yet concise treatment of Porter's life and writings, see Bertrand F. Richards, *Gene Stratton-Porter* (Boston: Twayne , 1980); for an in-depth biographical portrait, consult Long, *Novelist and Naturalist*.

2. David G. MacLean, *Gene Stratton-Porter: A Bibliography and Collector's Guide* (Decatur, Ind.: Americana Books, 1976), vii. For a discussion of Porter's wide popularity, her "Best-Sellerism," see Richards, *Gene Stratton-Porter*, 122–27.

3. Richards, *Gene Stratton-Porter*, 35.

4. Historical essentialism, the belief that women were innately drawn to the preservation of life, including plant and animal life, explains how many Progressive Era women justified their presence and leveraged power in the political realm of conservation. Historians who have effectively outlined this connection between established gender norms and the moral mandate to preserve nature include Vera Norwood, *Made from This Earth: American Women and Nature* (Chapel Hill and London: University of North Carolina Press, 1993); Jennifer Price, "When Women Were Women, Men Were Men, and Birds Were Hats," in *Flight Maps: Adventures with Nature in Modern America* (New York: Basic Books, 1999); and Carolyn Merchant, "Women and Conservation," in *Major Problems in American Environmental History*, ed. Carolyn Merchant (Lexington, Mass.: D. C. Heath, 1993), 373–82.

5. Richards, *Gene Stratton-Porter*, 19–23.

6. Long, *Novelist and Naturalist*, 45–52.

7. Richards, *Gene Stratton-Porter*, 22–23; Long, *Novelist and Naturalist*, 76–77.

8. Long, *Novelist and Naturalist*, 103–6.

9. Richards, *Gene Stratton-Porter,* 25.

10. Ibid., 29–30.

11. Sydney Landon Plum, "Introduction," in *Coming through the Swamp: The Nature Writings of Gene Stratton-Porter,* ed. Sydney Landon Plum (Utah: University of Utah Press, 1996), xii; Long, *Novelist and Naturalist,* 138.

12. Long, *Novelist and Naturalist,* 197–207.

13. Gene Stratton-Porter, "My Life and My Books," *Ladies' Home Journal,* September 1916, 13, 80, 81. In 1916, Porter published this autobiographical account of her life in an effort to control how the public viewed her, as increasing fame brought increasing scrutiny of her personal life.

14. Richards, *Gene Stratton-Porter,* 20.

15. Stratton-Porter, "My Life and My Books," 13, 80, 81.

16. S. F. E. [attributed to both Eugene Francis Saxton and Samuel F. Ewart], *Gene Stratton-Porter: A Little Story of the Life and Work and Ideals of "The Bird Woman"* (Garden City, N.Y.: Doubleday, Page, 1915), 32–33.

17. Long, *Novelist and Naturalist,* 146–47.

18. Stratton-Porter, "My Life and My Books," 13, 80, 81.

19. S. F. E., *A Little Story,* 22.

20. Richards, *Gene Stratton-Porter,* 32.

21. MacLean, *A Bibliography,* 84.

22. Edward Bok, a great promoter of nature conservation, used his editorial position at *Ladies' Home Journal* to convey his ideas about city beautification and wilderness preservation, for example. See David E. Shi, *The Simple Life: Plain Living and High Thinking in American Culture* (New York: Oxford University Press, 1985), 181–85.

23. Long, *Novelist and Naturalist,* 183–84.

24. In *Land of Little Rain* (Boston: Houghton Mifflin, 1903), a contemplative rendering of the desert Southwest (replete with scientific nature study and amateur anthropology), Mary Austin also valorized vultures and other carrion eaters as noble creatures. She appreciated these birds that so apparently participated in the recycling of nature, exemplars of nature's ecology in the unforgiving desert landscape. That two women, Porter and Austin, chose to dignify a bird whose character traits—preying on the helpless or, to put it another way, taking advantage of the weak—directly opposed gender norms may indicate a desire of both to consciously subvert gendered expectations and convey a countervision of what constitutes beauty and grace. As to Austin's influence, Porter borrowed her words to describe her own faithful recording of the Indiana landscape in *Girl of the Limberlost:* "As Mary Austin expresses it, I know 'the procession of the year.'" See,"Why I Wrote the Girl of the Limberlost," *World's Work* (February 1910): 12546.

25. MacLean, *A Bibliography,* vii.

26. Long, *Novelist and Naturalist,* 189–90.

27. Porter explained that in the novel *Freckles* the young hero was to be martyred after a tree crushed the life out of him. This maudlin ending was rejected and provides more evidence of the ongoing and often difficult negotiations that transpired between writer and publisher; see "My Life and My Books," 13, 80, 81.

28. Richards, *Gene Stratton-Porter,* 39. In the earliest biography of Porter writ-

ten during her lifetime (S. F. E., *A Little Story*), the author explained that her experience working for *Recreation* and *Outing* emboldened her to "turn her attention to what Porter apparently called 'nature studies sugarcoated with fiction'" (p. 22).

29. Although the critics panned most of Porter's novels for doing little justice to the craft of writing as well as for creating absurd situations and dialogue, almost every reviewer commended her for the one thing she did unfailingly well—make accessible to her audience the wonders and particularities of the natural world. *Michael O'Halloran*, published in 1915, received blistering reviews from the literary world, including the *Athenaeum*, a London literary journal. Yet, the *Athenaeum* ultimately resuscitated the novel and declared, "When dealing with the glories of the swamp flora or the mysteries of bird-music, the author shows an undiminished power in that better direction." One reviewer of *At the Foot of the Rainbow* (1907) struck an identical chord, claiming that if the book "is worth reading at all [and let us give the author the benefit of the doubt]," it is so "because of the background of outdoor life, nature, and of the changing pageant of the seasons"; see MacLean, *A Bibliography*, 3.

30. Gene Stratton-Porter, *Freckles* (New York: Doubleday, Page, 1904), 78–85.

31. Ibid., 31.

32. Long, *Novelist and Naturalist*, 224.

33. Ibid., 243.

34. In 1900, the outdoor magazine *Recreation* published Porter's "A New Experience in Millinery," an article that expressed outrage at the slaughtering of birds to furnish plumes and other winged finery for ladies' hats. While other women mobilized around this issue and launched group actions through Audubon Societies and Women's Clubs, Porter remained a maverick and demonstrated her opposition by buying a hat from a milliner and publicly destroying it with a pair of scissors in front of a stunned gathering; see Long, *Novelist and Naturalist*, 148. Also, with respect to this article, one biographer noted that in addition to nature study pieces, Porter wrote essays that had a "strong conservation intent" (Richards, *Gene Stratton-Porter*, 32).

35. Stratton-Porter, "My Life and My Books," 13, 80, 81.

36. Gene Stratton-Porter, "Gene Stratton-Porter Calls on Our Government to Curb Indecent Literature," *McCall's*, July 1922, 1, 18.

37. Stratton-Porter, "My Life and My Books," 13, 80, 81.

38. Ibid.

39. Gene Stratton-Porter, "A New Day in Pictures," *McCall's*, February 1923, 2.

40. Long, *Novelist and Naturalist*, 229.

41. MacLean, *A Bibliography*, 80–83.

42. Stratton-Porter, "My Life and My Books," 13, 80, 81.

CHAPTER ELEVEN

Nature's Lovers: The Erotics of Lesbian Land Communities in Oregon, 1974–1984

Catherine Kleiner

In August 1998, at We'Moon Women's Land in Estacada, Oregon, nearly forty women sat in a circle in the woods around a campfire. Celebrants had just finished with a potluck dinner prepared in the outdoor kitchen.[1] One woman announced that they were celebrating Lammas, the neopagan fall celebration of harvest, of particular interest to the many organic farmers attending the twenty-fifth anniversary of We'Moon Women's Land.[2] Gini, an African-American grandmother and mother of six grown children, danced rhythmically in the center of the circle to the improvised chanting and drumming of the women. Earlier, she had told the group that she was the reincarnation of an African goddess. They chanted:

> Gini, crossing over the water
> Come, come, sisterhood
> Leading the women across the wood
> Our love is mystical
> Our love is carnal
> We'll dance nimble,
> We'll be like Miriam
> Leading the women across the water
> Only Hecate, my mother, knows for sure
> Only Hecate, night rider, knows for sure
> By the new moon—by the half moon—by the full moon,
> Only Hecate, my mother, knows for sure.[3]

Gini's fire dance and contemporary rituals of feminist spirituality developed since the early seventies are legacies of the lesbian back-to-the-land movement, a national movement that began in California in the late 1960s.[4] Oregon was home to nine lesbian back-to-the-land collectives founded in the early 1970s.

An extended community of women experimenting with new forms of feminist spirituality and subsistence living incorporated nature worship with a commitment to living ecologically responsible lifestyles. Jean Mountaingrove, a longtime resident of lesbian land in Oregon, wrote, "We are organically grown. . . . if a woman decides she fits, she just keeps coming to the many open events. We welcome visitors, travelers, friends, and new settlers."[5] Lesbians living on land collectives in Oregon developed a "spirit politics" linking lesbian sexuality, lesbian feminist politics, feminist spiritual ritual, and nature as sites and subjects of their spiritual consciousness.

Land lesbian determination to live in a separatist lesbian world and to divest themselves of modern conveniences inspired a new kind of feminism and environmental politics, building on established ideas about women's distinctiveness, moral superiority, and a long-standing tradition of valuing a "female world of love and ritual."[6] Land lesbians gendered nature as a woman, becoming nature's lovers (both figuratively and literally) and moving beyond both deep ecology or ecofeminism. Their spiritual and sexual apprehension of nature was played out self-consciously in daily practical activities like composting, organic gardening, living "off the grid," and holding spiritual rituals celebrating their love for women and "mother earth."

Much of the lesbian nature writing from the seventies, published chiefy in *Womansprit* magazine, reflects a gynothromorphic sensibility. Nature is a woman, a gentle nurturer who needs protection and love that will be reciprocated in kind if she is treated with respect and love. The relationship between land lesbians and nature mirrors that of nurturer and nurtured, mother and child, and compassionate lover. This literature, like the chant at We'Moon land (see above), articulates the erotics of land lesbian spirit politics. Caring for the land is making love with a receptive woman. Spirit politics was a creative force, inspiring women to write about living close to the land without modern conveniences.

Like some other political radicals, by the 1970s lesbian feminists turned their attention to living their "personal" politics in countercultural experiments.[7] Nineteen seventy marked the beginning of the decade of the lesbian feminist. The new breed of political radical claimed that lesbians (women whose primary emotional and erotic attachments were to other women) were model feminists whose lives represented the ultimate in women's autonomy and power. Lesbian feminists believed that all women were potential lesbians and that lesbianism was primarily a political, not a sexual, choice.[8]

Most lesbian feminists came to political consciousness through urban-based political movements, such as the civil rights movement, the antiwar struggle, and women's liberation. Some women who adopted the lesbian feminist label had once identified as heterosexuals but chose lesbianism as the logical extension of their radical feminist politics. Other lifelong lesbians who became lesbian feminists never considered their sexual identity a choice but saw potential for lesbian empowerment in lesbian feminist politics.[9]

Among other political projects, lesbian feminists committed themselves to creating and sustaining separatist women's culture.[10] They argued that women and men share different values, whether as a result of inherent biological differences or socialization. Lesbian feminists argued that there are essential differences between the sexes and that men and women have separate values. Lesbians purported "women's" values such as nurturance, pacifism, egalitarianism, and cooperation rather than "men's" values of individualism, competition, and violence.[11] To create women's culture, lesbian feminists maintained that women had to separate themselves from men physically, emotionally, and sexually.

Land lesbians asserted women's sacred connection to nature, a contention they embraced as a central part of their spiritual beliefs.[12] Such beliefs are best described as "spirit politics," because land lesbians saw politics, spirituality, and sexuality as inextricably intertwined. In land lesbian culture, politics was religion, and religion was politics. Lesbian sexuality was a political *choice* expressed by making love exclusively with women. Going "back to the land" to create a separatist lesbian culture was also a political choice. Working and living close to nature was an expression of both ecopolitics and lesbian feminist sexuality. Both of these choices were predicated on the rejection of the patriarchal world, or the world that they believed men created. The difference between land lesbians and other deep ecologists is that they specifically blamed men and "patriarchal culture" for the violence and environmental degradation plaguing the planet.[13]

One of land lesbians' central beliefs was that nature had the power to unite women as women, providing an identity-based politics that encouraged them to minimize their differences and cooperate in the mutual enterprise of cultivating and caring for the earth. Land lesbians believed they could survive conflict with one another by making the land the main focus in their lives. As longtime land lesbian Bethroot Gwynn advised,

> Give a lot of attention to the land itself, the physical surroundings—befriend the land, and let it befriend you, so that no matter what goes on between you and other women, there's always . . . relating with the land. . . . I can endure almost any heartache such as a breakup because I am held by the land, and in time . . . the land will touch my pain, whatever it is.[14]

Land lesbians viewed nature as alive and knowable to women in a gynocentric and spiritual sense rather than from a distant and purely scientific standpoint. Land lesbians viewed the earth as a woman, and cultivating her soil to make her fertile and productive was an act of love for a woman.[15] The decision to move to the country to live and work with other women was initially a political decision, but it evolved into something much deeper: an immanent and sacred reverence for nature and women.

In the 1970s, Oregon was home to nine lesbian separatist collectives, ranging in size from three to thirty permanent residents. Eight of the nine early collectives were in southern Oregon. Still, the thirty-year history of lesbian land in the region is well known among lesbian baby boomers, even in urban areas, who came out as lesbians in the sixties and seventies. Women who read national lesbian publications today, like *Maize* and *Lesbian Connection,* will still come across articles and references to lesbian land. The definition of lesbian land has changed over the years, and it varies from woman to woman, but most lesbian feminists will agree that what lesbian lands share is a historical connection to the counterculture and radical political movements of the sixties and seventies.[16]

Of the nine early collectives, only three left in Oregon still function as intentional communities, housing three or more permanent residents. Although the number of lesbian lands is dwindling, their influence continues through articles in *Maize.* Residents still engage in group decision-making regarding how each land will be collectively managed. Most remaining lesbian lands host lesbian community functions and open their land to seasonal women travelers. Sometimes lands are held in trust as nonprofit corporations administered by a board of directors from the extended lesbian land community. Caretakers who live on the land are expected to abide by the rules of the trust's charter, attend open meetings, and oversee the upkeep of the land. These tiny enclaves continue to influence lesbian politics and culture.

Lesbian lands keep the cooperative tradition alive in the collective memory of lesbians. Most of those still living on self-designated lesbian land are engaged in the ongoing pursuit of potential permanent residents and still view collective living as an ideal to achieve. An organization called Lesbian Natural Resources (LNR) publishes national lists of lands looking for residents. They also provide grants to lesbians who want to start new lands or improve old ones. There is no documentation about the exact number of collectives functioning since the early 1970s, but Shewolf's *Directory of Wimmin's Lands* lists over sixty in the United States and Canada today. There is no comparable list of defunct communities, but records at the Knight Library at the University of Oregon document their history. Currently and for the past three decades, lesbian lands have hosted lesbian feminist spiritual gatherings and celebrations, advertised in national publications and in women's centers and bookstores. As a result of this publicity, Oregon remains an internationally known spiritual center for lesbians.[17]

Many lesbians moved to Oregon because of the distinctive spiritual/political culture and community that developed there over the last three decades. Land-based "community" once meant individual intentional communities, but the definition of "land community" grew to include residents in nearby towns and cities who visited lesbian lands as well as former members of land collectives who returned for seasonal celebrations and events.[18] Very quickly after the founding of the original collectives, any woman who went to celebrations, participated in community rituals, joined local lesbian organizations, and claimed to be a part of Oregon's lesbian land community was considered a member. Over the years, lesbian renters and private landowners who moved to the area to be a part of the culture also hosted spiritual rituals modeled on those of the original intentional communities of the 1970s.

Much like first wave feminists touting women's moral superiority in the nineteenth century, land lesbians and other cultural feminists emphasized women's difference from men and their "natural" superiority.[19] Women's culture in the twentieth century would be superior to patriarchal culture, they claimed, because of women's "natural" values of compassion, connection, and cooperation. Unlike radical feminists, cultural feminists believed that patriarchy, a mode of production and reproduction including but not limited to capitalism, had caused women's alienation from their "true selves" as powerful women. Cultural feminists invented a mythic women's spiritual tradition that envisioned a "golden age" of women's history when matriarchies dominated the political/cultural landscape.

Some scholars have criticized land lesbians for this cultural invention, and many doubt the existence of evidence supporting the myth. But the sapphic songs harking back to ancient Greece reflect more about rural lesbian culture and history today and the desire for cultural authority to shape their own identity and culture than they invoke an actual history. Goddess worship rituals are symbolic expressions of women's power, whether or not they are true.[20] Feminist spirituality is an amalgam of sometimes competing spiritual views that had direct ties to women's liberation and other radical political movements and to emerging New Age and human potential ideas and practices.

Land lesbian feminist spirituality provided the spiritual/political base from which to build the new lesbian feminist counterculture. Lesbian spiritual feminists believed they were building a new women's religion from the ground up—an invented tradition created by women, for women. Out of the ruins of this invented, mythic matriarchal golden age, lesbian feminists melded "ancient matriarchal traditions" with new ideas about women's power and potential.[21]

For land lesbians in Oregon, as in other regions of the country, coming to feminist spirituality was a gradual process. Land lesbians are the legacy of a long tradition of women questioning male supremacy in organized religion, as far back as Christine de Pisan in the fourteenth century and Elizabeth Cady Stanton in the nineteenth century. Women in 1960s and 1970s feminist consciousness-raising groups blamed Judeo-Christianity as a source of women's oppression and expressed interest in creating a new religion for women.[22] For land lesbians in Oregon, the unique women's spirituality that grew there was a continuation of the consciousness-raising process that began in the women's liberation movement and an outgrowth of the New Age spirituality movement.

Points of contest emerged among feminist spiritualists when various spiritual groups struggled for cultural authority to define the shape and direction of the feminist spirituality movement. Heated debates over what was politically acceptable spiritual practice for feminists divided the movement. Feminist spiritualists in the seventies and eighties can be divided into five general categories with considerable overlap between the groups: neopagans, goddess-worshippers, neo-Wiccans (women calling themselves modern-day witches), white Native American emulators, and cultural feminists building separatist culture. Lesbian feminists living in separatist communities in Oregon were closest in practice to the neopagans, but they also combined goddess spirituality with reverence for nature.

Radio journalist and author Margot Adler is the best-known feminist neopagan, whose book *Drawing Down the Moon: Witches, Druids, Goddess-Worshippers, and Other Pagans in America Today* introduced neopaganism (a religion based in nature worship) to broad audiences of both men and women. Adler described neopaganism as an anarchistic earth-centered religion with a wide variety of beliefs and spiritual practices, but she came up with a general set of basic beliefs:

> The world is holy. Nature is holy. The body is holy. Sexuality is holy. The mind is holy. The imagination is holy. A spiritual path that is not stagnant ultimately leads one to the understanding of one's own divine nature. Thou art Goddess. Thou art God. Divinity is imminent in all nature. It is as much within you as without. Neopagans may differ in regard to tradition, concept of deity, and ritual forms. But all view the earth as the Great Mother who has been raped, pillaged, and plundered, who must once again be exalted if we are to survive.[23]

Land lesbians in Oregon read Adler's book but criticized the equal attention she gave to neopagans of both sexes, claiming that an authentic feminist would focus on women only.[24]

The leader of the neo-Wiccan resurgence was Z. Budapest, a Hungarian immigrant who came to the United States in the sixties, founding the Susan B. Anthony coven in Los Angeles in 1971. Her book, *The Feminist Book of Lights and Shadows,* was a guide to Dianic witchcraft that inspired hundreds of imitators in cities across the country. Dianic witches were separatists who devoted themselves to goddess worship—the Greek goddess Diana, in particular.[25] The early coven's manifesto stated the following: "We believe [that] in order to fight and win a revolution that will stretch for generations into the future, we must find reliable ways to replenish our energies. We believe that without a secure grounding in womon's [sic] spiritual strength there will be no victory for us. . . . politics and religion are inter-dependent."[26] Land lesbians in Oregon adopted some of the rhetoric and practices of Dianic witchcraft, claiming to be performing "magic" in their ritual circles, but they rarely called themselves witches. Land lesbians objected to the hierarchies implicit in titles like "Grand Priestess" among practitioners of Wicca.[27]

Native American religion was the most popular source for religious appropriation among New Age spiritualists and some land lesbians. In land lesbian rituals, it was just as common to find feminist renderings of Native American spiritual practice as it was to find Wiccan or neopagan practice.[28] Women on lesbian land passed a rattle in ritual circles, adopted "spirit names" connected to nature, and in the early days used hallucinogenic drugs like peyote, mescaline, and LSD to bring "visions" in all-night spiritual circles. A few women on lesbian land, particularly in the Southwest, who had also lived on lesbian land in Oregon in the seventies participated (with Native American sponsorship) in the Native American Church, attended native peyote meetings, and brought some of the rituals to lesbian spiritual circles. [29]

Lynn Andrews, a key figure in the eighties New Age spirituality movement, claimed women had natural spiritual connections to Native American cultures and wrote many books on this supposed "relationship." Women on lesbian land, however, considered Andrews an apolitical opportunist pursuing her alternative spiritual course for the purposes of selling self-help books and making money, not helping women. Andrews was widely popular among New Age spiritualists (both men and women), who claimed she was a modern-day shaman. Her agenda was not explicitly feminist (or lesbian), but she claimed she was drawn to Native American spirituality because of the supposed central position of women in Native American culture. Andrews claimed to have Native American spiritual guides who anointed her a spiritual messenger among non-Indians. But it is never quite clear which Indians had made her their supposed messenger. She seemed unaware of cultural diversity among native people or the fact that the position of women varied from tribe to tribe.[30]

Academic feminists like Mary Daly and Charlene Spretnak explored feminist theology and wrote books and lectured on the topic, lending scholarly credence to land lesbians' way of life and spiritual views, but they never wrote specifically about lesbian land. None of these authors suggested going out to found lesbian separatist land, but lesbian separatists were encouraged and heartened by the books. They read and discussed Mary Daly's *Beyond God the Father* (1973) and Rosemary Radford Ruether's *New Woman/New Earth: Sexist Ideologies and Human Liberation* (1975). Merlin Stone's *When God Was a Woman* (1976) and Starhawk's *Dreaming the Dark: Magic, Sex, and Politics* (1982) targeted popular audiences but contributed significantly to the development of new forms of spiritual/political practice.[31]

Feminist spirituality in Oregon reached its peak in the seventies with the publication of *Womanspirit* magazine, the first national periodical devoted to feminist spirituality. Conditions of production reflected the editors' determination to live outside patriarchal power networks, "off the grid" from the morally bankrupt and oppressive American capitalist system. Remarkably, coeditors Ruth and Jean Mountaingrove and the women they recruited to help produce the magazine did so in an unfinished barn with no electricity, using marine batteries to power their typewriters. They eventually got electricity from solar panels. Jean argued that by publishing a quarterly magazine under difficult circumstances, women would realize that they could accomplish anything they put their minds to.[32] She described the magazine as a "down home" publication with a loose editorial policy and no "lofty aesthetic standards."[33]

In an article entitled "Why Womanspirit" in *Womanspirit*'s first issue, the editors articulated their purpose: "As we continue to tear down the institutions and relationships that oppress us, we are also building, making, creating. Because this process of taking and leaving, making a new culture, is so deep, so profound, and all inclusive, we are calling it spiritual. The sharing and caring in that process is the reason for this magazine."[34] The magazine documented the development and meteoric rise in popularity of feminist spirituality from 1974–1984.[35] Local lesbians in Oregon were the first contributors to the magazine, but the Mountaingroves recruited feminist spiritual luminaries like Merlin Stone, Mary Daly, Z. Budapest, and Starhawk to contribute as well.[36] Over time, the residents of rural lesbian land communities and like-minded lesbians in small towns in southern Oregon (and in other parts of the country) developed a shared value system that shaped the extended community of feminist spiritualists. The key ingredients of Oregon's regional variety of feminist spirituality were feminism, feminist neopaganism, lesbianism, separatism, and a deep reverence for nature.[37]

Individual lands differed from one another in spiritual practice, but the ritual practice most often used to honor Mother Earth, "her" change of seasons, and all women was the circle, a form modeled after the first consciousness-raising groups but later attributed to feminist reconfigurations of Native American and prehistoric European traditions. Women sat in a circle with a facilitator known as a "road woman" (a title borrowed from Native American spiritual practice), who opened and closed the circle. Women took turns passing a rattle and "sharing." As in consciousness-raising groups, the woman speaking could expect to have the full attention of all members of the circle. The road woman communicated the rules of the circle at the start of the ritual. Women could not interrupt one another, and they could not leave the ritual until the road woman released them after every woman had spoken. If a woman chose not to speak, the other women honored her decision. As each woman took a turn offering prayers expressing her hopes, thanksgiving, or distresses, she was said to be "channeling the goddess." For most of these women, the goddess was not a transcendent being, but the collective strength and support of the women in the circle.

Typically, women in the circle expressed themselves in some form other than talking, giving voice to a "spontaneous heartsong." This expression might include singing, chanting, drumming, or dancing, and everyone was invited to join her, intensifying the power of her "spiritual work." In early circles on lesbian lands in Oregon, women used marijuana, peyote, or other "medicine" as part of their ritual, a practice land lesbians brought from heterosexual communes and also from women visiting from lesbian lands in the Southwest.[38] Land lesbians held spiritual circles on each of the pagan holidays, including the summer and winter solstices, Candlemas (February), Hallowmas (October), Beltane (May), and Lammas (August). Land lesbians were drawn to neopagan holidays because of their historical association with animism and nature worship.

Bethroot Gwynn and her land partner, Hawk Madrone, are twenty-six-year veterans of lesbian land called Fly Away Home, an important lesbian spiritual center in Myrtle Creek, near Grants Pass, Oregon. Gwynn and Madrone, who had been radical political activists in Portland, devoted their lives to building women's culture on their separatist land and in the larger lesbian community. Gwynn came to southern Oregon because of *Womanspirit*. She knew from reading the magazine that Oregon was home to an extended community of women experimenting with new forms of feminist spirituality and subsistence living, incorporating nature worship and a commitment to ecologically responsible lifestyles.

Madrone and Gwynn are the only two permanent residents currently living at Fly Away Home. They are land partners who were at one time a couple but now occupy separate residences on the land. The women see themselves as "temple-keepers for the lesbian community," hosting spiritual celebrations on pagan holidays and performing ceremonies (funerals and "croning ceremonies," for example) for women who seek them out. Gwynn explained that "the kind of spirituality that we do here [in southern Oregon] that involves circles and singing is what compelled me to move to lesbian land and become a part of this culture." She explained that the reasons she moved to southern Oregon were that "I wanted to live closer to the magic of the natural world—and I wanted to grow food. . . . my passion was [also] about being able to create spiritual practice."[39] Madrone agreed that agriculture on lesbian land was both spiritual and political: "Now [living] closer to the earth, planting the seeds is political. Growing food is political."[40]

Land lesbians in Oregon expressed their spirit politics through a variety of creative channels. The songs they wrote and performed in ritual circles, the writing and artwork they shared with each other in art groups and writers groups, and the constructed landscape of individual lands reflected the spirit politics of land lesbians. The chant of the women at the We'Moon celebration, recounted at the opening of this chapter, is a prime example of the spontaneous creative expression of land lesbian spirit politics. What started as a rhythmic chant evolved into melodious song, complete with spontaneous harmonies. The song celebrated women's love for one another, love that circle participants characterized as both mystical and carnal. References to an all-knowing goddess-mother (in this case, Hecate) and "her" natural cycles of the moon express reverence for nature. Songs were an elemental part of land lesbian spiritual practice, and the recurrent themes of lesbian love, reverence for nature, women's unique powers, and self-sufficiency imbued lesbian songs and rituals with meaning. Land lesbians collected spiritual songs in songbooks and sometimes recorded them on tape.[41]

"She Changes" was (and still is) a song frequently performed at circle rituals and celebrations on lesbian lands.

She Changes

She changes everything she touches
And everything she touches changes
All that is gone comes around again
In a new time, in a new way.
We are changers and everything we touch can
Change us—touch us—change us—touch us—change us.[42]

If the circle symbolized the egalitarian connection between women, such songs imagine women's agency not so much in changing the wider world, but in dynamic interaction with each other and the lesbian culture of which they are a part.

A Womon's Voice

A womon's voice raised up in the silence can
Be heard a long way
A womon's voice raised up in the silence can
Be heard a long way
We don't need electricity to make our musical sounds
We just sit and sing in a circle
Passing the rattle around

Chorus: Revolution starts in a circle raising up from the ground
We believe in the power of wimmin to turn this world around

Firelight and moonlight shining in our eyes
Each one is special
Everyone is singing
Can't you hear the harmonies ringing
Women arise.[43]

An important component of land lesbian spirit politics was living sustainable, earth-friendly lives without electricity or other amenities—a source of pride and a mark of authenticity for land lesbians. Living one's spirit politics, while not always a cultural imperative, earned women respect in the extended community. Some lands had electricity and hot running water, like Womanshare and Rainbow's End, but in the early days, such luxuries were few and far between because most lands could not afford them. But many women chose to live simply because, as Ruth Mountaingrove put it, they were just more into "hairshirtedness" than others.[44]

Creative and expository writing shared at monthly meetings of the Southern Oregon Women's Writers group revealed more of the spirit politics of community residents in southern Oregon. In "Hawkwoman," a poem by Bethroot Gwynn, she remembers a happy time in 1975, when she and Madrone were lovers. Gwynn put sexuality at the heart of her mix of ingredients of the spirit politics of lesbian land:

Hawkwoman

Hawkwoman,
Last year today
Four of us came
With candles and karma
To haunt my new house
To hover round its spirits
To sign them gently but clear,
We are going to be here now.

We wise women
We cast our shadows into the shade
Mixed our shade with the shades already here.
Lest I be ambushed by the household spooks.

But I was
And so were you
The Eros Spook got us.
Boo!
Oh, oh Boo, and oh how the cave of your mouth kept on deeper
        and oh what an avid spelunker I was and oh
        finally what joy to be cavern again, probed and
        gentled in the hollows of my hollows

Hallowed, hallowed be.
We made hallow hallow . . .[45]

But Nature could also be a woman lover. In Equinox, a 1976 poem also by Gwynn, the poet engages nature as both mother and lover.

Equinox

Sitting in the oval meadow
I am the blue iris of a perfect eye
Black-capped, a pupil: I see and learn
Every growing thing is she
Watching her forlorn, blue, learning child.

The sun loves me
She kisses my neck,
My face
I smile at her.
This morning I wrapped myself
Around her round, flaming
I hugged her tight
Rubbed her burning with my breasts
Pushed my belly into her hot
Spread her fire between my legs
And thrust and thrust
For Glory.[46]

The poem reflects an explicitly sexual relationship with nature under-stood as female. Nature is mother and/or sexual partner—the two roles are not mutually exclusive or diametrically opposed.

    Hawk Madrone explores a similar theme in *Weeding at Dawn: A Les-*

bian Country Life.[47] The book is a Waldenesque ode to nature, with a lesbian twist—nature is female, and the author finds evidence of nature's womanhood in every tree, animal species, and mountain.[48] On a camping trip to a place called Squaw Mountain in the Cascades, Madrone saw the mountain as beckoning woman:

> I sat cross-legged on a large stump to meditate. Open-eyed, gazing at the white cliff, I smiled to discover the juxtaposition of the curved lines of the cliff, and the narrow road ending in front of it, formed gigantic eyes. There was a woman there, her left eye closed, winking at me. A very playful, trickster goddess, who had obviously been watching me since I arrived.[49]

Madrone cast her relationship with the beckoning woman as explicitly sexual. In the following passage she makes passionate love with nature:

> I decided to drive over to the cliff, to stroke the face of the winking goddess before I left. I was glad I did, for the view east from there was a grand expanse of ridges many miles away, with four mountaintops with ridges of snow. I sat bare-chested on a log in the hot sun, my spirit fed by the enormity of the scene. . . . Rhododendrons bloomed behind me, some of the flowers perfectly framed by the rock wall. So much beauty, and so liberally given, love lavished upon me by everything I saw. . . . I lay back on the log and, impassioned by the pink blooms, the sky, the birds, the mountains, I stroked myself to a singing orgasm.

    Madrone's relationship with nature is infused with romantic love and erotic passion, but the relationship she expresses is intensely personal. Her orgasm is a gift to herself, but she writes about it for other women and as a thanksgiving prayer to the female natural world she holds sacred. Land lesbians created rituals that reflected their profound reverence for nature and "mother earth." Madrone's sexual encounter in the woods was one such ritual.[50]

    Land lesbian spirit politics included living ecologically responsible lifestyles. Many women lived off the grid, using solar panels and kerosene lamps to light their cabins. Recycling was not simply an option for land lesbians, it was a requirement for "authentic" living. Lesbians practiced organic gardening, and their gardens and compost piles were shrines dedicated to the natural world. Kay Turner, a folklorist who wrote a book on women's altars, interviewed Jean Mountaingrove and Madrone. Mountaingrove claimed that her compost heap was her altar dedicated to Hecate, whom she contended was the goddess of decay, inviting the new to grow from the disintegration of the old:

My own altars are mostly made by nature rather than by human hands. . . . I love the vitality in nature, her sacred wildness. Yes, all the earth is a sacred altar bearing the mysterious and incomprehensible gift of life. By making altars here, I create more and more reminders of that sacred reality. When we mark a place as sacred and keep responding to it reverently, we are reminding ourselves that the earth is sacred, and that we, too are sacred beings. . . . and if we assemble a crate, a cloth, a candle, and a stone, we are setting up a miniature of the earth . . . to remind us of that deeper knowing that *all* of the earth is sacred.[51]

Turner's interview prompted Madrone to reflect on the meaning of the sacred in her life and to decide that altar should be a verb—altaring is was what she had done every day of her life since moving to lesbian land in 1976. The mystical and the mundane mingled in those altars. The altar in Madrone's home consisted of

a round piece of plywood covered by a large doily made by Beth-root's great aunt, and objects I am intimate with: rocks and crystals, locks of hair from each of the animal companions buried in the flower garden, a rattle made from a stick and large round seed pods—given to me by a dear friend—a bundle of sage from eastern Oregon, a pebble left a few years ago by my mother with whom I have a sometimes strained relationship. . . . I don't relate to these objects in a hocus-pocus way, don't imbue them with a magic any greater, or less than the magic of the seasons, of growth, death, and return.[52]

After musing for a while on what she considered sacred when she walked through the gardens and the orchard on the land she and Gwynn own, Madrone came to the realization that her altar was the earth itself. "Whether my heart sings in the area enclosed by rafter-holding posts, or the garden fence, or the ridge caressing sky, or the expanding boundaries of my philosophy, I am held and defined by concentric circles of altaring,"[53]

Environmentalist living was another way to love Mother Earth. Composting and recycling had spiritual significance for land lesbians who supplemented their diets with fresh produce harvested from their organic gardens. Composting was all-important for such production, even composted human waste. Residents used the plastic-covered two-seated "shitter" at Rootworks to collect compost. The garden plans from the land collective OWL reflect a vegetarian diet rich in iron (kale, spinach, and Swiss chard) and the use of herbs for medicinal purposes. The garden was divided into "realms" that separated vegetables from flowerbeds and herbs from vegetables. A large section was devoted to indigenous plants, called "where the wild things are" on the plans.

The Mountaingroves and other land lesbians religiously preserved and recycled gray water from dishes and the drainage from the solar-heated shower to water the garden. The contents of the outhouse at the Womanshare collective were also composted, and the same was true for other collectives in Oregon in the midseventies through the mideighties and up to the present day. In the early 1970s when many lands had animals like goats and chickens, the refuse collected from their pens was also added to the compost for the gardens.

Catherine Albanese, in *Nature Religions in America: From the Algonkian Indians to the New Age*, documents various nature-based traditions in American history, from the colonial period to the present day. Albanese includes nineteenth-century transcendentalists like Emerson and Thoreau, late-twentieth-century New Age "seekers" who adhere to reconstructed forms of indigenous spirituality, goddess worshippers, deep ecologists, and others inventing a "sustainable religion" as all of the same trajectory of Americans who believe nature is sacred.[54] Deep ecologists, like land lesbians, believe in the interconnectedness among all living things and repudiate human dominance over nature. Land lesbians have never been immune to earth domination—even while living lightly on the land, they still altered (or altared, in Madrone's words) the natural landscape when they planted their gardens, diverted springs to ensure reliable water supplies, or built woman-made structures on land they owned (albeit collectively). One could deduce that they think sustainable transformation is in harmony with Mother Earth.

In addition to earth worship, land lesbians created rituals to honor women's bodies and women's sexuality. In "Three Celebrations," an article in *Womanspirit* from 1977, Myra Quadrangle, a feminist spiritualist, encouraged women to hold sacred ceremonies commemorating the physical developmental stages in a woman's life. The first stage is defined as the menarche, or the first day of a woman's menstrual cycle. Judith Laura, publishing in *Womanspirit* in 1978, calls for a public ceremony, where the young woman dresses in red, to mark the occasion. She also suggests a celebration of the first self-proclaimed orgasm and menopause, complete with prayers to the "Great Mother." She suggests a prayer for the occasions:

> Praised be Our Great Mother who has this day brought me to know my fullness.
> Praised be Our Great Mother who has placed within me the rhythm of life.
> Praised be Our Great Mother who has made me in her image.[55]

In "Bless My Breasts," land lesbian "Mint" wrote about reclaiming her breasts as a symbol of her power and a marker of her sanctity as a woman: "Bless my bountiful, beautiful breasts. . . . I am my own Mama, my own lover, a caresser of breasts, and a lover of women with bosoms of all sizes and descriptions. O how I love to play upon and lay upon a woman's breasts, so safe a place to rest."[56] Like Madrone's expression of mountaintop orgasm, Mint's sexuality is portrayed as both spiritual and political and presumably "safe" because the sex she describes is with a woman, often the lesbian herself. Many land lesbians had suffered sexual abuse by men and viewed all men as potential sex offenders. Women at OWL Farm started an incest and rape survivors self-help group in the eighties.[57] They romanticized lesbian sex, just as they romanticized nature.

Land lesbian spirituality was a nature religion, but land lesbians would have resisted such a classification. To call it a religion might imply a formal system of beliefs to which all land lesbians subscribe. Most land lesbian spiritualists believed that there were multiple spiritual "truths"—that there were as many truths as there were women in a community of spiritualists. Various lands in Oregon developed their own traditions. Still, orthodoxies developed. Women who did not feel comfortable with the developing spiritual traditions associated with individual lands self-selected themselves out of participation in spiritual events. For example, in the seventies, when Fly Away Home began hosting all-day events and occasional all-night circles using drugs as "medicine," many women stopped coming, claiming they were getting too old to stay up all night or they had work commitments that precluded this kind of activity.[58] Furthermore, in the eighties, many land lesbians joined twelve-step recovery programs to overcome drug and alcohol addictions. Most lands and all national lesbian gatherings such as the Michigan Women's Festival are "clean and sober" places and events. Self-help philosophy became orthodoxy on many lesbian lands.

Noelle Sturgeon and more recently Catriona Sandilands have argued that ecofeminism must be understood as a distinct political movement that has various, often competing and contentious political (and spiritual) strands.[59] Some ecofeminists claim that women have a special connection to nature rooted in their reproductive capabilities, an "ethic of caring" that they "naturally" embrace as mothers (or potential mothers). Others (building on Carol Gilligan's work from the early eighties) argued that women inhabit a different culture than men, one that is based in caring and connection, not competition and domination.[60] Ecofeminists generally agree that the same forces of exploitation that oppress women also destroy the environment.[61] They subscribe to the basic tenets of deep ecology but add a further feminist critique of Western culture, arguing that the mainstream environmental movement is androcentric and male-dominated.[62]

Lesbians living on land collectives did not call themselves ecofeminists in the seventies, and few, if any, use the term to describe themselves now. Land lesbians associate ecofeminism with "overly intellectualized" academic theorists who know little about real women in land communities.[63] Land lesbians Jean Mountaingrove and Hawk Madrone resist the ecofeminist label because it fails to adequately emphasize the deep personal connections with nature that individual women found in community with other lesbians. The term also implies affiliation with political movements like the environmental movement that are conventionally political (involving direct action alongside men) rather than focusing on building separatist women's culture. Although some land lesbians in Oregon joined environmental actions, for the most part land lesbian political activism took the form of living and worshiping in close concert with their natural surroundings.

The lesbian land movement, like the counterculture homesteading movement during the seventies, is a tradition kept alive by a few aging but enthusiastic people who believe deeply in the possibility of living their ideals. Land lesbians longed for a resurgence of "new blood" on lesbian lands in Oregon to keep the culture alive. Although their numbers were small, they cast a larger shadow extending across the country in urban as well as rural areas. Land lesbian nature loving created a context and language for ecofeminism, feminist spirituality, and other continuing spiritual movements. What would it mean if we all, following land lesbians' lead, became nature's lovers and took care of nature as gentle nurturers and protectors?

NOTES

1. The deliberate misspellings of words that refer to men were common in cultural feminist writings and were attempts to reconfigure words seen as oppressive. Woman could become "womon" or "wombmoon," hero was often changed to "hera," and history might become "herstory."

2. We'Moon Women's Land is a working intentional women's community in Estacada, Oregon. It has been in operation since 1973 when a woman who calls herself Mu'sawa and her sister purchased fifty-two acres in the foothills of the Cascade Mountains. In the early days, the community was called Who Farm but changed its name in the late eighties when residents founded Mother Tongue Ink and began publishing the popular We'moon calendar, an astrological daily calendar and datebook for women. The We'Moon calendar is distributed in bookstores across the country. We'Moon is currently home to five full-time residents.

3. In Greek mythology, Hecate was a fertility goddess identified with

Persephone, queen of Hades and a protector of witches; taken from the personal journal of the author on the occasion of the twenty-fifth anniversary of We'Moon Women's Land, August 2, 1998.

4. Cynthia Eller, *Living in the Lap of the Goddess: The Feminist Spirituality Movement in America* (New York: Crossroad Press, 1993); Carol P. Christ, *Rebirth of the Goddess: Finding Meaning in Feminist Spirituality* (New York: Routledge, 1997); Charlene Spretnak, ed., *The Politics of Women's Spirituality: Essays on the Rise of Women's Spiritual Power within the Feminist Movement* (New York: Doubleday, 1985); Margot Adler, *Drawing Down the Moon: Witches, Druids, Goddess-Worshippers, and Other Pagans in America Today* (New York: Penguin, 1986), 176–229.

5. Jean Mountaingrove, "Notes on Community and Creativity," in *Community Herstories: Living in Southern Oregon*, ed. Tee Corinne, n.p., n.d., Southern Oregon Country Lesbian Archival Project (SOCLAP) files, special collections, Knight Library, University of Oregon.

6. Carroll Smith-Rosenberg, "The Female World of Love and Ritual: Relations between Women in Nineteenth-Century America," *Signs: A Journal of Women in Culture and Society* 1, no. 1 (Autumn, 1975): 1–29.

7. Raymond Mungo, *Total Loss Farm: A Year in the Life* (New York: E. P. Dutton, 1970); Stephen Diamond, *What the Trees Said: Life on a New Age Farm* (New York: Delacorte Press, 1971).

8. The New York Radicalesbians was one of the earliest groups in the women's liberation movement to not just acknowledge but also to celebrate lesbianism. They defined lesbian feminism as a political choice in an essay entitled "The Woman-Identified Woman" that first appeared as a mimeograph at the Congress to Unite Women in May 1970. The famous opening lines—"What is a lesbian? A lesbian is the rage of all women condensed to the point of explosion"— became an aphorism for lesbian feminists (Radicalesbians, "The Woman-Identified Woman," in *We Are Everywhere: A Historical Sourcebook of Gay and Lesbian Politics*, ed. Mark Blasius and Shane Phelan [New York: Routledge, 1997], 396–99). See also Adrienne Rich, "Compulsory Heterosexuality and Lesbian Existence," *Signs: A Journal of Women in Culture and Society* 5, no. 4 (1980): 631–60.

9. Although some lesbian feminists called themselves radical feminists, not all radical feminists were lesbians. For more on the rise of lesbian feminism in the feminist movement, see Alice Echols, *Daring to Be Bad: Radical Feminism in America, 1967–1975* (Minneapolis: University of Minnesota Press, 1989), 210–41. Radical feminists considered themselves revolutionaries, rejecting the reformist objectives of liberal organizations such as the National Organization for Women (NOW). They tended to be younger than their liberal contemporaries, and many had been involved in New Left and radical groups within the civil rights movement. Although a variety of radical feminisms existed, there were shared visions among them. Rather than seeking equality and an end to discrimination, their main objective was to destroy normative notions of family, love, and heterosexual sex. See Echols, *Daring to Be Bad*, 3–6; see also Sara Evans, *Personal Politics: The Roots of Women's Liberation in the Civil Rights Movement and the New Left* (New York: Vontage Books, 1979); Anne Koedt, Ellen Levine, and Anita Rapone, eds., *Radical Feminism* (New York: Quadrangle Books, 1973); and Arlene Stein, *Sex and*

Sensibility: Stories of a Lesbian Generation (Berkeley: University of California Press, 1997), 23–46.

10. Alice Echols, *Daring to Be Bad,* argues that there was a distinct difference between lesbian feminists and cultural feminists. Cultural feminists, she argues, emphasized the notion of a universal female experience, while lesbian feminists focused exclusively on their differences from heterosexual feminists. Although lesbian feminists may have stressed their differences from heterosexual women early in the gay/straight split in the women's movement, they made concerted (though unsuccessful) attempts to devise political rhetorics that would attract and include heterosexual women.

11. Ibid., 243–86.

12. Catriona Sandilands, *The Good-Natured Feminist: Ecofeminism and the Quest for Democracy* (Minneapolis: University of Minnesota Press, 1999), 3–27. Sandilands does not specifically refer to lesbian lands, but her discussion of the politics of cultural feminism makes it clear that land lesbians could be classified as cultural feminists.

13. Bill Devall and George Sessions, *Deep Ecology: Living As If the Earth Mattered* (New York: Peregrine Smith, 1985).

14. Bethroot Gwynn, quoted in Katharine Matthaei Sprecher, "Lesbian Intentional Communities in Rural Southwestern Oregon: Discussions on Separatism, Environmentalism, and Community Conflict" (master's thesis, California Institute of Integral Studies, San Francisco, 1997).

15. Devall and Sessions, *Deep Ecology;* Charlene Spretnak, *The Spiritual Dimension of Green Politics* (Santa Fe: Bear, 1986).

16. Joyce Cheney, ed., *Lesbian Land* (Minneapolis: Word Weavers, 1985).

17. La Verne Gagehabib and Barbara Summerhawk, *Circles of Power: Shifting Dynamics in a Lesbian-Centered Community* (Norwich, Vt.: New Victoria Publishers, 2000).

18. Catherine Kleiner, "Landdykes and Townies: Community Institutions and the Preservation of Lesbian Lands in Oregon, 1972–1995" (paper presented at the Western Historical Association's annual meeting, October 1998).

19. Kathryn Kish Sklar, *Catherine Beecher: A Study in American Domesticity* (New Haven, Conn.: Yale University Press, 1973); Barbara Welter, *Dimity Convictions: The American Woman in the Nineteenth Century* (Athens: Ohio University Press, 1976); Carol Gilligan, *In a Different Voice: Psychological Theory and Women's Development* (Cambridge, Mass.: Harvard University Press, 1982); Linda K. Kerber and Jane Sherron De Hart, *Women's America: Refocusing the Past* (New York: Oxford University Press, 1991); Lori D. Ginzberg, *Women and the Work of Benevolence: Morality, Politics, and Class in the Nineteenth-Century United States* (New Haven, Conn.: Yale University Press, 1990): Nacy Cott, *The Grounding of Modern Feminism* (New Haven, Conn.: Yale University Press, 1987).

20. Gerda Lerner, *The Creation of Patriarchy* (New York: Oxford University Press, 1986); see also Cynthia Eller, *The Myth of Matriarchal Prehistory: Why an Invented Past Won't Give Women a Future* (Boston: Beacon Press, 2000).

21. Charlene Spretnak, ed., *The Politics of Women's Spirituality: Essays on the Rise of Spiritual Power within the Feminist Movement* (New York: Doubleday, 1982).

22. Christine Pisan, *The Book of the City of Ladies* (London: Penguin, 1999); Elizabeth Cady Stanton, *The Woman's Bible* (New York: Arno Press, 1972).

23. Adler, *Drawing Down the Moon*, ix, 180.

24. Bethroot Gwynn, interview, August 6, 1998.

25. Adler, *Drawing Down the Moon*, 121.

26. Z. Budapest, *The Feminist Book of Lights and Shadows* (Los Angeles: Feminist Book of Lights and Shadows Collective, 1975).

27. Bethroot Gwynn, interview, August 6, 1998; Pelican Lee, interview, January 14, 1999.

28. Eller, *Living in the Lap of the Goddess*.

29. Pelican Lee, interview, January 14, 1999; Spes Dolphin, interview, December 15, 1998.

30. Lynn Andrews, *Medicine Woman* (San Francisco: Harper and Row, 1981), *Flight of the Seventh Moon* (San Francisco: Harper and Row, 1984), and *Star Woman* (New York: Warner Books, 1986). Philip Deloria writes of counterculture and New Age white "seekers" on identity quests who appropriate "indianness" as a badge of authenticity. Their spiritual practices have little to do with real Indians; see *Playing Indian* (New Haven, Conn.: Yale University Press, 1998).

31. See also Riane Eisler, *The Chalice and The Blade: Our History, Our Future* (San Francisco: Harper and Row, 1987).

32. Jean Mountaingrove, interview, August 6, 1998.

33. Jean Mountaingrove, "Jean on Community," cassette recording, n.d., SOCLAP files, University of Oregon.

34. *Womanspirit* 1 (1974), quoted in Micol Seigel, "*Womanspirit* Magazine: (Re-) Incarnating the Goddess" (senior thesis, Yale University, 1990).

35. Adler, *Drawing Down the Moon*, 185–86, 200, 204; Jean Mountaingrove, personal interview, July 26 and August 6, 1998; Ruth Mountaingrove, video autobiography, 1989 and 1993, Ruth Mountaingrove Collection, special collections, Knight Library, University of Oregon.

36. Zsuzsanna Budapest, "Beyond Ritual," *Womanspirit* (Summer 1984): 39; "Christian Feminist vs. Goddess Movement," ibid. (Summer 1980): 26–27; "My Salem in L.A.," ibid. (Fall 1975): 8–9.

37. Jean Mountaingrove, a seventy-seven-year-old resident of Rootworks, lesbian land in Sunny Valley, Oregon, observed that "feminism, lesbianism, separatism, spirituality, and creativity have been fundamental ingredients, their mix and proportions varying . . . from woman to woman" in land lesbian culture in southern Oregon; see "Notes on Community and Creativity."

38. Spes Dolphin, interview, December 15, 1998.

39. Bethroot Gwynn, interview, August 6, 1998.

40. Hawk Madrone, interview, August 4, 1998.

41. Land lesbians put together a tape called "Lesbians Singing Down Home" in the mideighties; SOCLAP files, University of Oregon. See reference to the tape in Gagehabib and Summerhawk, *Circles of Power*, 92.

42. Annie Ocean, ed., *Mother's Day Songbook* (1988), unpublished collection; author's copy given to her by Ocean in 1998.

43. Ibid.

44. Ruth Mountaingrove, video autobiography.

45. Bethroot Gwynn, unpublished poem dated 1975; given to the author on August 5, 1998.

46. Gwynn, unpublished poem dated 1976; given to the author on August 5, 1998.

47. Hawk Madrone, *Weeding at Dawn: A Lesbian Country Life* (Binghamton, N.Y.: Harrington Park Press, 2000).

48. Ibid., 103–14.

49. Ibid., 113. When Madrone wrote the book, she was single, though she has been in a short relationship since then.

50. Myra Quadrangle, "Earth Ritual," *Womanspirit* (March 1977): 3; Seaweed, "Tribal Stirrings," ibid., 4–5.

51. Quoted in Kay Turner, *Beautiful Necessity: The Art and Meaning of Women's Altars* (New York: Thames and Hudson, 1999), 33.

52. Madrone, *Weeding at Dawn*, 163.

53. Ibid., 164.

54. Catherine Albanese, *Nature Religions in America: From the Algonkian Indians to the New Age* (Chicago: University of Chicago Press, 1990), 153–201.

55. Judith Laura, "Three Celebrations," *Womanspirit* (March 1978): 8–9.

56. Mint, "Bless My Breasts," ibid., 16–17.

57. H. Ní Aódagain, interview, August 4, 1998.

58. Bethroot Gwynn, interview, August 6, 1998; Mountainspirit, "Hallowmas in a Peyote Circle," *Womanspirit* (Winter 1976).

59. Noelle Sturgeon, *Ecofeminist Natures: Race., Gender, Theory, and Political Action* (New York: Routledge, 1997), 24–58; for an overview of ecofeminist claims to women's "epistemic privilege" in their relationship, see Mary Mellor, *Feminism and Ecology* (New York: New York University Press, 1997), 102–26.

60. Carol Gilligan, *In a Different Voice: Psychological Theory and Women's Development* (Cambridge, Mass.: Harvard University Press, 1982).

61. Marti Kheel, "Ecofeminism and Deep Ecology: Reflections on Identity and Difference," in *Reweaving the World: The Emergence of Ecofeminism*, ed. Irene Diamond and Gloria Orenstein (San Francisco: Sierra Club Books, 1990), 127–37.

62. Deep ecology argues for the substitution of environmentally harmful worldviews with "biospherical egalitarianism" and the realization that "all things in the biosphere have an equal right to live and blossom and to reach their own individual forms of unfolding and self-realization. . . . all organisms and entities in the ecosphere are equal in instrinsic worth" (Devall and Sessions, *Deep Ecology*, 66–67).

63. Personal conversation with Jean Mountaingrove, October 15, 1998.

CHAPTER TWELVE

Saving Centennial Valley: Land, Gender, and Community in the Northern Black Hills

Katherine Jensen

Welcome to the Black Hills of South Dakota, translated literally from "Paha Sapa," the name the Lakota Sioux gave to the land they considered sacred ground. Included in the Great Sioux Reservation according to the Treaty of Laramie, it would be General George Custer's troops, assigned to keep the Indians on the reservation, that reported large quantities of placer gold and encouraged the encroachment by white settlers into the Hills in 1876. Homestake Mining Company (a Hearst enterprise) soon established the largest and longest running of the mines in the mile-high city of Lead. Most of the milling operations were built in its down-gulch neighbor Deadwood, which became the county seat of Lawrence County. The foothills community of Spearfish was soon established as the center of agriculture and ranching to feed the mining population, and the northern part of the county surrounding it contained those grain, hay, and cattle producing operations.

Lawrence County still embraces elements of the Old West as it struggles into a new century. In 2001 Homestake ceased to mine gold after 125 years, but a National Science Foundation–sponsored neutrino laboratory has been funded to occupy a portion of the mine eight thousand feet below the surface. Deadwood, the wide-open drinking and gambling town of the nineteenth century, falling into disrepair as a twentieth-century tourist town, decided in 1988 to revitalize itself, becoming the first community in the United States to adopt local option gambling since Atlantic City got into the business.[1] It turned its Main Street into a double facing row of casinos, cleaning up the downtown with the substantial portion of gaming taxes that must be spent on historic preservation. Even though the claim the Sioux tribes made for the return of the Black Hills has never been settled, the Santee Sioux tribe used profits from their casino in 1991 to purchase, for $230,000, 127.5 acres of forestland that they use for summer camps and powwows. And in 2002, the Cheyenne River Sioux obtained 400 acres of Homestake land in the Hills in an Environmental

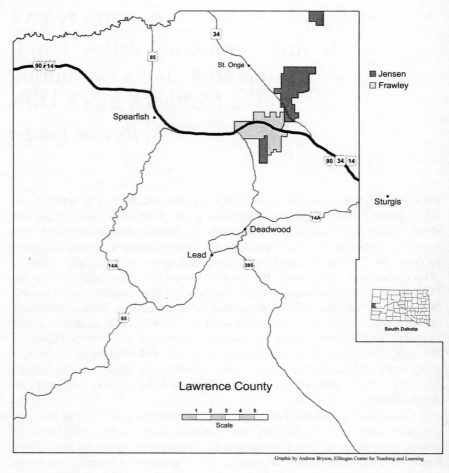

Legend:
- Jensen
- Frawley

Map locations: 34, 85, 90/14, St. Onge, Spearfish, Sturgis, 14A, Deadwood, Lead, 385, 90 34 14

South Dakota

Lawrence County

Scale: 1 2 3 4 5

Map of Frawley and Jensen Ranches, Lawrence County, South Dakota

Protection Agency settlement of a Homestake cyanide pollution case. The contest for land and land usage continues.

The biggest rendezvous in the Black Hills, however, has little to do with Indians, although it certainly draws traders when 200,000 bikers converge each summer for the Sturgis Motorcycle Rally at the site of old Fort Meade, the last cavalry post in the United States. And Spearfish has turned its attention from supporting agriculture to housing retirees, many of them from Deadwood and Lead, who have come down to the warmer climes of the foothills. Meanwhile, the ranchers in the Centennial Valley of northern Lawrence County struggle to keep from being swallowed up by Denver developers with German money, who want to build hotels, golf courses, and 450 houses on one large ranch at the intersection of I-90 and U.S 85 as it climbs up the hill to Deadwood and Lead.

This chapter is an attempt to understand the contested use of land in a dramatically changing economy and natural environment. It employs both historical and sociological perspectives, focusing on enactments of gender in a rural community and the course of a voluntary political organization to defend open space. Land use issues in the rural West are often construed as a battle between corporate developers and old-time ranchers, imagined to be men in suits and men in boots. And that is how the story appears on first telling. However, if we attend to a long-standing but dynamic sex-based division of labor among ranch families, this particular saga offers an example if not a prescription for social organization around the meaning of land in the rural West.

It is also a personal venture. I have been researching and writing about ranch women for two decades. I have been looking at various forms of community development for most of the last one. I was born in Lawrence County, and my family, including my parents and my two brothers and sisters-in-law, continue to ranch there, so this chapter is a test of a scholar's eyes meeting a local's heart. As James Clifford says, "A certain degree of autobiography is now widely accepted as relevant to self-critical projects of cultural analysis. But how much?"[2] We shall see, as this project has migrated much more in the direction of family history than I ever intended.

THE FRAWLEY RANCH DEVELOPMENT AND THE LAWRENCE COUNTY INITIATIVE

On February 1, 2000, 5,803 registered voters turned out for a special election on a proposed development of the Frawley Ranch in the northern Black Hills of South Dakota. The vote would attempt to determine the future of not only land development but also basic democratic process in

Lawrence County. The development proposal was defeated by a resounding 57 percent of the vote, but the more surprising number may be the 44 percent voter turnout, 3 percent greater than in the 1998 general election. While highlighting the historical context of the property and the surrounding communities, the rapid mobilization of this local population on a single issue also suggests an energetic confrontation between political actors rather than an archaic way of life meeting an inevitable force. It turns out that this would be neither the beginning nor the end, but rather the middle of the story, a story that is gendered, if unconsciously, at every turn.

The Frawley Ranch was established in 1877 at the first point at which ponderosa and granite turn to arable land in the Centennial Valley and had grown over the years to five thousand acres. Henry Frawley was a lawyer in Deadwood before statehood, before the military protection of white settlers, and had once argued for a $25 "abuse of animals" fine for a client charged with murdering a Chinese resident. The Frawley Ranch, always self-conscious of its historic significance, was made a National Historic Landmark in 1974 through the efforts of the founder's grandson, Henry (Hank) Frawley III.

Hank had been an attentive steward of the land's history, if not always of the land itself. In the 1970s, Homestake, under pressure from the Environmental Protection Agency to quit dumping cyanide tailings in Whitewood Creek, sought to build a large settling dam in Centennial Valley. Hank Frawley organized a local group called "Save Centennial Valley" to successfully stop the project. He had also worked to have Highway 85 declared a historic byway, preventing the erection of commercial advertising. Notably, in 1996, he and the current chair of the county planning and zoning board publicly protested a 240-acre development that would have contained seventy-five homes three miles from the current Spearfish city limits. Frawley was quoted in the newspaper as saying, "Commercial, industrial, or high density development—you can just go out and do it anywhere you want, I guess. We have lost control. We no longer have the ability to control and manage our growth and development."[3] Frawley successfully sued the city, the county, and the city's Extraterritorial Jurisdiction Commission for approving the Planned Unit Development (PUD).

Yet, in 1992, when chair of the county commission, he had pushed through his own PUD for a concentrated housing project on twenty-eight hundred acres of ponderosa-covered hilltops on the northern end of his property. He managed to sell only two lots before the project foundered on local opposition. The basic trouble was that Hank had never been a very successful rancher, despite the "Eastern degrees" his neighbors often mentioned with scorn, and he eventually went bankrupt. In 1998, forty-eight hundred acres of remaining ranch were sold to Union Park

Plaza Partnership, a front for Mike Kreke of Douglas Company, a German firm. In May 1999, Daryll Propp, a Denver developer, presented his plan for a $92 million development of the ranch to the Lawrence County Planning and Zoning Board. The plan included provisions for the "preservation of the ranch, a buffalo pasture, golf course, 450 homes, a campground, and a business complex." The proposal initially included a dozen rezoning requests. In the end, Hank was not only a bad rancher but worse, a bad neighbor.

THE JENSEN RANCH ADJACENT

The other ranching families in the northern part of the county were horrified and soon began to mobilize. Prominent in the effort to "save Centennial Valley again" were the three households constituting the Jensen Ranch, which abuts the Frawley place. My great-great-grandparents had immigrated from Schleswig-Holstein in 1880 and homesteaded in what would become known as "Little Denmark," still distinguished by the Little Dane Church building and cemetery at the top of the hill in the center of the Jensen Ranch. My great-grandfather, Ingward Weisman, had consolidated several homestead properties and delivered milk in Deadwood. When Grandpa Weisman retired, the ranch was run by my grandfather, Jens Peter Jensen, who had immigrated in 1911 and had married my grandmother, Katrina Weisman, in 1918. The ranch was divided among Katrina and her two sisters upon my great-grandfather's death. It was reconsolidated by my parents (who had met in high school in Lead and married after both had gone away to college—and my mother had worked as a welder in the Vancouver shipyards during World War II) and my brother Cliff, a veterinarian who had practiced in Utah and Colorado for ten years, and his wife Lonnie in the 1980s. I purchased most of a section of land originally homesteaded by "spinster sisters" on the northeast corner of the county about that time. Ten years later, my other brother, Karl, and his family returned from twenty-five-years' work in the Peace Corps (international development and rural banking in the Philippines, Indonesia, Egypt, and South Africa), so that their children could have some experience in American education before they went to college. They all live within two miles of each other, and the Jensen men and the hired man (who occupies the house where we grew up) rendezvous every morning at 7:30 around my parents' breakfast table over coffee and the day's plans.

The ranch looks very much as it did when I was a small child except that the houses have grown bigger and more luxurious and so has the machinery. The land is more productive as well after four generations of environmental stewardship, contemporary breeding techniques, in-house veterinary services, computerized production records, and careful business practices. During calving season in February and March, someone tours the calving barns every three hours, and often one of them is still on duty when the next labor watcher arrives.

When the (smaller) cattle operation was largely my nuclear family's responsibility, my mother used to have the three o'clock shift, I speculated because women were used to getting up with babies and getting back to sleep again,[4] and we all took turns when we were at home. But recently the women were mainly assigned to the sporadic jobs of vaccinations and record keeping when batches of cattle are "worked," going to town regularly for supplies, and meeting the very daily requirement of a large noon meal, even if you had a job in town.[5] (And Celia, my Filipina sister-in-law, has had to learn that neither rice nor garlic are yet very popular in large quantities, and you always have to have bread and jelly, no matter what.) As in other contexts, when organizations become larger and more formal, sex segregation of work often increases, even if irrationally. Gender expectations in neighboring families depend on the size of operation, presence or absence of children, and personal proclivities, but they are all well established and predictable. Work schedules and relationships with neighbors are based on the expectation of stability of rural family ranching operations in the rolling foothills of the Paha Sapa.

SAVING CENTENNIAL VALLEY AGAIN

Sociologists generally use three criteria to think about the concept of community. The most obvious is that of place or proximity of physical location in which people interact. The second is a shared sense of identity or identification of common interests of a group of people. And third is the organization or set of organizations through which a group of people meet their needs.[6] The Centennial Valley has long constituted a community under all three of these criteria and indeed may be more of an organized community now than it has been in a long time

Community is never so simple though. The recent mobilization of politics and labor in Lawrence County was ostensibly a matter of locals versus outsiders, most often expressed in the epithet "Denver Developer." But obviously, the question would also come down to recent or longstanding conflicts among locals as well, specifically relations among the five ranch properties adjacent to ("neighboring" in the vernacular) the Frawley Ranch. There would also be differences of opinion between rural residents and townfolk, particularly the realtors of Spearfish, and some interesting dynamics between pioneer families and some enthusiastic newcomers to Lawrence County. But we also need to understand the distinct if unarticulated roles not only of women and men but also of various generations of women and men in what most described as "the community coming together" around an issue of preserving the past while protecting the future.

Given the various interests in play, the process of organizing the valley to stop the Frawley Ranch development took place in a remarkably short period. The first time almost anyone in Lawrence County had heard about the development was at a county planning and zoning commission meeting May 6, 1999, when James Dascalos, president of Frawley Ranches, presented the corporation's request for a PUD and subsequent rezoning of the land currently zoned for general agriculture. At that first meeting, neighbors were already asking about water usage and sewage disposal for the proposed seventy-two-hundred-yard, eighteen-hole golf course surrounded by 58 "executive style" and 220 single-family homes and 148 multifamily homes. A representative of Hills Materials, the adjoining gravel company, asked how compatible an "upscale" recreational vehicle campground would be with their existing gravel quarry and rock crusher.

The Frawley Ranch's status as a national historic landmark also raised flags early on. The Midwest regional director for the National Park Service notified Lawrence County government that the development would result in a request to place the property on its annual list of most endangered national historic landmarks, since its designation was "for its association with the history of cattle ranching in the United States," and the South Dakota historic preservation officer wrote that state law required that the South Dakota State Historical Society office "be given an opportunity to investigate and comment upon a proposed zoning change for the Historic Frawley Ranch *before a decision is made regarding this project.*"[7]

Locals continued to be more concerned about environmental than historical issues. At a June commissioners' hearing, a dozen Centennial Valley residents expressed their concerns about the proposal, the lack of an environmental impact statement for the development, and the apparent deviations from the recently completed comprehensive plan for Lawrence County. A large contingent of real estate agents appeared to counter the criticism and support the proposed development at the continuation of the hearing. However, testimony at public hearings before both the planning and zoning commission and the county commissioners reflected overwhelming rural opposition to the development. The local daily paper asked whether the county commissioners should approve the development plan for the Frawley Ranch, and 96 percent of the calls said "no."

The trigger for the formation of an organization came after the October meeting of the commissioners at which a decision was expected. With the courthouse packed, the commissioners, without discussion, voted by acclamation to approve the development, adjourned the meeting, and then reconvened on the courthouse steps, with the citizenry left inside! Since neither subtlety nor civility seemed to be operating in Lawrence County, a week later, two dozen people, calling their organization the Save Centennial Valley Again Association (SCVAA), were circulating petitions to stop the development in order to protect open space and rural community. With twenty days to get the required 675 signatures of registered voters calling for a special election on the project, the women of SCVAA were primarily responsible for obtaining a whopping 1,659 signatures by the November 10 deadline.

Perhaps assuming that he was dealing with poor, uneducated, rural folk, within a week the deputy state's attorney for Lawrence County declared the petitions invalid, arguing that there should have been separate petitions for each of the six zoning changes actually approved by the county commission to accommodate the development.[8] Less easily discouraged than the county officials thought they would be, SCVAA immediately filed a writ of mandamus, and the Eighth District Court found in favor of the petitioners. The special election was scheduled for February 1, 2000; the issue had quickly galvanized the community in new and dynamic ways.

This standard chronological rendition demonstrates the rapid swell of local interest, but it provides little insight into the organization of labor of the Save Centennial Valley Again Association. Among other things, the description is nearly genderless except for the identity of the principal (male) players. In fairness, it must be said that the two newest members of the Lawrence County Commission were the first women ever elected to those positions; both had real estate interests. But it is in the work of SCVAA that a gendered division of labor is most apparent and most intriguing.

WOMEN AND MEN OF THE SCVAA

Because I was interested in the resistance to both the arbitrary power of local elected officials and the formidable power of international finance capital, I interviewed a majority of the organizers of SCVAA, usually described as "about ten couples." Indeed ten sets of names (his given name, then hers, then family name) and one widow are listed as signatories in the first letter to the editor sent to the local daily *Black Hills Pioneer* after the September planning and zoning vote. They were people who have ranched in Centennial Valley for more than fifty years or were men who have spent most of their lives in the county. Several of them had met their future "ranch wives" in college, and they eventually formed the partnerships commonplace among ranch family businesses.[9] The meetings of SCVAA were almost always in someone's home, usually on Sunday afternoons, the one sacrosanct rest/social period for ranch families. And in these domestic settings the division of labor became most apparent, although the public activities were gendered as well.

Besides the initial letter to the editor, SCVAA's first major effort had been the petition drive for the special election. The ranch wives of SCVAA started out going door to door to obtain signatures, but soon realized just how time-consuming that project would be in their sparsely populated environment and decided to move to public places frequented by both rural and town residents of the county. Lonnie Jensen described standing timidly outside the Family Thrift Center in Spearfish, waiting for people to inquire about her petition. Gradually, as she received generally positive responses, she became more assertive in asking people if they were willing to help put the Frawley Development on the ballot.

Kim Ridley, who organized the distribution of petitions, the mailings, and the phone calling before the election, repeatedly described the work the women did together as "so much fun" in part because neighbors who usually hadn't seen that much of each other, except when they met on the road, were suddenly working together. It may appear that they neglected to take themselves seriously in calling their assembly-line mass mailings "lick 'em and stick 'em" gatherings or referring to them as "hen parties," but they celebrated knowing that their work was primarily responsible for the success of the campaign, even if it was "gal stuff." I asked if they had food at these gatherings: "Oh, of course, Kathy, this was Christmastime! We always had food."

Only Lonnie seemed to have any consciousness of the sex-based division of labor, as she described one Sunday afternoon meeting when "couples" coming to the door would part, with the women taking a right turn into the kitchen and men turning left into the living room and only coming out to the kitchen occasionally to fill their coffee cups. I asked Andy Ridley, another fourth-generation rancher, what the men were doing while the women stuffed fifteen hundred envelopes. He said, "The other part, the talk," his quiet-spoken term for planning. Having spent two years on the new Lawrence County Comprehensive Plan Task Force, he was familiar with "talk."

The assignment the women claimed for themselves came not simply from assumptions about female dexterity but also from their prior political experience. Lonnie had worked on the presidential campaign of George McGovern twenty-five years earlier; Celia had worked for land tenure for sugar farmers in the Philippines when she was "an elite college student." Kim had seen rural Douglas County in Colorado turn into suburban development and factory outlet stores and "couldn't let that happen here." Other local women, including my mother Georgia, who were recruited to help make twenty-five hundred phone calls the last two days before the election victory, included several who had long-standing community experience on the cancer board, church boards, and county extension boards.

This spontaneous organization becomes particularly interesting in light of Robert D. Putnam's argument regarding the decline of social capital in contemporary American culture.[10] It is true that the old forms of volunteer organizations in the northern part of the county and elsewhere had disappeared or were on the decline, from the long-extinct Saddle Club and Commercial Club, which were mixed-sex organizations, to women's Extension Clubs, which had evolved into the awkward nomenclature of "Community and Family Education Leaders." There were no longer any rural schools to draw community people together. Some of the men got together regularly at the St. Onge Volunteer Fire Department, and the fire hall/community center would eventually be the Sunday night venue for SCVAA as the organization outgrew local living rooms. The Save Centennial Valley Again campaign clearly served a social function as well as its manifest political and economic purpose. And they always shared food.

In the same way that gender hierarchies are usually denied in these communities, participants in SCVAA resisted for a time acknowledging any particular leadership hierarchy in the organization. They did not initially elect a chair, although as they started to accumulate money for publicity, they did choose a treasurer. But Reed Richards, a local attorney who was born and still lives in Centennial Valley and practices law in Deadwood, provided much of the professional expertise enabling SCVAA's success in fighting the development and keeping a close eye on the county commissioners. Richards claimed no particular leadership responsibilities, even in calling meetings, and always referred to the organizational process in plurals. He insisted that, rather than an ostensibly similar group of ranchers, in fact SCVAA represented a "very disparate group of people, who all fell into our various notches, or traces, and pulled together. Everybody got along. There weren't any cliques or jealousy. Everybody, young and old, just got right into it."

Because the organization was so informal, so family based, differences in issues and responsibilities are difficult to dissect. Nevertheless, in observing the group over several months, gendered patterns of involvements emerge. Both women and men attended meetings of the planning and zoning board and county commission. Women as well as men are quoted in SCVAA's newspaper ads concerning the development of the Frawley Ranch. In the three weeks before the February election, letters to the editor of the Black Hills Pioneer included nearly equal numbers from proponents and opponents, but overall about four times as many were written by men as by women, and Spearfish realtors, calling themselves

"Ambassadors for Progress," were heavily represented in favor of the development. At the public forum sponsored by SCVAA the week before the election, all five of the scheduled speakers and the moderator were men, each with a specific topic ranging from concerns as an adjacent landowner, as a member of the Task Force on a Comprehensive County Plan, or as experts on particular issues, such as water availability and surface runoff. Nevertheless, some of the harshest questions for the three attending county commissioners came from women. My mother told me she was sitting in the back of the room but could clearly be heard when she asked, "The developers tell us there won't be any impact on the Spearfish school system because those home owners are going to be retirees, but I want to know who is going to build all those houses. Will they screen them for children?" Holly Baker, also in her seventies, appeared in a newspaper feature even as her husband was near death, describing her concerns about being an adjacent landowner and carrying on the fight for Glen.

And it may have been the SCVAA women, using their petitions and voter registration lists to take to the phones in the last few days before the election, that insured both a large and a positive turnout. Of the 5,832 votes cast from a possible 13,186 registered voters in Lawrence County, 3,294 rejected the Frawley development (57 percent) and 2,508 supported it, a difference of 786. The highest levels of support came from the three towns, with 48 to 51 percent "yes" votes in Lead, Deadwood, and the two Spearfish precincts. The five rural precincts ranged from 59 to 76 percent "no" votes, so the turnout in the rural areas was crucial to the defeat of the proposal.

But as decisive as the February vote seemed to be, the work of SCVAA was only beginning. Immediately after the special election, both Deadwood and Spearfish attempted to annex Centennial Valley (even though it is contiguous to neither), so sensing that the battle was far from over, SCVAA planned their next event, a "Ranch Get Together" at the Baker Ranch, adjacent to the Frawley buildings. Hoping to attract constituents from all over the county, it would be held on a Sunday afternoon in July. Blending the themes of preserving historic ranching enterprises with planning for the next century, SCVAA had erected a tepee on a hilltop outlook and a canvas tent housing geological maps of the area and the Lawrence County Comprehensive Plan, set up rope-making and blacksmithing demonstrations, laid out a walking tour of historic sites and a driving tour of the area proposed for annexation in a restored Model T, and offered a chance to meet SCVAA's candidate for county office. And, of course, there was lots of free ice cream, fruit, and cookies. The most interesting entertainment, however, was a prolonged and heated exchange between one of the SCVAA women and the male mayor of Spearfish. A large tractor-mounted V plow parked near the highway, which featured the word "Vote" painted in huge capitals before the election, now read "Welcome." But there were many more signs, some of them Burma Shave–style placards placed on fence posts by the SCVAA women reading, "Urban sprawl . . . Ain't too pretty. . . . Save our ranches . . . Build in the city," and hypothetical city limits signs for Deadwood and Spearfish sarcastically placed in the center of the gathering.

In the latter part of the summer, Carol Rahja and three other women of SCVAA including Celia Jensen set up a "Free Water" booth at the exit to Highway 85, polling fifty motorcyclists en route to the nearby Sturgis Motorcycle Rally to test whether, as the prodevelopment people had argued, commercial sites and a housing project would make the area more attractive to tourists. None of the bikers thought it would.

LAWRENCE COUNTY COMPREHENSIVE PLAN
AND LAND USE IN THE NORTHERN BLACK HILLS

Not only did the people of SCVAA bring different energies and resources to the effort, they also implicitly understood the Centennial Valley as a kind of ecosystem that encompassed values as diverse as open spaces, precious water, community infrastructure, and friendship, mutuality, and humor. The document they collectively relied upon for the serious part of their engagement was the recently completed Lawrence County Comprehensive Plan. Lonnie kept a copy of the plan in her file of letters and newspaper clippings documenting the endeavor.

Observed against the plan's "Vision Statement [setting] the framework for the future growth and development of the County," a complicated environmental history of the county emerges, part of which relates to the Frawley Ranch specifically and part of which questions the county government's handling of the proposed Frawley Ranch development. Over two and a half years, with $120,000 in expenses and nine public meetings, a citizens' task force that included Andy Ridley, one of the principals in SVCAA, had produced a planning document that was approved unanimously by the Lawrence County commissioners in December 1998, with the rules and regulations to follow. The Frawley Ranch development would be the first major test of its authority and its vision.

The plan described Lawrence County as a whole as a community rather than several towns and an agricultural area. But the vision statement also portrayed a rural future very much like the present. Lawrence County was to be a community where "the rural character is maintained in a relaxed, friendly atmosphere and a clean, safe environment throughout the county." So here the meaning of the word "rural" is as ambiguous as it almost always is, usually designating a negative: small size (towns of fewer that twenty-five hundred people) or a low population density (less than one thousand per township), but pretty clearly it means avoiding that which is "urban."[11] Most ranchers in Centennial Valley intend to keep ranching. When they pointed out that the Frawley development would make it the fourth largest town in the county, they did not see that new urban development as a mark of progress. Indeed, Doug Johnson, who had recently sold his Ford dealership in Spearfish, purportedly had offered to buy the Frawley Ranch in 1998, before it was sold to Union Park Plaza Partnership. Most locals thought that his offer was refused out of the fear that he could be successful ranching a property that Frawley argued could no longer support a family.

The planning document also emphasized a vision in which "the heritage is preserved and promoted in historic buildings, the western historic sites, historic open space areas, historic towns and historic activities and events" as part of its environment. This statement presumably would encompass the recognition of both the county's significance to American Indians as well as the long-standing celebration of "The Days of '76," the current massive contribution to historic preservation from Deadwood gambling revenues, as well as the protection of the agricultural history of Centennial Valley. But historic preservation in Centennial Valley and Lawrence County has some ironic elements, for it was Hank Frawley who had most singularly represented formal historic preservation efforts in the valley, initially with the designation of the original ranch buildings, later in the Centennial School building, and then, less successfully, with a stone dairy barn. Most of his efforts had been met with ridicule from his neighbors, first because he had secured public monies to preserve buildings on his private property, but second because many of his more progressive neighbors had been quite happy to tear down historic stone and wood frame barns to be used as salvage or simply to rid homesteads and pastures of deteriorating hazards to livestock and replace them with steel pole barns instead. More strikingly, Deadwood had turned itself into a gambling town on the legal pretense of historic preservation and then proceeded to gut every building on Main Street to make room for slot machines and mythical representations of "historic Deadwood." Now despite some nods to keeping part of the Frawley Ranch as a historic site, Frawley and his successors had become the threat to preservation, breaking a community trust and endangering a long-standing community agreement about living on the land, while the remaining ranchers had taken up the mantle of preserving not just buildings, but a way of life.

The plan also stated that Lawrence County was a place where "the natural environment is treasured and managed as a valued resource for its scenic beauty, wildlife habitat and multiple use opportunities." The statement reflected a long-standing effort to attract tourist trade through local identification with Black Hills National Forest land as well as the picturesque rolling foothill gateway to the towns in the county. The conjunction of a scenic natural environment and wildlife habitat with multiple uses has not, however, always merged perfectly in Lawrence County. Use of public (forest) land had long encompassed ample mining, timbering, and tourist opportunities. Mining had been its first and foremost enterprise; timbering had initially supported Homestake Mining Company with the Homestake-owned sawmill in Spearfish, which had recently been revamped into computerized operations by Pope and Talbot. By the 1920s auto tourism had made the Black Hills a destination; Deadwood capitalized on its Wild West image, while Spearfish became home to an Oberammergau-style professional depiction of the last week of Christ's life in its Passion Play on a four-hundred-foot amphitheater during the summer months.

Winter brought both hunters and skiers, and eventually snowmobilers, to the forestlands. Many local hunters preferred the grain- and grass-fed white-tailed deer of Centennial Valley to those that grazed on pine needles in the forest, and many ranchers willingly hosted wildlife on their lands and opened their land to hunters of deer, turkeys, and coyotes as long as they stayed away from the cattle herds and agreed to close the gates behind them. But recently some ranchers had granted exclusive lease rights to their land, and controversy erupted when a local hunter shot a deer on "open" property that jumped the fence to lease land before it died. Public and private had become more complicated.

Ranch land in Centennial Valley is privately owned, unlike most western ranches where the U.S. Bureau of Land Management, U.S. Forest Service, and even state-owned lands have always provided significant grazing for cattle and sheep. But in the last decade some Centennial ranches, including the Jensen Ranch, had acquired grazing permits in the adjacent national forest and found themselves, long regarded as careful stewards of the land, described instead as exploiters by environmental groups. Nevertheless, SCVAA activists now claimed protection of the natural environment as a reason for their quest to halt the urban/commercial development of the Frawley property. SCVAA raised concerns about "the protection of clean water and air, directed population growth and economic development, and assessing costs of infrastructure and services to new development" and accused the county commissioners of dereliction of duty in assenting to the Frawley development.

Water sources and potential runoff, issues with any large-scale development, may be particularly problematic in Centennial Valley. During the public meetings preceding the approval of Propp's plan, citizens questioned the lack of hydrology research for such a large development proposal and expressed concern about recharge of the proposed four

deep wells into the Madison limestone and the application for 1.2 billion gallons of water usage. Even more, because of well-known fractures in the gypsum layers of Centennial Valley and its Polo Creek flowing into Falsebottom Creek, which literally disappears for miles at a time, people worried about the effects of surface runoff from a highly fertilized, manicured golf course and miles of paved streets and the possible exchange with the Minnelusa and Madison formations from which most local wells draw their water.

Their concerns about circumventing the planning document falling on deaf ears with the county commissioners, SCVAA started another petition drive to put two initiatives on the November 2000 general election ballot. One would prohibit annexation of Centennial Valley by any Lawrence County municipality, and the other would require the completion of a U.S. Geological Survey water study before any zoning changes could be made in the valley.

THE ACTIVIST COHORT A YEAR LATER

SCVAA had no idea how appropriate the name of their organization would be; the effort would not be so easy, and the group would have to save the valley again and again. The petitions for the two planning initiatives were declared to have been submitted too late for the general election. Karl Jensen was not able to unseat either of the two incumbents, which may not have been surprising in a county that had not elected a Democrat to public office since someone had decided to "clean up the sheriff's office" in 1923. (He did, however, capture more votes in Lawrence County than Al Gore.) The day after the election, the county commissioners voted to allow Spearfish to annex the property. And exactly one year after the first development proposal was defeated in the special election, the commissioners approved a proposal from Daryll Propp for a Community Improvement District to manage a business park and campground development to be called Elkhorn Ridge; although piecemeal this time, the development carried a bigger price tag, $150 million. Since most properties in the area continue to be identified by the names of the original homesteaders, often three generations gone, the developer's attempts to change nomenclature was short-lived and unsuccessful. Newspaper text and their archives continued to refer to "the Frawley Ranch."

How had SCVAA held up after a year of reversals? Their resilience was reflected in making themselves a nonprofit corporation, requiring that they elect officers and form a board of directors, three men as president, secretary, and treasurer, and with only a small nudge my mother nominated a woman for vice president, all elected by acclamation. Of the thirty-two people at the St. Onge Fire Hall in mid-February 2001, two were women in their seventies; all the rest were middle-aged baby boomers, totaling fourteen women and eighteen men, including some new supporters. They variously argued that the development was contrary to the spirit of the comprehensive plan, that the February 2000 vote should be honored, that the land was protected by historic site designation, and that the campground would bring noise, traffic, and trash to the property lines of adjacent landowners.

The spring of 2001 looked like a rerun, with SCVAA supporters and placard-carrying demonstrators appearing at planning and zoning meetings, their presence and wishes being ignored, the commission approving the new development, and the petition drive for another special election launched. Not only was the organization and division of labor in place, but SCVAA had also collected considerable funds, including some from local businesses who wanted quietly to oppose the proposed development. On the same day in April that the South Dakota Supreme Court upheld the result of the previous special election, saying that the intent of the petition was clear even as its legal life had expired, SCVAA submitted three sets of petitions with nine hundred names each to call for a second special election to deny the approval of the campground and industrial park and to call for a moratorium on the ranch development for six years (long enough to replace the current county commissioners).

But the angle of vision was wider. SCVAA had forged links with other community organizations, notably Cows, Condos, Critters, and Community, a land-use organization based in Rapid City, whose mission is "to create partnerships that insure the future integrity of our quality of life and natural resources in the Black Hills region." Karl Jensen was interviewed by a Rapid City television station and asked to write an op-ed piece for the *Rapid City Journal,* as was Daryll Propp. Propp's piece emphasized jobs, tax revenues, and historic preservation of the remainder of the ranch outside the proposed development. Jensen's arguments included fighting urban sprawl, protection of water, potential competition with existing businesses, cost of public services, and the preservation of open space.[12]

Lawrence County also hosted a formal debate moderated by its local state representative, with two speakers from each side, all men. The paid publicist for Propp and the Spearfish economic development chair represented one side, while Karl Jensen and Mark Colby, as president and secretary of SCVAA, spoke for the other. More than four hundred local residents turned out at a rodeo arena to hear the discussion.[13] Meanwhile, the behind-the-scenes campaign was led by SCVAA's vice president, Kim Ridley, who again organized letter writing, phone calling, and advertising schedules. Cathy Morcum ran a door-to-door canvassing effort in Spearfish out of her physical therapy office, outfitting the volunteers in red T-shirts proclaiming "No, No, Yes," the votes SCVAA wanted on the two development proposals and the moratorium. This time they hired out the mailing. Envelope stuffing had become too tedious, even for the women.

The turnout for the June 2001 election was smaller than the February 2000 vote; still 37 percent of the registered voters of Lawrence County, more than fifty-four hundred people, were motivated to express their position on the single issue of the Frawley Ranch development and rejected both the industrial park and the campground by a 53 percent to 47 percent margin. The six-year moratorium on zoning changes passed by fifty votes. Vote counts show that the campground and industrial park proposals carried only in the three Spearfish precincts of the county's eleven, while the moratorium lost in Lead, Deadwood, and Spearfish, with the small town and rural votes bringing its small margin of victory. Propp's supporters gathered in Spearfish to hear him sympathize peculiarly: "I know this is the strangest thing you have all seen. It makes no sense. It is interesting . . . that communities that have nothing to do with it are allowed to block it." The statement from Karl Jensen expressed "delight" that so many people came out, sending a clear message: "You can't make decisions in the back room of the commissioners' offices."[14]

In the most recent celebration of "getting the job done," there was very little gender discussion; instead, everyone talked about how hard everyone else worked, and I had to ask oblique questions to avoid being embarrassed about wanting to know. It was still very much the situation of women "helping out" on the ranch and in the community that I started thinking about twenty years ago. And the arrangement still has demonstrable effectiveness. A small natural experiment as good as any a social scientist might imagine illustrated the way this division of labor worked at a May SCVAA meeting. Shortly after electing officers, sign-up sheets were put out for committee self-assignments on the election campaign. Men volunteered for fund-raising and speaker availability, women offered to do canvassing and mailing, and a mixed gender set of people enlisted to make signs in Karl and Celia Jensen's large dry shed.

It has also been interesting to observe a persistent voluntary community organization in the face of repeated obstacles. Part of the reflection is about generations. While the older generation has for the most part conceded defeat, and the youngest currently finds no obvious way to participate because they are currently "away" gaining their own professional experience, the cohort mainly involved with the ongoing effort to preserve agricultural space in Lawrence County is decidedly middle-aged people who came of age in the sixties. A majority of this group is college-educated, with many of its members having present or previous professional experience, in many cases away from Centennial Valley, indeed outside the country. They also have backgrounds in organizing political campaigns, economic development projects, and social services. These environmental activists (though they would not use that label) are, in many ways, "local kids" who had gone away at least to go to school or to work and have now come home to a place they cherish and intend to protect. In their interactions, their local histories are explicit; their "foreign" encounters are elided or blended in subtle ways, and they know "how gender works" in Lawrence County. But from this experience they have also gained a discernible new sense of who they are. In the past, they had seen themselves as the third or fourth generation of homesteader families with long complicated histories of alliances and toleration. Although the recent events have often been tension-filled and only sporadically celebratory, they now have a new sense both of the value of community and of political will and empowerment to protect a home on the range.

NOTES

1. Katherine Jensen and Audie Blevins, *The Last Gamble: Betting on the Future in Four Rocky Mountain Mining Towns* (Tucson: University of Arizona Press, 1998).
2. James Clifford, *Routes: Travel and Translation in the Late Twentieth Century* (Cambridge, Mass.: Harvard University Press, 1997), 88.
3. *Rapid City Journal*, June 20, 1996.
4. Katherine Jensen, "Mother Calls Herself a Housewife, But She Buys Bulls," in *The Technological Woman: Interfacing with Tomorrow*, ed. Jan Zimmerman (New York: Praeger, 1983).
5. Katherine Jensen, "Working Off the Farm to Save the Farm: Wage Work in Diverse Growth Situations" (paper presented at the Western Regional Science Association, Molokai, Hawaii, February 1990), and "Farm Women's Labor Contributions to Agricultural Operations," with Audie Blevins, *Great Plains Research* 2 (Fall 1991): 215–32.
6. Cornelia Butler Flora, Jan L. Flora, Jacqueline D. Spears, and Louis E. Swanson, with Mark B. Lapping and Mark L. Weinberg, *Rural Communities: Legacy and Change* (Boulder, Colo.: Westview Press, 1992), 14.
7. Letter, Jay D. Vogt, June 21, 1999.
8. "The goal of any election is to insure that a valid election occurs which results in a free and fair expression of the will of the voters. The issue as framed by Petitioners is fundamentally flawed. So much so that if this issue were presented to the voters it is doubtful that a free expression of the will of the voters could be expressed. . . . The end result would likely be the expenditure of $10,000–$12,000 for an election that is invalid" (letter, Bruce Outka, November 15, 1999).
9. The term "ranch wife" seems ubiquitous, especially in published autobiographies. See Jo Jeffers, *Ranch Wife* (New York: Doubleday, 1964; Tucson: Uni-

versity of Arizona Press, 1993); Mary Kidder Rak, *A Cowman's Wife* (Austin: Texas State Historical Association, 1993); Stan Steiner, *The Ranchers: A Book of Generations* (New York: Alfred A. Knopf, 1980); and unless you are a "cowgirl," Teresa Jordan, *Cowgirls: Women of the American West* (Garden City, N.Y.: Anchor Press, 1982). Only Linda Hasselstrom employs the term "woman" in *Going over East: Reflections of a Woman Rancher* (Golden, Colo.: Fulcrum, 1987), and *Windbreak: A Woman Rancher on the Northern Plains* (Berkeley, Calif.: Barn Owl Books, 1987), and also in her book of poems and essays, *Land Circle: Writings Collected from the Land* (Golden, Colo.: Fulcrum, 1991).

10. Robert D. Putnam, "Bowling Alone: American's Declining Social Capital," *Journal of Democracy* 6, no. 1 (January 1995): 65–78.

11. Janet M. Fitchen, *Endangered Spaces, Enduring Places: Change, Identity, and Survival in Rural America* (Boulder, Colo.: Westview Press, 1991).

12. *Rapid City Journal*, June 1, 2001.

13. *Black Hills Pioneer*, May 30, 2001.

14. *Black Hills Pioneer*, June 6, 2001.

CHAPTER THIRTEEN

Steps to an Ecology of Justice: Women's Environmental Networks across the Santa Cruz River Watershed

Giovanna Di Chiro

Human beings are natural forces of the earth, just like rivers and winds are natural forces.

—*Leslie Marmon Silko*[1]

They say that the TCE poisoning of the river and the groundwater is "historical," a thing of the past. I don't consider myself historical because I'm still alive! It always makes me laugh when they talk about looking for archaeological remains in order to protect the environment. What about the people who are living there now? Don't they matter?

—*Rose Marie Augustine*[2]

Chaos is a good place for evolution; I see chaos everywhere around us. There's a saying in Spanish, *en rio revuelto ganancio el pescador* ("fishermen thrive on a wild river"). We can use this chaos to coalesce in a holistic approach to saving the river, both for ample water supply and for quality of the water and the lives of the people.

—*Teresa Leal*[3]

Once cherished as *akimel,* or "revered river," the Tohono O'odham people now refer to the parched ravine, or what remains of the Santa Cruz River bordering their reservation in south-central Arizona, as *hik: dan,* a "cut in the earth."[4] As ancestors of the original inhabitants of the Tucson Basin, the Tohono O'odham are part of a diverse network of desert peoples seeking to "heal the river and themselves."[5] Restoring the purity and the perennial or intermittent currents of the Santa Cruz River, for many local Indian and Latino peoples whose livelihoods depend on its seasonal ebbs and flows or who have suffered health problems from drinking its polluted waters, are indisputable matters of environmental justice—"justice for the earth and all her children."[6] These grassroots actions to transform the biological and social nature of a degraded riparian environment constitute at least one story line in the environmental history of *El Rio* Santa Cruz.

In this chapter, I present a snapshot of the interlinked environmental justice politics practiced by members of a multiethnic and multinational network of women in the Sonoran Desert bioregion. Through a historical account of the everyday activism of one of these women, Rose Marie Augustine, I argue that their work is fundamentally about protecting the well-being of *la cuenca* ("river basin"). To sustain a healthy quality of life and secure livelihoods for all inhabitants of the semiarid desert ecosystem, these women activists fight for, among other things, revitalizing/recharging the local waterways and aquifers, improving water conservation and pollution prevention policies, and strengthening the environmental regulatory climate to encourage community participation and corporate accountability.

Like all dwellers of arid landscapes, Augustine and others express a heightened awareness of the sacredness of water, the lifeblood of daily existence. It would not be overstating the issue to say that for those people living in the Sonoran Desert, survival depends on the safekeeping of water. But in what ways are these women's actions for environmental change actually struggles on behalf of the river? I explore the question: how does the environmental justice work of women in the desert communities that straddle the Santa Cruz River constitute an environmental history of people's relationships with the waterways that sustain their lives?

Feminist historians have argued that insufficient awareness and attention to the theories and methods of women's history often result in a failure to recognize and document the productive and reproductive work of women as significant "interactions between people and all the other kinds of things on earth,"[7] one of the expressed objectives of the field of environmental history.[8] So, if one knows an environmental history of water when one sees or hears it (big dams, extensive irrigation canals, colossal diversion projects, stalwart salmon runs, intrepid canyon explorers or defenders), one might describe only some particular and culturally familiar human/nature relationships as being genuinely about people and rivers. In what ways can women's complex and interlocking struggles for environmental justice count as noteworthy narratives of historically specific "keepers" of a riverine community and thus emerge as a story about human interactions and transformations of water resources in the Southwest?

WATER, WATER EVERYWHERE, BUT WHAT OF THE SUBMERGED WOMEN?

It is by now a truism of classical environmental history that the history of the North American West, particularly the arid West, inescapably boils down to a story about water. The remarkable, epic environmental histories of western water, such as Worster's *Rivers of Empire* and Reisner's *Cadillac Desert*, attest to the determining role that the control of water played in the social and ecological transformation of this country west of the hundredth meridian.[9] The history of subduing and "improving" the desert to satisfy a seemingly unquenchable thirst for its scarcest natural resource is narrated by Reisner as a world "peopled by appropriators and diverters . . . by state engineers and water masters who wield the power of star tribunals."[10] The figure of water in the arid western states swirls at the center of a world-historical empire-building project spearheaded by both corporate and government backing and propelled by the manifold processes required to conquer and manipulate desert nature; the "development" of water proceeds by reclamating, damming, diverting, channeling, reservoiring, irrigating, pumping, trading, and so on.

What surfaces historiographically from these action-packed verbs are sensational histories chronicling the lives of, as Andrew Ross puts it, "Great White Dudes"—great in the sense of making their mark on both nature and history, but also great in the sense of championing noble causes, creating visions of the future, possessing strong moral fiber.[11] Moreover, what makes the histories of western water particularly compelling are the parallel tales of progress and decline—great engineering feats, great piles of money, great modern progress, great ecological disasters, great social injustices, great battles against all odds. The names of such men as John Wesley Powell, William Mulholland, Theodore Roosevelt, John Muir, and David Brower evoke unforgettable images of awesome power and dauntless determination. There is no doubt that the visions and actions of these men have had a significant impact on current social and environmental conditions of the North American West. But might there be other, perhaps less HBO-worthy yet historically and socially important parts of the story to tell?

As historian Virginia Scharff has shown, women are notably absent from the pages of the vast majority of books on the environmental history of the West, a phenomenon, she argues, that might lead a reader to conclude that "men's activities end up transforming 'nature' more than women's."[12] Mistaking "epic ecological events" for significance, she continues, blinds us to the ways that "women's actions, desires and choices have shaped the world, including the things men have done."[13] In agreement with Sandra Harding's concept of "starting from the lives of women" as a methodological accounting system to enhance the validity, or "strengthen the objectivity,"[14] of social research, Scharff asks us to imagine "an environmental history multiplied by the power of two, a history ever richer, more complicated, and yes, more fertile than we have seen so far."[15]

What would a more fertile environmental history of the desert Southwest look like? The environmental histories of desert transformation through manipulation of water resources provide us with unavoidably partial accounts of the past and necessarily limit their outlook to the particular events, moments, and characters that best weave together a story from the archival data at hand.[16] However, some historical data are notoriously self-effacing, especially those that on the surface appear to depict only tedious details of the overly mundane, boring, and inconsequential acts that support daily life. Indeed, it's not surprising that, in the interest of telling a good story, the redundancy of the everyday would be hardpressed to compete with "the heroic rendezvous between man and nature, dramas of dominance and submission, tragedies or triumphs."[17] Yet, history is not about skimming the surface, but rather about plunging into its depths to salvage that which may be submerged or lodged in the bottom sediments.[18] Launching an inquiry into the relationships between humans and their environments by starting from the marginalized, ecoepistemological standpoints of the lives of women may reveal those common, and sometimes repetitive, activities necessary to maintain the species, but it may also unearth some unexpected surprises. Focusing on the vernacular data produced through the daily movements of women activists raises the question: what new insights do we gain about how people have thought about, reacted to, and transformed the desert and its inhabitants in the Santa Cruz River basin?

A "POTTED" ENVIRONMENTAL HISTORY OF THE SANTA CRUZ RIVER

An arid to semiarid desert ecosystem typified by a mixed landscape of tree-sized mesquite bosques, palo verde, catclaw acacia, and saguaro cactus, the Sonoran Desert has sustained a long history of human settlements and environmental change, which include the vast irrigation canal systems of the Hohokam, the floodplain agricultural practices of the Tohono O'odham villages, and Mexican American communities' flower and vegetable gardens grown in terraced milpas shaded by the protective canopy of the once plentiful cottonwoods and willows lining the banks of the Santa Cruz River.[19] By the late 1600s, the Pimería Alta region, named after the local Piman-speaking Indian tribes by the Jesuit missionary Father Eusebio Kino, was transformed by the Spanish imperial program and, later, by Mexican and Anglo confiscations of Piman territory into a discordant landscape of missions, mining towns, presidios, and hacienda plantations and ranches—activities that all extracted more and more of the desert's limited supplies of water, yet continued apace owing to settlers' perception of the Santa Cruz Basin as an oasis with "no lack of water."[20]

The 205-mile-long Santa Cruz River, which "in the hierarchy of rivers . . . does not amount to much," served as the fragile lifeline in the Sonoran Desert that permitted early agrarian societies and later military, mercantile, and industrial colonies to take root and expand on both sides of the border of what is now Arizona in the United States and Sonora in Mexico.[21] Today, visitors to the Santa Cruz Valley find it difficult to imagine what an "oasis" the river once was. More than half a century of surface water drainage and groundwater overdraft to drive agricultural and industrial development as well as military base and weapons production expansion and to re-create Arizona as a tourist mecca and "desert playground" replete with verdant golf courses and swimming pools has taken a toll—the Santa Cruz River no longer flows.

A "cut in the earth" since the early 1950s, the Santa Cruz no longer supports the majestic groves of riparian cottonwoods that as early as sixty years ago flourished alongside its banks; because of many years of reckless pumping of the regional aquifer underlying the river, the water table has receded to a level below the reach of this hydrophilic species' roots. Groundwater depletion, however, is not the only problem that afflicts la cuenca Santa Cruz and the diverse human and nonhuman communities that depend on its ecological services. Years of illegal and unregulated dumping of toxic chemicals, copper mine tailings, and untreated sewage have percolated into the upper and lower levels of the unconfined aquifer, resulting in the contamination of the groundwater and forcing the closure of many wells in and around the metropolitan areas of Tucson, Nogales, and Nogales, Sonora. Fresh water, the most limiting and sacred of all resources in the Sonoran Desert, is being mined faster than natural hydrological recharge rates can keep up with and is being poisoned at a comparable scale.[22]

According to many concerned desert dwellers, "healing the river" and challenging the water politics that have shaped unsustainable development practices in the basin are central features of what constitutes environmental justice along the Santa Cruz "biological and social" corridor. This chapter delves into a piece of that history, starting from the lives of women environmental justice activists whose families and communities have for generations recognized and relied on the river's hydrological wealth.

TOXIC TOURING ALONG THE SANTA CRUZ RIVER

North-flowing rivers assume mythical dimensions in the popular imagination—a paradox of nature—even though there is nothing particularly mysterious about them, geologically and topographically speaking. With its headwaters in the Canelo Hills of the San Raphael Valley in southeast

Arizona, the Santa Cruz River discharges to the surface by a geological formation of impermeable basaltic dikes and commences its flow on a southerly course into Sonora, Mexico. Taking a wide U-turn near Paredes and redirected by the slope of the north- to northwest-trending fault-block mountainous terrain, the river begins its journey north approaching Ambos Nogales ("both" Nogales) and winding through Tohono O'odham territory up Interstate Highway 19 past Tucson to its confluence with the Gila River near Phoenix and eventually drains into the Colorado River.

I first learned about the southerly-northerly meanderings of the Santa Cruz River while attending a "toxic tour" of the maquiladoras in Nogales, Sonora.[23] It seemed to me absurdly ironic that U.S.-owned assembly and manufacturing plants that had relocated to these Mexican "free-trade zones," presumably to reduce both labor and environmental cleanup costs, would now flagrantly dump their industrial wastes into the river (albeit, to the naked eye, not an actually flowing one) that, instead of conveying the pollution out of sight and out of mind into the Mexican interior, was returning it across the border to the United States. I entertained fantasies of a vengeful Nature (perhaps in the guise of the benevolent serpent, *Quetzalcoatl*) rechanneling the toxin-laden river northward, thereby exacting natural law justice on the owners of those transnational corporations who had callously desecrated the river and its peoples in the name of profit.

As I listened, however, to the environmental history of the Ambos Nogales border region narrated by the two hosts of the toxic tour, Rose Marie Augustine and her *comadre* Teresa Leal, I realized that some of the environmental injustices we were witnessing on the tour could well be explained by the maquiladora owners' willful ignorance and disrespect for the ecological sensitivity of water in the desert. Augustine and Leal served as guides for the toxic tour bus, chock-full of academics attending the 1999 annual meeting of the American Society for Environmental History. As the bus followed the course of the Santa Cruz River, tracing the history of settlement and development patterns in the Sonoran Desert, the two women pieced together a story of the ecological predicaments that link the ever-multiplying maquiladoras of Ambos Nogales, Leal's native land, to the expanding metropolis of Tucson, Augustine's hometown. In their collaborative oral history, Augustine and Leal demonstrated to the tourists how the particular experiences of soil, air, and water pollution suffered by local communities were wedded to a larger story of environmental change in *la cuenca* Santa Cruz and, furthermore, to even wider transnational political and economic development policies. Just as the river, now a chimerical underground stream drifting in a northerly direction from Nogales to Tucson, connects their lives, Augustine's and Leal's toxic tour aims to show how the "invisible" processes of production and waste disposal are tied to consumption practices in far-away places, weaving together the threads that bind their communities to those of their guests.

The toxic tours are fatiguing and labor-intensive actions to organize, but Augustine and Leal insist that "this is a history that has to be told, and we decided that since this was a group of historians who might tell the story, it was worth it."[24] Like the submergence of women's experiences in many environmental history books, the environmental circumstances of the Mexican, Latino, Indian, and low-income communities living next to and drinking from this polluted river remain off the radar screen of many environmental agendas, even when it comes to the most widely cited scientific and journalistic reports on sustainable water resource management in the West.[25] When I returned to Tucson and the Santa Cruz Valley two years later, I spent a few days "on the move" with Augustine and other women activists in the informal *cuenca* network, who are striving to improve the environmental conditions of the valley and the quality of life of all its inhabitants. This is a small part of the story.

EVERYDAY ENVIRONMENTAL HISTORY

All in a Day's Work: Water, Workers, Weapons

In the 100-plus-degree weather typical of summers in Tucson (translated as "black spring" in Papago), water is obsessively on one's mind, yet, as in all arid environments, it is an ephemeral substance.[26] This morning, the oasis at hand was La Indita Café located on the lively Fourth Street promenade, a restaurant serving Oaxacan fare and noted for donating a portion of its profits to the Zapatista movement for social justice and indigenous people's land rights in southern Mexico. Drinking refreshing glasses of iced water and munching on chips and salsa, University of Arizona professor Joni Adamson and I met with social worker–cum–environmental justice activist Rose Marie Augustine to plan an itinerary for the days ahead.

Our agenda for the afternoon included a meeting of the Environmental Justice Action Group (EJAG), a coalition of concerned citizens and social justice organizations that formed in 1999 in response to an Environmental Protection Agency (EPA) request for public commentary on the water and soil remediation process under way at the local Superfund site. Listed on the EPA's National Priority List (NPL) in 1982, the Tucson International Airport Area (TIAA) Superfund site covers a ten-square-mile area and includes the Airport Authority, the northeastern portions of the San Xavier Indian Reservation, residential neighborhoods of the cities of Tucson and South Tucson, and the U.S. Air Force Plant No. 44–Raytheon Missile Systems Company (formerly, Hughes Missile Systems Company).[27]

Bordering the western edge of the site, the Santa Cruz River's groundwater resources provided drinking water for approximately fifty thousand people prior to the NPL listing of the TIAA. Since before World War II, a range of separate facilities engaging in aircraft and electronics production and military base training operations have discharged waste liquids directly into the soil or into unlined landfills, resulting in the long-term percolation into the groundwater of heavy metals such as hexavalent chromium and chlorinated solvents and volatile organic compounds such as trichloroethylene (TCE), tetrachloroethene (PCE), dichloroethylene (1,1-DCE), chloroform, and benzene. All of these substances are classified by the EPA's Carcinogen Assessment Group as hazardous to human health either as "suspected" human carcinogens or, as in the case of TCE, a "probable" human carcinogen.

The postwar economic boom brought even more industrial development to Tucson, including in 1951 the construction by Howard Hughes of an enormous government-owned, contractor-operated weapons production plant that amplified the relentless contamination of the increasingly limited surface and underground supplies of precious desert water.[28] Under direct supervision and control by the Air Force Command at Wright Patterson Air Force Base in Dayton, Ohio, the Hughes plant (purchased by Raytheon in 1997) manufactured tactical missile systems including TOWs, Mavericks, and Phoenixes, generating industrial wastewaters that had been treated on-site since 1951. Wastewater "treatment" up until 1962 largely consisted of diluting industrial acids and solvents in large vats and then discharging the liquid waste, about twenty thousand gallons per week, into natural drainage channels, or washes.[29] In desert ecosystems, washes (also known as arroyos), although parched for most of the year, make up the crucial network of ephemeral watercourses that capture and channel seasonal rainwater and return it back into the aquifer, thereby recharging the groundwater supply. Because they are the direct links to the thousands-of-years-old saturated layers of silt, gravel, and coarse sand containing the groundwater, dry washes, to the discerning eye of a desert dweller, reveal important signs of life made possible by the presence of water: in the alluvium composing the wash's floodplain, scrub mesquite and palo verde bushes persevere, and the songs of birds seeking shelter in the vegetation's cover fill the air. For Hughes and other electronics and military facilities that have set up shop in the deserts of the southwest, however, the intermittent streambeds of the Pantano Wash, Julian Wash, Arroyo Wash, and Rillito Creek become not sensitive, vital ecosystems, but convenient dumping grounds. Since the 1940s, these waterways steadfastly carried the toxic-laden water northwest to the Santa Cruz River and, ultimately, to the numerous municipal wells that served the low-income and 85 percent Hispanic neighborhoods of South Tucson, including the house of Rose Augustine and family.

Troubled Waters

Long before Rose's association with EJAG as a community adviser in the most recent phase of the EPA-supervised TCE-tainted groundwater remediation effort, she had earned her chops as an environmental organizer as one of the founding members of Tucsonans for a Clean Environment. After reading in 1985 the breaking news story by Jane Kay, an investigative reporter with the *Arizona Daily Star*, which revealed that the city's southside well fields had for years been polluted with chromium and the industrial degreasing solvent TCE, Rose and a group of other community residents including Marie Sosa, Ann Montaño, Sally Rendon, and Melinda Gonzales sprang into action to become what some county supervisors disdainfully referred to as "hysterical Hispanic housewives."[30]

As a social worker, Rose had plenty of experience helping people who were suffering, but she would not consider herself genuinely an activist until the moment she learned the water that she and her family had been drinking since the early 1940s had been poisoned with highly dangerous chemicals. In 1981 hydrologists James Angell and James Lemmon, both with the Arizona Department of Health Services, examined soil quality and aquifer depth records around the Hughes plant and conducted a flyover to take aerial photos of the wastewater treatment ponds. Around the settling ponds and dry washes, they found startling evidence of the desecration of the desert by this defense contractor: "The vegetation was just dead. If you see trees and bushes in the desert, they're usually green. They just don't get big and die. Something had happened."[31] Rose and her neighbors would learn, in Jane Kay's Pulitzer Prize–winning series in the *Arizona Daily Star*, that a number of private wells, including Hughes's own wells, and eleven municipal wells were contaminated with the carcinogen TCE. By the mid-1980s, the Tucson Water Department would close down these wells because tests had shown that some contained TCE in concentrations of up to forty-six hundred parts per billion—920 times the EPA's allowable levels of five parts per billion.[32]

Rose and the members of Tucsonans for a Clean Environment moved quickly to conduct their own informal health surveys in their neighborhoods. They found inordinately high rates of illnesses such as childhood leukemia and lupus in the city of South Tucson, where most of the con-

taminated wells were located.[33] Rose's own family endured a litany of serious health problems: she was diagnosed with lupus and had numerous
tumors removed, her son had a rare form of muscular dystrophy, her husband had bladder cancer, her daughter had disorders linked to heart
problems, her aunt had died of bone cancer, and her first grandchild was
stillborn. "That's four generations [of illnesses] that we have seen in our
family. . . . we bathed in and drank the water for over thirty years. . . . my
neighbors, my family, my friends have suffered greatly and our government has done nothing to help us," she explained.[34]

Rose had always supported social justice issues but would soon
learn that she was entering into the arena of environmental justice, a new
social and ecological framework through which "a whole mess of veils in
front of me were being removed."[35] A defining stage of this transformation occurred when she and the other women activists walked door to
door interviewing neighborhood residents to document their concerns
about TCE contamination and to survey their views on the government's
inaction. Rose found that her neighbors were cynical about the community's capacity to effect change: "They told me they knew what was going on but felt as though nothing they did would help because they were
Mexicans and their voices didn't count. They would say, 'Don't you
know that this happens because we are Mexicans and nobody cares?'"[36]

As Tucsonans for a Clean Environment continued its battle to gain
recognition, to demand compensation for the residents' illnesses, and to
struggle for the provision of health clinics in the neighborhoods, Rose en-
countered the term "environmental racism," a concept that helped explain the local health department's laxity and indifference to the welfare
of her Latino community. Faced with mounting evidence of the health
problems associated with TCE exposure in South Tucson, Pima County
Health Department director Patricia Nolan continued to insist that there
existed no conclusive scientific evidence linking TCE contamination to
the maladies afflicting southside residents. Nolan conjectured instead
that it was the lifestyles and "genealogy" of the people living in South
Tucson that caused elevated rates of bone and testicular cancer, childhood leukemia, heart valve defects, and neurological disorders such as
multiple sclerosis.[37]

Rose Augustine argued that blaming health problems on "our culture, on our heredity, on eating beans and chilies, rather than on the
chemicals in the water" was tantamount to environmental racism.[38]
Learning that other communities of color were facing similar battles
would propel her into the movement for environmental justice.

Glancing at our watches, we gulped a final mouthful of cool water
and exited La Indita Café into the blistering heat of the afternoon sun,
quickly moving on to our next destination—Kinko's Copies. In the car,

negotiating Tucson's late afternoon rush hour traffic as we hurried to make photocopies, Rose observed that in her many years of organizing she has relied heavily on the day-to-day groundwork carried out by women in the community: "Women are the ones who get things done; they are the ones who care. They are the ones who take care of the sick children, who take care of the sick parents, and they are the ones who get *angry*." Punctuated by the rhythmic syncopation of the copy machine, Rose recounted how she "felt powerless sitting on the hospital bed next to my sick child, not knowing if he was going to live through another attack, and I got *real* angry when I found out that someone had knowingly poisoned my child."[39] The upwelling of anger at the injustices committed against her family and neighbors was palpable in her voice, though it was fervent determination, not despair, that resonated in her words. Women environmental justice activists don't just get mad, they get moving. With a part of Rose's "groundwork" accomplished at Kinko's, we proceeded northwest on Interstate 10, armed with one hundred neon-green fliers announcing an upcoming community meeting hosted by the newly formed Rillito Residents for a Better Living Environment and PACE Local 8-0296, the union representing workers at Arizona Portland Cement Company.

Uncommon Alliances

Driving along the interstate, we followed the northwesterly path of the Santa Cruz River, which afforded us a panoramic view of the basin-and-range topography of the area. The Santa Cruz Valley is surrounded to the northeast by the Santa Rita, Rincon, Tanque Verde, and Santa Catalina Mountains and from the west rise up the Sierrita, Black, and Tucson Mountains. On the western side of the valley we passed expansive fields of pima cotton, an agricultural industry famous for its liberal use of pesticides and for contributing hazardous chemical runoff into the washes and creek beds that border the small town of Rillito.

Approaching Rillito via the frontage road, we saw the towering smokestacks of the Arizona Portland Cement (APC) Company silhouetted against the Tucson Mountains backdrop, a protuberant monument to the region's postwar industrial boom. Navigating the car through gritty clouds of cement dust billowing across the road, we came into Rillito, a town of approximately two hundred people encompassing a rural landscape of modest homes, backyards strewn with stockpiled paraphernalia, and patches of saguaro cacti. We stopped at the small, roadside building that operated as both a secondhand shop and a children's center run by Pat Grimmler, an energetic white woman who, after living in Rillito most of her life, was now standing up for the rights of its residents. Sitting together in the cluttered front room of her thrift shop, Pat recalled that when the cement plant came into town in 1949, the diapers she hung out on the clothesline would be stiff as a board in a few hours, encrusted with the fallout from the factory's stacks. The women in town, she recollected, did not bother to wash windows that had to be frequently replaced due to the relentless buildup of cement residue.

Rose's flier notified the community that the EPA had imposed stiff fines on APC for failure to notify its workers and the surrounding community of its releases into the air of the heavy metals cobalt and nickel in violation of the U.S. Federal Emergency Planning and Community Right to Know Act. By agreeing to ally with the small group of community members constituting Rillito Residents, the incipient environmental justice organization, the PACE Union local affirmed its commitment to protecting the health of the cement workers *and* the local residents, a diverse, working-class community of mostly African-American as well as Latino, white, and American Indian backgrounds.[40]

Rose had learned about the plight of the community of Rillito in 1998, through her affiliation with the Southwest Network for Environmental and Economic Justice (SNEEJ), a regional network of community-based environmental justice organizations. She had sought allies in the mid-1980s while trying to get local, state, and federal environmental health officials to act on the TCE contamination problems in South Tucson. Having requested technical assistance from the Citizens' Clearinghouse for Hazardous Waste,[41] the Virginia-based group founded by Lois Gibbs in the wake of the environmental disaster at Love Canal, New York, Rose realized that her small organization would need to reach beyond the boundaries of the polluted wells of South Tucson to gain recognition:

> I knew at the time that if I was going to do something, it would have to be outside of Tucson. It would have to be at a national level. I had no money, no connections. All I had was here, and the people I was working with were so sick. About that time one of our group members told me about the Southwest Organizing Project in Albuquerque. They provided us with scholarships and we went up to a meeting in New Mexico ready to tell them, "look what's happening in Tucson." I was prepared to tell them this whole story about Tucson, and I just sat there because as everybody was telling their story, my mouth was just open. I couldn't believe that this was happening in other parts of the country, and it was all communities of color. Lo and behold, I didn't know at that time that what I was getting into was the environmental justice movement—I haven't stopped since then.[42]

Through their association with the Southwest Network and other regional and national organizations, Rose and Tucsonans for a Clean Envi-

ronment began to see their families' and community's woes as the negative consequences of industrial development and "progress" rather than
as retribution for the "sins they had committed."[43] The group became a
force to be reckoned with in the late 1980s and 1990s in local, regional,
and federal environmental health circles. As an active leader in the Southwest Network, Rose has spent sixteen years traveling across the country,
speaking on behalf of her community, and advising other groups with
similar problems. What keeps her going, she says, is that "I'm tired of going to funerals, I'm tired of going to the hospital, the only thing I can give
is to fight to get medical services and recognition for the problems that
come from contamination in communities, not only in Tucson, but everywhere. . . . I'm not satisfied to leave this kind of inheritance to my children and my grandchildren or *anybody's* children."[44]

Unwilling to adopt a particularist NIMBY (not in my backyard)
stance in her environmental justice organizing, Rose decided to come to
the aid of the community of Rillito when she learned at a regional Southwest Network meeting that a Title VI[45] antidiscrimination suit was being
filed by PACE Union members on behalf of APC workers and the local
community to force the company to clean up its operations.[46] For Rose,
the town of Rillito ("little river"), together with its desert washes draining northwestwardly into the Santa Cruz River, was encompassed within
la cuenca, the river basin in which she lived. Although she had no prior
connections to the small town, she "hates injustice wherever it is," and so
used her skills and knowledge to help organize this predominantly minority community nestled nearby the dry creek bed of the "little" Rillito
River.[47]

The lawsuit initiated by PACE Union was consistent with the concept of "Just Transition," a new strategy devised by the Southwest Network to promote more sustainable environmental and economic
development policies. The "Just Transition" argument, otherwise known
as the "Superfund for workers," or the "GI Bill for workers," was the
brainchild of Oil, Chemical, and Atomic Workers' (OCAW) Union member Anthony Mazzocchi, who in the 1960s and 1970s fought for worker
health and safety concerns in the nuclear weapons production industries.[48] In the 1980s, when OCAW was challenged with possible phase-
outs and banning of many of the products their workers manufactured,
including chlorinated chemicals and carbon- and nuclear-based fuels,
Mazzocchi argued for a creative process to grapple with the painful up-
heavals that would result from massive job layoffs. Similarly, local
"fence-line" communities, who make up the core of environmental justice
organizations, are concerned both with the economic devastation
wrought by large-scale job losses and with the serious health impacts
their communities endure living adjacent to the polluting facilities. The

Just Transition strategy aims to establish an equitable transition process toward more sustainable production practices in the hazardous industries sector in order to protect the livelihoods and environmental health concerns of workers and the neighboring communities so that they do not bear an unfair share of the costs of moving toward a more sustainable society.[49]

Progressive unions like PACE, environmental justice organizations like the Southwest Network, and residents of toxic-damaged communities have thus exposed the shrewd corporate tactic of pitting jobs against the environment, workers inside toxic-producing facilities against the community, and workers on one side of the border against those on the other.[50] Instead, they "demand the creation of a National Just Transition Fund to provide full income protection, access to sustainable jobs and education for workers in toxic industries, and economic support for impacted communities."[51] A Just Transition Alliance is developing training manuals and workshops to build bridges between workers and communities and to draft a framework for the Just Transition Fund, a proposed federal program modeled on the GI Bill for servicemen returning from World War II. The fund would provide full wages and benefits plus tuition costs for displaced workers and financial and educational support to aid in relocating to find a new job. Operating through a consortium of government, labor, industry, community, and environmental entities, the fund could also provide technical assistance and low-interest loans for research and development on alternative technologies and sustainable jobs for workers. Funding would be raised from surcharges and taxes on materials and products slotted to be phased out or eliminated, such as dioxin-producing organochlorines or fossil fuels contributing to climate change.[52]

"This Just Transition approach is a great opportunity for the workers and the community to talk about their commonalties," Rose exclaimed, "and the point is to eventually bring in the industry to work with communities and the workers to clean up the environment—so far it's been so interesting, it's such a new concept."[53] Excited by the PACE Union workers' Title VI lawsuit, Rose and other members of the Southwest Network saw an ideal opportunity to unite the cement workers and the people of Rillito by foregrounding their shared environmental health interests and, in the process, broadening and deepening the environmental justice movement.

For two and a half years, Rose persevered in her attempts "to break into the community" to inform them about the health risks they faced due to APC's toxic releases and to raise their awareness of the environmental rights to which they were entitled. She explains: "I made phone calls, nobody would answer the phone or return my calls, nobody would open their doors, but I kept going there to Rillito. It's a very close community, a community that's been dumped on for so many years, and they really don't understand what is happening. They've lived so far out of town that they've been isolated, but they're not isolated anymore."[54] Rose's first opening came when she knocked on the front door of Pat Grimmler, the local resident and shopkeeper who would soon become an active participant in Rillito's environmental struggles. "Are you Carl Grimmler's wife?" she ventured. Rose knew that Carl and her husband, Ben, had been acquainted with each other since the 1950s. "Oh, how is Ben?" Pat asked and promptly invited Rose in for a visit. Relieved that she had finally made a promising contact with a long-standing community member, Rose smiled, "It's a good thing I know a lot of people in Tucson!"[55] But there were more people to bring into the fold.

Rillito had long operated its own water company, so, on a tip, Rose decided to contact Jesse McKnight, the president of the Water Board, to ascertain his thoughts on APC's effect on the town's water quality. After leaving a series of lengthy messages on his answering machine, Rose finally heard from McKnight, an African-American resident who "wasn't too sure what this lady was up to" but, impressed with her perseverance, agreed to a meeting. Given that none of the cement workers lived in the community itself, McKnight was interested to hear that "the workers know there's a problem here and they want to get involved and help the community."[56]

McKnight and Augustine agreed upon a neighborhood cleanup as a way to "bond the workers and the community" in a joint activity that would also begin the process, if only symbolically, of environmental remediation. Rose contacted the president of the union local, David Garcia, and organized a daylong event in which workers brought out front-loaders and hauled trash, yard waste, and discarded debris into seven large dumpsters. Afterward, the community residents and workers celebrated with barbecued hot dogs, potato salad, drinks, and lots of laughter. "It was a great day, just great!" Rose exclaimed. "Everyone wanted to get involved, and the workers really helped out the elderly people and bonded with the community." "Now," she continues, "we have to educate the community about what's happening, they have to get organized because more development is coming here, like the Department of Transportation's expansion of the frontage road that will take a hundred feet more of their property and bring more traffic and pollution. And Portland Cement has been importing hazardous waste from the Virgin Islands. . . . But we're getting organized!"[57]

Chuckling at the gaudy green color of the fliers and discussing how they would be distributed around Rillito, Pat and Rose talked excitedly about the approaching meeting between PACE workers and Rillito Residents for a Better Living Environment. It was getting late, and we needed to return to Tucson in time to make the meeting of EJAG, the environmental justice group that was battling the Brush Wellman Corporation to force it to adopt a zero-release policy for the highly toxic metal beryllium. Rushing out the door of Pat's thrift shop, Rose spied and was beguiled by an antique, chipped piggy bank that had been Pat's grandmother's and was lying unceremoniously in a box filled with stuff. Pat happily unloaded the pig and we got back on the road, stopping only to buy bottles of water to quench our incessant thirst.

Militarized Borders

Heading toward the city of South Tucson and the El Pueblo Community Center, our meeting destination, we crossed imperceptibly into the TCE groundwater contamination zone, now in the seventh year of a thirty-five-year proposed remediation process. Advancing at a rate of three hundred to one thousand feet per year, the five-mile-long, one-mile-wide, and up to one-hundred-feet-deep toxic plume of groundwater radiates northwestwardly from its "headwaters" at the U.S. Air Force Plant No. 44–Raytheon Missile Systems site. Smaller plumes emanate from the other facilities in South Tucson listed by the EPA as "potentially responsible parties" (PRPs), including the defense contractors McDonnell Douglas Corporation and General Dynamics Corporation. These PRPs manufactured high-tech weapons systems during the Cold War and, more recently, supplied what Hughes labeled the "missiles of victory"— long-range, rocket-propelled, air-to-surface missiles vital to Operation Desert Storm.

The spreading TCE groundwater plume and the environmental illnesses it has spawned, Rose argues, are the hidden legacies of a silent war perpetrated on poor people and communities of color in the United States and abroad. Speaking of her family, friends, and neighbors in South Tucson, Rose articulates the linkages between the civilian casualties in Third World nations—women, children, the elderly—in modern wars like Desert Storm and the victims of the lethal by-products of military facilities scattered across the United States, disproportionately located in communities of color. "Even though we didn't go to war," she says, "we were victims of war."[58]

Defense contractors are a prime source of toxic pollutants in the low-income Latino neighborhoods of Tucson's south side. Since the late 1940s, the Brush Wellman Corporation has supplied the Pentagon, NASA, and the Department of Energy with the metal alloy beryllium, a highly toxic substance critical to the production of nuclear weapons. The company took advantage of the tax benefits offered to attract businesses to the

South Tucson "enterprise zone" and opened a plant there in 1980. Calling Brush Wellman's move to the south side "a stepping stone to Mexico," Rose argues that these hazardous industries "are here just for that corporate welfare." She continues: "As soon as all these tax incentives are exhausted, and there's nothing to keep these plants here anymore, they just leave. Look at all the hundreds of people they leave behind. 'Free enterprise zones' are, in fact, sacrifice zones—an enterprise for the industry but a sacrifice for the community."[59]

Maneuvering through the maze of roadwork detours along South Sixth Avenue to get to the El Pueblo Center and the EJAG meeting, we entered the neighborhood where Rose spent her youth. Locals contend that the border (la frontera) begins here, not sixty miles to the south at the official national boundary between Mexico and the United States. Representing the unofficial boundary demarcating Tucson's rich and poor districts, city administrators describe South Sixth Avenue as the "bad side of town," crime-ridden and overrun with Latino gangs. Colorful storefronts advertise their wares in Spanish, and the busy sidewalk scenes are in fact more reminiscent of a south-of-the-border town than they are of the ersatz, hacienda-style modern architecture that dominates Tucson's new city center, the outcome of the urban renewal/gentrification projects that razed the downtown's Old Pueblo.[60]

In 1967, the city of Tucson demolished twenty-nine city blocks of prime real estate to erect the sprawling Tucson Convention Center and its adjacent parking lots, along with a host of upscale office complexes and condominiums. Rose and Ann Montaño, her childhood friend and fellow Tucsonans for a Clean Environment activist, remembered the former barrio as a warm, lively community where "everyone looked after each other." City planners and administrators, however, saw skid row, a dilapidated enclave of poverty that threatened to "spread like a cancer" throughout the city.[61]

"They said it was a slum filled with prostitutes, thieves, and drug addicts," Ann recalled, dismayed at the image that the city fathers used to justify the downtown's demolition, razing her own grandmother's house.[62] In an unfortunate chain of events, hundreds of displaced Mexican American residents of the downtown barrio were relocated predominantly to South Tucson where, unawares, they would live atop the TCE-contaminated groundwater plume and drink its deadly waters.[63] "This is environmental racism two times over," Rose contends, "and now, these people are dealing with berylliosis from the Brush Wellman Plant— it's the same story again and again."[64]

Parking the car and stepping out into the desert heat, Rose directed our attention to a small Honda station wagon whose roof was adorned with a five-foot-long cardboard nuclear missile and an attached sign proclaiming, "Star Wars: A 60 billion dollar HOAX." "That's Pat Birnie's car, and does she get a lot of stares on the street!" Rose laughed.

Pat Birnie, a soft-spoken septuagenarian and one of the founders of EJAG, cut her teeth on the 1970s peace movement and, as a longtime member of the Women's International League for Peace and Freedom (WILPF), argues resolutely that the fundamental cause of militarism and war is racism. "As long as you can have an 'us and a them' mentality, as long as we train people to believe in an 'us' and a 'them,' then people will do irrational things," Pat says. In the low-income neighborhoods of South Tucson, she explains, such irrational acts include exposing workers and neighbors to beryllium dust in the production of the trigger mechanisms for nuclear warheads built to kill people in distant lands.[65] Pat first became aware of the struggles against environmental racism when, in 1997, WILPF invited Rose Augustine to speak at one of their meetings. "Rose has a stick-to-it-ness that doesn't quit," Pat admiringly remarked. "She seems to find what motivates people, and she has the courage to speak the truth to the seats of power."[66] This and her "ever-questioning mind," Pat claims, drive Rose's persistence to fight for environmental justice, "for communities here in Tucson who are in danger from TCE or beryllium dust exposure . . . and for people struggling in any community."[67]

Beryllium is a metal alloy that is three times lighter than aluminum and six times harder than steel. Its unique properties, first discovered in the early 1940s, have made it attractive to the aeronautics, space, and nuclear weapons industries. Consequently, it is a "strategic metal," critical to the U.S. government's military policy. By 1941, beryllium production plants had sprung up in Ohio and Pennsylvania to supply the voracious appetite of the Manhattan Project after atomic bomb scientists had demonstrated that the metal enabled a more efficient chain reaction in the fission process. In a few years, medical doctors in Ohio were seeing a range of mysterious respiratory symptoms in patients who worked at what were then the Beryllium Corporation plants in Cleveland and Lorain. In 1943, a Cleveland-based scientist determined that beryllium was toxic to the lungs. Lung damage occurs when the microscopic particles of the metal lodge themselves in the alveoli, the lungs' minute air sacs. Eventually, the injured lungs produce scar tissue, which surrounds the beryllium dust particles and impairs the delicate alveoli membranes, preventing the exchange of oxygen and carbon dioxide gases to and from the bloodstream. There is no cure for beryllium disease, and it is most often fatal.[68]

By the mid-1940s, dozens of beryllium workers and their families (including nuclear scientists) had become seriously ill with berylliosis, and the newly formed Atomic Energy Commission (AEC) realized it had both a public health and public relations problem on its hands. The fed-

eral government had known for years that the metal was toxic at infini-
tesimally small doses, yet, in the name of national security, the AEC continued to support production, to overlook Occupational Safety and
Health Administration (OSHA) inspections, and to kill plans to
strengthen regulations.[69] Despite considerable epidemiological evidence
and a mounting death toll, only once in the last fifty years has OSHA
tried to impose stricter exposure limits: in 1975, OSHA scientists proposed cutting the exposure level in half. At the time, Secretary of Energy
James Schlesinger warned that the new regulations "would seriously
limit our ability to develop and produce weapons for the nuclear stock-
pile," and, with the endorsement of President Jimmy Carter, the OSHA
plan to more tightly regulate beryllium was abandoned.[70]

While compiling their public commentary on the most recent phase
of the TCE groundwater remediation plan, a public participation process
mandated by the Clean Water Act of 1972, the members of EJAG learned
about the case of twenty-five workers falling ill with chronic beryllium
disease and many others at risk at the Brush Wellman plant on 6100 South
Tucson Boulevard. The company claims it has complied with all EPA and
OSHA guidelines and argues that some people are "genetically susceptible to beryllium disease."[71] Invoking the "genetic disadvantage" argument also used by Hughes's spokesmen and the Pima County Health
Department, the Brush plant refused to investigate the claim that workers might have been overexposed to beryllium dust because of the company's negligence.

At this evening's meeting, EJAG members discussed whether to participate in the community advisory board (CAB) that Brush was interested in establishing. Most members of EJAG were unimpressed with the
company's agenda, as CABs are regularly deployed as rubber-stamp
mechanisms to co-opt community members into thinking they are being
consulted and to reassure them of the benevolence of the company. Rose
interjected that she had served on a CAB handpicked by Hughes in the
1980s and 1990s, an experience that left her skeptical about the good "la-
bor/neighbor" assurances of Brush Wellman plant managers. Consequently, she recommended that EJAG remain independent. Rather than
sign on to the CAB, therefore, EJAG called for Brush to demonstrate its
good faith by installing air monitors around the plant and in the community, committing to a zero-release policy, and agreeing to treat the
workers humanely.[72]

During the TCE battles, Rose and Tucsonans for a Clean Environment had built solidarity with the ailing Hughes plant workers, many of
whom where women, but that strategy was proving difficult in the beryllium campaign against Brush Wellman. "Most of the line workers are
Hispanic women, who don't speak English, or don't speak very well, and

so are apprehensive about complaining," Pat explains. "Some of them were mothers who Brush took in on the 'welfare to work' program, and many of them have come down with berylliosis."[73] Recalling the tribulations of trying to organize the TCE campaign while sick with the debilitating symptoms of lupus, Rose expressed how difficult it would be to build bridges with the women beryllium workers. "Even so," she underscored, "we have to bring these women along."

To "bring along" and educate the workers and neighbors about the hazards of inhaling beryllium dust, EJAG members discussed strategies to expose Brush Wellman's and the county health department's lax monitoring procedures. Demanding more careful and accurate monitoring of beryllium emissions, EJAG followed the lead of the Ohio Citizen Action Group protesting Brush Wellman's Ohio plant and decided to conduct their own "swipe" tests of a twelve-block radius of the facility to measure the extent and scope of beryllium fallout in the community. Abiding by the sample collection protocol of the Severn Trent Laboratories in Westfield, Massachusetts, the group has swiped a series of metal surfaces, including those at the six elementary, middle, and high schools that encircle the plant. The activists use scientific methods in their community-based monitoring to determine whether Brush Wellman can fulfill its promises to protect workers and neighbors from the harmful dust.

After the meeting, Rose led us on a mini "toxic tour" of the Sunnyside neighborhood to see how close Brush's elevated smokestacks stood next to school grounds, child care centers, and residences. Staring up at the beryllium plant's stacks while leaning against the adjacent schoolyard fence, it was not hard to imagine how the powdery emissions from the factory might drift silently onto the playgrounds and buildings that house the South Side's children.[74]

The dusty bed of the Santa Cruz River winds its way not far from the Brush Wellman plant. To date, there have been no studies examining the fate of the waste beryllium that empties down the drain into the sewer system and ultimately finds its way into the river channel.[75] Recharged wastewater from two Pima County tertiary treatment plants flows through the Santa Cruz waterway for a short distance and then evaporates into the dry atmosphere or percolates through the sand and soil into the upper groundwater layers. EJAG activists wonder whether the crystallized beryllium particles left behind attach themselves to tiny grains of sand and soil eventually to be blown into the regional airshed with the prevailing winds. The arid winds and the ephemeral water of the Sonoran Desert knit together this system of circulation, disseminating innumerable military and industrial poisons imperiling the health of the desert ecosystem and its inhabitants.

Polluter Pays?

The pastel colors of the early evening light soften the craggy mountainous landscape of the Tucson Basin. We drove to a city park situated along the banks of the Santa Cruz where, as a child, Rose and her family took refuge from the hot sun under the shady stands of cottonwood trees that once lined the riverbed. These days the trees are gone. Either they died with the disappearance of the river's surface water due to decades of overdraft, or they were cut down, Rose laments, because "the city said the trees drank up too much water."[76]

As the sun set behind the Tucson Mountains, bringing welcome relief from the scorching heat, we ventured out onto the walking trail that curved along the river in view of one of the out-of-service South Side wells encircled by barbed wire. Further downstream, the trail offered a display of the large cylindrical holding tanks of an "air stripper," one of the Tucson Airport Remediation Project's (TARP) water treatment facilities funded by the Tucson International Airport Area Superfund site PRPs as a result of a 1987 consent decree and a $28 million settlement with the EPA.[77]

TARP consists of three thirty-five-foot air-stripping towers that aerate contaminated groundwater, releasing volatile organic compounds (VOCs), especially TCE, into the air and then trap the air emissions through granular-activated carbon filters.[78] The "rinsed" water, treated at a rate of three thousand to five thousand gallons per minute, is then blended with other water and released into the municipal water distribution system. The Tucson Water Company, which oversees the project, has been forced to respond to objections by customers to drinking previously tainted water and so has also considered the alternative option of recharging the detoxified water back into the aquifer.[79] According to EJAG, the EPA-mandated TARP project is evidence of federal regulators assuming some responsibility to enforce the nation's antipollution laws, considering that an earlier "remediation" proposal would have stopped at supplying southsiders with bottled water rather than cleaning up the groundwater.[80] In its report to the EPA on the groundwater remediation process, however, EJAG found it "unacceptable that the agency was allowing some polluted sites to be considered 'technically infeasible'" to detoxify and, therefore, would remain public health hazards well into the future.[81]

As we gazed at the postindustrial scene before us— the desiccated riverbed, the condemned city well, and the shiny white treatment plant— the folly of the history of water "management" in the Tucson Basin, from unrestrained pumping to toxic dumping to costly cleanup projects handling a gargantuan quantity of underground water, was mind-numbing.

Rose shook her head, "They kept pumping more and more water all those years, forgetting that it was a desert, and then Hughes was told there was a shallow well field under their site and they needed to be careful, but they didn't care, and now they want to take CAP [Central Arizona Project][82] water from the Colorado River to recharge the groundwater!"[83] One of the consequences of Hughes/Raytheon's and Brush Wellman's efforts to ignore the hazards of their actions stood starkly before us in the form of the multimillion-dollar TARP structure. Another outcome of despoiling desert water was one that neither the defense contractors nor the public health officials had anticipated—that the "hysterical Hispanic housewives," shifting their attention from cooking "beans and chilies" for their families to protecting their children from TCE-contaminated well water, would slap them with an $84.5 million lawsuit.[84]

In 1985, a small group of residents initiated a lawsuit against Hughes Missiles Systems for contaminating their water and causing personal injuries. By 1991, the number of plaintiffs had grown to 1,620, and Hughes agreed to settle out of court by awarding the $84.5 million sum to the residents, which was described by the plaintiff's lead attorney as "the largest settlement offered in U.S. history in a suit involving groundwater contamination."[85] Although twenty of her family members were plaintiffs in the lawsuit, Rose argues that "the book in this case is not closed because of the settlement. It has no provision for illnesses that appear in the future, and it doesn't address the cleanup."[86] Other suits are pending, including a tentative $35 million settlement with the City of Tucson and the Tucson International Airport Authority.[87]

Although Rose supports "people having their day in court" to gain monetary compensation for TCE victims (even though the individual payments, based on the nature of the individual's illness, were in the $3,000 to $17,000 range—not sufficient to pay for most medical bills), she knows "nobody will ever go to jail or be held accountable for poisoning the water, and that's injustice."[88] Instead, she pushes public health bodies, like the Agency for Toxic Substances and Disease Registry (ATSDR), to address the current and future health needs of contaminated communities. Her organization, Tucsonans for a Clean Environment, lobbied hard for a public health clinic staffed by practitioners who would be trained to recognize and treat TCE-related maladies. In 1992, the Arizona Senate, with objections from a number of Republican senators to paying for the "phantom illnesses" of South Tucson, appropriated $250,000 to establish the El Pueblo Health Clinic to serve the poor and low-income residents of the community.[89]

Rose insists that in a "real democracy" the government would not "protect industries, but the people."[90] Although widely lauded for her civic participation and activism on behalf of her community, Rose is not content to sit back complacently after winning a few battles. After their success in forcing the departure in 1988 of Pima County health director Dr. Patricia Nolan for ignoring evidence of TCE contamination for eight years, Tucsonans for a Clean Environment continues to pressure the ATSDR, the agency that holds primary responsibility for conducting health assessments at Superfund sites, to include socioeconomic and cultural factors in their community health surveys, thereby ensuring a more useful understanding of the multiple risk factors facing south side residents.[91] "We're fighting for a better kind of government," Rose explains. "What's happening here in Tucson is happening throughout the country. If the people sit back and let the government 'protect' them, it's not going to happen. . . . with enough people, the government is going to have to listen."[92]

Border Crossings

The shrill ring of my cell phone (one of the "peacetime" technologies manufactured with beryllium) pierced our sunset litany of environmental transgressions perpetrated on the rivers and peoples of the Sonoran Desert. On the other end of the line was Rose's colleague, Teresa Leal, calling to arrange a meeting at the Pimería Alta Historical Society in Nogales, Arizona, where she compiles archival and anthropological data on the multicultural history of the region, including the history of environmental injustice. I recalled my first meeting with Teresa on the toxic tour I had attended two years earlier. She and Rose impressed me as formidable coconspirators in their multifaceted campaigns to fight for environmental justice along the Santa Cruz River corridor, from the *colonias* huddled alongside the polluted Nogales Wash in Sonora, Mexico, to the Latino neighborhoods perched atop the regional aquifer's "deadly plume" in South Tucson.

Both active members of the Southwest Network, Rose and Teresa's collaborations originated in the early 1990s when an organization in Nogales, Arizona, known as LIFE (Living Is for Everyone) contacted Rose and Tucsonans for a Clean Environment soliciting their technical expertise regarding a planned community health survey. LIFE had formed in response to residents' observations of rising incidences of specific and rare forms of cancer—multiple myeloma and pancreatic cancer—in neighborhoods that drank from wells sunk in the groundwater near the Nogales Wash, a principal tributary draining northward into the Santa Cruz River. By the mid-1980s, the Nogales Wash flowed year-round with the wastewater from the hundreds of hillside shacks of the shanty town *colonias* that had sprouted up along its banks with the expansion of the maquiladora industrial parks in Nogales, Sonora. Flowing north into Nogales, Arizona, the Nogales Wash carried, in addition to untreated wastewater and raw sewage, runoff from the overfull "sanitary" landfill located on the Mexican side of the border and industrial effluent from the maquiladora plants contaminated with TCE, PCE, chloroform, cyanide, mercury, chromium, and copper.[93]

Teresa Leal, a Mexican Opata Indian born in Sonora and living on the Arizona side of Ambos Nogales, worked with the LIFE group and with Rose to develop a binational survey to document health issues related to drinking polluted water, a matter of concern to poor communities on both sides of the border.[94] In her efforts to "protect our Mother Earth" and her children, Teresa founded the organization Comadres ("co-mothers"), a group of women who work in the maquiladoras and whose health is endangered both by the toxic substances they handle daily in the primarily U.S.-owned factories and the water they use at home in the colonias. Employing "popular education" methods, Comadres designs training strategies to help women workers maintain the quality of the water that is delivered weekly by pipas, private water vendors who procure clean water from distant wells and transport it by truck for a fee to families living in the colonias.[95] Among other things, Comadres secured plastic liners for the fifty-five-gallon drums, most of which had previously contained hazardous chemicals, that women salvaged from the maquiladoras or from the dump to store water.[96]

Expanding her community-based struggles to protect the health of maquiladora workers, Teresa has worked in what she terms the "cuenca network" with local and state organizations such as the Friends of the Santa Cruz River and the Sierra Club. The coalition fights to force the International Boundary Water Commission (IBWC), the City of Nogales, Arizona, and the EPA to fulfill their statutory obligations to regulate the quality of the wastewater discharged into the rivers and washes and to upgrade the shoddy operations of the Binational Wastewater Treatment Plant, located a few miles north of the border.[97] Because Comadres does not have formal legal standing, Teresa chose to enter the lawsuit as an individual, arguing "if that's what it takes to move these agencies to do a better job, if the decay of our river basin is out of control, then we have to do all that is in our power to help. . . . these entities are not omnipotent and they can be challenged in their own realm."[98] Rose's and Teresa's transcommunal and transborder organizing in the diverse communities that constitute la cuenca Santa Cruz make visible the fluid interconnections of hydrological and biological systems and, likewise, of the fates of the people whose quality of life and livelihoods depend on the sustainable use of those systems.

From Dawn 'til Dusk: Building "Community" in the Santa Cruz Basin

To take advantage of the relative cool of the morning air, desert inhabitants tend to rise early. The women environmental justice activists of the Santa Cruz Valley get an early start on the day because there is so much work to be done. I met up with Rose again several days later. On that morning, she needed to attend to some family problems that had arisen overnight; as a mother, grandmother, great-grandmother, and full-time activist, her multiple obligations regularly collide. Women activists, often dealing themselves with debilitating illnesses, assume a considerable share of the burden of caring for their community writ large, which includes their immediate and extended families, their friends, their neighbors, their neighbors' children, the workers in the factory next door, and the health of the water, air, and land that sustains them.[99] Rose and Teresa and the many other women who participate in the cross-basin *cuenca* network have a "stick-to-it-ness" that anchors them to the cause of environmental justice long after frustration sets in or the media lose interest. Men tend to disappear, Rose contends, "when the going gets tough and the wives and children are sick. Who takes the husband or the child to the hospital or to their chemotherapy? It's the women."[100]

Beyond contending with the skewed gender dynamics of the family, women environmental justice activists experience the trivialization or erasure of their concerns and organizing approaches as they leave the home and enter the political arena. They endure the impediments and humiliation of blatant sexism not only when confronting a company CEO, lobbying in a roomful of county supervisors, or testifying before a panel of EPA scientists, but, disappointingly, also working among the male members of their own organizations. "It's that machismo thing. It keeps men from respecting women and taking what they say seriously," Rose asserts. In times of urgency, women activists explain, many men in the movement insist that decisions must be made fast and efficiently rather than inclusively and democratically. Rose challenges this stance as flawed political leadership: "You have to bring the whole community along, people have to feel they have a say in where you are going."[101]

Rose cites the powerful influences of the women in her life—her mother, her grandmother, her aunt—for instilling in her "pride, honor, and respect for other people."[102] She recalls that "our living conditions in South Tucson were hard, like the *colonias* in Mexico, but my mother worked for thirty-five years at El Charro [a downtown Tucson restaurant] to support the family. My grandmother would take a wagon to town to sell vegetables and eggs."[103] Rose takes seriously her role as a mentor to other women of color, urging them "to not quit, to keep going, keep strategizing, keep having faith."[104] Resisting any romanticization of the life of an activist, she cautions, "It's a hard job, it's a lonely life, you lose some of your friends because you don't have the same interests anymore. Sometimes I just want to quit, I don't want to know anything more, I'm sick of it all. But I can't, I can't stand injustice."[105]

After resolving the morning's dilemmas, Rose drove to meet me in her dependable 1983 Toyota Tercel with 245,000 miles on the odometer and no air conditioning. We zoomed off to South Sixth Avenue to the small house that was the office of the Indigenous Alliance for Border Justice and the *Coalición de Derechos Humanos*. Rose's concept of her "community" as spanning the Santa Cruz Basin led her to an affiliation with organizations working for social and environmental justice in the immigration policies of the federal Immigration and Naturalization Service and its enforcement wing, the Border Patrol. This afternoon's meeting was of the group Derechos Humanos ("human rights"), a coalition that split from the sanctuary movement of the 1980s over the issue of what constitutes defensible unsanctioned immigration from Mexico and Central America. Arguing that positing an "artificial distinction" between political and economic refugees was indefensible, Derechos Humanos formed to elucidate the human rights, and later environmental justice, impacts of the neoliberal globalization policies at the core of the U.S. border control program. Providing documentation of the human rights abuses of Border Patrol operations and exposing the "low intensity conflict" shoring up an increasingly militarized zone along the border, Derechos Humanos also aims to confront the racist stereotypes of border crossers as ruthless outlaws endangering American national security and stealing jobs.[106] Through educational campaigns, the organization raises awareness of the interconnected political and economic reasons, directly related to U.S. "free trade" policies eviscerating local economies in Mexico, that men, women, and children seek, against all odds, to immigrate across the unforgiving desert with no water, food, or shelter in sight.

"Rose pops up everywhere in the community!" exclaims Maritza Broce, a twenty-six-year-old member of Derechos Humanos. "It was her influence as an environmental justice activist that helped us see the connections between human rights abuses on the border and environmental destruction that's happening at the same time."[107] According to Maritza, Rose's "holistic approach" to environmental justice allowed the members of Derechos Humanos to link the harassment, beatings, and murder by U.S. military forces of Mexican nationals and indigenous peoples crossing the border with the wholesale destruction of the ecological integrity of the desert environment. Unique and sensitive wildlife and riparian habitats are damaged or threatened by military missions including building twelve-foot-high steel walls, installing high-power stadium lighting, using infrared surveillance technology, constructing roads and helicopter landing pads, and defoliating desert vegetation using toxic herbicides that result in the poisoning of desert washes and the underlying aquifer.[108] "From her own experience," Maritza explains, "Rose knows that you can't talk about deaths in the desert without talking about destruction of the environment, and you can't talk about destroying the environment without talking about deaths in the desert—they're linked, and her willingness to form coalitions with different groups has made us much stronger."[109]

Rose's "popping up" in many local organizations in the region has brought the "much needed" environmental perspective to human rights activism, argues Maritza. As one of the elder stateswomen of the local activist community, Rose possesses an intergenerational consciousness that conceives of environmental justice organizing as incorporating the "entire community." Maritza asserts that Rose is "one of those people in the community who not only has a lot of wisdom to share but she shares it actively. She has a strong commitment to young people and the strengths they bring to the community—I always see her with new faces, she brings people along."[110] For Rose, building a sustainable community requires recognizing the complexity of the cross-generational, multicultural, and local and nonlocal constituents of her community. "Bringing along" children, women factory workers, Tohono O'odham and Yacqui peoples, Mexican immigrants, and environmentalists, among others, Rose constructs a global sense of place that understands her locatedness within a set of entangled local, regional, and transnational political and economic forces.[111] By revealing the linkages between local living conditions and global socioeconomic processes, Rose connects her immediate environmental predicaments to those of the heterogeneous communities, human and nonhuman alike, living within the Santa Cruz River watershed, her biocultural ecosystem.

Common Visions

Bright neon-green fliers in hand, members of Rillito Residents for a Clean Living Environment and PACE Union workers began arriving at the community recreation center in Rillito. In the spirit of "bringing people along," it was clear that Rose's organizing strategy for this evening's meeting was to assemble two groups of people with very different relationships to this small town off the interstate frontage road, up in the northern reaches of the Santa Cruz Valley. In the shadow of the incinerator stacks of the Arizona Portland Cement Company (APC), the unassuming Rillito Vista Recreation Center was packed with a mixed crowd of local residents including a row of smartly dressed, elderly African-American women and a handful of children, some patiently listening to the adults at the front of the room and others getting bored and restless. After an introduction by David Garcia, the PACE local president, followed by remarks by two leaders of Rillito Residents (Jesse McKnight, the Water Board president, and Mary Cooley, an African-American woman whose eighty-five-year-old mother still lives in town), Rose shared with the group her own community's experiences battling a large corporate polluter. "By working together and getting organized," she declared, "the community and company could work together for a better quality of life." Encouraged by the attendance of about a half dozen union workers and a community turnout of close to thirty people, the leaders of the meeting rallied the crowd by exhorting, "We've been dumped on too long!"

Many local residents, who had never in their lives attended a political gathering, asked questions about the status of APC's air monitoring system and wondered about the dangers to their health of emissions containing heavy metals such as nickel and cobalt. The EPA had recently fined the company a total of $82,442 for discharging nickel and cobalt contaminants at levels above the allowable threshold; many attendees felt this result explained the complaints by both workers and residents of health problems commonly associated with heavy metals poisoning—allergic reactions, reduced lung function, and lung cancer.[112] The community also raised concerns about the proximity of their homes to the cotton fields west of town and the contamination of the Rillito River and their drinking water with pesticide and herbicide runoff. McKnight and Cooley diligently recorded the community's concerns, while some union members noted that they had learned that the company's air monitoring technology screened only for pollutants categorized as PM-10, that is, for particulate matter larger than ten micrograms in size. The EPA regulates air emissions of hazardous primary and secondary air pollutants such as nitrogen dioxide and sulfur dioxide, both measuring in at a miniscule PM-2.5 micrograms and therefore undetectable by APC's monitoring equipment. Why, the community wanted to know, was the Arizona Department of Environmental Quality overlooking the inadequacy of the company's air monitoring system and, hence, permitting the release into the environment of these asthma- and cancer-causing pollutants?

Rose was heartened to see the workers and community members sharing information and expressing a common sense of outrage at the apparent indifference of the local and state regulatory agencies to the welfare of the people in Rillito, both inside and outside APC's plant. PACE Union leaders have argued that "we believe the company doesn't do more to clean up the dust because Rillito is a small minority community."[113] Echoing this view, the community residents worried that "we don't have any political clout." How might workers and neighbors join forces and augment their political power "to make their voices heard?" Some members of Rillito Residents for a Clean Living Environment had regularly joined the weekly picket at APC's gates, brandishing signs in support of the PACE Union members' contract negotiations and grievances against the local plant manager's antiunion tactics. Rose was working to organize a trip to Los Angeles to attend the PACE Union's West Coast regional convention. Some members of Rillito Residents were "at first apprehensive to go to a union rally," but in the end, they agreed to accompany her.[114]

"Another way to get political clout," Rose asserted, "is to make your voices heard at the voting booth." Soon after the meeting, she learned that very few of the two hundred residents of Rillito were registered to vote, and many had never voted in an election. Some of Rillito's senior citizens stayed away from the polling place because of "the shame of not being able to read and write."[115] In another "uncommon alliance" between the workers and the community, the PACE Union local and Rillito Residents for a Clean Living Environment plan to organize a voter registration and voter assistance drive in the community.

Rose enthusiastically welcomed the presence of the children at the meeting, explaining that "they need to know what's going on early, so they know how to make sure it doesn't continue to happen in their lives, or any children's lives." Currently, she is helping Rillito Residents plan a fun event to bring together the children from the community with the children of the workers. Rose's commitment to intergenerational and transcommunal organizing encourages her to develop strategies that expand the community spirit, a "natural force" that she believes is the foundation of social and environmental change.

Moving Forward

On my final evening in the Santa Cruz Valley, Rose and I met up with fellow TCE activist Ann Montaño. Ann treated us to a memory-laden tour of the site where the Old Pueblo once thrived, and where the Tucson Convention Center now stood. Not far from the Convention Center parking lot, the land on which Ann's grandmother had raised nine children, and in striking distance of the now cement-lined levees corralling the seasonal monsoon flooding of the eroded banks of the Santa Cruz River, we stopped at El Minuto, a corner restaurant on South Main that, according to Rose and Ann, had been spared the wrecking ball because the mayor liked the food. On the south side of the restaurant, we passed by *El Tiradito* ("the castaway"), the small, tucked-away shrine "to all those who are lost," where earlier we had attended an ecumenical vigil for the Mexican immigrants who had lost their lives crossing the vast, blistering, Sonoran Desert in the hopes of earning a decent livelihood.

After our festive dinner of chili verde and guacamole-filled enchiladas, we strolled out into the coolness of dusk concluding yet another full day. But, as usual, the day's work was not ending for Rose. She would spend the evening planning a telephone conference call with her fellow members of the National Environmental Justice Advisory Council (NEJAC), a group of scientists and activists who advise the EPA on upholding its mandate to ensure the equal protection of all racial and socioeconomic groups in the implementation and enforcement of environmental laws. Chairing NEJAC's subcommittee on health and research, Rose is composing a set of guidelines for community-based environmental health research to "assess the full impact and numbers of people who are affected by contamination" all over the country. Without a research method that is capable of uncovering the "larger impact" on the health of people and the environment of modern industrial and military activities, she knows, "these things will happen over and over again."[116] Rooted fundamentally in her community, as broad and diverse as that may be, Rose understands that to "help her community," she would need to extend her reach and engage a wider political sphere. Onetime "castaways" in the racial and class-based policies of modern "progress" and military supremacy, Rose and other women activists have multiplied their voices against environmental injustice. Recasting the gendered tools of the housewifely trade, they have forged multicultural networks that, like capillaries or tributaries, permeate the many interstices of the diverse communities radiating throughout *la cuenca* Santa Cruz.

CONCLUSION: THE RIVERKEEPERS OF LA CUENCA SANTA CRUZ

Environmental justice activists like Rose Augustine struggle persistently to save the precious, water-limited desert bioregion that is their home. They adopt an inclusive stance toward ecosystem preservation, understood in the terms of sustaining the long-term health and integrity of people, surface and underground water resources, the economy, and ecological stability. Organizations such as Tucsonans for a Clean Environment, Environmental Justice Action Committee, Coalición de Derechos Humanos, and Rillito Residents for a Clean Living Environment fight for the safekeeping of the Santa Cruz Basin to defend the health and livelihoods of its diverse human and nonhuman inhabitants from the onslaught of corporate, government, and military "progress" in the region. These environmental justice activists contend that because the biological and social diversity of the Sonoran Desert thrives on account of the Santa

Cruz River, protecting its watershed requires more comprehensive and sustainable approaches to economic development.

Women activists like Rose Augustine demonstrate the stalwartness required to safeguard the mixed social and ecological communities that constitute a riverine ecosystem. Much of this "riverkeeping" relies on *la cuenca* networking and is about the mundane, day-to-day upkeep of daily life—securing potable drinking water in the *colonias*, helping a sick neighbor suffering from TCE-related lupus to a doctor's appointment at the El Pueblo Health Clinic, sitting at the kitchen table talking with residents about their children's health problems. Paying attention to the constancy of the everyday environmental activities of these women, we uncover stories that are much more than mundane and no less gritty, bold, and world-making than those found in the pages of the epic works of environmental history.

Struggling against imposing odds, "ordinary" women in the Tucson Basin craft a transnational environmental network one piece, one step, one person at a time. Every meeting or rally, every xeroxed flier, every trip taken to an ill neighbor's house, and every testimony before an official government body are all strands knitting together a new social and ecological vision for the desert ecosystem in which they live. Like the "natural" flows of rivers, air currents, and toxic chemicals within and across geographical landscapes, political borders, residential neighborhoods, and bodily tissues, the "extraordinary" circulation of women's environmental networks reveals the quintessential ecological threads connecting desert-dwelling peoples and desert nature.

This is the stuff of remarkable, and even more "fertile," environmental history. It is the rub with the everyday, close-to-home experiences of an unjustly contaminated environment that propels these predominantly working-class women of color out into the farther reaches of the Santa Cruz Valley and across wider realms still. Heartache and anger are emotions the women of *la cuenca* network in the Santa Cruz River basin share. Yet, as the daily environmental actions of Rose Augustine demonstrate, these painful encounters with environmental injustice are resisted and reshaped into political strategies to ensure that no other beautiful, ecologically and culturally unique watershed endures the same fate.

NOTES

1. Leslie Marmon Silko, *Yellow Woman and the Beauty of the Spirit* (New York: Touchstone, 1997), 123.
2. Author's interview with Rose Marie Augustine, Tucson, Arizona, June 15, 2001.

3. Author's interview with Teresa Leal, Nogales, Arizona, June 13, 2001.

4. Arizona Historical Society Museum, exhibit on "Life of the Santa Cruz River," Tucson, April–June 2001.

5. Ibid.

6. Silko, *Yellow Woman*, 153.

7. Virginia J. Scharff, "Man and Nature! Sex Secrets of Environmental History," in *Human/Nature: Biology, Culture, and Environmental History*, ed. John Herron and Andrew Kirk (Albuquerque: University of New Mexico Press, 1999), 39.

8. See, for example, Vera Norwood, *Made from This Earth: American Women and Nature* (Chapel Hill: University of North Carolina Press, 1993, and Carolyn Merchant, *Earthcare: Women and the Environment* (New York: Routledge, 1996).

9. Donald Worster, *Rivers of Empire: Water, Aridity, and the Growth of the American West* (New York: Oxford University Press, 1985); Marc Reisner, *Cadillac Desert* (New York: Viking-Penguin, 1986).

10. Marc Reisner and Sarah Bates, *Overtapped Oasis: Reform or Revolution for Western Water* (Washington, D.C.: Island Press, 1990), 5.

11. Andrew Ross, "The Great White Dude," in *Constructing Masculinity*, ed. Maurice Berger, Brian Wallis, and Simon Watson (New York: Routledge, 1995), 174.

12. Scharff, "Man and Nature!," 38.

13. Ibid.

14. See Sandra Harding, *Whose Science? Whose Knowledge? Thinking from Women's Lives* (Ithaca, N.Y.: Cornell University Press, 1991).

15. Scharff, "Man and Nature!," 45.

16. Patricia Nelson Limerick, *Desert Passages: Encounters with the American Deserts* (Albuquerque: University of New Mexico Press, 1985), offers a fascinating and unique approach to the environmental history of the arid West—a series of stories of eight men's thoughts, actions, and reactions to the desert experience. One can imagine the use of this "individual" approach to history writing in chronicling the experiences of women.

17. Scharff, "Man and Nature!," 44.

18. The work of scholars writing on water struggles in the Southwest that do uncover some of the experiences and life histories of marginalized groups include Devon Peña, ed., *Chicano Culture, Ecology, Politics: Subversive Kin* (Tucson: University of Arizona Press, 1999); Robert Gottlieb, *A Life of Its Own: The Politics of Power and Water* (San Diego: Harcourt Brace Jovanovich, 1988); and Helen Ingram, Nancy Laney, and David Gillilan, *Divided Waters: Bridging the U.S.–Mexico Border* (Tucson: University of Arizona Press, 1995).

19. Joni Adamson, *American Indian Literature, Environmental Justice, and Ecocriticism: The Middle Place* (Tucson: University of Arizona Press, 2001).

20. Thomas Sheridan, "Sonorenses, Tucsonenses," in *Tucson: A Short History*, ed. Southwestern Mission Research Center (Tucson, Ariz: privately published, 1986), 66. New technological advances introduced by the arrival of the Southern Pacific Railroad's steam-powered locomotives in 1881 facilitated the extractive capacity of water pumping by harnessing the power of steam. For a detailed history of settlement patterns in the Santa Cruz River basin, see Michael Logan, "Head-Cuts and Check-Dams: Changing Patterns of Environmental Manipula-

tion by the Hohokam and Spanish in the Santa Cruz River Valley, 200–1820," *Environmental History* 4, no. 3 (July 1999): 405–30.

21. Logan, "Head-Cuts and Check-Dams," 405.

22. For a more extensive study of the status of groundwater resources in Arizona and New Mexico, see *Sacred Waters: The Life-Blood of Mother Earth,* ed. Southwest Network for Environmental and Economic Justice and the Campaign for Responsible Technology (Albuquerque, N.M.: privately published, 1997).

23. I attended the "Environmental Justice Tour of the Biological and Social Corridor of the Santa Cruz River" in April 1999, which was one of the field trips offered at the annual meeting of the American Society of Environmental History in Tucson. For a more detailed analysis of the use of toxic tours by environmental justice activists, see Giovanna Di Chiro, "Bearing Witness or Taking Action? Toxic Tourism and Environmental Justice," in *Reclaiming the Environmental Debate: The Politics of Health in a Toxic Culture,* ed. Richard Hofrichter (Cambridge, Mass.: MIT Press, 2000), 275–99.

24. Author's interview with Teresa Leal and Rose Marie Augustine, Tucson, Arizona, April 16, 1999.

25. For example, see *Water in the West: Challenge for the Next Century,* a report of the Western Water Policy Review Advisory Commission, Albuquerque, New Mexico, June 1998.

26. Charles Polzer, "Blackrobes, Black Springs, and Beyond," in *Tucson: A Short History,* 22.

27. See Environmental Protection Agency, Region 9 Web site, Pima County, Tucson, Arizona, EPA ID no. AZD980737530.

28. For an exhaustive history of industrial development in Tucson, see C. L. Sonnichsen, *Tucson: The Life and Times of an American City* (Norman: University of Oklahoma Press, 1982).

29. Later, Hughes put in place a series of treatment processes including batch treatment and flow-through treatment, which are intended to detoxify hazardous substances such as chromium and cyanide. In the late 1970s, wastewater ponds and sludge-drying beds were added. In the mid-1980s (after its Superfund site designation), the treatment ponds were retrofitted with double liners and a "leak detection system." See "Evaluation of Hughes Aircraft, U.S. Air Force Plant No. 44," Hazardous Waste Ground-Water Task Force, EPA, 1988, 12–13.

30. Usha Lee McFarling, "Poor, Minorities Seek Role in Environmental Justice," *Boston Globe,* February 13, 1994.

31. Jane Kay, "Hydrologist's Hunch Led to TCE Discovery," *Arizona Daily Star,* May 18, 1985.

32. Jane Kay, "A Deadly Plume Threatens Tucson," *High Country News,* May 25, 1987, 10.

33. Keith Bagwell, "Four New Studies Tie Southside Ills to Tainted Water," *Arizona Daily Star,* July 7, 1991, 1A.

34. Mary Benanti, "Environmental Conclave Airs Tucson Woes," *Tucson Citizen,* October 26, 1991, 6A.

35. Monica Spann, "Holding the Government Accountable: Founder of Tucsonans for a Clean Environment Shares Her Story," *National Wildlife Federation Superfund Justice Newsletter* (Winter 1993): 4.

36. Ibid.
37. Bob Christman, "Panel Chief Opposes Southside TCE Study," *Arizona Daily Star,* April 12, 1986, 1B.
38. Author's interview with Rose Augustine, Tucson, June 11, 2001.
39. Ibid.
40. "Arizona Cement Workers Continue Contract Battle," *United Paper Worker's International Union Reporter,* November 1999.
41. Now called the Center for Environment, Health, and Justice, located in Arlington, Virginia.
42. Fran Buss, "Rose Augustine and Her Fight for Environmental Justice" (presentation to the Arizona Historical Society Conference, Tucson, 1999).
43. Ibid.
44. Spann, "Holding the Government Accountable," 6.
45. Environmental justice groups have appealed to the Civil Rights Act of 1964, and especially the Title VI amendment, to file legal claims against polluting facilities for violating the civil rights of communities of color. Title VI prohibits discrimination on the grounds of race, color, and national origin by any program or activity receiving federal funds. See Luke Cole and Sheila Foster, *From the Ground Up: Environmental Racism and the Rise of the Environmental Justice Movement* (New York: New York University Press, 2001).
46. PACE (Paper, Allied-Industrial, Chemical, and Energy) International represents 320,000 working men and women in the United States and Canada. The union was formed in 1999 from a merger of the United Paper Workers International Union (UPIU) and Oil, Chemical, and Atomic Workers Union (OCAW). The union is notable for its commitment to environmental justice causes and for fighting for a safe and clean workplace and environment on behalf of both workers and local communities.
47. Author's interview with Rose Augustine, Tucson, June 11, 2001.
48. David Moberg, "Brothers and Sisters, Greens and Labor: A Coalition That Gives Corporate Polluters Fits," *Sierra* (January/February 1999): 46–51, 114.
49. Karen Gventer, "Just Transition: Greening the Work without Grounding the Worker," *PIC Press* (March 2000).
50. The European Trade Union Confederation also supports policies consistent with "Just Transition" including the participation of workers in the introduction of new, cleaner technologies and provision of training to employees concerning environmentally friendly production; see *Hazards, Trade Unions, Health, and Work* 72 (November 2000).
51. "Just Transition Movement for Jobs and the Environment," handbook produced by the Public Health Institute and the Labor Institute, 1998.
52. Ibid.
53. Author's interview, Rose Augustine, Tucson, June 11, 2001.
54. Ibid.
55. Ibid.
56. Ibid.
57. Ibid.
58. Bill Turque and John McCormick, "The Military's Toxic Legacy," *Newsweek,* August 6, 1990, 22.

59. Author's phone interview, Rose Augustine, Tucson, January 19, 2001.

60. For a social and environmental history of urban renewal in Tucson, see Michael Logan, *Fighting Sprawl and City Hall: Resistance to Urban Growth in the Southwest* (Tucson: University of Arizona Press, 1995).

61. Margaret Regan, "There Goes the Neighborhood: The Downfall of Downtown," *Tucson Weekly,* March 6–12, 1997, 16.

62. Author's interview with Ann Montaño, Tucson, Arizona, June 15, 2001.

63. Joyesha Chesnick, "Plagues on their Houses," *Tucson Citizen,* February 9, 1999.

64. Author's interview, Rose Augustine, Tucson, June 15, 2001.

65. Author's interview with Pat Birnie, Tucson, Arizona, July 28, 2001.

66. Ibid.

67. Ibid.

68. See the reprint of the six-day series on the story of beryllium in the United States by Sam Roe, "Deadly Alliance: How Government and Industry Chose Weapons Over Workers," *Toledo Blade,* March 28–April 2, 1999.

69. Exposure limits to beryllium set by OSHA stand at two micrograms per cubic meter of air.

70. Sam Roe, "Decades of Risk: U.S. Knowingly Allowed Workers to Be Overexposed to Toxic Dust," *Toledo Blade,* March 28, 1999, 7.

71. David Sanders, "Protection Didn't Work: 25 Workers Poisoned by Beryllium Now Risk Death," *Arizona Daily Star,* May 9, 1999; Sam Roe, "Deadly Metal's Use Endangers Workers," *Chicago Tribune,* July 29, 2001.

72. Author's phone interview, Pat Birnie, Tucson, July 28, 2001.

73. Ibid.

74. See the report compiled by sixty-seven grassroots environmental groups, *Poisoned Schools: Invisible Threats, Visible Actions* (Arlington, Va.: Center for Environment, Health, and Justice, 2001).

75. Author's phone interview with Rob Kulakovsky, Sierra Club, Tucson, July 27, 2001.

76. Author's interview, Rose Augustine, Tucson, June 11, 2001.

77. The potentially responsible parties for the TIAA site identified by the EPA are the city of Tucson, Raytheon Corporation, U.S. Air Force, McDonnell Douglas Corporation, Tucson Airport Authority, and General Dynamics Corporation.

78. Kay, "A Deadly Plume Threatens Tucson," 12; Keith Bagwell, "Tucson Water Plans $100,000 Tower to Cleanse Southside Well of TCE," *Arizona Daily Star,* December 10, 1986, B3.

79. Joe Gelt, Jim Henderson, Kenneth Seasholes, Barbara Tellman, and Gary Woodward, "Water in the Tucson Area: Seeking Sustainability," report by the Water Resources Research Center, University of Arizona, 1996; John Schaefer, "Dumping Treated TCE Water Considered a Waste," *Arizona Daily Star,* August 9, 1998.

80. The Resource Conservation and Recovery Act (RCRA) of 1976 regulates how solid and hazardous wastes should be managed to protect human health and the environment. The Comprehensive Environmental Response, Compensation, and Liability Act (CERCLA), or "Superfund," of 1980 becomes relevant after the

occurrence of a release of a hazardous substance that presents a threat to human health.

81. Author's phone interview, Pat Birnie, Tucson, July 29, 2001. The TARP facility was installed to treat the main groundwater contamination plume north of Reales Road. There are other air strippers and water treatment operations located on-site at the various PRP's plants including hundreds of monitoring wells. Additionally, the EPA has determined whether soil remediation was necessary at the different sites, and some, including Air Force Plant No. 44–Raytheon, are undergoing soil cleanup to remove VOCs and metals from contaminated soils and sludges. The EPA has designated the detoxification of some PRP's sites as "technically infeasible" and so instead has ordered the "hydraulic containment" of the contaminated groundwater in perpetuity, relying on the "impermeability" of the clay sediments surrounding the plume.

82. The Central Arizona Project (CAP) is a project of the Bureau of Reclamation, first conceived of in 1947, to set aside a share of the Colorado River for Arizona's dry interior and the mushrooming metropolises of Phoenix and Tucson. A multibillion-dollar water diversion project, CAP was designed to carry Colorado River water from Lake Havasu via an intricate system of dams, power plants, pumps, and aqueducts to central Arizona. To get from the Lake Havasu reservoir, water would have to be pumped nine hundred feet uphill to its final destination of Tucson. Slated to start delivering water to Tucson in the 1990s, the CAP project has run into a series of obstacles, including the bad taste of the water and its high mineral and saline content, which proved corrosive to water pipes and home appliances. See Reisner, *Cadillac Desert*, Gottlieb, *A Life of Its Own*, and Wendy Nelson Espland, *The Struggle for Water: Politics, Rationality, and Identity in the American Southwest* (Chicago: University of Chicago Press, 1998).

83. Author's interview, Rose Augustine, Tucson, June 11, 2001.

84. Des Ralles, "$84.5 Million Offered in Tainted Water Case," *Arizona Republic*, February 26, 1991, 1A.

85. Keith Bagwell, "1,620 May Get Hughes Payments on TCE Suit in June," *Arizona Daily Star*, March 31, 1991, 4B.

86. Ibid., 1B.

87. Ibid., 4B.

88. Author's interview, Rose Augustine, Tucson, June 11, 2001.

89. Mary Reinhart, "Senate Panel OKs $250,000 for Southside Center for TCE Victims," *Arizona Daily Star*, February 29, 1992, 1B.

90. Author's interview, Rose Augustine, Tucson, June 11, 2001.

91. Bill Scanlan, "Group Blasts New Health Director," *Rocky Mountain News*, January 24, 1992.

92. Margo Nikitas, "The Silent Bomb: Racism, War, and Toxic Wastes," *WREE View of Women* 16, no. 3 (Spring/Summer 1991): 15.

93. Miriam Davidson, *Lives on the Line: Dispatches from the U.S.–Mexico Border* (Tucson: University of Arizona Press, 2000), 55–56.

94. Author's interview with Teresa Leal, Nogales, Arizona, June 12, 2001. The LIFE group succeeded in getting the ear of state and federal authorities, although they ran into many barriers from the medical community about the feasibility of a health study to demonstrate with certainty that the water was causing

the high rates of cancer. President Clinton told one of the LIFE members when asked what he was going to do about the toxins from the maquiladoras flowing into Arizona, "That's what NAFTA's for" (Davidson, *Lives on the Line*, 76).

95. Ingram, Laney, and Gillians, *Divided Waters*, 76–78. The price of delivered water ranges from 4.5 to 5.0 pesos ($1.32–$1.47) per two hundred liters of water.

96. Author's interview, Teresa Leal, Nogales, Arizona, June 13, 2001.

97. Teresa is currently a plaintiff in a lawsuit filed jointly by herself and the Sierra Club–Grand Canyon Chapter to force the defendants to abide by their "non-discretionary mandate to act upon consistent violations at the wastewater treatment plant in order to avoid contaminating the river and to efficiently clean the residual waters that come into the waste water treatment plant as best they can" (author's interview, Teresa Leal, Nogales, Arizona, June 13, 2001, and author's phone interview with Sandy Bahr, Sierra Club–Grand Canyon Chapter, Tucson, July 25, 2001).

98. Author's interview, Teresa Leal, Nogales, Arizona, June 13, 2001.

99. For analyses of the triple-shift labor burdens on women grassroots activists, see Nancy Naples, *Grassroots Warriors: Activist Mothering, Community Work, and the War on Poverty* (New York: Routledge, 1998).

100. Author's interview, Rose Augustine, Tucson, June 11, 2001.

101. Her unflagging commitments to "bringing the community along" and "fighting injustice wherever it is" have earned her numerous accolades including, among others, the prestigious 1993 Jefferson Award, a national honor bestowed by the Washington, D.C.–based American Institute for Public Service, the 1995 Arizona Woman "The Power of One" distinction, and a highly selective fellowship for community activists granted in 2000 from the Bannerman Foundation.

102. Author's interview, Rose Augustine, Tucson, June 14, 2001.

103. Ibid.

104. Author's interview with Edna San Miguel, Tucson, Arizona, June 14, 2001.

105. Ibid. Author's interview, Rose Augustine, Tucson, June 14, 2001.

106. Low intensity conflict (LIC) is official Pentagon policy intended to create a climate of fear among civilians living along the border and to represent the region as a war zone requiring military occupation. LIC results in the use of high-tech surveillance apparatuses and the wholesale destruction of the desert environment through defoliation and clearing of wildlife habitat. An atmosphere of intimidation is deployed to discourage people from resisting the human rights abuses perpetrated by military (Joint Task Force–6) missions and local law enforcement agents, including increased physical and sexual assaults against women. For more on LIC, see Timothy Dunn, *The Militarization of the U.S.–Mexico Border, 1978–1992: Low Intensity Conflict Doctrine Comes Home* (Austin: University of Texas Press, 1996).

107. Author's phone interview with Maritza Broce, Tucson, Arizona, August 8, 2001.

108. George Kourous, "Border Patrol Conducting Environmental Impact Assessment in Arizona," *Borderlines Updater*, November 15, 2000.

109. Author's phone interview, Maritza Broce, Tucson, August 8, 2001.

110. Ibid.

111. See Doreen Massey, *Space, Place, and Gender* (Minneapolis: University of Minnesota Press, 1994),146–56.

112. Michael Graham, "Cement Plant to Pay $82,442 in Toxic Case," *Tucson Citizen,* June 5, 2001.

113. United Paperworker's International Union, "Arizona Cement Workers Continue Contract Battle," *IPIU Newsletter* (1997).

114. Author's phone interview with Rose Augustine, Tucson, August 13, 2001.

115. Ibid.

116. Author's phone interview with Rose Augustine, Tucson, January 19, 2001.

CONTRIBUTORS

PETER BOAG is professor of history at the University of Colorado, Boulder. He is the author of *Same-Sex Affairs: Constructing and Controlling Homosexuality in the Pacific Northwest* (2003), and *Environment and Experience: Settlement Culture in Nineteenth-Century Oregon* (1992).

ANNIE GILBERT COLEMAN is assistant professor of history at Indiana University–Purdue University, Indianapolis. She is currently working on a book that explores the intersections between sport, landscape, and identity through the history of Colorado skiing.

GIOVANNA DI CHIRO teaches in the women's studies and earth and environment departments at Mount Holyoke College. This chapter is part of a larger project, *Uncommon Expertise: Women, Science, and Environmental Politics,* that focuses on women activists' approaches to reshaping science and technology within the environmental justice movement.

AMY GREEN is an independent scholar living and teaching in Northampton, Massachusetts. She is currently finishing a book, *Savage Childhood: The Scientific Construction of Girlhood and Boyhood* (Berkeley: University of California Press, forthcoming).

MARIL HAZLETT received her Ph.D. in history from the University of Kansas in 2003. Her fields of interest include Rachel Carson and *Silent Spring,* pesticides and human health, gender and technology, and the history of horticulture.

KATHERINE JENSEN is professor of sociology and women's studies at the University of Wyoming. She has published extensively on rural women's work, international development, and community development.

CATHERINE KLEINER received her Ph.D. in 2003 from the University of New Mexico. She has written on the history of lesbian sexuality and more generally in American women's history. Her dissertation examines lesbian back-to-the land communities in Oregon from the 1970s, 1980s, and 1990s.

NANCY LANGSTON is associate professor of environmental studies at the University of Wisconsin–Madison. Her first book, *Forest Dreams, Forest Nightmares: The Paradox of Old Growth in the Inland West* (1995), examines the history of forest health, while her second book, *Where Land and Water Meet: A Western Landscape Transformed* (2003), explores the changing relationships between water and land. She is currently working on *Polluted Bodies*, a book that examines the connections between human and ecosystem health, focusing on the history of endocrine disruptors.

PAIGE RAIBMON is assistant professor of history at Simon Fraser University in Burnaby, British Columbia. Her research deals with questions of colonialism, culture, and indigenous peoples.

DOUGLAS C. SACKMAN is assistant professor of history at the University of Puget Sound. He is the author of *Orange Empire: California and the Fruits of Eden* (Berkeley: University of California Press, forthcoming).

VIRGINIA J. SCHARFF is professor of history and director of the Center for the Southwest at the University of New Mexico. She is author of *Twenty Thousand Roads: Women, Movement, and the West* (2003), *Coming of Age: America in the Twentieth Century* (1998), *Present Tense: The United States since 1945* (1999), and *Taking the Wheel: Women and the Coming of the Motor Age* (1991). She also writes mystery novels under the name of Virginia Swift.

BRYANT SIMON, associate professor of history at the University of Georgia, is the author of *A Fabric of Defeat: The Politics of South Carolina Textile Workers, 1910–1948* (1998), and coeditor of *Jumpin' Jim Crow: Southern Politics from Civil War to Civil Rights* (2000). Currently, he is writing a history of tourism, fantasy, and urban development in Atlantic City, New Jersey.

MARK TEBEAU is assistant professor of history at Cleveland State University. An urban historian, Tebeau is the author of *Eating Smoke: Fire in Urban America, 1800–1950* (2003).

INDEX

323

"Cottonwood Anniversary CCC, The,"
    89(fig.)
Counterculture, 186, 187, 207, 245, 261n30
Country Life Commission, 181
Cows, Condos, Critters, and Community,
    278
Crane, Stephen, 87
Croning ceremonies, 251
Cronon, William, xiii, xxiin3, 13, 14
    on consumerism/materialism, 172
    index of, 11
    on masculinity, 188n8
Crosby, Alfred, 10
Cryptochidism, 132
Cuenca network, 288, 305, 306, 311, 312
Cultural capital, 173
Cultural changes, 179
Cultural norms, 24, 74, 170–71, 174, 231
Culture, xx, 65, 107
    consumption-oriented, 179
    environmental history and, xix, 171
    gender and, 198
    history and, 120
    lesbian, 245, 246, 251
    nature and, xvii, 40–41, 104, 106, 113,
        120, 169, 171, 188, 222, 239
    snowboarding, 207, 211, 212–13
Currier and Ives, 74, 78n19
Curtis, Edward, 232, 236
Custer, George, 263
Custer State Park, 41
Cyanide, 305, 314n29
Czekalinskis, 184, 185

Dairy industry, realities of, 172
Daly, Mary, 248, 249
Dandridge, William, 29–30
Darby, William J., 117
Darktown Comics, 74, 79n19
Darktown Fire Brigade, The, 74
Darwin, Charles, 6
Dascalos, James, 269
Davis, Barbara J., 149
Davis, Mike, 12
Davis, Natalie Zemon, xv, 3
Dawes Act (1887), 47
"Days of '76, The," 275
DDE, 147, 151
DDT, 147, 150
    endocrine disruption and, 142
    estrogenic effects of, 141

exposure to, 131–32, 151
impact of, 109, 141, 142
outlawing of, 105
reproduction and, 141–42
sex hormones and, 133
Deadwood, 263, 265, 266, 267, 272, 274
    gambling in, 275
    image of, 276
    voting in, 273, 279
Declaration of Independence, 43
Deep ecology, 243, 256, 257, 262n62
Degeneracy, 49, 222
    urban, 86–87, 99n30
Degeneration (Nordau), 49
DEHP, effects of, 149
Deloria, Philip, 261n30
Democracy, 44, 53, 303
Dental sealants, 145
De Pisan, Christine, 247
DES, 143, 147, 150
    approval of, 138, 139
    daughters, 138
    endocrine disruptors and, 138
    exposure to, 140, 160n46
    in food supply, 140
    mothers, 138, 139, 140
    problems with, 138–41
Desert, xxii, 312
    environmental history of, 284
    industrial poisons and, 301
    transformation of, 284, 285
    See also Sonoran Desert
Dharma Bums, 186
Diana, worshipping, 248
Dichloroethylene (1, 1-DCE), 289
Dieldrin, 114
Di-ethyl phthalate, 146
Dioxins, 142, 143, 149
    in breast milk, 150
    sex hormones and, 133
Directory of Wimmin's Lands (Shewolf), 245
Division of labor, sex-based, 265
"Division of Labor in the Home" (Porter),
    235
Dodds, Edward Charles, 138, 143
Domesticity, 15, 48, 113, 179, 193n67, 222
    agriculture and, 189n22
    cult of, 235
    feminine, 115
    redefining, 226–28
Donation Land Act (DLA) (1850), 47, 48

gender and, xx
postwar, xviii
Silent Spring and, 104
Environmental justice, 282, 283, 293, 295, 308, 311–12
toxic tours and, 314n23
women and, xx, 292, 306
Environmental Justice Action Group (EJAG), 288, 299, 301, 302, 311
Augustine and, 290
CABs and, 300
meeting of, 297, 298
Environmental Justice Tour of the Biological and Social Corridor of the Santa Cruz River, 314n23
Environmental Protection Agency (EPA), 306, 311
APC and, 293
beryllium disease and, 300
endocrine disruptors and, 152
fighting, 305
fines by, 309
groundwater remediation process and, 302
Homestake and, 263, 266
NPL of, 288
PCBs and, 151
phthalates and, 146
soil remediation and, 317n81
South Tucson and, 297
TCE and, 290
TIAA sites and, 316n77
Environmental racism, 291
Environmental stewardship, xxi, 266, 267–68, 283
Epidemiology, 152
"Equinox" (Gwynn), text of, 253
Erikson, Erik, 169
Essay on Man (Pope), 5
Estradiol, 135
Estriol, 135
Estrogen mimics, 137, 148, 151
Estrogen receptors, 135–36
Estrogens, 130, 133
alcohol and, 137
carcinogens and, 138, 143, 144, 145
compound, 150
contraceptive, 129
environmental, 141, 150
exposure to, 143, 147–48, 150
formation/regulation of, 141

in formula, 151
gender and, 135, 136
increase in, 132, 136, 137
leaching, 146
premature puberty and, 148
sex hormones and, 137
synthetic, 137, 138, 140, 144, 148, 158n31
Estrone, 135
Ethnic differences, 84, 85, 95, 233
Ethynylestradiol, 130, 155n3
European Trade Union Confederation, 315n50
Eve, 27, 34n6
Evolution, chaos and, 282
Extension Clubs, 272
Extraterritorial Jurisdiction Commission, 266

Families
alternative, 187
biological/social reproduction and, 187
changes in, 179
companionate, 180
consumer, 170, 180, 184
cooking by, 173–74
gender dynamics of, 306
gendered identities and, 187
moral/physical growth of, 185
nuclear, 54
ranch, 265, 268
See also Farm families; Ranch families
Family life
economic conditions/normative prescriptions of, 174
family labor and, 180
image/reality in, 190n24
model of, 177, 180
nature and, 173
"Family Status Must Improve: It Should Buy More for Itself to Better the Living of Others" *(Life)*, 184
Family Thrift Center, 271
Family values, 175, 181
Farm families, 170, 171
celebrating, 180
(Euro)American, 176
image of, 175, 176
nature of, 174–79
as social organism, 180
subordination in, 175
trade/social relationships and, 175

Nature, 32, 41, 117, 221, 224, 231
awareness of, 104
bodies and, xvii, 108, 119
CCC and, 94
commodification of, 173
consumption of, xix, 187, 188n10
culture and, 40–41, 104, 106, 113, 120,
169, 171, 188, 222, 239
defining, 4
desert, xxii, 312
dominating, 94, 118, 174, 197
environmental history and, xix, 3–4, 8,
10, 171
family life of, 170–74
farm families and, 175
as female/feminine, xix, 11, 253
foods and, 181
gender and, xiii–xv, xix, xxi–xxii, 74, 76,
106, 120, 173, 187, 225
humans and, xvi, 4, 104, 107, 112, 118,
120, 188
kinship and, 173
knowing, xviii, 188
land lesbians and, 244–45, 258
Madison Avenue and, 186
man and, xiv, 4, 9, 16, 285
midwives and, 177
moral character and, 233
photography and, 233
preservation of, 222, 234, 238, 239n4
reverence for, 100n34, 245, 247, 254
romanticization of, 257
separation from, 154
sexual relationship with, 253–54
transformation of, 10, 186
using, 180
vengeful, 287
vision of, 113–14
women and, xxi, 11–12, 107, 115–16, 178,
238, 239
Nature (journal), 143, 148
Nature Religions in America: From the
Algonkian Indians to the New Age
(Albanese), 256
Nature's Metropolis (Cronon), xiii, 11, 172
Nature's Nation, xviii
Nature study, 230, 231
lesbian, 243
male world of, 223
Nelson, Dana D., 38n81
Neopaganism, 247, 248, 249

Neurological disorders, 291
New Deal, 54, 88
CCC and, xvii, xviii, 80, 82, 85, 87, 91–92
public art and, 95
Newlands Act (1902), 47
New Woman/Earth: Sexist Ideologies and
Human Liberation (Radford Ruether),
249
New Yorker, Silent Spring in, 110
New York Fire Department (NYFD), 64, 69,
72
New York Radicallesbians, 259n8
New York Times, on Old World fire, 63
Nogales, 286, 287–88
maquiladoras in, 305
Nogales Wash, 304, 305
Nolan, Patricia, 291, 304
Nonylphenols, 129, 144
Norbeck, Peter, 43
Nordau, Max, 49, 58n20
North by Northwest (movie), 54–55
Northwest Ordinance, 47
Norwood, Vera, 9, 12, 112, 178
Now They Are Men (McEntee), 82
Nutrition, 170, 183

Oates, Cherie, 199
Occupational Safety and Health
Administration (OSHA), 300, 316n68
Oelschlaeger, Max, 17n8
Ogburn, William F., 94
O'Harra, Cleophas C., 44
Ohio Citizen Action Group, 301
Oil, Chemical, and Atomic Workers Union
(OCAW), 294, 315n46
Old World Building, fire at, 63, 64, 72
O'Leary, Catherine, 11, 13–14, 16
O'Leary, Patrick, 11, 13, 13–14
"On Being Civilized Too Much" (Merwin),
50
1, 1-DCE. See Dichloroethylene
Open spaces, defending, 265, 275, 278
Operation Desert Storm, 297
Organic compounds, 289
Organic Machine, The (White), 12
Organochlorines, 141, 295
Ortner, Sherry, 11
O'Sullivan, Timothy, 236
Our Stolen Future, website of, 146
Our Synthetic Environment (Herber), 109
Outing, Porter and, 228